The Fourth Economy

Inventing Western Civilization

By Ron Davison

ISBN: 978-0-9838232-0-9

Contact: ron@thefourtheconomy.com

To Sandi who has waited for what must seem like centuries for this book to be done.

To Jordan & Blake who grew up with the story of the fourth economy and will hopefully grow old with the reality of it.

Table of Contents

Introduction

There is nothing new about claiming that the West has advanced through agricultural, industrial, and information economies. The new claim of this book is that beyond these three there is a fourth, entrepreneurial economy. The basis for making such a claim comes from seeing a pattern in the changes from one economy to the next.

The pattern involves big social inventions like the nation-state or corporation, and revolutions like the Protestant and democratic revolutions. It involves a host of changes that have helped the West to overcome one limit to economic progress only to face yet another. This pattern can be used to predict the future of the West, a future that includes the transformation of the corporation in response to yet another new limit to progress.

There is a big difference between an agricultural economy and an industrial economy. One has people scratching out a living with hoes and the next has factories billowing smoke. Among other things, the industrial economy automates work and makes people richer. In an agricultural economy, it might take 90 percent of the population to work farms to feed everyone. In an industrial economy, that percentage might drop to 30 percent or less, freeing up people to make new products.

But there is so much more to a change from an agricultural to industrial economy. Society is hugely different. In the history of the West – and even around the world so often today – the transition from agricultural to industrial economies fed and was fed by a rise in banks and financial markets and a transformation from tyranny to something more democratic.

Economic change is never just about economic change.

The progress from agricultural to industrial and industrial to information economies have transformed how the West defines religion, politics, and finance. It has repeatedly changed how people think about the world and even the purpose of life. This kind of disruptive transformation is not done yet.

Back in 2005, there was a tsunami in the Indian Ocean. It began with an underwater earthquake that nobody noticed and ended with a tsunami that no one could avoid. Economic change seems to work in the same way. The underwater earthquake that gets little noticed is the shift in the limit to progress; the tsunami that no one can avoid comes in the form of social change that triggers the invention of new institutions, and revolutions of others, and even a change in how people think. In the West, for instance, the change from an agricultural to industrial economy gave us more than just machinery: it gave us the bank, democratic revolution, and the Enlightenment. This second economy changed the daily experience of life.

The book you are about to read is a history book that uses a pattern of change to predict the future.

The introductory section explains some ideas that help to tease out the pattern of progress from history. In the first chapter, I argue that social invention is as important to progress as is technological invention and describe what it is. In the second chapter, I define the limits to progress and how and when they can shift. In the third and last chapter of the introductory section, I share the pattern of social invention and revolution that has defined progress in the first three economies, a high level overview of the next three sections.

After that introductory section, I have four sections to tell the story of the four economies. The first three economies likely describe some mix of fresh and familiar stories from history but told as part of a pattern of change, all stemming from a shift in the limit to progress triggering a wave of social invention and change. The last section predicts the future through roughly 2050 based on the pattern of progress that seems to have defined the West since the beginning of the first market economy in about 1300.

The next chapter you will read explores the acts of social invention that give us institutions like the nation-state, bank, or corporation. Social inventions are the creative acts that have defined and invented what we know as Western Civilization. Understanding social invention does not just help us to understand how the world we live in was created; it suggests something big about our future. Traditional entrepreneurship is a form of social invention. If the new limit to progress is entrepreneurship, we'll have to become as adept at social invention in this century as we became at technological invention in the last. Social invention is not just helpful as a way to understand our past; it is key to creating our future.

1 Social Invention

Social invention is the oft-overlooked companion to technological invention in the story of economic progress. Yet social invention is key to understanding progress both past and future.

There are these two young fish swimming along, and they happen to meet an older fish swimming the other way, who nods at them and says, "Morning, boys, how's the water?" And the two young fish swim on for a bit, and then eventually one of them looks over at the other and goes, "What the hell is water?"

— David Foster Wallace

Progress has always depended on technological invention. It is pretty obvious that the wheel and pottery made life better for early man. It is sometimes less obvious that social inventions like the tribe or city were just as important to early man's progress. The history of Western Civilization is punctuated by really big social inventions like the nation-state and corporation that have defined our world and stimulated progress as much as the steam engine or computer. Such social inventions will become even more important in the next economy.

Social Inventions

The philosopher John Searle makes the distinction between brute facts and institutional facts.[1] Brute facts – the sun is 93 million miles from earth, hydrogen has a single atom – exist independent of what we think

[1] John R. Searle, *The Construction of Social Reality* (The Free Press, New York, NY, 1995), mostly drawn from the first two chapters, "The Building Blocks of Reality" and "Creating Institutional Facts."

or agree. Institutional facts, by contrast, depend upon agreement. "The meeting is adjourned," for example, is a fact because it was declared and cannot exist independent of such a claim.

Searle further makes the distinction between rules that create behavior and thus reality and rules that merely regulate.[2] Rules regulate the fact of people driving cars. Rules create the game of chess. Driving might be chaotic without rules but it could exist. Chess, by contrast, depends on rules. People were not pushing wooden pieces around on a checkered board when someone came along with the rules of chess to regulate what they were doing.

When an offensive linemen pulls off the line to block a defensive end, his action makes no sense – indeed, has no purpose – independent of the team. His actions are part of a collective effort and only make sense within that context and the rules that create the game of football. Even his competition against the other team makes sense only within the context of cooperating with that other team in order to play a game. Most economic behavior is like this – meaningless on its own. Imagine the lineman "pulling off the line" without any other players or a person trying to use money to "buy" something among people who have no concept of money. The fact that the offensive lineman pulled off the line is an institutional fact, dependent in this case on the institution of football.

Economic behavior is an institutional fact. Money is only money because we agree it is money. As soon as we all agree that Confederate currency no longer has any value, it no longer has any value. When we agree that information on magnetic strips affixed to plastic has value, it has value. Whether someone is a slave, employee or part-owner of an enterprise is not inherent in any physical reality or dependent on any brute facts, but is – instead – true only as an institutional fact.

I'll piggyback on Searle's distinction between brute facts and institutional facts to make a distinction between technological invention and social invention. A technological invention results in a product that can be seen independent of any agreement about it. While its use might require some instruction, instruction that might be something akin to declaration or agreement, its existence does not. A steam engine translates heat into motion and even if it requires an operator to do

[2] Rules that create reality Searle calls constitutive and those that regulate it he calls regulative.

this, its existence falls more into the category of brute fact than institutional fact. By contrast, a home loan is an institutional fact. Without a contract specifying terms and even who owes what to whom, the loan makes no sense. Further, the loan assumes a whole other set of institutional facts, from money to banks to a real estate market to determine the value of the home for which the loan exists.

Invention and Progress

When we step into a car, we're fully aware that we have entered into a piece of technology. We know that someone once invented this. Social inventions are more subtle. When you come home to your family, you're less aware that family is something that's also invented. In some tribes, children from numerous families grow up around common fires while the couples retire into private huts outside of these circles. In 80-some percent of cultures, some form of polygamy was – and is – practiced,[3] and while most of the world defines family as only two parents, an increasing percentage of children grew up in families of just one parent. Families in different cultures and households have three generations or one, adopted children or only biological, same sex couples and no sex couples. Family, nation, culture, workplace, and gang are all invented, but seem less obviously like inventions than simply the way things are. Social inventions less obviously exist "out there" and more subtly take root in our minds, and as such are more like an operating system that is just there when we boot up than an application we intentionally open. They are not so much things that we're aware of as things we simply wake up to.

The claims of this book rest on two points.

The first is that progress depends as much on social invention as it does on technological invention. To provide a simple example, think about the chaos that would ensue if there were only technological invention and no social invention when it comes to cars. Imagine driving in cars but having no roads, no speed limits, no conventions for

---

[3] Laura Fortunato, "The ancient roots of monogamous marriage," http://www.santafe.edu/news/item/fortunato-origin-monogamous-marriage/ 8 July 2011.

passing on the left or right, and no agreements about right of way through property or what drivers had to know in order to be safe to license. Just learning how to use technology like a car or computer often requires changes in behavior that more neatly fall under the umbrella of social change or social invention than technological invention.

The second point is that we're entering a century in which social invention will become as intentional and as normal as technological invention became in the last century. There are lots of reasons to make such a claim, but for now simply think about the consequences of that. Imagine social invention applied to schools, with people designing, creating, and customizing learning around individual children, an explosion of educational entrepreneurship that means more options for more kinds of learners. Imagine employees who act like entrepreneurs, creating new products, markets, and business units from within their corporations. Imagine government agencies that adapt and respond to specific events and opportunities, facilitating the creation of communities that raise quality of life without clear causation from business developers, government agencies, or city planners, communities that emerge from coordination rather than control. Imagine communities intentionally shaping and transforming their defining institutions. But I'm getting ahead of myself.

The past is a foreign country. They do things differently there.

— L. P. Hartley

Our prehistoric ancestors had to worry about wild beasts crashing through the bushes. They did not have to worry about being late for work. We begin our day alarmed, our bodies' natural processes truncated by a ring or radio. From our first stirring of consciousness, we're plunged into a world that's made up. We use a razor to shave (a technological invention), shampoo to wash our hair (more technology), and a brush to comb it (technology) so that we'll look fashionable (a social invention), and we do it quickly (social invention) in order to be on time (social invention) and seem like a good employee (social invention). Inventions technological and social affect every part of our lives, though they are so ingrained into the fabric of our daily lives that we give them little notice.

Social inventions, especially, often fly beneath the radar of our awareness. Children learn stories about technological invention. Ford invented the assembly line (as with so much history, a fact that is not true but is close enough and commonly taught). Alexander Graham Bell invented the phone, and Thomas Edison the light bulb. By contrast, typically not even adults are told stories about social invention. Who invented the nation-state or corporation? Such things seem to have always existed, at least in our minds.

Social inventions are as essential to progress as are technological inventions, even if they seem less intentional. Like the microwave oven and air conditioning, churches, banks, and corporations have made this a different world. In fact, social inventions like churches, ATMs, jobs, roads, and department stores have become such ingrained parts of our lives that we can scarcely imagine a world without them.

One consequence of overlooking social inventions as inventions is that we are less inclined to think about the need to change them. We are used to technological inventions continually changing: we shop for new cars, new computers, and new clothes that reflect the latest and greatest idea and execution. We don't have this same expectation with social inventions; we somehow are startled whenever the norms and practices for religion, government, or business change. In fact, while we expect a stream of new products, we tend to consider social inventions so disruptive that we give them labels like revolution.

Inventing Civilization

Initially, change was defined only by the programming of biology, changes in DNA that occurred through biological evolution. Starting about a million years ago, cultural evolution began to have greater influence on behavior change than biological evolution. Instinct was supplemented by imitation and then instruction. Today, biology evolves so slowly as to be nearly invisible in a lifetime, whereas cultural and social evolution are not only visible but accelerating. Still, the idea of social invention and evolution is largely neglected.

After curing polio, Jonas Salk had a blank check to essentially pursue whatever he wanted. As it turns out, he wanted to establish an institute across the street from the University of California at San Diego on the cliffs of La Jolla, overlooking the Pacific Ocean. He wanted to populate this institute with some of the most interesting and eclectic minds on the planet. (For instance, James Crick, co-discoverer of DNA, spent his last years working at the Salk Institute.) And he wanted to base this institute on two principles: one, it would be devoted to the study of social evolution (or what he called meta-biology), and two, it would be democratically run. Sadly for Salk–and for us–he did not clearly subordinate the one goal to the other. That is, he did not say, "We will pursue the question of social evolution in a democratic way." So, once he'd assembled his great minds, they listened to his goal and quickly dismissed it. Social evolution was not, it appears, either interesting enough or real enough to be made a proper object of study. This author would beg to differ.

Among the lessons of history is this–although social inventions are just made up, the consequences of adopting or discarding these social inventions are not. At one level, declaring "this meeting is adjourned" seems arbitrary; at another level, though, even a social invention as simple as declaring a meeting adjourned depends on layers of social inventions as varied as the idea of a chairman with the authority to make such a claim and, of course, the idea of a meeting or even an authority. At one level social invention might appear to be just made up, but as with technological invention it is involved and always depends on a sequence of previous inventions and the context of the times.

A tyranny and a democracy are both "just made up" and involve different rules and expectations. But the consequences of adopting one or the other are very profound for a community and lead to very different experiences for the individual living within them. A tricycle and a luxury car, too, are both "just made up," but that doesn't make them any less real or the differences between them any less stark. And just as someone who has only known a tricycle can't just declare that they're going to invent a luxury car without lots of intermediate inventions, so it is with simple communities that have only known tyranny and want to create a modern democracy. Inventions are complex and seem to evolve.

Things that are made up can create experiences that are quite real. The people on Easter Island somehow "made up" a religion of ancestor worship that led them to decimate all the trees in order to build statues. The ensuing loss of resources and topsoil that wiped out a huge percentage of their population was not made up; it was very real. There are very real rewards for getting social invention right and very real penalties for messing it up. The success of a plane doesn't depend on imagining a world without gravity any more than the success of an economy depends on imagining a world without greed. Inventions have to deal with reality as it is in order to change it or rise above it.

It is not just the things that we can see that are made up. Even the way that we see is made up. An ATM is a technological invention yet the idea that we need money (even the idea of money itself) to buy something as essential as food is a social invention. In a village centuries ago, a hungry person would not be sent away for lack of money. The way we see the world, our worldview, has changed. The medieval mind made sense of the world very differently than does the modern mind. (Well, than do some modern minds.) Among other things, we invent meaning, explaining our world and our roles in it. Social norms, too, are just made up but have very real consequences.

The medieval mind believed that man had fallen from grace and, now expelled from the garden, was destined to a life of misery as a test of worthiness for the afterlife. The Enlightenment mind, by contrast, believed that progress was possible and desirable, believed that this life could be good and made even better. These beliefs, too, are social inventions. Whether we call them beliefs or philosophies or mental models, these might be the most subtle yet pervasive social inventions of all, changing how we make sense of the world and even what we think is possible or desirable.

A set of inventions defines a culture or civilization.

We recreate civilization in each child. We call it education. Look at the huge amount of time and attention we devote to "civilizing" a baby to become a member of society. The gross effort it takes to recreate society in each child should be testament to the fact that a culture is not a "natural" or spontaneous state; it is, instead a social invention that takes great effort—every time. Language and manners, what we question and what we accept, social roles—all of these end products represent the teaching of parents, teachers, and even the media and are essentially conventions that work to construct meaning, to create the modern life.

Rather than see them as inventions, we often see social inventions as simply "the way things are." Should you want a reminder that social inventions are just made up, however, raise a child. Mothers know that the curious, rebellious, stubborn, and lazy child will challenge social inventions. My family lives close to the Mexican border and when my daughter was protesting her car seat, she would say, "Mexican kids don't wear seat belts." She, like every child, knew that things could be different and questioned why they were not. And of course, travel, news reports, novels, and history all remind us that our social inventions are not universal or even stable. What makes you successfully fit into your neighborhood in Manhattan would make you stand out in Afghanistan. Or even Montana. What made you fashionable in 1972 makes you look silly in 2012.

The Need for Social Invention

Perhaps teachers and parents should add this to their list of admonitions and lessons: "Warning: contents of this society have been known to create feelings of anomie and alienation; provoke wars, homicides, and suicides; and pollute the habitat you need for survival. Most of what we tell you should be questioned and could be improved upon. This is, really, just the best we've been able to do up until now and it could be that improvement will actually overturn much of what we now accept and advocate. Learn about your culture and your place in it, but don't cling too tightly to it. What we're teaching you probably needs to change, and soon."

History is not a set of static stories about the way the world once was. Told right, history is the story of how we came to live the way we do, and it might even predict our future. Most of us define our lives by the social inventions that define us. I'm an American, we might tell people, or a Baptist, or young, or an engineer, or an employee of IBM, and yet this is as often a phase we are going through as a defining part of who we are. We had the potential to be something more or perhaps someone different, and had we been born into a different time or place we would have been. Through history, the ways of being—the options for how we live our lives —have changed dramatically. What is perhaps most interesting about this change is that in each succeeding generation, one's way of being has been defined less by the society one is, by chance, born into and defined more by personal choice. There is little reason to believe that the ratio of intentionality and choice to chance and destiny won't continue to rise. Increasingly, individuals will define their lives rather than leave that definition to the society into which they're born. This is already happening.

Change Consensus – Invent a New Social Reality

A $20 bill is worth exactly $20 for no other reason than this: we all agree that it is worth $20. As soon as we stopped agreeing that it was worth $20, it would no longer be worth $20. One day a Confederate dollar is worth a dollar and the next it is worthless. The thing itself did not change—only what everyone agreed about it.

This is an oddity of social reality. It is not made out of a material like wood or metal. Instead, it is made out of consensus.

One day, everyone agrees that a certain amount of gold is worth $20. The next day, everyone agrees that mere paper will be worth $20. One day the world is populated by polygamists and the next by monogamists. This is called progress.

Of course, there are limits to social invention. Like technological invention, it is not magic. A group of people can't just gather around a fish and declare it to be a desk. (Well, unless they are merely changing its name.) But a group can gather around one man and say he's a king and around another and say he's a president and then agree that the two have very different rights and responsibilities. Or groups can gather around one woman and say she's a slave and around another and say she's a wage earner, and explain the demands that can be made of each, the rights each does or does not have, and the compensation each deserves.

Charles Tart makes the point that a hypnotist, in a matter of minutes, can program you to do things you don't normally do and to believe what is not so.[4] He then asks, how much more powerfully can society program you during the course of your life, given that it has so much more time and so many more persuasive tools at its disposal than does a hypnotist?

Without going too far into this now, the fact that the self is itself a social invention suggests something curious about the next stage of progress. If social invention is to become more widespread, the individual will have to become more aware of how his or her life is also an invention. Up until now, it is the few who have defined society and the many that have been defined by it. A few receive divine revelation and many receive Mass. Think about a world in which the

---

[4] Charles Tart, *Waking Up: Overcoming the Obstacles to Human Potential* (New Science Library, Boston, MA, 1987) 98-100.

direction is increasingly reversed, a society in which the individual is less social invention than social inventor. Or, rather, imagine a world in which more people engage in acts of social invention. If social invention becomes to this century what technological invention was to the last, we'll witness such a change. Or, rather, we'll create such a change.

If daily life is an invention, the question is, whose invention is it? It is hard to underestimate the importance of inertia in defining society. Yet entrepreneurs challenge this inertia and invent something new.

As I left school, the headmaster told me, "Branson, I expect to either see you on the cover of a business magazine or in jail."

— Richard Branson, founder of Virgin, who has, incidentally, been on the cover of quite a number of magazines

Entrepreneurs

We've been intentional about technological invention through much of the twentieth century. Corporations budget for it and assign project teams to develop new products. By contrast, social inventions come from entrepreneurs and revolutionaries—from outside the system. Social invention is not planned for. It receives little support. People seem to think that the social inventions through which we currently work and govern will not change, in stark contrast to their expectations about technological inventions. I think that notion will radically change within our lifetimes.

It seems as though we're about to enter a new economy, one in which the act of social invention will become as normal as the introduction of new products. At first, this will seem disorientating, but our grandkids will think it is normal. New ways to learn, to work, and even to worship will be invented and evolve at unprecedented rates. This will be a period of unprecedented prosperity and individual freedom. It will also be unsettling.

For centuries, if you were to ask the average person in the West to articulate the purpose of life, you would probably hear a response that had to do with being a good Christian, a good citizen, a good employee. That is, purpose has been given to the individual by social institutions. The big social inventions provided meaning and purpose and the criteria by which people judged their lives.

It is difficult to distance ourselves from our big institutions and do the hard work of defining self. It is much easier to be an employee than to be an entrepreneur. It is much easier to be a good Catholic than to be the first Protestant, or to be a good government bureaucrat than to be a revolutionary.

Society teaches us many things, but one thing it does not teach us is how to change society. Every society is born out of some revolution and yet no society actually teaches or encourages revolution.

Entrepreneurs start businesses, and I'm going to expand the term to essentially say that an entrepreneur is a social inventor. Their work is to create a new social invention, an organization, an institution, a new market, or a new business. Social entrepreneurs might start a new non-governmental organization (NGO) or nonprofit or charter school. I'm going to include under my broad umbrella of entrepreneurs not just business entrepreneurs like Bill Gates and Henry Ford but political and religious entrepreneurs like Thomas Jefferson and Martin Luther.

The next economy will popularize entrepreneurship in the same way that the Information Age popularized higher education and knowledge throughout the twentieth century. As entrepreneurship becomes more popular and diverse in its expression and application, social invention will become as normal as technological invention.

For centuries, social invention was more often the product of revolutionaries than something societies intentionally encourage. Yet social invention is at the root of social progress. The first communities to successfully encourage social invention as they now encourage technological invention will be the first to create the next economy, ushering in a time of unprecedented social progress.

The next chapter explores why some social inventions give communities more wealth and power.

2 Limits to Progress

> An economy is defined by its limit. If you want to understand an industrial economy, predict what people will do to overcome the limit of capital. If you want to understand the fourth economy, predict what people will do to overcome the limit of entrepreneurship—the act of social invention.

Not every invention leads to progress. At the dawn of an industrial economy, a community is limited by capital; without machines or money people have to make things by hand and, as a result, have very few things. By the end of an industrial economy, by contrast, they have enough machinery and money to make lots of products. The limit has shifted from capital to knowledge workers who - among other tasks - can create advertising that creates demand for all the products that capital can make. At different stages of development, economies have different limits and those limits define them. Once a limit is overcome, though, a community has a choice: stagnate by continuing to focus on what used to limit or reinvent itself by shifting its focus to a new limit.

Fad or Fundamental?

Social inventions like the church or state define lives for generations. Others, like pet rocks and the Macarena, are just fads. So why has the Catholic Mass been persistently more popular than the twist? (And if you think that this is an absurd, glib, or intentionally irreverent comment, you underestimate the oddity of history. For a long time, dance was quite common in church as a means of celebration and expression. And yes, I do mean dance in what came to be known as the Catholic Church, not some obscure pagan sect.)

The reason that some social inventions have a lasting influence and some are thrown onto the scrap heap of nostalgia and history is fairly simple: some inventions are more effective at helping communities get what they want.

Imagine that a tribe in the American Northwest lives in an area rich with beavers and has lots of furs but is often hungry. A neighboring tribe lives in an area rich with salmon and has lots to eat but is often cold. A social invention that lets the two tribes swap excess furs for excess salmon would improve the welfare of both tribes.

Given that you live in modern times, when thinking about a social invention to solve this exchange problem your mind probably immediately goes to the idea of a market like the mercantile exchange market, or barter, or eBay. Those social inventions are indeed possible solutions but the tribes in the Pacific Northwest developed an interesting alternative: the Potlatch ceremony. Two tribes would meet for a feast and "gift" each other with their excess. This became competitive and did a lot to establish status. Giving "gifts" also created a sense of obligation and mutual care that sales or barter would not. Not only did this make them both better off, as should all trade, it also created a sense of obligation that helped to maintain peace and ease the request for help in the future. To prove their wealth, chiefs would not just make gifts to others but might even throw gifts into the fire in a display of conspicuous consumption likely to make even someone joy-riding in a Hummer scratch his head. (Social inventions often look silly to people outside of the culture. This is one reason that university students can sometimes be so annoying: not yet vested in the system, they're more likely to see and mention the obvious flaws in the society in which they live.) An economist would likely point to the inefficiencies of the Potlatch ceremony but the rituals probably helped the tribes to bond. The ceremonies also resulted in the exchange of surplus in ways that led to specialization and an improvement of life for both tribes. And given that the Potlatch ceremony solved the problem of hunger or cold (for our fictional tribes; exchange between actual tribes was more complex), this social invention would become institutionalized. Communities would likely resist attempts to change it because it worked. Why did the Potlatch ceremony become such a big deal? It got the tribes what they wanted. If people see an invention as a means to get something as vital as food or clothing, it will become important. It will become something mythologized through stories or advertisements, which are, of course, themselves social inventions.

Every society is limited in its ability to get what it wants. Any social invention that helps a community to overcome these limits becomes important, and in economies, the limits that matter most are the limits to economic progress.

In the simple example of the two tribes who need only salmon and fur, once they have the Potlatch ceremony that lets them trade, their access to natural resources no longer limits them. They have enough salmon to eat and enough furs to keep them warm. Sort of. Once communities overcome one limit, though, a new one appears. Development continually shifts the limit, whether it is from toilet training to managing tantrums in public or from a need for natural resources to a need for capital.

The tribes with enough salmon and furs experience a shift from the limit of natural resources to the limit of technology to process these natural resources. They need what economists call capital: tools that require an investment of time, problem-solving, and creativity. They have plenty of salmon but only when it is in season. If they want enough to eat in the off-season, they need new techniques and tools for preserving salmon. This requires some experimentation and investment of time and resources. Until they develop this ability, they're not limited by the natural resources but by a process that can preserve their salmon. And perhaps they have a similar problem with the furs, which are hard to link together well enough to keep out drafts on cold and windy days. You can stack only so many furs on your shoulder before cold legs are all you think about. Their limit to progress is having the knowledge, tools, and processes to smoke the salmon and stitch the furs. More abstractly, their limit is capital. Until our tribes have that, life doesn't get much better in spite of an abundance of furs and salmon. Overcoming their new limit requires a new batch of inventions, some technical and some social. (Technical inventions might include the actual hooks that work as needles and threads for stitching, while social inventions might include agreements about how to divide the work of stitching and smoking salmon and how to divide the "profits" from the work.)

When social inventions help communities overcome limits to progress, they become important. They make the community richer and more powerful. The people who control these inventions gain wealth and power, and the better these inventions are at overcoming the limits to progress, the more rich and powerful is the community.

What happened in the history of the West is more complex than our simple example of fictional tribes who are lacking only fish and furs. But the general theme is the same. Progress depends on overcoming limits. Economies—and the communities they are in—are largely defined by the limit they're focused on overcoming and the success they are having in doing so.

Systems Dynamics and Strange Attractors

Complex systems can be defined by relatively simple dynamics. Communities focused on overcoming the limit of natural resources are going to have a very different set of behaviors than communities focused on overcoming the limit of knowledge workers. The degree of competitiveness, the tendency towards dogmatic religious beliefs, and levels of toleration for divergent thinking are just a few of the very pervasive things that will be different in these two communities. Economic limits are not the only things that define a community, but they have a huge and pervasive influence, working like Mandelbrot's strange attractor. Picture how a whirlpool in a draining tub shapes the water; other currents and eddies are at play, but it's the dynamic leading to the whirlpool that does the most to shape and direct the flow. Or think of how the sun anchors the movement of the planets in the solar system. So it is with the limits to an economy and, by extension, a community. It is never just one social invention that allows a community to overcome a limit; that effort is pervasive and defining.

As complexity rises, precise statements lose meaning and meaningful statements lose precision.

— Lofti Zadeh

What is Bald?

A quick aside about baldness. If you have a full head of hair, you're obviously not made bald by someone plucking a single hair from your head. That would be ridiculous. Even if they took two hairs from your head, still you would not be bald. But at some point in the process of plucking hairs, there would be a general consensus that you were now bald. The way that the term is generally used, bald is rarely an all-or-nothing state. So it is with so many of the concepts that I'm writing about in this history of the West. In a traditional economy, people generally choose a trade, say, because of tradition. The baker's son becomes the baker. By contrast, in a market economy people's actions and career choices have far more to do with market forces, attempts to maximize salary or lower costs. But such terms are terribly imprecise. To this day, there is economic activity defined by tradition rather than pure market forces. For instance, someone took over the family farm not because it offered the best economic opportunity but because it was family tradition. Yet such events don't make our market economy a traditional economy. And during the time that we generally label the economy as traditional, before 1300, there were lots of examples of towns formed by trading and where market forces defined what people did for a living. Yet that – alone – did not make it a market economy. Did the West suddenly go bald in 1300? Or, rather, did it suddenly become a market economy? No, but the influence of markets became more obvious. It might be more accurate to say that in 1000 there was little evidence of the West being shaped by market forces, and by 1500 there was quite a lot of evidence. It's just simpler to say that in about 1300, the West became more of a market than a traditional economy. And throughout this narrative of Western civilization, I'll continuously opt for such simplifications of reality rather than attempt to exactly capture reality. For instance, I'll talk about the first economy as something that started in 1300 and ended in 1700—a sort of convenient precision that is fairly absurd at one level and yet good enough at another. So, back to our story.

The Theory of Constraints

Eli Goldratt developed and popularized his Theory of Constraints through books like *The Goal* and *Critical Chain*. Put simply, he claims that any system with a goal has one constraint to getting more of that goal. If one focuses anywhere but on that constraint, any "improvements" will not actually get one more of the goal. His own focus has been on the business world and some of the world's biggest companies have applied his ideas to factory floors and product development.

To illustrate how his approach might work, imagine the world's simplest factory. This factory has just two workstations. The one workstation takes ten minutes to process a piece of inventory. The other takes only five minutes. To make the product, the factory has to move inventory through both process steps. The factory, or system, can produce only six products an hour because of the first stage. This is the constraint to making more products.

To "improve" the speed of the second stage would really be no improvement at all. The limit to making more products is in the first step. Double the speed of the second step and you don't improve your ability to create more products at all. Double the speed of the first step and you double the number of products you can make in an hour. Now that both workstations take only five minutes to process each part, the system, or factory, can make twelve products an hour. Focus on the limit and you get more of your goal. Diffuse your attention elsewhere and you get no improvement.

Double the speed of the first step one more time, though, and you get no increase in ability to make products. Once your first step takes, say, just two minutes, the limit has shifted from the first step to the second. If you want more products now, you have to shift your improvement efforts to the second stage, which still takes 5 minutes.

Now in this example, the limit is obvious. That's not the case with a factory floor with dozens or hundreds of steps, each worked by someone who wants to "do their best." Yet any person doing her best to improve who is working at the station that is not the limit will do nothing to improve the output of the system. Best efforts are not enough. The only way to make more products per hour is to improve the speed of the limit. The whole factory improves when we focus on the limit; "improvements" elsewhere in the system are illusions.

Goldratt's theory of constraint and its focus on limits can apply to any system, from traffic flows, to projects to launch new products, to economic systems.

A central premise of *The Fourth Economy* is that economies are generally limited by, and therefore defined by, one factor of production at a time. But before an economy faces a limit to progress, it has to be making progress. Progress starts when a community changes from a traditional to a market economy.

Economic Limits

At one stage in development, an economy is mostly defined by tradition. The village has a baker because the baker's son fills the role, and prices are set by tradition. Guilds protect prices and process. Not much changes in this world. At the next stage of development, markets primarily define the economy. The village may or may not have a baker, and he'll fill the job if he can charge prices high enough to make a living that keeps him in that village and out of another job or profession. To accept a market economy is to accept a disruptive dynamic. After 1300, the West was more obviously defined by a market economy than by tradition.

The West's first market economy was agricultural. Neither capital nor knowledge workers were the limits to progress. There was almost no talk about the need for more machinery or the need for better universities. In 1300, progress was mostly limited by access to natural resources and products of the land.

Communities in 1300 didn't rely much on genetics, fancy fertilizers, or machines and didn't even have much in the way of plows and seed drills. If they wanted more, there were essentially two ways to get more: one was to conquer and rule more land and the other was to trade surplus with other regions, trading fish for furs or wool for grapes. Natural resources, or what economists call land, were the limit to progress in this first economy, and at the beginning of the first economy, communities most often got those through conquest or trade.

To simplify, I'm going to refer to an economy based on land as an agricultural economy, to contrast it with an industrial or information economy. But if we're talking about an economy limited by land, it could get its wealth from any number of sources, including agriculture (most likely), fishing, mining, forestry, oil, or any natural resource. Practically speaking, the economies of the West during this first economy were essentially agricultural, and a huge majority of the workforce was engaged in some kind of farming.

Economy	First	Second	Third
Period	1300 – 1700	1700 – 1900	1900 - 2000
Limit to Progress	Land (Natural Resources)	Capital	Knowledge Workers
Type of Economy	Agricultural	Industrial	Information

If land is your limit to progress, you might do well to invent a nation-state with a standing army to protect your land and a navy to explore and conquer (or at least establish and protect trade with) distant lands. Of course, the notion of a nation-state with a standing army represents a big jump from tribes wearing furs, which is one reason that the story of the first economy plays out over roughly four hundred years. It doesn't just take a long time to bake this cake, but there are many layers to it; the series and layers of social inventions that brought societies to a place where they could field a standing, national army—inventions as varied as stable borders, taxation, and a sense of nationalism and patriotic duty—didn't unfold in a single generation.

Defined by Limits

The community whose economy is limited by land is likely to be very religious, for instance. They rightfully see that the natural resources they enjoy have their origins in something other than man's efforts. The fish, the fertile land, and the seasons are all blessings that they can do little to control or influence. Even today, agricultural or rural communities throughout the West are generally more religious than urban communities. The oil-rich nations in the Middle East, whose wealth is based on natural resources—or land—are also more religious than the more economically developed European nations where communities' welfare is not so obviously dependent on the blessings of nature.

An economy limited by land is ready for war. Members of this community know that any acre you rule is an acre that they don't. The competition for control of natural resources is zero-sum. (Control of resources is win-lose, or zero-sum. Trade of resources can be win-win, or variable sum. [5]) Communities whose progress is limited by land are prepared for war and put a great deal of effort into military preparations and actual war.

The communities whose economy is limited by land find ways to

---

[5] Robert Wright's *Non-Zero: The Logic of Human Destiny* (New York: Pantheon Books, 2000). The first half of the book is a marvelous explanation of how variable sum games contributed to cultural evolution. Pages 31–37 tell the story of trade among the Northwest Indian tribes.

enhance the value of their goods through trade. The further you are from the apple orchard, the more an apple is worth. When all you have is natural resources, you have incentive to trade. Within their borders, communities working to overcome the limit of land might create free trade zones (a social invention). Outside of their borders they might fund navigation and exploration to find new sources of goods and new markets in which to sell or trade. (And in the process may even discover new continents.)

During the first economy, social and technological inventions that helped communities to overcome the limit of land made them wealthier and more powerful. Furthermore, the social inventions that helped were the ones that became important and were institutionalized. That is, they became a way of life, they defined for these people, "who we are." The good thing about this is that once communities had institutionalized these inventions, they were less likely to be lost. The bad thing about this is that once communities had institutionalized these inventions, it was harder for these communities to let go of or change them in order to focus on overcoming a new limit. Change required revolution. The kings who invented the nation-states and were able to make the land prosperous early in the first economy (around 1300) were beheaded late in the first economy (around 1700) when the monarchies they'd invented as part of the nation-state were overthrown.

The West has overcome a series of limits through a series of inventions and revolutions. In the process, western economies have transformed from agricultural to industrial and then from industrial to information-based. In transforming from an agricultural to an industrial economy, the limit of land gave way to the limit of capital. At one point, trade in cotton made communities wealthy and it was enough to sell cotton to the households that were left to process it into clothing. As the West moved into the next stage of economic development, however, the limit of land, of natural resources like cotton, was overcome. What then limited the new economy was capital to process that cotton into garments that could be sold. If you want to be wealthy in an agricultural economy (the first economy), when land limits, you might focus on conquest and trade. If you want to be wealthy in an industrial economy (the second economy), when capital limits, you focus on investment and process. The strategies for attaining affluence and progress change as the limits shift.

The main thread of the narrative for the first economy, from 1300 to 1700, is one of overcoming the limit of land. It is a story of global exploration and conquest. It is a story of shifting power from church to state because the state is an institution better able to adapt to the demands of overcoming the limits of land, an institution better at managing, ruling, and extracting value from land. The most important social invention of the first economy was the modern nation-state, an invention of entrepreneurs like Henry VIII and King Louis XIV. The world of 1700 was very different from that of 1300. One simple but dramatic difference reveals the magnitude of the change in mindset that occurred over the course of these four centuries: around 1300, spices like pepper were rumored to come from lands just across from the Garden of Eden, lands so distant as to be mythical; by 1700, spices were likely to come from foreign colonies that had been conquered, mapped, and largely "civilized." And much of the progress that occurred during this four-hundred-year period of history was clearly driven by a set of social and technological inventions—as diverse as the compass and the notion of private property—that allowed the populace to overcome the limit of land.

Since the beginning of the eighteenth century, Western economies have been limited by two other factors: capital and knowledge workers. These two limits have created two new kinds of economies: an industrial economy focused on overcoming the limit of capital, and an information economy focused on overcoming the limit of knowledge workers.

After 1700, the limit to progress shifted from land to capital, and the West was transformed by a new set of social and technological inventions. Inventions as diverse as the steam engine and bank clearinghouses, factories and bond markets helped communities to overcome the new limit of capital. The agricultural economy was transformed into an industrial economy and once this occurred, capitalists dictated to kings.

After 1900, a third economy—an information economy—emerged. It was limited by knowledge workers. The story of the last century is a story of a new set of social and technological inventions like venture capital and computers. Again, a wide and disparate range of events can be given coherence if seen as an attempt to answer the question of how to overcome the limit of knowledge workers. How do communities create more of them? How do they get more from them? How do they create tools to maximize their productivity? The answers to those questions bring us inventions like MBA degrees, the Multinational Corporation, and personal computers.

When the factors limiting society shift, communities have two choices. They can struggle to invent their way into the future by creating new social inventions better suited to overcoming this new limit, even if this means transforming or toppling the old social order, or they can remain stagnant, continuing to do well what matters less and less, gradually losing power and wealth over time. And lest you think that the abandonment of social inventions is something simple or abstract, know that it involves things as wrenching as beheading kings and being branded a heretic. We tend to define ourselves by the work we do inside of the corporation, the beliefs we have within a church, the citizenship we have within a country; to transform or invent the institutions that in turn define us is to challenge our very notion of self, our very definition of community, our meaning of life. Social invention and social change are disruptive. When limits shift, inventors, entrepreneurs, and revolutionaries create a new society in response to the new limit. They reinvent civilization. And this disruptive, awful, and wonderful process that has unfolded three times in the history of the West has just begun for a fourth time.

Progress

If we talk about the limit to progress, it is worth defining progress. Obviously it is progress when a tribe goes from hungry to having enough to eat or from cold to having warm clothes, but progress is more comprehensive than merely meeting physical needs.

Progress gives the individual more autonomy, more freedom to live a life of his own choosing. A person with shoes has more choices about where to go than a person in bare feet; a person with a car has even more autonomy than a person who has only shoes. The person living in a modern democracy has more autonomy about how—or even if—to worship than someone living under a theocracy. Progress follows from social or technological inventions or—most often—some combination of the two.

At a really large scale, the social inventions that have helped communities to overcome the limits to land, capital, and knowledge workers have also given the individual more freedom in religion, government, and finance. This might be the most fascinating thing about how social invention has changed the world so far.

In a sense, the West is an odd experiment in placing trust in the individual. Progress has given choice and autonomy to people who hold no titles or formal authority. This is a hard experiment to justify, but it has created the most phenomenal results in history. And while people have done things with religion that popes disapprove of, things with government that kings don't like, and things with credit that would make J. P. Morgan's face turn red, the net effect has been quite wonderful.

The more choice and freedom we give the individual, the more interesting the world is, and the better life is for nearly everyone. Inventions that give us progress are the ones that give us, along with generations to come, more autonomy and more choice about how to define and live our lives.

So What Really Limits?

One way to distinguish between what limits and what is necessary is to ask whether acquiring more of it will help. Air could limit survival but once you have enough, another roomful of it will do little to change things. Once you have enough air, it could be that you need water. And, again, water might limit survival only up to a point and then you might need food and then warmth. The limits to progress, like the limits to survival, can shift, and acquiring more of a limiting factor, once the limit has shifted, may have little effect.

The limit to progress does not shift because the old limiting factor is no longer necessary or because the old social inventions haven't done well at addressing the old limit. Air still matters when you start drinking water. Success at the old limit gives you a foundation for addressing the new limit. Factories that define the industrial economy could do little without natural resources, which defined the limits of the agricultural economy, to process.

Yet, after a time, acquiring more of the limiting factor does little to further progress. We reached that stage around 1700, when conquest and trade had opened access to essentially all of the natural resources this planet had to offer. At this point, the limit shifted to capital that could be used to process these natural resources into higher value products. From that point, wars of conquest were more likely to impoverish rather than enrich communities. We reached the stage of diminishing returns with capital shortly before 1900, when factories could produce more than communities were prepared to consume. Now, we have reached that stage in our information economy, a stage in which information no longer limits, a world where a fourteen-year-old with Internet access can get more information in an hour than could the head of the KGB in a month at the height of the Cold War.

What limits us now is not land, capital, or knowledge but entrepreneurship. The story of the economy during the first half of the twenty-first century will be the story of how communities invent their way past this limit, building on what we've learned in overcoming the limits of land, capital, and knowledge work but still ready to overturn the social inventions that defined communities within the agricultural, industrial, and information economies.

Entrepreneurship

We've typically thought of entrepreneurship as the act of starting a new business. It is. Yet I think that the fourth economy will reveal how narrowly we have thought about entrepreneurship. Entrepreneurship is an act of social invention. By this definition, when Martin Luther and Joseph Smith each started a new religion, they were engaging in an act of entrepreneurship. Thomas Jefferson and Giuseppe Garibaldi were also entrepreneurs, helping to create the nation-states of the United States and Italy.

Entrepreneurship has always been with us, just as land, capital, and knowledge workers have. But entrepreneurship was not a limit to us as long as our economies were constrained by these earlier, simpler limits.

Entrepreneurship is social invention that creates new systems. And one bit of evidence that we're entering a new economy that needs a new approach is that everywhere we look we face failing—or at least faltering—systems. We live in a world dependent on systems and yet we know little about them, their dynamics, or how to create, manage, or sustain them. We question the sustainability and efficacy of systems as varied as our financial systems, industrial systems, ecosystems, and educational systems. Entrepreneurship in the fourth economy will be about creating new businesses and creating equity, as it always has been. And it will be about popularizing that so more people engage in acts of entrepreneurship. But it will more profoundly be about creating sustainable social systems through some combination of technological and social inventions. Focusing on overcoming the limit of entrepreneurship will reinvent civilization as much as any previous shift in limit. And then it will reinvent it again. And again. Entrepreneurship will be to the fourth economy what technology was to the third economy.

The set of activities societies use to overcome limits is complex but falls into a pattern. This pattern of revolutions and invention will be explained in the next chapter.

Progress doesn't just happen. Communities that actually transform the lives of average people are the communities that focus on overcoming the limit to progress. Within a stable economy—within an industrial or information economy, for instance—progress comes from focusing on a single limit. During a time of transition into a new economy, progress requires shifting the focus from one limit to the next. That's more than a little unsettling.

The next chapter traces the pattern of progress from about 1300, tracing the combination of social invention and revolution that marks the transition from one economy to the next. It gives a very high level summary of the tsunami of change that follows from a shift in the limit to progress.

3 The Pattern of Social Invention & Revolution

The history of the West is punctuated by big changes and revolutions that have defined and redefined religion, politics, and finance. These are not random events but seem to fall into a pattern that emerges as communities focus on overcoming limits to progress.

Patterns

Western Civilization has been reinvented on three separate occasions, and has each time created a distinctly different economy and society. Each time, a wave of social invention has helped the West to overcome the limit to progress. History is composed of more than just economic progress, but some of the biggest and most defining events are captured in this pattern of progress.

Patterns allow prediction. Because patterns repeat, someone can tell you the exact time the sun will rise tomorrow. Because of patterns, we can define the major trends of the next few decades.

During the last seven centuries, a big pattern has been repeated three times. Savvy readers will point out that this is hardly the basis for a statistically significant conclusion but in fact the pattern is a bit like Mandelbrot's fractals. Mandelbrot discovered shapes that repeated at small and large scales: a fern leaf has a shape that is similar to the larger shape of the fern plant and also to just a portion of the leaf. Fractals repeat patterns at different scales. The pattern of revolution in the West that has played out three times in really broad strokes has also played out in smaller domains than the whole of Western Civilization quite a few times. Communities, countries, and regions have all gone through similar stages of development enough times to give

the pattern credibility.

This pattern also has logic behind it. In the sense that this represents a progression, this pattern of economic and social progress echoes natural evolution. Plants had to develop before herbivores could develop and, of course, herbivores had to develop before carnivores could. That's logical. It also seems logical that an economy would first need some raw materials, some natural resources, before it would have much incentive to develop capital and machinery to process those materials. And then you could say that the complexity of the machinery, markets, equipment, and products of this industrial economy would generate increasing incentive to develop ways to manipulate symbols of these things first, which is the work of knowledge workers. (It is much cheaper to re-arrange the blueprints of a factory than the actual walls, and much cheaper to learn what a focus group wants when you are still designing the product than to learn what a market wants after you've already made one hundred thousand units.) Raw materials give machines something to work with and machines give knowledge workers something to work with. The progression from a resources or agricultural economy to an industrial or to an information economy is not only logical but seems to be supported by lots and lots of examples in many different regions, communities, and countries.

The Pattern of Revolutions

This book covers more than seven hundred years of history and predicts the next half-century. It tends towards sweeping generalizations.

If you want a book on the particulars for starting a business in California in the second decade of the twenty-first century, you'll need something about a thousand times more detailed. With that said, this section is going to be the most sweeping of all. I'm going to talk to a pattern that plays out over centuries and ignore about a thousand details that might be worth examining—if I had dozens of lives in which to research and write about the West and you had decades in which to read about it.

Our starting position before 1300 was one of squalor, starvation, superstition, short lives, and short people. In this period, nobody knew anything about anything and even sections of Europe that would later fall within the same national boundaries were shrouded in mystery from one another. Distant continents were known mostly by rumor, if at all. The dominant institution was the church and there weren't any nation-states. There weren't really even any nations, and the states (mostly city-states) were capriciously governed. After the collapse of the Roman Empire, Europe had shrunk to the size of small villages and, in more prosperous regions, city-states. Even things like the Roman formula for making concrete were lost, and Europeans used the Roman roads for centuries, unable to build anything better. The church was the one institution that gave Europe a common identity or any kind of coherence during this time.

Limits

There was no limit to progress, because there really was no progress. Life was static. Ninety-five percent of Europeans never traveled more than five miles from their homes during the course of their short lives. Many were serfs, meaning that they were bound to the land by law anyway, and could not travel even if such a thing occurred to them.

Although there might be markets here and there, this was not a market economy. It was a traditional economy. Centuries went by and nothing changed. Life was not particularly complicated, and even as late as the seventeenth century, the main pastime of French peasants was little different than the grooming behaviors of other primates: they spent most of their free time combing lice from each other's hair.

A market economy is dynamic. As technologies and competition and fashions change, whole industries rise and fall. A market economy unleashes gales of creative destruction and it is not just companies or industries that are created or destroyed. Worldviews, dominant institutions, and a sense of self and community can also be made or lost in these gales. A society with a market economy is dynamic, and once the West transitioned into a market economy, change rippled through every facet of life.

I'm not saying anything new when I claim that industrial economies follow agricultural economies and information economies follow industrial. That these economies are part of a larger set of changes is less often noted. The process that leads to the creation of a new economy does not create only a new economy: it also creates an entirely different culture, society, and people. This is, for our generation, no mere historical curiosity; another new economy, and all the sweeping changes it will provoke, is about to emerge.

The pattern of economic change starts with this: when a community focuses on a new limit, it starts the process of creating a new economy. As with natural evolution, there is no precise period of transition from one species, or one economy, to another. And as with natural evolution, social evolution seems to carry forward elements of the last economy into the next. As communities focus on specific social inventions, the broader forces of social evolution occur.

Economy	First	Second	Third
Period	1300 – 1700	1700 – 1900	1900 - 2000
Limit to Progress	Land (Natural Resources)	Capital	Knowledge Workers
Type of Economy	Agricultural	Industrial	Information

As mentioned in preceding chapters, an economy is defined by its limit. An agricultural economy is defined by the limit of land and an industrial economy is defined by the limit of capital. Less obviously, an information economy is limited by knowledge workers. (This will be explained in more detail later but suffice it to say that information has little value without knowledge workers to transform it into, well, knowledge. Until it is acted upon, information has only potential.)

The world we have made using one level of thinking creates problems we cannot solve at that same level of thinking.

—Albert Einstein

Intellectual Revolutions

It is not enough to use the same approach with a new limit that you used with the old one. It's a "new wine in old bottles" or "old minds in new worlds" problem. Getting communities to shift is problematic for lots of reasons. One is that the very fact that a community is facing a new limit is proof that their strategies were good. These strategies took them up to the new limit, and it's hard to abandon the tried and true. But you have to crawl out of the boat that got you to the new shore in order to walk around to explore the new land; the old strategies don't work on the new terrain. A community facing a new limit has succeeded at overcoming the old limit. This alone is proof that its approach, its culture, its worldview, and a myriad of social inventions are successful. But this success renders much about the old economy obsolete. Or, more accurately, renders it necessary but no longer sufficient. Worse, some of the most defining pieces of the old economy have to be transformed.

The most subtle but probably most profound social invention changes how we think about the world. It's an intellectual revolution. Intellectual revolutions change how problems are framed, how problems are solved, and even what communities consider to be problems. Until about 1100, in the West it was widely thought that humanity had been created to replace the fallen angels who'd been kicked out of heaven along with Satan. Limits to material or economic progress were not even considered problems for the simple reason that progress was not the goal of life. Salvation was. It might take a great deal of intelligence to debate about how many angels fit on the head of a pin, but winning or losing such a debate did little to bring milk to the table. Life was thought to be only a test by which one could win or lose salvation. Nothing else mattered. Without a change in thinking, an intellectual revolution, issues like conquest, capital, or information technology had little hope of seizing the popular imagination. Breaking with the obsession with spiritual matters required a new way of thinking, something the Renaissance provided.

In the history of the West, three great intellectual revolutions have changed how elites and laymen alike have seen the world. The Renaissance shifted attention from heaven to earth, reviving interest in the work of the Greeks and Romans and even the idea of progress. This life—and not just the next—became important and this was represented even in the art of this period, which depicted real (if idealized) people rather than the less realistic people or things, icons, and symbols that were common in the art of the medieval period. Following the Renaissance, Enlightenment thinkers transformed science and politics, subordinating monarchs and miracles alike to law. Finally, most recently, pragmatism has become the watchword. These days, most people claim to be pragmatic, many unaware that they're describing a philosophy rather than a sentiment hammered out in woodshop. Pragmatism is to most people in the West not a philosophy but instead, just the way things are. "I'm pragmatic," business or political leaders tell us, as if that refers to the world itself rather than a lens through which we look at the world. The Renaissance, Enlightenment, and Pragmatism each represent a distinct philosophy, and each will be explored in its own chapter. What they each have in common is that they were useful constructs for addressing the limit of their time.

Economy	First	Second	Third
Period	1300 – 1700	1700 – 1900	1900 - 2000
Limit to Progress	Land	Capital	Knowledge Workers
Type of Economy	Agricultural	Industrial	Information
Intellectual Revolution	Renaissance	Enlightenment	Pragmatism

Transforming Work

The pattern of revolution also includes a change in the definition of work. Before 1300, the role of workers was essentially that of slaves. (The term "slave" comes from the word "Slav," in reference to the fact that Central Europeans would make "recruiting" runs into the east to kidnap Slavs whenever they needed more workers.) Serfs were bound to the land, unable to live anywhere else. The agricultural economy saw a growing number of freemen, workers who were free to lease their own land and choose how and where to work. The manual work of the agricultural economy was eclipsed in the industrial period by factory work and then, in the information age, by knowledge work. At each new stage, the experience, productivity, and even products of workers radically changed. It probably seems obvious to say that work changes as an economy changes. This "obvious" point should be remembered, though, if we're going to seriously think through the implications of what it means to create one more new economy. A new economy suggests that how we define and think about work will change again.

Economy	First	Second	Third
Period	1300 – 1700	1700 – 1900	1900 - 2000
Limit to Progress	Land	Capital	Knowledge Workers
Type of Economy	Agricultural	Industrial	Information
Intellectual Revolution	Renaissance	Enlightenment	Pragmatism
Work	Manual (manipulate things by hand)	Manufacturing (manipulate things by machine)	Knowledge (manipulate symbols of things)

Big Social Invention

Economic changes are never neatly contained within the workplace, however. A community does not change how it thinks about the world and leave its institutions as they are. The rewards for inventing a new institution able to overcome the new limit to progress are huge. The leaders in this process are inevitably the richest and most powerful communities. They are also the ones most willing to make wrenching changes to their dominant institution.

The first economy emerged at a time when the church was at the peak of its power. With everything from church bells to papal bulls, the church defined daily life. One little-known fact about medieval popes is that much of their time was spent resolving property disputes. Without agreed-upon government officials, the pope was the ultimate authority. (In fact, many of the property disputes were between barons, counts, and various-named "authorities" who were the closest thing to government officials but were nonetheless arguing amongst themselves about who had jurisdiction, given that political authority was not yet defined and settled.) Yet the church was poorly suited for overcoming the limit of the first economy. Europeans were never really comfortable with the idea of a pope riding out to battle with a sword on his hip in order to claim land (something that actually happened). Nation-states were a much better social invention for conquering and protecting land. Nation-states could provide a navy able to protect trade routes on the open sea, an army to protect and expand borders, and police and courts to protect private property. By the end of the first economy, the nation-state had eclipsed the church as the most powerful institution in the West. One simple reason for this (although the process itself was anything but simple) is that the nation-state is better suited for overcoming the limit of an agricultural economy than is the church. If a community is serious about overcoming the limit of its economy, it needs to be serious enough to cede control from a previously dominant institution to a new, more effective one. This process alone makes for wrenching social change.

The second economy saw the rise of capitalism and financial markets, and once again a new institution came along to eclipse the power of the old. The bank was better at overcoming the limit of capital than was the nation-state, and soon governments were shaping their policies to win the approval of bond markets and bankers, eager for the financing that would allow them to keep power, even while it hastened their loss of relative power to the banks and the market they represented.

In the twentieth century, the multinational corporation became the most powerful institution in the West. These corporations grew to define our work-family balance, our options for products and services, our incomes, our capital returns, our landscapes, and even the quality of our environment. The corporation is simply better at overcoming the limit of knowledge work than is the church, the state, or the bank. As with every economy before, in the third economy the institution best suited (or, really, designed and invented) for overcoming that economy's limit to progress was the institution that became most powerful.

Economy	First	Second	Third
Period	1300 – 1700	1700 – 1900	1900 - 2000
Limit to Progress	Land	Capital	Knowledge Workers
Type of Economy	Agricultural	Industrial	Information
Intellectual Revolution	Renaissance	Enlightenment	Pragmatism
Big Social Invention	Nation-State	Bank	Corporation

Institutional Transformation

Of course, these newly dominant institutions do not emerge in a vacuum. They have to wrestle against the old, previously dominant institution. Furthermore, these new economies don't displace the old economies; they build upon them. You can't manufacture without natural resources to process. Knowledge workers manipulating symbols need actual things to which those symbols link. (As Peter Drucker quipped, even the grandest strategies eventually devolve into actual work.)

As previously mentioned, there is a very real difference between something that is necessary and something that is a limit. The newborn needs air, but once it is breathing, it needs food and rest. The need for food doesn't assume that the baby no longer needs air—just that the air is a given. So it is with economic progress. Communities working to overcome a new limit do not assume that the old limit goes away but rather, that this old limit is no longer a limit.

When the limit to progress shifts to capital, there is still a need for natural resources. In fact, demand for them grows. This suggests that the social invention able to overcome the limit of a preceding economy is even more effective and more broadly used in a new one. That is, the previously dominant institution does not go away when a new one takes over the dominant role, but instead becomes the tool of the many.

One repeating pattern throughout the history of the West is the dispersal of power. “We are all priests,” cried Martin Luther as he wrested authority away from the pope and gave it to every Bible-reading Christian. “All men are created equal,” wrote Jefferson, the slave owner. Such sentiments speak to real changes in what it meant to be a Christian or a citizen. Such sentiments also describe the democratization of power.

The Protestant Revolution ultimately shifted power from church authorities to the Bible. Catholic authorities warned that in this direction lay massive splintering of the church, as any Bible reader could claim a revelation about what a particular verse meant and start his own denomination. As it turns out, they were right. Thousands of Protestant denominations now pepper the religious landscape, but this is a consequence of the dispersal of power. Today, each individual can decide how—and even whether—to worship.

But the new nation-state quickly escalated in size and its armies alone were enough to drive innovations in finance like the emergence of bond markets that could feed the nation-states voracious appetite for previously unimagined sums of money. The nation-state’s dependence on money made it dependent on financial markets, and eventually presidents danced to the rhythm of bond markets.

Finally, and less obviously, the power formerly held by the bank has been dispersed over the last century. Not only do corporations dictate terms to banks (rather than vice versa, as in the early days of capitalism) but rather than beg for credit, the average household regularly rejects offers of it, discarding credit offers that seem to come daily in the mail. In this way, households now have the power over credit that bankers once held: they decide whether to accept or reject loans requests. Stock markets have become investment vehicles for the average person and not just the elites. During the last century, mostly through pension and mutual funds, the average person has become the majority stockholder in the United States. Households have been given easy access to credit and investments. As with the church and state before it, the bank has become a tool of the masses.

Economy	First	Second	Third
Period	1300 – 1700	1700 – 1900	1900 - 2000
Limit to Progress	Land	Capital	Knowledge Workers
Type of Economy	Agricultural	Industrial	Information
Intellectual Revolution	Renaissance	Enlightenment	Pragmatism
Big Social Invention	Nation-State	Bank	Corporation
Social Revolution	Protestant Revolution	Democratic Revolution	Financial Revolution

The Fourth Economy

Our generation gets to add a fourth revolution to this fascinating adventure. The fourth economy will result as we invent our way past the new limit of entrepreneurship. We will discover a new way of thinking that is better suited to entrepreneurship and the creation and management of systems and social inventions. The new economy will change work again, popularizing entrepreneurship rather than leaving it to the elites. It will transform today's dominant institution, making the corporation the tool of workers and their communities, rather than the other way around. Finally, it will mean a change in how we define institutions and how we delineate our relationships to them.

One constant through this thread of progress is the rise of the individual over the institution. At the rise of each new economy, the average person is seen as subject to that economy's dominant institution, and is used as a tool by it. The individual is a subject of the state, for example. By the close of the economy, things have been reversed: the institution has become a tool of the individual. The king's subjects become citizens.

There is one other point worth making, a point so obvious that we nearly overlook it. Social invention—this story of the rise and transformation of institutions—offers the potential for huge and powerful payoff. The walls of Oxford's Christ Church College Dining Hall are covered with portraits of luminaries who have attended Oxford. John Locke is among them. Even if every other graduate of Christ Church had been a slacker who smoked opium rather than accomplish anything in business or politics, England would have seen a positive return on their investment in the whole of Oxford. It would be difficult, if not impossible, to calculate the extent of the benefit we have received as a result of John Locke's ideas, which did so much to create modern democracies. Social invention has huge potential, and because of its track record we've come to nearly deify social inventors like America's founding fathers. And here's the point: if social invention can make so much difference, why not make it an intentional part of life rather than something that happens only on rare occasion? When we create institutions to overcome limits, we make progress. When we transform institutions to make them tools available to many, we are better off. Social invention, just as assuredly as technological invention, facilitates progress. It makes little sense to confine it to history books when we can make it a part of our lives.

When a community transforms from an agricultural to an industrial economy, or from an industrial to an information economy, it is not just the economy that changes. There is a pattern of revolutions that sweeps through society to change the major institutions and even how people think about the world. That pattern suggests that when the next economy emerges, its impact will not be neatly contained with cubicle walls but will require a change in our thinking and dominant institution.

The next section delves into the first economy, a time that brought us out of the Dark Ages and transformed how we think about religion. The pattern of progress touched on in this chapter will be explored in more depth.

The First Economy

The first economy was a time when tradition gave way to markets. The first economy was crude, with little machinery and few knowledge workers. What limited economic progress was land, or natural resources. By the end of the first economy, the land from which the West drew included Africa, the Orient and the Americas. It included, that is, the whole world. What it took to explore and conquer so much of the planet is outlined in these chapters.

Chapter 4, Land, explores and defines the limit to progress in the first economy and briefly touches on how we could again change our relationship to nature in the next economy.

Chapter 5, The Agricultural Economy, lists some of the highlights of the new economy, some of the major turning points in the transition from a traditional economy to the first market economy.

Chapter 6, The Renaissance, introduces some of the thought leaders and artists of the time who changed the West's worldview.

Chapter 7, Inventing the Nation-State, introduces some of the defining social inventors who did so much to create the institution that would come to define Europe.

Chapter 8, Protestant Revolution, gives an overview of how the emergence of the first economy changed the church and the definition of religion in the West.

Chapter 9, The State Trumps Church, gives a few examples of the battle between church and state, and how the nation-state replaced the church as the West's dominant institution.

4 Land

In the first economy, land was the limit to progress. This is to simply say that natural resources were the source of wealth before the West developed the machines and financial markets of capitalism.

Economy	First	Second	Third	Fourth
Period	1300–1700	1700–1900	1900-2000	2000-2050
Limit to Progress	**Land**	Capital	Knowledge Workers	Entrepreneurship
Type of Economy	Agricultural	Industrial	Information	Entrepreneurial
Intellectual Revolution	Renaissance	Enlightenment	Pragmatism	Systems Thinking
Big Social Invention	Nation-State	Bank	Corporation	Self
Social Revolution	Protestant Revolution	Democratic Revolution	Financial Revolution	Business Revolution

God blessed them and said to them, "Be fruitful and increase in number; fill the earth and subdue it. Rule over the fish of the sea and the birds of the air and over every living creature that moves on the ground."

- Genesis 1:28

Eventually the earth said, “Alright already! That’s enough. I’m subdued. Go work on another commandment, like love your enemy.”

Land was the limit to progress in the first economy. Wealth followed directly from conquering land or trading its products. Although many of the major players during the first economy may not have articulated the notion that land was the limit to progress, trade and conquest were central objectives to the budding nation-state.

Nature vs. Natural Resources

The natural environment of medieval times was as rich as the social environment was impoverished. People reported hiking through forests on the European continent with overhead foliage so thick that they did not see the sun for days. The new lands they discovered were even richer.

James Gustave Speth wrote about North America when the Europeans first arrived, giving a vivid example of abundance through a story about passenger pigeons:

It is difficult to appreciate the abundance of wild nature in the world we have lost. In America we can think of the pre-Columbian world of 1491, of Lewis and Clark, and of John James Audubon. It is a world where nature is large and we are not. It is a world of majestic old-growth forests stretching from the Atlantic to the Mississippi, of oceans brimming with fish, of clear skies literally darkened by passing flocks of birds. As William MacLeish notes in *The Day before America*, in 1602 an Englishmen wrote in his journal that the fish schooled so thickly he thought their backs were the sea bottom. Bison once roamed east to Florida. There were jaguars in the Southeast, grizzly bears in the Midwest, and wolves, elk and mountain lions in New England.

Audubon described the breathtaking multitudes of the passenger pigeon migration as well as the rapacity of their wild and human predators: "Few pigeons were to be seen before sunset; but a great number of persons, with horses and wagons, guns and ammunition, had already established encampments. ... Suddenly, there burst forth a general cry of 'Here they come!' The noise which they made, though yet distant, reminded me of a hard gale at sea. ... As the birds arrived, and passed over me, I felt a current of air that surprised me. Thousands were soon knocked down by polemen. The current of birds, however, still kept increasing. ... The pigeons, coming in by thousands, alighted everywhere, one above another, until solid masses ... were formed on every tree, in all directions. ... The uproar continues ... the whole night. ... Toward the approach of day, the noise rather subsided. ... The howlings of the wolves now reached our ears; and the foxes, lynxes, cougars, bears, raccoons, opossums, and pole-cats were seen sneaking off from the spot. Whilst eagles and hawks, of different species, accompanied by a crowd of vultures, came to supplant them, and enjoy their share of the spoil. It was then that the authors of all this devastation began their entry amongst the dead, the dying, and the mangled. The pigeons were picked up and piled in heaps, until each had as many as he could possibly dispose of, when the hogs were let loose to feed on the remainder."

The last passenger pigeon on earth expired in a zoo in Cincinnati in 1914.[6]

We have so tamed and subdued nature that it's hard for us to imagine how threatening the wilderness would have seemed to the average person at the beginning of the first economy, around 1300. To venture into the forest or ocean was to court death. The forest had bandits who were happy to steal from the poor as well as the rich, and wild beasts that could tear you apart. It also had elves, fairies, and demons. The community, too, discouraged venturing too far into the wilderness; many medieval towns had curfews and if you came back inside the city gates after dark you could be fined a day's wage.

Before the invention of the compass, it was dangerous to lose sight of shore. Storms could easily swallow boats and everyone on board. Maps, if they existed at all, were invariably sketchy and often missed what they didn't distort. Sea monsters rose out of the water just beyond the horizon.

Nature did not need protection from people; people needed protection

---

[6] James Gustave Speth The Bridge at the Edge of the World: Capitalism, The Environment, and Crossing from Crisis to Sustainability (New Haven, Conn.: Yale University Press, 2008), 2–3.

from nature. There didn't appear to be any real limits to how many fish could be hauled out in nets or how many birds could be snared or shot with arrows. For instance, in New England there was such a proliferation of number and variety of fish—fish that today we've never seen—that it was illegal to feed one's servants lobster more than twice a week. Lobster was considered a garbage fish. The limit was not in nature. The limit was what people could take from nature.

Farming and fishing were perhaps the most obvious ways that communities sought to extract value from nature, but mining and logging were also common.

Starvation, too, was common. Life was hard and nature gave up her bounty reluctantly. The world's population in 1300 was roughly one-twentieth of today's population, and life expectancy was roughly twenty years in the year 1000.

To turn nature into a source of natural resources required a confluence of technological and social inventions. There is a profound difference between nature and natural resources. A man who lives in the forest approaches it differently than the man who makes his living from the forest. Animals live in the forest but they don't make and sell timber, don't convert it into goods to be sold in markets.

Throughout the first economy, communities in the West focused on overcoming the limit of land, creating a host of technological and social inventions able to better navigate, measure, conquer, and extract value from the land. The result was that nature was transformed from a wild and intimidating force that was little understood into natural resources that had been tamed into regularly providing returns.

The Invention of Land

In the half millennia between 800 and 1300, Europe's population grew from about thirty million to eighty million. Never had so many lived on that land, and traditional agricultural could not keep up. By 1300, the population was so chronically malnourished that it was even more susceptible to the plagues that regularly swept across it. [7] This put pressure on communities to get more from land, pressure that rewards inventions, whether they are technological or social.

By 1305, King Edward I had made a really important social invention: he'd standardized measures like the yard and the acre. This, in turn, helped with the invention of private property, turning land into acreage. Nature can't be subdivided or bought and sold. Land can be. More importantly, people don't really invest in nature or improve its yield. An acre of private property, though, well that's a different thing.

Sometimes similar inventions occur in different places. The same little communities that had invented the role of serf invented and began to adopt the role of freeman. A serf is owned by the land; a freeman owns the land. A serf's welfare changes little as the land yields more; not so with the freeman.

It wasn't until about the twelfth century that the Catholic Church accepted the legitimacy of private property, previously holding to the notion that "the earth is the Lord's and the fullness thereof, and its fruits belong to all His creatures in common."[8] Private property better lent itself to a market economy than did nature or communal property.

Traditional vs. Market Economies

Throughout history, people worked, used tools, and had access to natural resources. People did not become labor, tools did not become capital, and natural resources did not become land, though, until they began to operate within a market economy.

A traditional economy is fairly stable because actions are defined by tradition. A market economy is dynamic because actions are defined in response to shifting and evolving market forces.

In a market economy, people become labor. That is, how they work is

---

[7] Hagen Schulze, *States, Nations and Nationalism: From the Middles Ages to the Present*, trams/ William E. Yuill (Malden, Mass.: Blackwell Publishers, 1994), 27–28.

[8] Jack Beatty, ed., *Colossus: How the Corporation Changed America* (New York: Broadway Books, 2001), 21.

defined by labor markets. A baker is not a baker because his father was, but because he sees it as the best job given his options. Nature becomes natural resources. That is, how a product like timber, fish, or ore is used is determined by commodity markets, and these natural resources go to the highest bidder. When communities transition from traditional to market economies, they create land and labor out of natural resources and people. For this reason, the transition to a market economy requires the invention of land. Now that's an important social invention.

It was not until the eighteenth century that the field of economics was considered a branch of study in its own right rather than a branch of ethics. At the beginning of the first economy, how prices were set and resources were used was determined by what was considered right, by traditions rather than market forces, making these decisions ethical rather than economic issues. While this may sound nice in theory, in practice it tends to mean that vested interests get to define what is allowed to happen and how much can be charged. Such an arrangement tends to favor the status quo (for good reason it is called a traditional economy). Land had been a source of value since life emerged but became a factor of production only with the emergence of a market economy. This changed everything.

To illustrate the difference between land as a source of value and land as a factor of production, let's take a simple example. As I write, California is in the midst of huge budget problems. Among the many solutions being considered, no one mentions the possibility of selling San Diego County to Mexico, or selling the Redwood National Forest to Oregon. Real estate within California is bought and sold all the time, but the state's border has remained unchanged for more than 150 years. The land as claimed by a state is not subject to market forces, not treated like a factor of production. Now imagine a world like that, a world where all property is tied up with identity and the claims of rulers. That was the world at the beginning of the first economy.

Markets and Trade – Maximizing the Value of Goods

Markets maximize value. At the risk of stating the obvious, when you sell to the highest bidder you tend to get more for your product. In addition, the further the apple is from the orchard, the more it is worth. Prices tend to rise with scarcity and the further you get from the source of a thing, the scarcer—and hence more highly priced—the item becomes. Curiously, it's a tiny black seed that illustrates how this dynamic works, and how this dynamic, once set in motion, can change how the world is defined.

To find a good reason why the waiter might think it would impress your date to offer her freshly ground pepper from what appears to be a small table leg, you'd have to go back centuries to medieval Europe. (Of course, Freud might have as much to say about what this conveys as any historian. Lasting rituals rarely make sense at only one level.) In medieval times, pepper and other spices were status symbols, highly coveted, exotic, and expensive. So much so that pepper's special place in our diet has carried over into today's fine restaurants.

Spices were ideal for trade. They didn't spoil and were light in weight. Essentially, foreign trade at the start of the first economy meant spice trade. And the foreign lands from which the spices came were so remote as to be shrouded in mystery. By at least one estimate the average European never traveled more than five miles from home during his entire life, and places as remote as Asia were romanticized. To medieval Europeans, America was unknown but Atlantis was real, as was Paradise. And yes, by Paradise they meant the Garden of Eden. Medieval Europeans believed that "pepper ... grew on a plain near Paradise [and that] ginger and cinnamon" had been carried by the Nile straight from Paradise.[9] Spices were so aromatic, so rare, and so special that they were thought to come from Eden. (It seems reasonable to assume that traders who were happy to enhance demand for their product would make little effort to clarify that pepper actually came from what we now know as India and the Maluku Islands in Indonesia.)

European food had yet to be infused with so many of the exotics to come from later stages of world trade, and spices were coveted for the simple fact that they enhanced the taste of food. Given that the trade route was so long, spice prices were high and the products were essentially reserved for the elites. "In fact, pepper frequently took the place of gold as a means of payment."[10] And as with any highly priced item, spices conveyed status; they meant it literally when they said that

---

[9] Wolfgang Schivelbusch, *Tastes of Paradise: A Social History of Stimulants, and Intoxicants*, trans. David Jacobson (New York: Vintage Books, 1993), 6.

[10] Schivelbusch, *Tastes of Paradise*, 7.

a man had good taste.

By the fifteenth century, new rulers along the long trade routes were charging traders more and more costly tariffs, and growing wealth among Europeans meant increased demand. As a result, spice prices went up thirty-fold. If a person could find a better trade route to India, perhaps a sea route that would circumvent the Oriental land routes that required the payment of so many tariffs, he would be rich. Columbus ventured out into unknown seas in search of just such a route.

So, it was a taste for spices drove explorers to find a new continent. For all that makes modern America different from Renaissance Europe, perhaps one of the details that would most impress Columbus is that of a waiter coming to one's table to offer unlimited quantities of fresh ground pepper.

But perhaps it is time to update the definition of progress from Columbus's time to incorporate what we've learned in the five hundred years since. Maybe we could consider an economy that doesn't depend on the process of transforming more and more nature into more and more stuff. Moving in that direction might start—curiously enough—with an acknowledgement of psychology.

From Quantity of Goods to Quality of Life

Throughout the first three economies, the initial approach to land has never changed. If anything, we've gotten better at conquering it, exploiting it, and turning nature into natural resources. And just as it seems that we've perfected our methods for overcoming the limit of land, bringing us into an economy of unprecedented abundance, we are becoming aware that natural resources are limited. We can no longer predicate progress on getting and using more natural resources: the next economy will have to design systems that respect the limit of nature rather than treat it as unlimited. For the first time since the dawn of the first economy, we may have to change how we design products and production systems, working to make our use of natural resources as sustainable as the cycles of nature.

To again quote Speth,

Half the world's tropical and temperate forests are now gone. The rate of deforestation in the tropics continues at about an acre a second. About half the wetlands and a third of the mangroves are gone. An estimated 90 percent of the large predator fish are gone, and 75 percent of marine fisheries are now overfished, or fished to capacity. Twenty percent of corals are gone, and another 20 percent severely threatened. Species are disappearing at rates about a thousand times faster than normal. The planet has not seen such a spasm of extinction in sixty-five million years, since the dinosaurs disappeared. Over half the agricultural land in drier regions suffers from some degree of deterioration and desertification.[11]

We've faced such issues before, but never at a global scale. In fact, the very first civilization seems to have eventually clashed with natural systems. Theirs were ingenious inventions but, in the end, their systems were not compatible with nature. The Sumerians invented the city and writing, professional soldiers and hereditary kings. They also invented irrigation. [12] This irrigation helped them to overcome the limits of land for a time, but eventually turned productive farmland into salt pans, maximizing short-term returns at the expense of the carrying capacity of their farmland. The result? "Even after four thousand years, the land around them remains sour and barren, still white with the dust of progress. The desert in which Ur and Uruk stand is a desert of their making."[13] What was the first great civilization in the history of the world became a desolate desert in Iraq.

Just as with money, there are two ways to respect the limit of nature. One way is to respect limits and budget now. This is uncomfortable but sustainable. The other is to overspend to the point that all reserves are gone and one is left bankrupt. This is painful and can be disastrous. What's true of households with money is true of communities with natural resources.

The foundational assumption of economics is that more is possible. Although theoretically most people would tell you that resources are finite, that is not the assumption behind daily actions. For instance,

---

[11] Speth, The Bridge at the Edge of the World: Capitalism, The Environment, and Crossing from Crisis to Sustainability (New Haven Connecticut, Yale University Press, 2009), 1.

[12] Ronald Wright, *A Short History of Progress*([Cambridge, Mass.: Da Capo, 2004), 70–71.

[13] Wright, *A Short History of Progress*, 79.

even if you don't believe in climate change and believe we have plenty of oil, you'd have to acknowledge that we will run out eventually (even the most optimistic forecasts assume this will happen by century's end) and that our economy is today based on it. More is not possible indefinitely. At some point, we will need to do one of two things: shift over to different sources of energy or learn how to get more from less.

Some suggest that progress is at odds with nature. It's possible. It might be that we're in some utopian period between taming nature and destroying it. Yet we do know that given nature has limits there are only two choices: either we seal our fate by destroying nature or we find ways of building sustainable systems that allow us to coexist with nature indefinitely. Fortunately, a curious fact about human psychology might actually help with the transition to a more sustainable economy.

Philosophers talk about three kinds of goods: goods to have, goods to do, and goods to be. Each is considered to be at a higher level than the last. To date, it is just assumed that any reference to economic goods is a reference to economic *goods to have*. Given that Western civilization came out of a background of scarcity even in this time of abundance, we assume that more *goods to have* are a sign of progress. We assume this even as we know that the rate of consumption is not sustainable. By some estimates, if the entire world consumed resources at the same rate that we Americans do, we'd need half a dozen earths. More, in any case, than we have. We can no longer assume that we've overcome the limit of land, not as long as we continue with an economic model that assumes all economic goods are goods to have.

To shift from quantity of goods to quality of life will mean broadening our definition of economic goods to include economic *goods to do*. This gets to the definition of happiness and work. William James wrote that "Lives based on having are less free than lives based either on doing or on being."[14] It seems like a bad idea to destroy our habitat in the process of creating economic goods to have. It seems like a tragic idea to destroy our habitat in the process of creating economic goods that do little to make us happier.

Some studies suggest that after about $20,000 per person, increases in income don't do much to improve people's level of happiness, which raises the question of what it is that does make people happier.

---

[14] Robert D. Richardson, *William James: In the Maelstrom of American Modernism* (Boston: Houghton Mifflin, 2006), 411.

Flow and Happiness

Mihalyi Csikszentmihalyi has spent decades studying happiness[15]. He got started by trying to understand why people might paint. Behaviorists inspired by B. F. Skinner thought that people must paint with the expectation of reward—hoping for money or fame. But when Csikszentmihalyi talked to amateur painters, they didn't seem the least deluded about their prospects of such rewards. Freudians postulated that their painting had something to do with sublimated desires, something about trying to find an appropriate way to express inappropriate feelings. Csikszentmihalyi found this implausible. As he talked to them about their painting, though, he continually heard painters use terms like "flow," as in, "I got into the flow." He adopted that term to describe a particular psychological state.

People in flow lose track of time; lose self-consciousness; are not distracted by thinking about something other than what they are doing; experience a perfect synchronicity of what they are doing, what they are thinking about, and what they wish they were doing; and end the activity feeling better about themselves and more capable. The activity that creates a sense of flow is one that strikes a balance between challenge and skills. (If the task is too challenging, people experience stress rather than flow; if they are too skilled for the task, they experience boredom.)

What is curious about this finding of Csikszentmihalyi is that it flies in the face of much of traditional economics. It suggests that what matters is intrinsic rather than extrinsic motivation, motivations that come from the experience of the task itself rather than the rewards for the task. That is, it is not what the person is paid for the task that makes him or her happy but, instead, the experience of the task.

This suggests that if we're intent on using our economy to make people happier rather than just make products, we'll focus more on creating economic *goods to do*, and move to include a higher level of economic good. The corporation has risen to become the most powerful institution of the modern world in no small part because of its

---

[15] See, for example, Mihalyi Csikszentmihalyi, *Flow: The Psychology of Optimal Experience*.

ability to cater to and stimulate the desire for goods to have. For all its flaws, it does a brilliant job of appealing to consumers. But behind every consumer is a producer. Consumers have money because they—or someone sponsoring them—also wear the hat of producer, creating goods and services. In the fourth economy, the corporation will become more adept at creating goods to do, at creating work that is meaningful and creates flow. It will do as much to design work as it now does to design products.

Shifting the focus from goods to have to goods to do, from quantity of goods to quality of life, will be one key to creating a sustainable balance between the economy and ecology. It also suggests something significant about how the corporation will be transformed, but that gets ahead of the story, leaping as it does to the set of social inventions that will transform the corporation in the fourth economy. For now, we'll focus on the social inventions that defined the first economy and helped society to overcome the limit of land when nature seemed unlimited.

The period of the first economy, from 1300 to 1700, was an incredibly chaotic and disruptive time. A certain order and simplicity emerges, though, if we focus on the efforts of communities to overcome the limit of land. The efforts to overcome land defined the economy, a new way of thinking, the big social inventions and the big revolution that transformed religion in the West.

The next chapter highlights a few of the defining periods of the first market economy, what we now simply refer to as an agricultural economy.

5 The Agricultural Economy

Trade and markets disrupted the Old World. How could that be a big deal?

Economy	First	Second	Third	Fourth
Period	1300–1700	1700–1900	1900-2000	2000-2050
Limit to Progress	Land	Capital	Knowledge Workers	Entrepreneurship
Type of Economy	**Agricultural**	Industrial	Information	Entrepreneurial
Intellectual Revolution	Renaissance	Enlightenment	Pragmatism	Systems Thinking
Big Social Invention	Nation-State	Bank	Corporation	Self
Social Revolution	Protestant Revolution	Democratic Revolution	Financial Revolution	Business Revolution

While tradition impeded progress at every turn, beginning about 1300 the West began to adopt a market economy. This agricultural economy depended on conquest to extend and protect borders and on trade to enhance the value of the products of land. Because communities that seriously pursued trade and conquest became more powerful and wealthy, this forced players from throughout the West to adopt similar strategies and objectives, if only to defend themselves.

The real animating force of the emergence of the agricultural economy was the shift from economic activity guided by tradition to economic activity driven by profit maximization. The first economy was the first *market* economy. This didn't just radically change the West: it put in place a dynamic that continues to this day.

Crusades as a Catalyst to Change

It seems fitting that it was religious excess that ultimately triggered changes that were to radically change religion. Christian crusaders intent on conquering the Holy Land returned from their journey seduced by new ideas and products. They brought back from the Arabs their numerical system, their nautical and astronomical knowledge, and new luxuries. The numerical system was used in bookkeeping and business. The nautical knowledge helped spur navigation that enabled exploration and trade. The luxuries, of course, became the initial impetus for trade.[16] The crusaders found the Promised Land but it was a little different than what they expected, the lasting impression seeming to be one of sales rather than salvation. The trip to Jerusalem curiously enough ended up more like a trip to the mall, leaving Europeans wishing they had more money for their next trip and knowing just what they'd buy next time.

"The religious crusades helped to awaken desire in Europe, desire for gold and silver cloth, cotton, silk ... glassware, porcelain ... rugs, gems, drugs, pepper ... and perfume."[17] As advertisers know, people want only what they know about. Once exposed to these new goods, Europeans were ready to pay for them. Not just a new market was born; in a sense, the crusades helped to awaken a market economy. The crusades became history's most important shopping excursion.

Marco Polo

At the beginning of the first economy, Europeans had no clear concept of world geography, and the outside world was full of mystery. There were no good maps, no accurate reports, and no TV broadcasts to bring the faraway into the living room. There weren't even living rooms. Although popes and emperors were, in name, the rulers of little villages

---

[16] Schivelbusch, *Tastes of Paradise*, 8.

[17] Jacques Barzun, *From Dawn to Decadence: 500 Years of Western Cultural Life, 1500 to the Present* (New York: HarperCollins, 2000), 169.

and towns scattered throughout Europe, there is little evidence that their proclamations were even heard there. Many Europeans were not just unaware of far off places like India, but knew almost nothing about towns and villages just over the mountains. The reports of distant lands came in distorted and hazy and it took centuries before the exchange of rumors about these remote places evolved into the exchange of goods with them.

Marco Polo did more than open up trade routes with the Orient. That alone would have been transformative, creating a steady stream of new products into Europe and making Venice incredibly wealthy. But his stories about the Orient proved more fantastical than any rumors about it. His book changed European minds perhaps as much as the products he brought back.

Marco Polo's trips to the Orient[18] overlapped with the final crusades (he returned to Italy from his final trip in 1295) and opened up trade routes with Cathay (a kingdom roughly coincident with China) and Cathay's "Emperor of the Universe," Kublai Khan. He traveled widely through Asia, India, and the Middle East and then, while sitting in jail back home in Italy, dictated his stories to a cellmate who wrote romance novels. The book seduced Europeans, who were fascinated to learn of distant lands with exotic customs. They read of Pem, a place where a woman was legally entitled to take a new husband whenever hers was gone on a trip of twenty or more days. They learned of the funeral procession of the Mongol's Great Khans "anyone unfortunate enough to encounter the funeral cortege was put to death to serve their lord in the next world."[19] Mangu Khan's funeral procession collected twenty thousand victims en route to the grave. Yet it might have been the reports of great wealth that most captivated their imagination. Marco Polo inspired generations of explorers.

Christopher Columbus, for one, carried a copy of Marco Polo's account with him on his journeys across the Atlantic. Marco Polo changed the geography of the imagination of younger explorers, changing what they thought was possible and desirable, and this transformation of the possible, as much as anything, helped to change world geography.

With a monopoly on Marco Polo's trade routes, Venice became the

---

[18] "Orient" refers to a region that includes what we now call Asia and the Middle East.

[19] "Marco Polo and His Travels," <http://www.silk-road.com/artl/marcopolo.shtml,> Silk Road Foundation.

gateway between Europe and Asia and gained enormous wealth and power through trade. To this day, Venice is one of the most beautiful cities in the world, its architecture a curious blend of the Arabic, Asian, and European. Its beauty, for the most part, traces back to the trade routes that Marco Polo did the most to create. Venice was made so rich and powerful by this trade that it was not until the 1700s that it lost land that spread into Central Europe, and even then only in battle against a coalition of forces. Only when the center of trade shifted from the Mediterranean to the Atlantic did Italian city-states like Venice lose much of their wealth and power.

The Oceanic Search for New Trade Routes

The search for new trade routes was continual and was, in a sense, just a variation on the search for profits. Looking for short cuts and ways to avoid tariffs and trade monopolies inspired ventures and invention. The trade that wound its way from India through many empires enriched many a ruler who collected tariffs en route, and there was strong incentive to avoid these tariffs.

As with so much of progress, these ventures resulted from a combination of social and technological inventions. Technological inventions in use by 1300 included the compass and the astrolabe, aids to navigation beyond sight of land. The Spanish and Portuguese used these technologies to explore the coast of Africa and venture out into the Atlantic Ocean. One defining social invention of this particular phase of the economy is something that remains with us to this day: venture capital. Columbus needed Isabel and Ferdinand to finance his venture across the Atlantic. (And it is hard to think that any venture capitalists ever got a higher return on their investment than these monarchs did.) As so often happens, the confluence of these social and technological inventions resulted in something no one could have predicted: Columbus discovered a new world.

This new land—the American continents—had been unreported in earlier literature. Not even the Bible made mention of it. And yet this land was populated not just by savages but also by huge empires, complete with ruling classes, religion and priests, economic activity, and other defining features of the West. Perhaps it is no exaggeration to say that the equivalent shock to conventional wisdom today would require the discovery of life and civilization on another planet. This discovery alone opened Europeans up to new possibilities they'd never before considered.

The Dutch were probably the first to fully exploit the new patterns of trade that spilled outside of the Mediterranean and across the Atlantic, doing as much as any people in Europe to let the search for profits define them. Trade – even more than conquest – was the way to riches in the first economy.

Trade: Even Better Than Conquest

There are two dimensions to gaining value when land is the limit to progress. One is zero-sum. If you conquer or claim land, no one else can claim that land. You win and they lose. The other is variable-sum. In order to receive value from your land, you have to bring its goods to market, trading them for money or other products. Negotiations might determine who gains the most from markets, but if they truly are free markets with full information, everyone gains. In zero-sum games, any gain I make comes at your expense. In variable sum games, it is possible for both of us to gain. One tribe gains furs for warmth and the other gains fish for food. Both win.

The Dutch, like any economic power of the first economy, engaged in both zero-sum and variable sum economics, conquering and putting their names on territories as far away as the Dutch East Indies, and trading goods with lands they had not conquered or ruled. For a time, this trade made the Dutch the richest community in the world.

The Dutch were not bound by tradition. The Netherlands was a fiercely commercial community that didn't let traditional religion or politics get in the way of profits. Rather than kings and priests, merchants essentially governed the nation. These merchants were so driven by profits that when they were at war with Spain the Dutch even sold military stores to the Spanish army.[20]

Although they were able farmers, the Dutch made most of their money by buying, selling, and transporting goods. As middlemen, they profited

---

[20] Richard S. Dunn, *The Age of Religious Wars, 1559–1689* (New York: W.W. Norton & Company, 1970), 100.

from about every kind of shipping trade, and Amsterdam was the busiest port in Europe. "They bought great quantities of spices, tea, china, and cotton in Asia, and of sugar, tobacco, and furs in America. They bought even greater quantities of lumber, grain, cattle, and copper in northern Europe, and of wool, wine, silk, silver in southern Europe."[21] Crops in the field or gold in the mine have no value; it is only when they are brought to market that they have value. The Dutch, by connecting so many different parts of the globe, created markets that enhanced the value of the goods they bought, sold, and manufactured.

Probably no community was more shaped by trade than the Netherlands, and in the latter part of the first economy, no community was richer.

Crude Goods

Land, or natural resources, was the basis of value. Most trade goods at this time were in pretty much the same form as nature made them: wheat was ground, wool was spun, and grapes were crushed and aged. The goods traded within Europe included timber, grain, wine, wool, herring, and the like.[22] Fish and whale oil, sugar, rice, and furs were all part of the growing trade between continents. If you had the products of land, you had value. Most manufacturing was actually done by hand (as the term "manu" suggests). There were very few factories and certainly none on the scale—much less at the level of mechanization—of factories in the nineteenth century. Goods were more often processed in homes than in workplaces. When value resided in products little changed from their natural state, people had incentive to explore, conquer, and claim land in order to expand their access to these products and thus increase their wealth and power.

Natural resources so defined value that in the late 1700s, the first philosophers to be called economists, the Physiocrats of France, introduced the term *laissez faire* and

---

[21] Dunn, *The Age of Religious Wars*, 99.

[22] Paul Kennedy, *Rise and Fall of the Great Powers: Economic Change and Military Conflict from 1500 to 2000* (New York: Random House, 1987), 19.

Held simply that all wealth originated in agriculture, none in any other industry, trade or occupation. Merchants, in particular, bought and sold; it was the same product before and after; nothing was added to it in the process. And the case was ... the same in industry—in manufacturing. Manufacturing merely added labor to the products of the soil; nothing new emerged."[23]

Although the Physiocrats' theory of economics was developed just in time to be made obsolete by the industrial revolution, it would have seemed a perfectly good explanation to the average person living in the first economy.

Trade from this time introduced products like the potato, maize, and chocolate and made goods like sugar and rice more plentiful. Perhaps the most interesting and transformative trade, however, was of crops, plants that originated in the New World but began to be farmed in the Old. After the discovery of America, Europeans soon added "potatoes, tomatoes, squash, beans, vanilla, avocadoes, pineapples and maize"[24] to their diet. Imagine Italy without the tomato, Ireland without the potato, and England without tea to get some sense of how indelible was the mark of foreign products on European cultures. It wasn't just the change in ideas resulting from exposure to foreign cultures, the new products they desired, or the knowledge about the outside world and new peoples that changed the West. Very simply, and very profoundly, the change in diet stimulated by trade transformed the lives of Europeans. As Europeans began to overcome the limit of land, the continent was able to support far more than the roughly eighty million that had so strained the limits of agriculture at the dawn of the first economy.

Europe Sobers Up

Trade with the New World changed diets and that likely transformed Europe as much as the political and religious revolutions of the first economy. But it didn't just change the population of Europe. It shifted

---

[23] John Kenneth Galbraith, *Economics in Perspective: A Critical History* (Boston: Houghton Mifflin Company, 1987), 52.

[24] Barzun, *From Dawn to Decadence*, 101.

consciousness. Sort of.

When communities are small, they can find fresh water in rivers and streams. Water is essential to life, and good water is prized. Yet European towns and cities grew, they put a strain on the fresh, flowing water. Alcohol was important because it was a way to make drink safe for people who could no longer just walk to a freshly flowing stream.

Yet while alcohol may have aided the growth in the European population, it seems likely that it had another, more inhibitive effect as well. Before trade with the New World brought Europe the potato, only bread provided Europeans more calories than did beer. (In northern Europe, most calories came from bread and beer. In the south, most came from bread and wine.) As late as the seventeenth century, every man, woman, nun, priest, and child in England drank about three liters of beer each day. [25] Beer soup was a typical German breakfast. The traditional economy in Europe was not the only thing that discouraged progress or change; the European population was probably a little buzzed for a few centuries. You may love your stoner friend but likely wouldn't expect him to start a new business. Alcohol may have improved public health, but it likely also took an edge off drive, reason, and energy levels.

The potato's yield was about double wheat's. After the Irish incorporated the potato into their diet, Ireland's population exploded, from about 2.5 million to 8 million. In retrospect, it almost seems too obvious that in response to the great potato famine so many Irish would leave their native land for the potato's native land, migrating to the United States in large numbers.

There are always hard-to-predict consequences to change. Population growth might seem an obvious consequence of the introduction of new foods to Europe, but by alleviating hunger these new foods might also have made Europe a less mystical place. One theory is that even as late as the sixteenth century most people lived in a state of perpetual hunger that often led to hallucinations.[26] In such a context, the church's attempt to claim a monopoly on true revelation seems justifiable, competing as it must have with every crazed and hungry visionary.

Between 1500 and 1600, in the wake of the discovery of the New

---

[25] Schivelbusch, *Tastes of Paradise*,, 22.

[26] Barzun, *From Dawn to Decadence*, 112.

World, the population of Italy and England rose by about a third and Germany's rose from about twelve million to twenty million. In 1378, London's population was only 46,000 but by 1605 it was 225,000.

Some argue that economic progress as measured by rises in per capita income did not really begin until the dawn of capitalism in the late 1700s and early 1800s (during what I'm calling the second economy). Given how narrowly gross domestic product measures wellbeing (and, of course, how crude our estimates are of GDP centuries before governments made serious attempts to measure it), this might be. Yet a measure of prosperity that discounts an increase in the number of people who could live in a region seems somewhat flawed. The first economy changed the population in many ways; perhaps the most obvious was in their sheer number.

Tradition Gives Way to Market Dynamics

Trade and the profit motive behind it shattered old traditions.

A traditional economy is, well, traditional. The feudal relationships of medieval times, for instance, were nonfinancial, and almost all exchange was done by barter. By some estimates, about 70 percent of the money in circulation was controlled by the church. Most daily activities required no money. Serfs were bound to the land and guilds defined "fair" prices and practices. At the dawn of the first economy, there were not many product options and there was almost no accumulation of wealth.

To state that land, or natural resources, was the limit to progress in this first economy is accurate, but it misses an important point. The first limit to progress is the recognition that a limit to progress exists. That land, or anything else, would become a limit to progress required that communities find themselves straining *against* limits. It is possible that people could go for generations with little or no expectation of progress. In the fourth century, one of the early church elders articulated his belief that

Men were inherently disobedient and "the cause of their own corruption in death. Things were not getting better but worse. ... These were important and enduring shifts in perspective, and they contrast strongly with the earlier optimism of Greek thinking."[27]

Lack of an expectation of progress might be the simplest definition of a traditional economy, and in such a situation the "limit" to progress is not realizing the possibility or even desirability of more. The medieval church focused Europeans on eternal riches and an acceptance of God's will, not striving for more goods. To covet (arguably the force at the root of most consumption) was a sin.

As Venice became a conduit for trade from one continent to another, creating a flow of precious goods between Asia and Europe, money did begin to seep into Europe. Soon, the gold and silver from the new world dwarfed this initial trickle and prices throughout Europe rose, stimulating economic activity. People with money look around for more things to buy, and when they do, the people around them who can provide these new things now have money too. Venice became wealthy, as did other city-states like Florence and Genoa. Enterprising merchants in places like Bruges, Antwerp, Lyons, and Geneva invented the trade fair, which was the equivalent of a shopping mall that opened for business just once or twice a year, and this helped trade to spread from the Mediterranean to other regions of Europe. These trade fairs were a transformative social invention that—like any market—gave people an opportunity to buy things they'd once been ignorant of and sell things they'd only recently acquired or just learned how to make. Inevitably, markets introduce new ideas and new possibilities, and perhaps the most overlooked resource in any economic progress is possibility. As trade exposes more people to more goods and ideas, they begin to consider more and more possibilities. And a growing population meant more people with whom to trade; even today, as the population in cities grows, incomes and levels of innovation grow even faster. Trade is transformative.

Man's mind stretched to a new idea, never goes back to its original dimension.

- Oliver Wendell Holmes

Trade is disruptive. It changes industries, expectations, and knowledge.

---

[27] Charles Freeman, *The Closing of the Western Mind: The Rise of Faith and the Fall of Reason* (New York: Vintage Books, 2005), 188.

It is no accident that on 9-11 fundamentalists attacked the World Trade Center. Trade links communities in ways that invariably bring in more of the foreign culture than first bargained for. You open a trade route for spices and your children are soon buying oriental rugs and using arithmetic to calculate their profits. A new computer delights a devout Muslim until he sees his daughter imitating Britney Spears's dance moves.

The movement from a traditional to a market economy disrupts all of society. In a traditional economy, markets do not shape the community. Serfs, for instance, are bound by law to serve the landowner and markets do not define the tasks these serfs perform. They don't choose careers based on wages or skills and would probably find the very concept of "choosing careers" confusing. "The essence of the feudal relationship was that it was *nonfinancial*. The manor yielded little excess produce for sale, and almost all exchange was done by barter."[28] In a market economy, by contrast, wages determine the use of labor, interest rates the use of capital, and prices the use of natural resources. Tradition gives way to market forces as the community seeks the greatest returns from limited resources. This transition is an essential part of the emergence of a market economy.

One of the more curious disruptions to tradition came from the popularization of private property, one of the most transforming social inventions of the first economy.

Private Property

The enclosure movement was particularly important in England. Essentially, this movement turned commons into private property, making pasture lands that communities had previously shared into private land that could be turned into pasturage for sheep or acreage for crops. Before the enclosure movement, communities shared access to land. Afterward, individuals owned land. This was a huge impetus for investment. (And even in this first economy, it helped to make poverty a twin to wealth as some gained the benefits of enclosures and some were closed out of them.)

---

[28] William J. Bernstein, *The Birth of Plenty: How the Prosperity of the Modern World was Created* (San Francisco: McGraw-Hill, 2004), 28.

Drawing from common resources tends to make people more shortsighted. During colonial times, there was such a profusion of wonderful fish in New England waters that lobster were considered undesirable, garbage-eating creatures. The number of fish and the variety of types of fish has dropped since colonial times, a consequence of what systems thinkers call the Tragedy of the Commons.

Imagine a community with one hundred fishing boats, all drawing from the same waters. No one "owns" the ocean but anyone can profit from fishing the waters and bringing back their catch to market. If, say, 100 boats fish the waters off the coat, the fishing population will remain stable, able to keep up with what fishermen draw out. But if that number increases to, say, 200 boats the population of fish might collapse, unable to keep pace as their numbers are deleted.

The problem is that each fisherman wants just a little more—or even just to continue making a living at fishing regardless of whether there are more fisherman entering the waters. He could refrain from fishing but then someone else will take "his" fish. Self-interest leads the fisherman to take what he can, but when everyone does this, the result is an outcome that no one wants. Communities generally overexploit and underinvest in commons. If the individual *gives* something to the commons—effort, fertilizer, new crops—everyone shares in the benefit. If the individual *takes* something out of the commons—a fish, or pasture for his sheep—he alone gets the benefit. The benefit is private and the investment is public: given this fact, individuals take out too much and invest too little. The value of the commons dwindles over time.

One advantage of private property over commons is that private property gives one the incentive to invest. If you sacrifice something today to make things better tomorrow, you are the one who gets that return. This alone is one reason that private property was one of the most important social inventions of the first economy.

The enclosure movement (most active in England during the first economy) turned commons into private property. This proved an important element in overcoming the limit of land. There were two consequences to this: one was that many peasants were displaced and forced into poverty; the other was that land became something people had incentive to invest in. In the long run, this created wealth. Lots of it. And it made communities more prone to invest.

These economic changes like establishing private property, global trade, and exploration, put in place a dynamic that challenged tradition and promised something better in this life and not just in the next. Economics is rarely just about economics, though. The market dynamic would overturn both aristocracy and the church. Accommodating this new impulse would require a set of social inventions that would change how Europeans thought, felt, and identified themselves.

And, these new realities changed the perception of reality. The change from a focus on the supernatural to a focus on the natural fell under the heading of the Renaissance, something defined and explored in the next chapter through characters like Michelangelo and Machiavelli.

6 The Renaissance

Progress called for a philosophy that shifted focus from the supernatural to the natural, from spiritual revelation to seeing the world as it is. The Renaissance was a time when many of the ideas of the ancient Greeks and Romans were revived and attention shifted from the afterlife to this life.

Economy	First	Second	Third	Fourth
Period	1300–1700	1700–1900	1900-2000	2000-2050
Limit to Progress	Land	Capital	Knowledge Workers	Entrepreneurship
Type of Economy	Agricultural	Industrial	Information	Entrepreneurial
Intellectual Revolution	**Renaissance**	Enlightenment	Pragmatism	Systems Thinking
Big Social Invention	Nation-State	Bank	Corporation	Self
Social Revolution	Protestant Revolution	Democratic Revolution	Financial Revolution	Business Revolution

The Renaissance revived interest in Greek and Roman art and ideas but more importantly, it shifted the West's attention from the next life to this life, from the super natural to natural resources, from the spiritual to the sensual. The art of the Renaissance was not just beautiful – it represented a focus on what could be seen with one's own eyes.

Disruptions to the Old

There are only two states of mind that precede learning, and neither is particularly pleasant. Before you learn something, you are either ignorant or confused; or, put differently, before you receive answers you have to question what you know. There were two huge events in the first two centuries of the first economy that created mass confusion and revealed great ignorance, two events that made Europeans question what they knew and opened them up to the a new way of thinking.

These two influential events were the Black Death, which began in 1348, and the discovery of America. Try for a moment to imagine the incessant coverage today's media would give to the discovery of a "new world" populated with people with many of the same social structures that we use and yet very different rituals and behaviors. Now add to that the nearly apocalyptic coverage of a pandemic that mysteriously killed nearly a third of the population. Imagine what absurd speculation we'd hear on talk shows, the banter between "experts" whose expertise in no way prepared them for this, and the callers who would begin to question everything. These two events were gales of destructive creation, destroying much of what Europeans believed and opening them up to the new.

A World Disrupted: Pandemic as a Social Earthquake

As it turns out, spices like pepper and nutmeg were not the smallest items traders imported to Europe. A microscopic bacterium was brought back with Genoese sailors in the middle of the fourteenth century. This might have easily derailed the new economy, but it seems, in retrospect, to have helped instead to erode the old order to make way for the new.

Saul Alinsky writes that someone pushing for social change will rarely have a majority on his side.[29] Change is too uncertain and people are busy with their own lives. The best one can do is to get the majority feeling like the status quo is so bad that they won't work to defend it. When this happens, you can make changes. In a sense, the Black Death did just that, not only making Europeans feel ambivalent about the status quo but actually making them ready to embrace change.

The scale of devastation from the Black Death was immense. In some parts of Europe more than half the population was killed, and across Europe as a whole between one-quarter and one-third of the population died. For all of our scientific advances, today we still struggle to understand and treat viruses like AIDS. These poor Europeans did not even have the right model for beginning to understand the plague in which they were caught. Accounts from the time showed ignorance of disease and the supremacy of the church, as most of the cures and preventatives were religious, involving prayer, penance, and admonitions to live a better life. Evil spirits or God's wrath and disapproval of social change were often cited as reasons for the widespread death and grief. Riots and the liberal slaughter of Jews, witches, and other suspicious people added to the death toll.

Seeing the ravages of the Black Death, Petrarch envied "happy posterity who will not experience such abysmal woe, and will look on our testimony as fable!" A Carthusian monk, after attending the burial of his prior and all thirty-four others in his monastery, with only his dog for a companion, went searching for a refuge. "No bells tolled and nobody wept no matter what his loss," a Sienese chronicler reported, "because almost everyone expected death ... people said and believed, 'This is the end of the world.'"[30]

As it turns out, it wasn't the end of *the* world, but it did prove to be the end of *a* world.

Imagine that even one-quarter of the people in your world die of some horrific disease that you don't understand the cause of, and certainly not the cure for. Have every person you know flip a coin twice: if they get tails twice in a row, they're dead. Doing this simulation for my children's universe of aunts, uncles, grandparents, cousins, siblings, and parents, the result was six dead and sixteen left alive. (Chance is a

---

[29] Saul D. Alinsky, *Rules for Radicals: A Pragmatic Primer for Realistic Radicals* (Vintage Books, New York, NY, 1971)

[30] Daniel J. Boorstin, *The Creators: a History of Heroes of the Imagination* (New York: Random House, 1992), 267.

harsh arbiter of justice: one family of four was left completely intact and another lost all their children. People whose religion gave more credence to the supernatural than the natural would make this mean something and seek to discern what bad thoughts, spirits, or actions made the difference. It is not that religious people don't understand causation; it is just that in their minds the cause of natural effects is often supernatural.) Not only would the deaths in this year be emotionally devastating but, to make matters worse, imagine that something like this repeats itself every two to twenty years. The first wave of the Black Death hit in 1348 and the second wave hit just two years later, in 1350. Incidences of the plague recurred repeatedly into the eighteenth century, with more than one hundred plague epidemics[31] sweeping across Europe before the illness died out in the late eighteenth century. Recently, millions of Americans were traumatized when, on 9-11, about one one-thousandth of *one* percent of the population was killed. By contrast, Europeans in this time watched about every third or fourth person they knew die. Imagine how disruptive Americans would have found a pandemic that killed about 100 million when the country was so horrified at the death of 3,000.

Living through the plague would leave your emotions and worldview shaken, and the pandemic would leave villages in ruins as surely as an earthquake. Your baker lives but the cobbler dies, as does your spouse and both of your parents and one of your children. Even the baron of the manor has died and no one is quite sure who has inherited his authority because he did not have any surviving heirs and the priest who would normally explain who is now in charge and how things should work has also died. A person has been sent out to one of the larger communities to learn more about what is going on, but this person has not returned. He, too, may have died from the plague or been killed by robbers in the forest or simply found that conditions were so much better in the next town that he chose not to come back. Obviously, there is no way to phone to inquire, no Facebook status through which one can inform. Normally, your life as a serf is determined by tradition and defined by the baron and priest. All of that has broken down. You might decide to venture out yourself and so follow the roads to another community. You might find a baron who has lost a third of his serfs, but he, of course, has no real claim over you. He might be desperate enough for help that he actually offers you a wage and more freedoms and rights than you've ever had before. You, suddenly, are free to move with the markets rather than being

---

[31] http://en.wikipedia.org/wiki/Black_Death

tied to the land. For that reason alone you and your children may never again look at life in quite the same way. And should all that not do enough to disrupt your life and sense of what's normal, imagine this repeating itself at random intervals for the next several hundred years. It was not until 1550 that the European population returned to its pre-plague levels.[32] Between 1300 and 1500, England's population dropped from five million to three million.

The Black Death helped to weaken the old social order and make way for a new one. Those who lived through it did not expect life to ever be the same.

The forces of trade and change that were slowed by the plague resumed with greater force afterwards. The plague so decimated the population that it shifted some power to the serfs, who were now relatively scarce. Among other things, this helped to erode the old feudal system and usher in new social constructs. Serfs were increasingly free to follow opportunity wherever it led them as communities struggled to adjust to the drop in population.

The plague helped undermine the church's hold as well. In 1378, about a quarter of a century after the first wave of the Black Death ended, the Great Schism of the West began. This was a period in which two popes competed for rule of the church. The Great Schism would finally end in 1417, when the (by now) three popes were all forced to abdicate and Rome was again recognized as the "official" throne of the papacy. This schism did little to enhance either England's or Germany's respect for the papacy and probably helped lay the foundation for the Protestant movements that would convulse those regions a century later.

A World Discovered

About 150 years after the start of the Black Death, Europe was faced with something new: the New World. In its own way, this was as disruptive as the Black Death.

---

32 Southern Utah University, "Topic 2: The Black Death," <http://www.suu.edu/ced/distance/hist4440/topic2.htm>

The Black Death—or something like it—was inevitable. When two human communities come into contact for the first time, both groups will suddenly be exposed to diseases which are new to them but for which the other has already developed immunities. And as terrible as the Black Plague was, Europeans had an easier time of it with their pandemic than did the Native Americans. When Europeans like Cortez and Pizarro came to the Americas they brought guns with them, but this was not what gave them enough advantage to conquer entire empires. Instead, it was smallpox, bubonic plague, influenza, and measles that killed huge swaths of Peruvians, Mexicans, and North Americans and many of their leaders. The Americans' experience of these diseases was worse than that of their European counterparts, coming as it did with not one plague but many, and with conquering armies in the wake of these germs. Europeans suffering the Black Death were traumatized, but once the population began to recover, they still found themselves in possession of their own lands and institutions. The invasion Europeans suffered was microscopic only, while that the Americans suffered was both microscopic and militaristic. Europeans found their society transformed; Americans found their society destroyed. But while European discovery and exploration of the Americas mostly obliterated American culture, it also radically changed European culture. Western Civilization moved west.

"What took place in the early 1500s was truly exceptional, something that had never happened before and never will again. Two cultural experiments, running in isolation for 15,000 years or more, at last came face to face. Amazingly, after all that time, each could recognize the other's institutions. When Cortes landed in Mexico he found roads, canals, cities, palaces, schools, law courts, markets, irrigation works, kings, priests, temples, peasants, artisans, armies, astronomers, merchants, sports, theater, art, music, and books. Higher civilization, differing in detail but alike in essentials, had evolved independently on both sides of the earth.

"The test case of the civilizations in America suggests that we are predictable creatures, driven everywhere by similar needs, lusts, hopes, and follies."[33]

In discovering America, Europeans discovered a world that paralleled their own. They found this both fascinating and horrifying, feeling at turns pity for (the priests practiced human sacrifice!) and envy of (so much gold!) the Indians but also continually found it jarring that people

---

[33] Wright, *A Short History of Progress*, 50–51.

might live so differently from—and so ignorantly of—the West.

The flow of gold and silver alone from the New World was enough to change Europe, where prices rose. Furthermore, in order to have items to trade with the Americans (now colonialists rather than natives), Europeans were driven to manufacture items, helping to push Europe towards a nascent capitalism. Europeans did not just redraw their world maps to accommodate the Americas but also changed how they thought about the world and what they thought was possible.

The disruptions of trade and gold and exposure to new civilizations created both new possibilities and stress. The possibilities were everywhere: Spanish adventurers, after 1492, had the promise of American gold; the Germans, after 1494, had the lottery. Not everyone was able to adapt to these new, jarring realities. It hardly seems surprising that by 1533 Europe had its first lunatic asylums.

Those who did not go crazy in the face of all this change had a new way to look at the world.

Look at this!

We talk about how we "see" the world, but the Renaissance was, of all the intellectual revolutions, the most obviously visual. Although the Renaissance brought about a change in how the West thought about the world, we immediately think of art when we hear this term.

Institutions are social inventions. Although it is less obvious, so are worldviews. All social inventions exist in the mind, but a worldview is probably the most subtle. We see through eyeglasses, but have to remove them to actually see them. Worldviews are difficult to remove, and given that we see through them but don't really see them, we could live a life unaware that we have a worldview, like the man surprised to learn that he has spoken in prose. Our worldview defines how we solve problems and even what we consider to be problems. The problem of the Black Death, for instance, is one that an authority from 1300 would probably try to solve through prayer and that an authority from 2020 would probably try to solve through science.

It takes little exaggeration to characterize the Renaissance as a shift of concerns from heaven to earth, from the spiritual to the sensual, and by sensual I mean the world of the senses. Renaissance art helped to focus attention on the world as it was, rather than how religious leaders thought it should be.

This is the paradox of change: the best starting point for change is acceptance of the world as it is, yet only those who find the world unacceptable attempt change. At some point in life, one stops working for life as it should be and accepts it as it is. As it turns out, life is more extraordinary than any model of it. Letting go of how it should be lets us better see it as it is, and that inevitably gives us more richness and complexity and resources than we'd have inside the confines of our own head.

One way to characterize the world before the Renaissance is as a world of should. The dominance of the church, in particular, meant that the social world was defined less by how people were than by how they should be. Because the church denied the world and people as they were, the medieval population made little positive change, or progress. Into this world came the art of the Renaissance, which did not depict mere religious icons but instead depicted real men and women.

We apply the term "the Renaissance" to a sprawl of events, people, and products, but I'm going to focus on the three elements of it that I think were the most transformative: the art of the likes of Michelangelo and da Vinci; the proliferation of books in Europe triggered by Guttenberg's press and the fall of Constantinople; and the philosophy and science of Machiavelli and Galileo. The art represented an embrace of the sensual world. The proliferation of books not only spread non-Christian ideas, but also, by allowing individuals to own a Bible, democratized the interpretation of scriptures, a prelude to undermining the power of the church. The philosophy and science of the time focused on the observable world rather than the unseen one, and the study of power separate from ethics. If the Black Plague destroyed the old world, these three elements helped to create the new one.

The conquest and use of natural resources required a more sensual and less spiritual philosophy than that which had dominated the Dark Ages. What actually *was* began to matter more than what the authorities said *should* be. Even the political philosophy of Machiavelli focused on what he saw as the reality of power and its use, rather than on ethics, or what *should* be. In this way, Machiavelli's study of power was similar to Copernicus's and Galileo's study of the heavens, beginning as it did with reality as it was rather than reality as people thought it ought to be. (To this day people think of Machiavelli as amoral, and they are right. He's amoral in the same way that Newton and Einstein were amoral.) And of course the Guttenberg press helped to spread radical ideas—most subtly the radical ideas buried in various verses of the Bible. But we'll start with the art that represented an embrace of the sensual world—again, the world of the senses rather than that of Platonic ideals and spirituality.

That Amazing Art

The soul is content to stay imprisoned in the human body ... for through the eyes all the various things of nature are represented to the soul.

—Leonardo da Vinci

When we think of the Renaissance, we first think of the art. And for good reason. No period has produced art more extraordinary or more highly valued. Works by Michelangelo, da Vinci, and Rafael are considered priceless, and if you were in a position to sell one, you and your great grandchildren would be set for life. The Renaissance got its name because it revived an interest in Greek and Roman art, but it soon went beyond simple imitation of classic thought and art. Brunelleschi, for instance, moved beyond the imitative perspective of the ancients to introduce a geometric perspective that was informed by math, more accurately capturing reality as it was. This enabled him to create structures that not only were better than any built during medieval times but eclipsed even those that the ancients had made. To this day, tourists come to Florence to see the beautiful Cathedral dome he designed and engineered.

Michelangelo, da Vinci, and Botticelli, were born into a world where art had already been gaining influence and attention for about a century. These artists mastered techniques that had already been revived and improved upon from the times of the Greeks and Romans. Daniel Boorstin writes that "there is no doubt of Giotto di Bondone's (1267?–1337) role as a creator of modern painting. He transformed schematic religious symbols into warm living figures and so showed the way for creating human figures that transcended religion."[34] Although Giotto's figures might look a little crude in comparison to those of Botticelli or Michelangelo, his are real people. Boorstin calls him an "empirical" artist whose paintings viewers might actually confuse for reality. It was not just Brunelleschi's architecture that showed an appreciation and mastery of reality; so did the art of these masters.

Although Donatello had carved Europe's first nude since classic times about seventy years before him, Michelangelo's *David* dared to depict the biblical figure as a man rather than a mere boy. If all men looked like Michelangelo's *David,* women would likely have never asked men to put on clothing. Michelangelo's art represented technical expertise, to be sure, but it also represented a desire to capture reality rather than rely on mere icons, continuing in the vein that Giotto had pioneered. Although he was still a biblical subject, Michelangelo's David was not a mere visual reference to a religious figure that would help the church to instruct an illiterate people. This David represented an idealized man who would have won Erasmus's admiration, representing a man who saw no conflict between the spiritual and the natural.

Botticelli's Venus took this even further. While this Venus, like Michelangelo's David, also represented a natural ideal of beauty, Venus was not a biblical character, but a character from a time and a mythology preceding Christ, and so removed from any connection between art and the church whatsoever. Botticelli's depiction of a pagan goddess would have been more controversial than her dress—or lack thereof.

Art of the medieval period was crude and almost symbolic by comparison to Renaissance art. Renaissance art, in contrast, caused people to *see* the world. Although beautiful, even idealized, the characters in the art of the Renaissance were real.

In another change, Renaissance artists began to sign their art. In earlier periods, art had been dedicated to the church. Artists were anonymous. Michelangelo's family was upset about his choice to become an artist because it was considered a common profession, like bricklayer. Artists were craftsmen, not people who changed community's way of seeing. During the Renaissance, artists began to make a name for themselves, famous for their mastery because they did change how people saw the

---

[34] Boorstin, *The Creators*, 382.

world.

Thus, the art of the Renaissance helped to fuel the idea of this world, this life, as something beautiful and worthy of adulation. This art was not like the earlier religious art that looked forward to paradise: it showed beauty in this world.

The shift in art from emphasis on the spiritual to emphasis on the sensual helped to shift public consciousness towards a focus on the natural world rather than on the supernatural, a necessary part of the shift in the West's attention as the economy shifted to a focus on natural resources. It's hard to overcome a limit one's not looking at.

Science and Philosophy

It is easy to blame the church for the obstruction of science, but it may be that Plato had as much to do with the adherence to authority and revelation rather than actual data. Platonic Forms are idealized representations of things that exist here on earth, and knowledge of them could be gained through revelation or reason. In his allegory of the cave, Plato essentially likened the observation of what we could see on this earth to the observation of shadows against the wall, with the Forms representing the objects casting those shadows. Plato thought "knowledge gained of the Forms was so significant that observations of the actual world should be disregarded if they were in conflict with the reality of the Forms. 'We shall approach astronomy, as we do geometry, by way of problems, *and ignore what's in the sky* [Freeman's italics], if we intend to get a real grasp of astronomy,' as [Plato] puts it in *The Republic*, his most famous work, on the nature of good government."[35]With this sort of sentiment, it is not hard to imagine whose side Plato would have taken in the debate between the church's revealed truth and Galileo's observed truth.

Plato's allegory of the cave is a powerful metaphor about essential truth that has lasted for millennia. The real lesson of the allegory is that you can't trust what you see, a lesson that Ockham, for one, chose to ignore.

---

[35] Freeman, *The Closing of the Western Mind*, 31.

William Ockham is perhaps best known for Ockham's razor, his admonition that when confronted with two explanations for a phenomenon it made sense to accept the simplest explanation. His was the kind of advice that helped to undermine convoluted superstitions. If a cow dies, it is probably easier to blame the heat than a witch's spell, however much more alluring the latter may be.

Ockham was an intellectual, brave enough to challenge the pope's conclusions. Like Roger Bacon before him, he advocated an empirical method. Further, he separated logic and faith, essentially saying that the realm of the spiritual, since it could not be observed, should not be considered the same as events that could be observed. Scientists who took his advice, quietly reasoning through issues that could be observed, were to overturn accepted wisdom about the very planet on which we live.

It was obvious to medieval man that the sun rose and set, moving around the earth. And as if one's senses were not enough instruction, they also had this verse from the book of Joshua, chapter 10 and verse 13, that clearly states that it was the sun that stopped moving, not the earth. "So the sun stood still, and the moon stopped, till the nation avenged itself on its enemies, as it is written in the Book of Jashar. The sun stopped in the middle of the sky and delayed going down about a full day." Of course, what was obvious to someone just looking around became less obvious to someone looking into space.

Copernicus was trying to make sense of orbits based on data he'd collected rather than casual observation, and could make the numbers work only by assuming that the earth orbited around the sun. Once he made that shift, all of his numbers fell into place. The more one knows the more difficult it is to maintain simply obvious but obviously simple theories.

This question about whether the sun orbited around the earth or the earth orbited the sun was not some curious academic argument removed from daily conversations. This was a time before light pollution, and Europeans knew their nighttime sky the way that you and I know our local grocery store.

When he chose to argue for Copernicus's conclusion, the problem that Galileo had was the same problem that Darwin faced centuries later: Galileo had only theory and observation on his side, whereas the church had intuition and tradition on its side. Oh, and authority.

"Not until 1822 did the church permit books to be printed which accepted that the earth's motion was real, a delay which fatally damaged Catholic science and likewise church prestige. And so, despite the evidence, it took two hundred years for Copernicus to be fully accepted."[36]

Copernicus and Galileo helped to literally change how we see the world. Copernicus argued that the earth was revolving around the sun (giving us the connotation of revolution as central to overturning authority) and Galileo helped to popularize this idea with his telescope and his writings. Renaissance art drew the individual's attention to representations of the world as it is; Copernicus drew the individual's attention to the universe as it is. Both were revolutionary. Copernicans were called atheists and the Catholic Church did not just force Galileo to recant but forbade any readings that described the earth's motion.

It seems a simple thing to go where the data takes you, yet this was perhaps the most revolutionary thing about Renaissance thinking. Even Aristotle was so revered that there is one story about a group of monks who were trying to recollect how many teeth Aristotle had said horses had. One of the younger monks said, "We rode here on horses. Why don't we simply go out to the stables and count the number of teeth in their mouths?" For this he was derided. It is like the old Marx brothers quip: "Who are you going to believe, me or your own eyes?" Before the Renaissance, the general rule was to side with tradition. After the Renaissance, the general rule was to side with observable facts. Just as following profits in adopting a market economy put in place a dynamic that led to changes and discoveries as disruptive as new continents, so did this seemingly simple approach to science disrupt the West in ways that still affect our thinking today.

Books, Books, Books

1453 was a great year for books. Guttenberg used his new press to print the bible at Mainz and the Fall of Constantinople triggered a flood of books and antiquities into Italy that exposed Europeans to the inquisitive minds of Greeks and other pagans. By roughly 1500, one thousand printing offices had produced ten million copies of thirty-five

[36] Peter Watson, *Ideas: a history of thought and invention, from fire to Freud* [Harper Perennial, New York, NY, 2006], 518–19.

thousand books. The Dark Ages that so depended on ignorance and superstition had little chance against this onslaught.

When Guttenberg made books affordable, he didn't just accelerate the spread of ideas: he allowed ideas to spread outside of any institution. In a sense, affordable books meant the birth of the intellectual.

Richard Hofstadter says that intellectuals aren't necessarily smarter than other people. What characterizes an intellectual is his or her willingness to follow ideas regardless of whether the conclusion supports or overturns existing institutions. A priest who supports the church may be as brilliant—or even more brilliant—than the man who simply follows observation, reason, and conscience to a conclusion that might challenge—or affirm—the church's claims. What makes them different is that the priest begins with a foregone conclusion: support for the church. The intellectual lets ideas take him where they will, whether the result is revolution, revelation, or confirmation. His is not a foregone conclusion.

Given that Guttenberg made books affordable outside of institutions, he helped to create the intellectual. (Well, this is an exaggeration. Obviously, by Hofstadter's definition, people like Socrates and Jesus were intellectuals.) Yet there is no doubt that Guttenberg's actions led society in this direction. By doing so, he helped to create social change.

It was not just that these books exposed people to new ideas. They changed their ideas about the very purpose of ideas. Through medieval times, philosophy, knowledge, and theology were all aimed at preparing man for a safe death. Montaigne (1533 – 1592), who used the new popularity and affordability of books to popularize the essay, rejected this notion, "arguing that the purpose of knowledge is to teach men how to live more adequately, more productively, more happily, right here on earth. ... This was in effect the birth of the human sciences." 37

---

[37] Watson, *Ideas*, 515.

Erasmus

Books are dangerous, and the man who may have done the most to subtly challenge European thought through his books was Erasmus. Perhaps the gentle Erasmus did as much as any writer to challenge the assumption that daily events were largely defined by supernatural causes. Like Da Vinci, Erasmus was illegitimate. The Renaissance helped open up possibilities for those who were not of noble birth. Erasmus was, for a time, a monk but soon left because of "horror of ceremony and love of freedom." [38]

He argued in *Against the Barbarians* that even though the fall from the Garden of Eden had diminished man's virtue and intellect, it had not completely extinguished it. For Erasmus, the ideal was to use the best of classical and Christian teachings as a means to realize the potential of the individual. To his thinking, the spiritual and the natural were not at odds, and improving one's natural state did not mean deviating from God's will. Erasmus's easy balance of the simultaneous pursuit of secular and spiritual goals would likely put him at ease with many contemporary Americans, but certainly made him unique among the Europeans of his day. So unique, in fact, that the West's most powerful emperor (Charles V) and the King of England (Henry VII) sought his advice.

Erasmus's approach to changing minds was less jarring than that of Machiavelli, who challenged the easy acceptance of fate as the determinant of outcomes.

During medieval times, the typical European saw natural outcomes as the product of either God's will or sorcery. An obstinate mule, bad crop, or fatal virus put the neighbor woman under suspicion of witchcraft. As late as 1545, when the plague returned to Geneva, it was blamed on witchcraft and thirty-four people were executed. As arbiter of good and evil and interpreter of God's will, the church played a vital part in a community anxious to align its actions with the judgments of heaven, and through most of the medieval period the Church seemingly had more competition from local superstitions than reason.

Labeling a phenomenon, however, doesn't necessarily change it. It is one thing to say that drought is the result of witchcraft and another to expect rain after burning witches. By contrast, to attribute a

---

[38] "Desiderius Erasmus," <**http://www.ucl.ac.uk/~uctyaev/erasmus.pdf**>

phenomenon to physical causes suggests the possibility of physical intervention. Some beliefs and explanations suggest acceptance and others action. It is only the latter that trigger change—a key predecessor to progress.

A particular approach to Christianity breeds, at best, an acceptance of fate and at worst, irresponsibility. To quote one Jesuit, "One of the great consolations of the monastic life is the assurance that we have that in obeying we can commit no fault." The uncertainty of salvation can be absolved simply by doing one's duty, for that is all that God could ask. Or, as Charles Freeman puts it, "Here the abdication of the power to think for oneself is complete."[39] The Renaissance shattered this easy reliance on fate, and Machiavelli probably did as much as anyone to change this.

Machiavelli penned a passage in *The Prince* that urges Europeans to seize the reins of fate. This has become a classic in part because the sentiment he expresses here is so modern. Given that we live in a world at least partly shaped by this sentiment, we might fail to realize how different such ideas were from what came before.

"I realize that it has been and still is widely held that the affairs of this world are so strictly governed by Fortune and Providence that human wisdom cannot modify them, or provide any remedy whatever; from which it might be concluded that it is better not to devote too much effort to affairs, but to let everything be governed by chance. This opinion has gained ground in our own times, from the many strange upheavals which have happened and still happen every day, beyond what anyone could imagine. These considerations have sometimes made me inclined to that opinion myself. To avoid eliminating human free will altogether, however, I think it may be true to say that Fortune governs one half, or thereabouts, of our actions, but that she allows us to control the other half, or thereabouts. For Fortune may be compared to one of those terrible rivers which rises up in its wrath and floods the plains, destroys trees and buildings, takes the soil away from one place and deposits it in another; everyone flees from the waters, and yields to their power, without being able to put up any resistance whatever. But for all that, it is still possible, when conditions are normal, to make suitable provision with dykes and embankments so that, if there is another flood, the water will be contained to a single channel, or at least the flooding will be less uncontrolled and damaging than before. It is the same with Fortune: she shows her power where

[39] Freeman, *The Closing of the Western Mind*, 250.

there is no organized, vigorous resistance, and consequently directs her attacks where she knows no dykes or embankments have been built. ... Any prince who relies entirely on Fortune will come to grief when Fortune changes. I also believe that success awaits the man whose actions are in accordance with the times, and failure the man whose actions are out of harmony with them. I must add that it is better to be bold than cautious; for Fortune is a woman and must be mauled and beaten if you want to keep her in subjection."[40]

It is this sentiment that animated the most visible actors of the times. Violently seizing gold and glory rather than awaiting God's reward in this or the next life became characteristic. This shift from awaiting Fortune to pursuing Fortune lies at the crux of the difference between a traditional and an economic society. The purpose of a theocratic society is people pleasing God; the purpose of an economic society is people pleasing people. To accept the latter as a purpose for society is to accept that the desires of a layman with a coin are just as important to respond to as the desires of a priest with a cross.

Machiavelli also wrote about the state, a political entity never really described before. That is, he wrote about a region ruled by a public official who exercised authority throughout a region irrespective of exactly what person held that public office. [41] The position had authority regardless of who held it.

The issues of state were not unique to the political turmoil of Italy. Thomas More wrote *Utopia* about the same time (1516 vs. 1513). The state was struggling to emerge at this time and matters of state mattered. Greatly. The invention of the nation-state was of huge importance and has its own chapter in this section on the first economy.

The individuals most inspired by Machiavelli's work were the modern princes, a select few of whom pioneered the modern nation-state, the first institution to challenge the Church for centuries. These princes and kings took on the work of defining and ruling these emerging states that were so much better suited to overcoming the limit of land than was the Church. It was Renaissance philosophy that focused on reality both brutal and sublime that would shape the minds of these inventors of the nation-state.

---

[40] Niccolo Machiavelli, *The Prince,* trans. Bruce Penman (Rutland, VT: Everyman's Library, 1981) 98–99, 101.

[41] Schulze, *States, Nations and Nationalism,* 31.

The historian Will Durant argues that the rediscovery of Greece and Rome was as important as the discovery of America, claiming that "the literary and philosophical transformation had far profounder results for the human spirit ... [because it] liberated man from dogma, taught him to love life rather than brood about death, and made the European mind free." The Renaissance was a rebirth of interest in the secular, the basis for the first economy.

In Conclusion

The Renaissance shifted attention from the afterlife to this life, from the supernatural to the natural, from what should be to what is. This focus was crucial to overcoming the limit of land. But it was not enough to merely change how people thought. The West needed a new social invention that could realize the goals Machiavelli laid out in *The Prince* – the conquest and rule of land.

The next chapter will tell the story of some of the major steps and characters in the invention of the nation-state.

7 Inventing the Nation-State

The church wasn't such a great way to overcome the limit of land. For that, the West needed a new social invention.

Economy	First	Second	Third	Fourth
Period	1300–1700	1700–1900	1900-2000	2000-2050
Limit to Progress	Land	Capital	Knowledge Workers	Entrepreneurship
Type of Economy	Agricultural	Industrial	Information	Entrepreneurial
Intellectual Revolution	Renaissance	Enlightenment	Pragmatism	Systems Thinking
Big Social Invention	**Nation-State**	Bank	Corporation	Self
Social Revolution	Protestant Revolution	Democratic Revolution	Financial Revolution	Business Revolution

States had existed for thousands of years but the new nation-state was something different. The nation-state was invented to encourage trade and economic development within its borders and to protect and expand borders. The nation-state helped communities to overcome the limit of land in a variety of ways, from private property to the removal of trade barriers within its borders. Nations of people had previously existed, as had states; during the first economy, these two were combined into the modern nation-state.

A New Economy

Even before the discovery of the new world with its new sources of gold and silver, money, rather than personal duties, was becoming the medium of exchange in agriculture.[42] Property rather than jurisdiction defined ownership, and the enclosure movement meant that the commons were converted into private property that would attract investment and enhancement rather than exploitation and depletion. The emerging nation-state could facilitate both of these trends. It could coin money and enforce property lines.

The church had not been invented to overcome the limit of land: the nation-state was. The church resisted so many of the impulses behind a market economy, from the impulses for acquiring more goods and money to the embrace of progress and innovation. Empires and city-states were only slightly better suited to overcoming the limit of land, but both lost in competition with the newly emergent nation-state. In the four hundred years during the first economy, entrepreneurs like Henry VIII and Louis XIV helped to invent the nation-state. This would redefine daily life and make possible previously unknown levels of affluence.

Social Invention Writ Large

The media commonly report on nation-building efforts and then proceed to describe state-building efforts: creating stable administration, administering justice, and securing the peace. Yet there is a difference between a nation and a state, and the nation-state is, in the history of the world, a relatively novel invention. It emerged in the West during the first economy.

To begin, some clarification of terms. The word "nation" refers to a people with a shared sense of identity. Usually this stems from a

---

[42] http://en.wikipedia.org/wiki/Holy_Roman_Empire

shared language and literature, culture, and history. In a sense, a nation is a group of people who, by default, tend to think about the world in similar ways and see themselves as having shared interests and a shared history and future.

The word "state" refers to a government and could be a subset of a nation (as in an Italian city-state) or include numerous nations (as with the Indian, Roman, or Hapsburg empires). A state usually defines and enforces law and taxation and creates a shared defense against outside enemies (at a minimum).

Early in the first economy, the most notable states were city-states like Venice and Florence and the Holy Roman Empire. There wasn't much in between the sprawl of empire and the local governance of city-states. As land became more important to wealth, however, the city-states were unable to hold their own against emerging nation-states that were able to field larger armies and thus claim more land. This was a time of increasing emphasis on private ownership, and empires did not tend to give their subjects (subjects, that is, not citizens) a sense of ownership. Empires generally hired mercenaries, and they, too, had difficulty competing with the nation-states, who offered ownership of land and, thus, a stronger incentive for their soldiers—who were often landholders—to fight. The nation-state had the potential to combine the best of the city-states' sense of participation and ownership with the empire's resources and large population.

The word "nation-state" refers to a community that shares both culture (the nation) and a political system (the state). It combines social and political bonds, and separates a community from its neighbors who are subject to different laws and rulers and often have a different sense of identity.

James Kurth summarizes the importance of the nation-state:

"The nation-state was the most distinctive and effective form of social organization in the modern era, that great epoch that began half a millennium ago, and has only recently come to an end. Each of its elements, the nation and the state, was the product of that era. In most places, the modern era brought only one or the other of these elements: some places developed a nation but no corresponding state (e.g., the Arab world); others developed states but no corresponding nations (e.g., Latin America, Sub-Saharan Africa). But the most effective social organizations were created, and the most explosive energies were released, when these two elements were fused together into the nation-state."[43]

Nation-States as Social Invention

Europe itself is a great example of a social invention. What's curious is that it's an invention that exists only in people's minds. Of course, it exists in the minds of billions of people, so that makes it real. Still, it's a consensus reality that does not exist independent of agreement. Even a border is a construct, and border disputes can tip into wars, which are not settled until the border is again clear and stable. The border is a social construct and, of course, so is most everything to do with nation-states, from citizenship to tax rates and laws to governance.

The difference between technological inventions and social inventions is their durability once consensus is lost. If you erased the memories of people in a modern city, they would still be surrounded by technological inventions and might even intuit what some of them do. Technological inventions might not work, but they would still exist. By contrast, social inventions would dissolve like cotton candy left out in the rain if the people using them suddenly had their memories wiped clean.

To say that Europe—or any of its nation-states—is a social invention is not the same as saying that it is not real. It is. And its existence is not just arbitrary, proclaimed into being in the same manner as a child who suddenly announces herself to be Cinderella.

Today's Europe includes social inventions like France and England, Germany and Italy, the Netherlands and Spain. It also includes technological inventions like nuclear power plants, toasters, and bicycles. At the start of the first economy, none of these had yet been invented. These countries did not exist in the year 1000. Even as late as 1300, only someone who knew how the story would end (or, more accurately, how it would look early in the twenty-first century) could confidently predict that these countries would emerge from the swirl of tenuous empires and emerging city-states. (England was more readily discernible by 1300 than the others, in no small part by virtue of its

[43] James Kurth, "The Post-Modern State," *The National Interest* Summer 1992: 26.

geographical status as an island.)

A technological inventor can retire to his lab or garage and tinker with reality until he has something to debut. He does not have to unveil his gadget until he's proven that it works. It is different with social invention.

A social inventor works through consensus, conversation, and coercion. He or she can't disappear away from the crowd to prove his or her invention. The crowd is the medium for the invention and the inventor has to work with them. It's a different kind of magic trick, one in which everyone peers into the hat with you to help you pull out the rabbit, or even decide if it's a dove rather than a rabbit or if the rabbit should be up your sleeve instead of under your hat. One day a group of people feel like Venetians or Virginians, and the next they think of themselves as Italian or American. And this is something they come to believe with as much conviction as their own name. That's the kind of magic a hypnotist couldn't perform.

There is something remarkable about creating a nation. One hardly knows whether to admire or be horrified at the effects of nationalism. Tell someone that one hundred people were killed in a plane crash in a faraway country and they listen distractedly. Tell them that three of the people were from their home country and suddenly they listen a little more intently. Vaguely sad news is suddenly made tragic. It is easy to be horrified at such a shift in emotion (all one hundred were both real people and complete strangers). Yet there is also something admirable about this. Woody Allen once quipped that he can't enjoy a meal if he knows that somewhere people are starving. Things like national identity seemingly make the world of seven billion people less huge and abstract and make it easier for many of us to empathize.

It is really remarkable that people take so to nationalism. Csikszentmihalyi opined that the flag might have been the most important invention of civilization. It is one thing for people to rally around their clan but quite another for them to rally around a flag that gives them a shared identity with people they've never even met. We kill one group of strangers and die for another. Perhaps it is just me, but again, this seems like something akin to magic.

Inventing the Nation-State

Not only did the countries in Europe not exist at the start of the first economy; there wasn't even an accepted notion of stable borders. The kingdom of the West Goths, for example, jumped from region to region over the course of a few generations, migrating from the Baltic to the Black Sea to the Bay of Biscay. Before the institution of the first economy, a kingdom actually centered on a king and not a place, and alliances were made between individuals—alliances that could change with deaths, war, and shifting fortunes. If you were to draw a map of Europe over the years prior to the fourteenth century, it would probably look like a lava lamp, shapes shifting over time as pieces are absorbed and broken off, people and regions becoming part of one kingdom and then another, some disappearing altogether and others growing. It would, in a sense, be much like a map of today's modern corporations. Villages and hamlets, even, might move with the villagers, who might even take the village name with them to a new location.

Borders were not the only dynamic part of the medieval world. Even the social glue that held people together was subject to change. As late as around 1500, Machiavelli experienced Florence as a republic, a monarchy, and a dictatorship. Politics and governance were chaotic. If we define a state as "persisting in time and fixed in space, [and including] the development of permanent, impersonal institutions, agreement on the need for an authority which can give final judgments, and acceptance of the idea that this authority should receive the basic loyalty of its subjects,"[44] it is clear that states did not suddenly appear, fully formed, but instead emerged gradually between about 1100 and 1600 in a slow, violent, and messy process.

Nation-Building as a Modern Problem

Nationalism does not just happen. While it is true that the nation-state is a social invention, it is not one you can easily and hastily cobble

[44] Joseph R. Strayer *On the Medieval Origins of the Modern State* (Princeton, N.J.: Princeton University Press, 1970), 10.

together. The question no one asks about Afghanistan as I write this (early in the second decade of the twenty-first century) is what sort of state makes sense, given there is no Afghan nation. You cannot force a nation into being, and attempts to do so generally mean imposing a state—something that ends up looking a tad imperialistic. Social inventions need to be at least as carefully constructed as technological inventions. Some of the major elements of nation-states were invented during the first economy.

Nothing Personal

France today is France, whether Chirac or Sarkozy is president. The borders don't change with the migration or death of its president or citizens. By contrast, medieval alliances were personal and changed upon the death of vassal or lord. "In most of Europe political power was based on the feudal system: medieval Europe was unfamiliar with the idea of states on a purely territorial basis, it acknowledged only personal bonds based on an oath of allegiance. States, as we know them, are built to last, they are impersonal and linked to institutions: the medieval personal bond, however, was limited in duration, it came to an end with the demise of the overlord or his vassal, and had to be repeatedly renewed."[45]

With the birth of the nation-state, the administration of the state became separated from the person who headed that state. When the French king would die, officials would announce, "The king is dead! Long live the king!" This was a reiteration of the fact that even though the man had died, the position survived. This was a big change from the model that defined much of medieval Europe prior to 1300.

Institutionalization of the Justice System

There was no single way that communities within Europe were governed

---

[45] Schulze, *States, Nations and Nationalism*, 7.

at the start of the first economy, but historians make some generalizations.

Medieval society was closer to anarchy than anything we know of as a modern nation-state. Force was used to settle issues and anyone could wage war against anyone else. Feuds were common. Although clergy were prohibited from bearing arms, everyone else was expected to be armed and prepared to defend him- or herself. Rights were not guaranteed, but had to be fought for, and "war" regularly broke out between families, groups, and even individuals.

Furthermore, justice was a personal thing. Conflicts between people were settled personally, by the parties involved, rather than by any state agency or bureaucrat. While this political chaos might have sufficed in a primitive society where rule and ownership of land was collapsed together, it didn't much work to promote the private property rights within a functioning state. And that made it not only difficult for individuals but untenable as a lasting solution for communities committed to overcoming the limit of land.

Peace and order result from the state claiming a "monopoly of power" and not allowing its citizens to kill who they would (something prosecuted as murder in the new nation-state) and instead ordering them to kill who the state would (something prosecuted as war).

Chief among the services of the emerging nation-states was the administration of justice. If people were not allowed to settle their disputes through force on their own, they had to have someone to whom they could turn. We use the term "court" today to refer to the office that settles criminal and civil issues. This use evolved from the king's "court," the officials who could be petitioned to settle a grievance. Kings were happy to provide this service because it meant that their authority was acknowledged. Gradually, communities were happy to turn to the king for this service because it meant that there was an ultimate authority able to resolve disputes. Kings made peace within their kingdom because they offered a final authority to settle disputes.

It took some time, however for a centralized justice system to overcome the medieval practice. It was not until 1495 that the Emperor of the Holy Roman Empire (itself a continually evolving set of territories and peoples) tried to outlaw the feuds that defined justice by declaring a Perpetual Truce for the people within his realm. Note that he wasn't declaring truce with another empire, just within his own. And, like so much social change, this only gradually became effective.

Implementation of Taxation and Tariffs

Courts and other administrative offices were not cheap. Turning property into land also changed how kings received revenue. When there was no state to administer, kings essentially got their revenue from their own lands. But as the king's jurisdiction spread to encompass property that others owned, a different relationship emerged. The king's law and courts had jurisdiction in defining the boundaries of property, and also overseeing what went on inside them. The kings began to tax all the people and economic activity in their realms, in order to govern them.

A European merchant in 1550 might have to contend with custom tolls about every six miles. Within an area the size of a modern country there were hundreds of different measurement standards and a multitude of currencies.[46] It was expensive for merchants to do business because there were hosts of lesser nobility who were so eager to receive revenues from trade tariffs. One reason that merchants favored the jurisdiction of kings was that under this new system they could pay just one tax, rather than many tolls. King Louis XIV, for instance, made France a free trade zone in order to encourage trade and business. Louis also instituted a host of taxes to fund his new government (and, of course, Versailles and a lifestyle of unprecedented opulence).

Policies like a free trade zone both made France more affluent and put it at the forefront of the invention of the nation-state.

"The first modern state to come into perpetual existence in Europe was France. . . . By the beginning of the fourteenth century, at the latest, the main features of the modern, centrally governed state had begun to emerge, in a form that we subsequently find well-nigh perfected in the France of Louis XIV."[47]

---

[46] Robert Heilbroner, *The Worldly Philosophers*, 5th ed. (New York: Simon & Schuster, 1980), 20.

[47] Schulze, *States, Nations and Nationalism*, 15, 17.

Development of a Standing Army

The nation-states made knights obsolete. Armies had convulsed Europe since the first time that a group of men got together to fight another group. But a standing army was a different thing, suggesting as it did money enough to have men stand around waiting to attack or defend. As with so much of social invention, standing armies required predecessors. In this case, the two most obvious were a regular source of taxes (to pay a regular expense like soldiers' salary) and armaments like guns and cannons.

Social and technological inventions often work together. The struggle to monopolize power coincided with the spread of guns and cannons. The gun shifted power from knights to armies, from skill and strength to whoever had money enough for armaments. A bullet could pierce armor and made knights obsolete. It is harder to think of further proof of this shift from skill and strength to resources than in the simple fact that the term "infantry" comes from the French reference to youth, or infants. Military success wasn't even dependent on full-grown men. Even the castles of lesser nobility—the aristocrats who held titles like baron and count—were subject to attack with the introduction of the new cannon. Ferdinand and Isabella used cannon in the conquest of Granada, the Muslim's last stronghold in what was to become Spain. Suddenly, impregnable walls were quite vulnerable and thick walls were not enough to resist armies with guns and cannons. This change in weaponry allowed a change in governance.

During medieval times, kings were generally the first among equals and generated money from their own land. They were generally called upon only in emergencies, when the landholders needed someone to lead them into battle. Once technology changed, land was vulnerable to conquest by anyone who could gather and equip an army. The king became a monarch who could resist or lead invading armies, and the king was gradually made a ruler over everyone—even the aristocracy who had once considered him nearly an equal.

Guns entered the battlefield early in the fourteenth century and in 1445[48] the French king established the first standing army, an invention that he managed in no small part because he was nearly as aggressive

---

[48] Schulze, States, Nations and Nationalism, 36.

in taxation and establishing the bureaucracy to administer these taxes as he had been in military affairs. By the time of Louis XIV, the French army numbered one hundred thousand.

Development of a Navy

Given the importance of trade routes, a strong navy became as important as a strong army. Dutch and English ships continually harassed Spanish ships bringing back gold and silver from the New World. There was, initially, a fine line between pirates and the British Navy. (A friend whose father was a Tijuana policeman told me that his father was paid $5 a day and had to pay the police chief $50 a day for his job. While such an arrangement would not ensure corruption, it would suggest that a certain entrepreneurial flair was needed. In a day of loose regulations and uncertain taxes, looting and piracy might be more promising than reliance on pay from a shaky government.)

Henry VIII, who may well have done as much as anyone in history to lay claim to the title "inventor of the nation-state," was among the first to build a navy. Among others, he commissioned the *Harry Grace a Dieu*, which carried 186 guns. By contrast, the Spanish required their merchants to be ready to convert, upon demand, into "navy" ships. The Spanish had not established taxation as had the English, and the result of not having a standing navy was that their ships were not quite suited for either commerce or war, but were compromised for both purposes. Ultimately, the British were to defeat the Spanish in the realms of both commerce and battle.

Increasing Trade under the Nation-States

The gradual shift from tolls to taxation helped to encourage trade. When barons charged tolls to each passing merchant, trade was stunted. When, instead, taxes were levied against any sale or even charged per person, trade was not penalized and it was easier and more profitable to trade. By establishing justice and order and removing tolls, the rise of nation-states actually encouraged commerce. Coupled with strong navies to protect trade routes outside the nation-state, the result was a steady rise in trade, the key to creating value in this first economy.

Nation-Building

The marriage of Ferdinand of Aragon and Isabella of Castile, uniting as it did the people of two different regions, was a significant step in the invention of Spain.

When Europeans of the first economy spoke of Germans or Italians, they were referring to a people who (mostly) shared a language and culture but did not share a state. Germany was formed out of the union of more than twenty kingdoms, duchies, and principalities in 1871. Italy was formed in the same year.

As it turns out, the nation-state so defined reality for twentieth-century Europeans and Americans that not only could they hardly conceive of Europe without nation-states, but they could hardly look at the world without projecting this new social invention onto it. Sadly, the process that generally began with some semblance of shared nationality and then morphed into state-building in Europe was reversed in places like the Middle East and Africa, a reversal that creates political turmoil to this day.

We send troops into Iraq for nation-building, but the truth is they are, at best, engaged in acts of state-building. Saddam Hussein ruled over three peoples, three nations, with tyrannical force. The nation-state of Iraq did not arise organically, if you will, out of a desire of one people to share one state or government. Iraq arose—as did so many countries around the world—from a British administrator's decision about how to divide that region.

Nations are very much a social invention, an extremely soft and malleable concept. Clans based on kinship are fairly obvious. Family bonds are strong and I'll leave romantics and evolutionary psychologists to explain why. Even a city-state as a basis of shared identity and governance makes sense. Florence, around 1400, was a town of about thirty thousand, and a sense of shared identity in such a town would not seem difficult to maintain. But to extend a sense of shared identity and fate to millions within the borders of a region that most people have never traveled would seem a little preposterous. And yet, through the work of aspiring political leaders and shared literature and media, as much as anything else, a sense of nationality did emerge. King Arthur legends and Grimm Brothers Fairy tales played a part in the definition of an England or Germany.

The nation-state was by no means a strictly sequential invention in which first the nation emerged and then the state was established. Yet, nations could not be ignored or glossed over, and if a state wanted to be perceived as having imperialist pretensions, it had only to get too far ahead of the process.

Isabella and Ferdinand knew this, at some level. The decision to send Columbus west in search of a trade route to Asian spices was part of a set of policies that they thought would purify Spain and create a coherent nation.

Trade makes the products of the land valuable. The tribe with excess furs trades with the tribe with excess salmon and both walk away happier, each now both warm and fed.

Trade also suggests diversity. If each person had exactly the same assets and products, there would be nothing to trade. It's hard to improve your lot when everyone has the same things. Without diversity, trade offers little value.

Ferdinand and Isabella understood the need to create a sense of nationality, but they didn't appreciate the importance of diversity for trade. The two were known as the Catholic Monarchs but (the region that was to become Spain) also contained plenty of Jews and Muslims at the start of their reign.

"By turning their backs on the peninsula's multicultural heritage, in order to consolidate political power and stabilize the united territories into a single Spanish state, Ferdinand and Isabella effectively proclaimed a non-reliance on that colourful traffic in goods and commodities which we have seen animating the cultural life of Europe in the second half of the fifteenth century. Instead they announced an official policy of homogeneity of cultural practices, dress and religion, and the ruthless suppression of local custom, ritual, and belief. In spite of the fact that the growing prosperity of Spain, as of other European nations, depended on vigorous and heterogeneous trade throughout the known world, and in spite of the fact that the artisanal skills which supported lucrative industries like carpet manufacture, ceramics or brocade-weaving were tightly associated with specific ethnic and religious groupings, the victorious Spanish regime declared ethnic and doctrinal purity as the foundations of the stability of the new state. By sponsoring a daring and improbable attempt to forge an entirely new set of trading routes westwards and thereby arrive at the same desirable commodities and sustain the same vigorous trade without recourse to the existing network of Christian, Jewish, and Islamic agents, merchants and middlemen, Ferdinand and Isabella ostentatiously set their sights on an ethnically cleansed "new world"—one in which Spanish might would be unhampered by other interests, and one in which the Christian faith would inevitably dominate."[49]

Creating a nation-state meant creating a sense of shared nationality. If we want to see what happens when that idea is taken too far, we have to look no further than Spain.

After conquering Granada, the last Muslim stronghold on the peninsula, Ferdinand decided to finance Columbus's venture. They had purchased a copy of Ptolemy's *Geography* and confirmed what Columbus told them about how short a route he might find to the Indies. (Ptolemy had made a little miscalculation in his estimate of the circumference of the earth, persuading readers that the distance from Europe to Asia by heading west was about as far as the distance from Europe to America.) The decision to finance this venture seemed to be part of their decision not to rely on so many nonbelievers. They knew that they needed economic breakthroughs to replace the infidels who formed such a big part of the economy.

God smiled on Spain and gave them new worlds and more silver and gold than any country had ever before had. God, they believed, was obviously happy with Ferdinand and Isabella's decision to purify their new country of Jews and Muslims. It is easy to believe that the two died convinced that they'd made the right choice not only for Spanish souls but for their pockets as well.

Sadly, the Spanish model, while extreme, was not unique. Most monarchs thought that it was their responsibility to care for the souls of their subjects. Between the establishment of standing armies that seemed to get tired of just standing around and the perceived high stakes for getting religion wrong, religious wars roiled across Europe for centuries. This was a tragedy of major proportions.

---

[49] Lisa Jardine, *Worldly Goods: A New History of the Renaissance* (New York: W.W. Norton & Company, 1996), 86–88.

Not until the Treaty of Westphalia finally acknowledged the sovereignty of nation-states did Europe have relative peace (for a time—always for just a time) and a new, generally recognized, ultimate authority. The year of the Peace of Westphalia, 1648, is probably as decent a time as any to date the completion of the social invention called the nation-state. Yet this nation-state had to compete with the last claimant to the role of ultimate authority in Europe: the church. The revolution that shifted power from nation-state to church is the story of social earthquake. It is, in fact, the most fascinating story in all the first economy. If you simply turn the page, you'll begin the chapter that shares some of the highlights of this curious and violent revolution and the invention of a new kind of religion.

8 Protestant Revolution

The first economy transformed religion. The West that had once been united by a common, enforced definition of faith and religion became a place where individuals were able to define those concepts for themselves.

Economy	First	Second	Third	Fourth
Period	1300–1700	1700–1900	1900-2000	2000-2050
Limit to Progress	Land	Capital	Knowledge Workers	Entrepreneurship
Type of Economy	Agricultural	Industrial	Information	Entrepreneurial
Intellectual Revolution	Renaissance	Enlightenment	Pragmatism	Systems Thinking
Big Social Invention	Nation-State	Bank	Corporation	Self
Social Revolution	**Protestant Revolution**	Democratic Revolution	Financial Revolution	Business Revolution

In order for the nation-state to emerge as the new, dominant institution in the West, the previously dominant institution had to be transformed; this transformation came in the form of the Protestant Revolution. Although the individual still had little choice about his own religion unless he was a prince or monarch, this revolution made religion a local affair and was the first – and most important – step towards making religion a personal rather than public matter. The invention of the nation-state, the changes brought by global trade and conquest, and the new Renaissance thinking were all forces that transformed the medieval church. Most interestingly, it was forces from within the community of believers (essentially a group that included everyone at the dawn of the first economy) that most changed the church.

Order from Chaos: The Church in a Post-Roman World

Roman Catholic priests, perhaps unsurprisingly, dress like Romans. Well, except for the shoes. I can't think of another profession that has a dress code that dates from the height of the Roman Empire. Yet the church maintained more than fashion. Amid the chaos of the post-Roman world, it was the church that sustained the administrative structure of the Roman Empire over much of the same domain as the old empire.

The Renaissance revived the art and ideas of Greeks and Romans. The church was one reason why those ideas needed reviving.

In the centuries after the fall of Rome, the Western church had rejected much of the pagan literature of the Greeks and Romans. But early in the first economy, Christians in the east—essentially Greek Orthodox—petitioned Rome for help in defending against the Turks. During the talks that opened up to discuss bringing these churches together, the eastern Christians visited Florence to attend a conference hosted by the Medici. Even the pope was there. The Italians, living in a part of the Christian world that had banned the ancient literature, were extremely impressed and very jealous of the libraries the eastern scholars had.

Later, when Constantinople fell to the Turks in 1453, many of these eastern scholars, with fond memories of Medici hospitality, took refuge in Florence. They brought their books with them. This is one big reason that the Renaissance began in Florence.

Before the Gutenberg press made books affordable, a library was a sign of great culture and affluence. (And Gutenberg's press did not immediately change that. Guttenberg first used his press to make extra profit, not to lower prices.)

The confluence of the Gutenberg press and the re-introduction of Greek libraries to Italy meant that soon new ideas (that were actually very old) were circulating around in Europe. Initially, even the popes were as smitten with this as they were with the Renaissance art.

Nicholas V (pope from 1447 to 1455) loved these new books and began a collection even before becoming pope. Once he had the papal budget at his command, he didn't just collect more books but he began to commission translations of many great works, like the *Odyssey* and *Iliad*. His private library and the books he collected and commissioned as pope became the start of the Vatican Library. In this way the Vatican helped to fund the Renaissance directly. It indirectly funded it in a myriad of other ways. For instance, the jubilee that Nicholas called in 1450 brought such a flood of pilgrims and donations to Rome that Nicholas was able to deposit one hundred thousand florins into the Medici's bank.[50] The Medicis, of course, were big sponsors of the books and art of the Renaissance.

These books from an earlier time suggested that the West before Christianity was more advanced and open. Since the time of the Romans, faith had seemingly displaced reason, and individuals had learned to conform. Medieval thought was generally directed at discerning God's mind rather than nature, and focused on obedience to God's will rather than thinking for one's self.

This emphasis on obedience seemed to put the West on intellectual auto-pilot for centuries. But as these books filtered into the West, minds were beginning to question again. Once started, the questioning would not end until it had transformed the most powerful institution in the West.

The Medieval Church: A Necessary Evil?

Since about the time that Gibbons published *History of the Decline and Fall of the Roman Empire* between 1776 and 1788, it has been fashionable to say that the rise of Christianity undermined reason and brought Europe into the Dark Ages. There is some truth to this claim, but it doesn't address another issue. Without getting into the flaws of

---

[50] Will Durant, The Renaissance: A History of Civilization in Italy from 1304–1576 A.D. (New York: Simon and Schuster, 1953), 380.

the Roman Empire (it, for instance, depended on conquest and slavery to maintain an impressive lifestyle for a few), it is worth saying that the conquerors of Rome probably did more than Christians to plunge Europe into the Dark Ages. Tribes like the Huns, the Visigoths, and the Vandals who gradually dismantled and conquered the Western part of the Roman Empire knew more about conquest than about creating and sustaining a society as complex as the Roman Empire. They may have conquered the Roman Empire, but they were not equipped to manage it. Europe descended into the Dark Ages as Rome disappeared beneath the weight of barbarians who happily raided the restaurant but had no real idea how to cook. The world created by these conquerors was awful, really. It takes different skills to conquer than it does to develop. It is one thing for armies to know how to raid a village to take the food and women. It is another to know how to raise crops and children. Life was brutal and short and reliant on force. The medieval church may seem oppressive, but its emphasis on caring for the weak and its insistence on order in thought and deed might have saved lives in such a milieu. The church was not exactly competing with the government of modern-day Sweden.

If we compare quality of thought and life under the church with that during the era of the Greeks and Romans before, the church obviously did Europe a disservice; if we compare it with life under barbarian invaders, the church might have helped. Theocracy was not ideal, but it—or something like it—might have been a necessary step in development. Religion makes sense of the world and, in bleak times, offers enough hope to help sustain some order and cohesion.

Still, while the medieval church may have been a lesser evil, but it was, nonetheless, evil. It was an institution that killed people for unconventional thinking. It wasn't just because the church was so poorly constructed to overcome the limit of land that it needed to be reinvented: it oppressed the individual and economic progress is about giving more autonomy to the individual. This was not something the medieval church encouraged.

The Inquisition & the Origins of Evil

The Inquisition was administered by priests, not barons, princes, or sheriffs. The inquisitor who had refused to offer evidence, even to make a specific charge of heresy, while insisting that the suspect answer vague and open-ended questions was a priest. The men who tortured the suspect with a method called the *stappado* were priests, tying his hands behind his back and raising him in the air by his wrists, the angle and the weight dislocating his shoulders. Then they tied weights to his feet and let the rope go, catching it before he hit the floor, and the combination of the jerking motion and weights dislocated his knees and ankles. Finally, the men who now tied him to the stake, piling wood around him to burn this suspect to death in the village square, were priests. They usually picked a market day so that the number of spectators would be higher than normal. Throughout the ordeal, the priests were police, judges, and finally, executioners.

If the wood was damp, the heretic's death would be even more painful and drawn out, but no matter how quickly he expired in the flames, punishment wouldn't end once he died. His wife and children would be automatically disinherited simply because they were heirs to a heretic. Instead, his estate would be divided amongst the church, the local prince, and, yes, the inquisitors. He did not have a lawyer for a very simple reason: any lawyer who would dare to defend a heretic would have his own faith called into question. His family would have trouble finding anyone to help them, fearful that help would be construed as sympathy for the heresy of which he was accused. This was not an age of affluence. It was conceivable that one or more of his children, even his wife, would now die of starvation, illness, or simple exposure. Even his home was to be razed. Heirs were never secure. People who had died one or two generations earlier could be suddenly exposed as heretics and even their heirs would lose all their wealth and property, which would be given to the church, the state, the inquisitors, and the people who first brought the charges against the dead heretic. The dead heretics—decomposed by decades—would be disinterred and paraded to a pyre. Even the ashes of the body would be dumped into a stream, leaving behind no trace of the heretic.

What was the crime of the heretic? The word "heretic" comes from the Greek and refers to a choice. The heretic chose to believe something other than church dogma. Worse, the Inquisition set out to prove what people believed—a particularly difficult task—and thus not only persecuted some who had exercised their reason and conscience to arrive at a belief other than the church's, but some who still held to the church's teachings and yet had been targeted by secret witnesses or even the inquisitors themselves. These poor people might eventually confess to end torture. The church considered the rack to be one of the milder forms of torture and used it extensively. The nude victim of the rack was stretched out, as ropes tied around wrists and ankles like tourniquets were gradually tightened to the point that muscles and ligaments tore and bones broke. Other tortures included ripping the skin from the body (torturers learned that victims would stay alive until the skin was ripped down to the waist), wedges that smashed leg bones until bone marrow spurted out, slathering the feet and legs in lard and then putting them in the fire, and the water board, which simulated suffocation and was used, at a minimum, to create panic and at times led to rupture of the stomach. In addition to the tools of torture, the inquisitors could hold prisoners indefinitely, sometimes waiting decades for them to confess.

The inquisition squelched expression and free thought. No one could be certain who might volunteer a report to the inquisition and whose words might be construed to convict one of heresy. Accusations and confessions would sweep through families and networks of friends. When imprisonment and trials could last years, suspicion was nearly the same as guilt—and trials rarely resulted in acquittal.

This was life at the dawn of the first economy, a time when the church's power was perhaps at its peak and the individual's was at its nadir. Fortunately, the church that perpetuated this was about to dramatically change.

The medieval church was evil because it dismissed the individual. It repressed freedom of thought and perpetuated its own survival by turning generations into believers who taught their children to teach their children to believe in the church. As with any powerful meme, it programmed programmers to program more programmers. And while it had the power to coerce believers, it used it.

Why the Medieval Church Became Evil

Quite simply, when individuals are forced to conform to the institution, rather than the institution to the individual, the institution starts down the path to evil. Human beings are real; institutions, by contrast, are just social inventions.

The Roman Empire was formed atop many nations, and the Romans often just incorporated the local god into their pantheon. Religious tolerance was a given and variation in beliefs was expected.

We now know that in the centuries after Christ, a great number of gospels and letters were written. Some, like Paul's letters to the Galatians or Matthew's gospel, became part of the canon that defines modern Christian thought. Others, like the gospels of Thomas and Judas, disappeared completely until they were rediscovered just last century.

Yet the variation in religious thought that defined both the Roman Empire and early Christianity was squelched. Forcefully. The Inquisition was instituted in 1233, and by 1252 the church had authorized the use of torture to impose conformity of thought. As late as 1600, Giordano Bruno was burned alive for sharing his beliefs about moving atoms, an infinite cosmos, memory, and imagination. The goal was to crush heresy, defined as any dissent or deviation from church teachings, and the church was not squeamish about the use of force to protect its dogma.

Torture was consistent with the teachings of St. Augustine, who felt that the "main point was 'not whether anyone is being forced to do something, but what sort of thing he is being forced to do, whether it is good or bad.'" Punishment was justified "because 'the unrighteous man's grief in his punishment is more appropriate than his rejoicing in sin.'" Torture was of little consequence in comparison to an eternity in hell; if pain caused one to recant from heresy, it was a gift.

Once a community accepts the notion of one truth about eternal salvation and one authority entrusted with its revelation, every kind of coercion and evil naturally follow. And seriously, if you honestly believed that someone you loved was going to spend an *eternity* in torment, wouldn't you do anything you could—including creating some temporary torment—to dissuade him of his ways? For the medieval mind, so reliant on faith and distrustful of reason, conviction was more powerful than proof.

The evil crept into the church in steps. It wasn't evil for individuals to say, "I believe in the authenticity of the gospel of Matthew but not the gospel of Thomas." It didn't seem particularly evil for a group of individuals to get together in a council to reach an agreement about which books to include and which to exclude to promote a "right" way and to create a holy scripture. And once that was in place, it did not seem so evil to urge conformity on the congregation, or to resort to expulsion or even force to spare the congregation from the influence of a heretic. Over the centuries, though, the cumulative effect of these little steps became clear. The individual "disappeared," to borrow a term from South American tyrannies.

This meant that before real progress could begin in the West, the church had to be radically changed. The revolution that overturned its monopoly on thought and action would prove even bloodier than church oppression. Encompassed in the Protestant Revolution and Reformation, this challenge to the medieval church offered the individual opportunities never before available to the common man.

Ockham

As the fourteenth century, there were philosophers, theologians, and priests who challenged the church. William Ockham (or Occam, 1288–1348) was an original and influential mind. Among other things, he separated faith and logic. H helped to free reason from church authority. Ockham himself was confident enough in his own reasoning to accuse the pope of heresy and while he was excommunicated, he fled to the protection of an emperor. Unsurprisingly, he was one of the first philosophers to advocate a separation of church and state and even got involved in the early development of property rights (making him perhaps the first philosopher to see the link between church reform and new kinds of governance as issues that were linked through the definition of land).

Even though Ockham had state support, his challenges to the church did not catch on quite like Martin Luther's would more than 150 years later, in part because there was, in his time, no printing press available to spread his ideas. Furthermore, while ideas like his were beginning to percolate, before such ideas could gain traction, Europeans had to take offense at a few popes.

The Popes

Bad popes and CEOs, while not a sign of the apocalypse, are a sign that an institution has gone rogue. When the church's main focus is the glorification of the pope, or the corporation's main focus is enriching the CEO, it is an institution in dire need of reform or reinvention. It is hard to imagine three people who did more to dissuade Europeans of respect for medieval authority than the three Renaissance popes.

Think of the fun Fox and MSNBC would have reporting on these popes. There were theological arguments against the papacy but for most Europeans the indictment was against personal behavior rather than abstract notions of power and its abuse.

Alexander

Pope Alexander purchased the papacy in 1492. As Columbus was discovering a new world, Alexander was bribing fellow cardinals for their vote, an investment that he and his children would recoup.

The pope had incredible resources at his disposal. Europe was becoming more secular and wealthy but it still tithed somewhere between 10 percent and a third of its income to the church, a good deal of which made it from the local churches to Rome. By one estimate, 70 percent of the money in circulation was in the hands of the church.

Alexander was not the least shy about having children, and their welfare was a key focus of his papacy. Where a modern CEO might think it fun to throw multi-million-dollar parties for a child, Alexander's gifts were more creative. He didn't just buy his children lavish wedding parties and private bull fights, but also political positions and even armies with which to conquer new territory. Alexander had at least seven known illegitimate children, a natural enough product from a man who seemed so at ease with sex. Once, when leaving Rome for three months, he left administrative matters to his daughter Lucrezia, to whom the College of Cardinals was subject in his stead. He awarded the position of cardinal to his son Caesar when he was only eighteen and not yet a priest. Caesar's military campaigns and willingness to murder without compunction (even his own brother and brother-in-law, if one were to believe persistent rumors) terrified the Romans.

As a cardinal, Alexander was once admonished for participating in an orgy. As pope, according to at least one source, he hosted a party that included a contest matching his guests with prostitutes and then dispensing gifts to the guests who demonstrated the most impressive feats of virility. Fittingly, this earthy man took his name from the conqueror Alexander the Great rather than a Christian saint.[51] And it is not as if Alexander's ease with sex made him terribly unique. In 1414, a council was called to end the schism that led to the rule of competing popes. About five thousand attended this, the most important council since the Council of Nicaea in 325 defined the church. Among this collection of cardinals, priests, and doctors of theology was a small army of people there to provide services to the luminaries: physicians, secretaries, and 1,500 prostitutes.[52] About this time the closed confessional box was instituted to protect women; previously, men and women knelt at the knees of the priest and priests were known to proposition women confessing and promise forgiveness after.

The stories of Alexander's debauchery and excess were likely embellished by his enemies, but one didn't have to embellish much to arrive at a picture of a pope who left Europe dismayed and confused about the extent to which they should respect a position that would hold such a person. The debate about Alexander's reign is not whether it included excess and violence, but merely the specifics of that excess.

Julius

The man who was next pope had once tried to depose Alexander. For that reason, Alexander attempted to assassinate the cardinal. (Imagine Pope John Paul trying to survive in such a world.)

In the section on Fortune in *The Prince*, Machiavelli wrote favorably of Pope Julius II as "impetuous in all he did" and cited a military campaign that the pope himself had led. The thought of a pope riding out to battle, sword on his hip, urging on his soldiers with curses did perhaps as much as the reports of Alexander's excess to make Europeans question the papacy. Yet it did verify something: even the pope felt that the church was less without land and would go so far as

---

[51] Barzun, From Dawn to Decadence, 64.

[52] Durant, *The Renaissance*, 365.

to lead campaigns to protect and capture it. More fundamentally, it also demonstrated the church's lack of trust in the states around it to protect it; not wanting to be dependent on the good graces of worldly dukes and princes meant that the church had to be able to conquer and rule its own lands. One of the reasons that Italy did not match the pace of France and England for state formation was that the church controlled a swath of land right through the heart of Italy.

Julius was an executive. He led armies. It seems fitting that he ordered that St. Peter's Basilica be razed in spite of warnings not to destroy this sacred place. (And although it took more than a century to replace it, the Vatican now has the largest church in the world—a place that can seat sixty thousand, making mass in Italy nearly as popular as football in Texas.) He rather famously commissioned Michelangelo to paint the Sistine Chapel's ceiling and was the fiery pope who so exasperated Michelangelo with his constant interruptions to the work he had ordered.

The pope might have had the most power in Europe at this time, but this did not save him from mockery. Erasmus, who did so much to open the door to secular learning, penned a satire after Julius's death titled "Julius Exclusis." In this piece, Julius protests St. Peter having the nerve to block his entry to heaven:

Peter: Is there no difference between being holy and being called Holy? . . . Let me look a little closer. Hum! Signs of impiety aplenty.. . . Priest's cassock, but bloody armor beneath it; eyes savage, mouth insolent, forehead brazen, body scarred with sins all over, breath loaded with wine, health broken with debauchery. Ay, threaten as you will, I will tell you what you are.... You are Julius the Emperor come back from hell....

Julius: Make an end, or I will excommunicate you....

P: Excommunicate me? By what right, I would know?

J: The best of rights. You are only a priest, perhaps not that you cannot consecrate. Open, I say!

P: You must show your merits first....

J: What do you mean by merits?

P: Have you taught true doctrine?

J: Not I. I have been too busy fighting. There are monks to look after doctrine, if that is of any consequence. ... I have done more for the Church and Christ than any Pope before me.

P: What did you do?

J: I raised the revenue. I invented new offices and sold them... I recoined the currency and made a great sum that way. Nothing can be done without money. Then I annexed Bologna to the Holy See.... I set all the princes of Europe by the ears. I tore up treaties, and kept great armies in the field. I covered Rome with palaces, and left five millions in the treasury behind me....

P: Why did you take Bologna?

J: Because I wanted the revenue....

P: And how about Ferrara?

J: The duke was an ungrateful wretch. He accused me of simony [purchasing his office], called me a pederast.... I wanted the duchy of Ferrara for a son of my own, who could be depended upon to be true to the Church, and who had just stabbed the Cardinal of Pavia.

P: What? Popes with wives and children?

J: Wives? No, not wives, but why not children? [53]

To head the church meant more power and riches than any other position could offer, and it is unsurprising that the position attracted alpha males with little compunction about how to acquire or exercise power. To this day there seems to be confusion between the skills needed to rise to the top of an organization and the skills needed to make that organization effective. Also, it was not surprising that in a Europe becoming more secular and wealthy, its most powerful institution would also become wealthier and more secular. It's not surprising but, of course, people were and still are surprised.

Because of the poor behavior of the Renaissance popes, Luther's protests about the excesses of Rome found ready ears. In Erasmus's account, Peter expresses dismay that there is no way to depose such a pope and in this he speaks for many Europeans. Although revolutions may seem obvious in retrospect, people do look for a variety of options before they consider the overthrow of the social order. It took a lot to embolden Europeans to give up on their church and the popes.

In *The March of Folly*, Barbara Tuchman defines folly as the pursuit of

---

[53] Will Durant, *The Reformation: A History of European Civilization from Wycliffe to Calvin: 1300–1564* (New York: Simon & Schuster, 1957), 279–82.

policy that is to the detriment of the institution. Among her examples are these Renaissance popes who inflamed the Protestant Revolution. Previous popes lived more circumspectly, but I'm sure Alexander would tell you that they missed an amazing opportunity. And while it might be true that what they did was harmful to the church, Alexander and Julius's actions did not hurt them as individuals. When power and privilege rest with elites, this drives a wedge between the fate of the institution and that of its leader; a modern CEO can make hundreds of times what his employees make while pursuing policies that hurt the company.

Alexander and Julius convinced many Europeans that the papacy—and by extension the church—was corrupt and no longer deserved respect. This provoked two responses that undermined the grip of the church. That story can be told through the third of our popes.

Leo

If Alexander and Julius fueled the Protestant Revolution, Leo struck the match. Leo was born a Medici, the Florentine family that did more than any other to trigger the Renaissance. It is hard to fathom any firm or family showing more wisdom in hiring practices: the list of Medici employees included Galileo (hired to tutor the kids), Donatello, Raphael, Michelangelo, and Leonardo da Vinci. The Medici family collected ancient Greek manuscripts, helping to introduce and popularize the ideas of the ancient Greeks, and then funded artists who would meet and surpass the artistry of Greek and Roman art.

Pope Leo was born and raised a Medici and it is no wonder that as son of Lorenzo the Magnificent Leo knew so little of limits. Of course, his ignorance of limits couldn't last. Within two years of his election as pope he had gone through the money Julius had left in the treasury. Two years after that, in 1517, Leo resorted to aggressively selling indulgences to help with church finances.

At the time, some Christians believed that the soul did not directly ascend to heaven after death. Time spent waiting in purgatory was proportionate to the sins committed on earth—unless, that is, one was able to make an indulgence, a gift of money to the church. Suppose your father was dead; if you were to purchase an indulgence for him, his soul might immediately fly from purgatory to the comfort of heaven. Or it might at least commute his sentence. One could even anticipate one's own sins: an indulgence would "forgive" these sins, freeing the soul from any fate but paradise. It was a clever idea of Leo's to sell indulgences, but this was to prove a social invention with terribly unfortunate consequences for the church.

The Rise of the Protestants

Unlike Italy, Germany hadn't been terribly renown for religious leadership. It had, about 1200 years before the first economy, developed bowling as a religious ritual in monasteries. Then Tetzel preached and sold indulgences in Germany, where Martin Luther heard him.

Luther saw in Tetzel's teaching and Leo's eager attempts to procure funds a corruption of the true faith.

There is at least one account of a man who lived in medieval times who sold his house in order to buy a Bible. Often the priest was the only literate one in the village. (Given that Bibles were written in *scripta continua*, literacy was not as much of an issue as we would consider it today; words ran together, without space between them, and it was when they were read aloud that the ear naturally separated the words, as it does in everyday speech. It was not until the early Renaissance that any Bibles were written with spaces between them and, if you will, silent reading was invented, or made possible. Only then did reading become a private rather than a social activity.) For centuries, the clergy were rarely challenged in their teachings. Yet by the time that Tetzel was selling indulgences that anticipated sin, Luther had read one of these new, affordable Bibles and was able to point to Scriptures that contradicted these teachings and could expect that some who heard him would be able to confirm his claims by reading their own Bible. The Guttenberg Press made Bibles more affordable, and the Scriptures emerged as a new source of authority that could be used to contradict the church. (Luther's thoughts were themselves the beneficiary of the printing press. He had not even seen a Bible until he was twenty, and his own religious education had before that been based on biblical excerpts selected by church fathers. [54])

[54] Barzun, *From Dawn to Decadence*, 27.

Much of the trouble for the church began with the spread of Scriptures in local languages. Able to read the Bible for themselves, many began to question the basis for so many church decisions. "Many other practices and traditions, sanctified by time, and which the laity assumed were in the scriptures, were actually nowhere to be found. These included papal authority, the celibacy of priests, transubstantiation, infant baptism, the canonization of saints and the impossibility of salvation outside the Catholic Church."[55] The Bible, which had been the source of power for the church, now began to erode that power.

Many, like Machiavelli and Erasmus, were less concerned about the excesses of the church than about the need to complement religion with secular teachings and human will. Machiavelli actually admired Julius's boldness. And even though Erasmus satirized Julius, he seemed more aligned with the Catholic Church than the Protestant movement. These men seemed comfortable with the secular, but didn't seem to think that such progress meant abandoning the church. They challenged the status quo but it didn't necessarily want a new church. Theirs was a call for reform. By contrast, Martin Luther and John Calvin advocated revolution.

Luther and Calvin did not approve of the church's secular tilt and sought, instead, to create a new church based on biblical truths rather than tradition, something uncorrupted by so much power and money.

As it turns out, these two approaches had more in common than an opposition to the status quo. A church that kept itself pure by letting others care about secular things like money and the rule of territory proved a perfect complement to the newly emerging nation-state, which was secular in its interests and focus. If Europe was to be controlled by the church, the church was either going to be an obstacle to progress or it was going to become increasingly secular along with Europe. But if the church was to focus on religious matters and leave affairs of state to the emerging nation-states, this would result in the birth of a new kind of world, one as different from the world before it as America was from Europe.

---

[55] Watson, *Ideas*, 513

Ultimate Authority?

Perhaps the simplest contrast between the Protestants and the Catholics has to do with the Bible. Both believe it is the word of God. The difference between them lies in their opinion about the ultimate source of authority. Catholics believe that the Bible could be interpreted in a variety of ways and that there needs to be an ultimate authority to declare which verses are to be taken literally (should one actually pluck out his eye if he lusts after a woman?) and which should be taken figuratively (does the phrase "men consumed in their lusts for one another" really refer to sexual acts?), which are true historically (was it only in Christ's time that one had to love his enemies?) and which apply today (is it still a good thing to kill Philistines and to enslave enemies?). Without an ultimate authority to interpret it, the Catholic Church feared that the Bible would lead to an explosion of denominations and interpretations. (And of course the Catholics were right; there are, today, thousands of Protestant denominations.) Protestants, by contrast, believe that the Bible itself is the ultimate authority, and of course in practice that means that as soon as one group decides that this verse is literal and that one is figurative, in contrast to another group that decides the reverse, the world suddenly has a new denomination. There is no outside authority to tell the individual that his interpretation is wrong. Martin Luther was apparently surprised that so many people would interpret the Bible so differently.

Furthermore, once verses were numbered (a practice that started in 1551[56]), it was easier for people to find verses and create disagreements. The Protestant revolt set in motion a diversity of thought about religion, laying seeds for the diversity of thought that would come to characterize the West, in domains as different as politics, science, philosophy, and fashion.

Martin Luther

Martin Luther was doubly offended by indulgences. He was offended first because the church seemed to be both sanctioning sin and selling

[56] Watson, *Ideas*, 513

entry to heaven. He was also offended because the church advertising its ability to send someone to heaven as the result of buying an indulgence seemed to make entry into heaven the result of what the church did rather than the result of what Christ had done. Luther's outrage was not limited to outbursts at the local bar or pulpit. Able to make use of the printing press, Luther turned what might have been a local issue into something that spilled across all of Europe.

Luther had the protection of German princes (Germany, like Italy, had yet to unify into a single country and was divided into hundreds of regions and city-states at the time), and thus was assured of some safety. He was not the first to challenge the church, but he was among the first to do it and live.

Before Luther's time, John Wycliffe (1324–84) was an Englishman who did not just challenge the church's authority, but had the audacity to translate the Bible from the Latin into English. When servants to the English queen returned her body to her homeland of Bohemia for burial, they shared what they'd learned about Wycliffe's teachings. Jan Hus (1369–1415) heard this and founded a movement that rejected any church teachings that were not grounded in the Bible. He was executed for heresy, burned at the stake like a banned book. (And, in fact, the fire used to burn the poor man was started with kindling made from Wycliffe's translated Bibles.) Wycliffe, in England, was free to speak and write in opposition to the church, much like Luther. Hus, on the continent, was not; on the continent around 1400, the state was less evolved and rulers were less able and willing to resist the power of the church. The church was not going to be challenged by individuals but it could be challenged by individuals backed by the emerging states.

When Luther published his ninety-five theses in Wittenberg in 1517, German princes were still paying a tribute to Rome. Luther's woodcuts illustrating his conviction that the papacy was the antichrist included an image of the German emperor lying on the ground with the pope's foot on his neck, showing "Luther's belief that the papacy was trying to control secular authority throughout the world."[57] Luther appealed to his fellow Germans' economic interests in his challenge to the papacy, writing

"Some have estimated that every year more than 300,000 gulden find

---

[57] KPBS, Frontline, Mark Edwards Jr., "Apocalypse!" <http://www.pbs.org/wgbh/pages/frontline/shows/apocalypse/explanation/martinluther.html>

their way from Germany to Italy. ... *We here come to the heart of the matter.* ... How comes it that we Germans must put up with such robbery and such extortion of our property at the hands of the pope?"[58]

Luther was a theologian who helped to create the German language by translating the Bible into it, but he also knew the importance of money in the newly emerging market economy. Luther helped formulate a religion that depended on Scriptures rather than on Rome for its authority. Many rulers saw in this the opportunity to gain independence from the church, and some seized on this. It would, among other things, save them money.

Some of the rulers made their territories Protestant and some made them Catholic. Originally, freedom of religion just meant that a ruler was free to choose the religion for his realm. Although Luther wrote that "A Christian man is a perfectly free lord, subject to none,"[59] in truth a common person freed from the rule of pope was still subject to the rule of the prince or monarch.

Where Erasmus tried to introduce reason and could see in many biblical stories allegories rather than actual events, Luther believed in elves and demons, claimed to have seen Satan several times, and also claimed that once the devil threw nuts at him. At times Luther charmed the devil by playing the flute and at other times frightened him away by calling him filthy names.[60] Luther was brilliant but still rooted in a time of superstition and belief in the supernatural.

Church & State

Martin Luther was part of a larger movement of unrest and reform that spread throughout Europe. In England, Tyndale used Erasmus's translation as a starting point for a more contemporary (than Wycliffe's) translation of the Bible into English. (Tyndale's use of thee's and thou's became so associated with biblical language that later, when

[58] Durant, *The Reformation*, 353 (emphasis added).

[59] Barzun, *From Dawn to Decadence*, 6.

[60] Durant *The Reformation*, 372.

King James authorized a new translation, these already obsolete forms were preserved. Even today some see this older form of English as somehow more representative of the speech of Jesus and Moses than contemporary English.) The authorities knew that once households got their hands on a Bible written in their own language, it would be hard to maintain a monopoly on "truth." To escape prosecution, Tyndale was forced to flee to the Continent. This, however, did not stop Henry VIII from having him executed for the crime of printing the Bible in English.

At about the same time as Tyndale and Luther, the Anabaptists, showing up across Europe, were also challenging the church, claiming their right to interpret the Bible without guidance from Rome. They thought it was silly to baptize infants, who didn't know what was happening, and they expected people to choose baptism as adults (hence the name Anabaptists, taken from the Greek word that means re-baptism.)[61] The Anabaptists (evolved today into the Amish and the Mennonites) had the misfortune to suffer persecution from both Catholics *and* other Protestants, such as the Calvinists.

"Don't baptize babies" seems like reasonable advice. Yet even this criticism of the church was a sign of how growing affluence was rendering old ways irrelevant and even incomprehensible. During medieval times, infant mortality rates were so high that a mother had only about a 50 percent chance of celebrating her baby's first birthday. Concerned about what happened to the souls of these poor infants, mothers inquired of priests who, rather kindly, began the practice of infant baptism to assure these mothers than their little ones would be safe in heaven. (It is only in our own time that the pope declared that Limbo, the place where infants and small children awaited judgment, no longer exists. For popes, social invention is easier than it is for guys at the diner counter.) As infant mortality rates dropped and literacy rates increased, what had formerly made perfect sense suddenly seemed like nonsense. Progress does that.

The emerging governments of the first economy challenged the medieval church everywhere—not just in Germany and England. Switzerland had two great religious entrepreneurs: John Calvin and Ulrich Zwingli. Zwingli seems to most clearly illustrate the shift in authority from the church to the state. Faced with the question of who had the authority to interpret the Bible, the conclusion in Zurich was as

---

[61] Alister McGrath, *Christianity's Dangerous Idea: The Protestant Revolution—a History from the Sixteenth Century to the Twenty-First* (New York: HarperOne, 2007), 79.

follows: "The city council, seeing itself as a duly elected representative body of the Christians of Zurich, declared that it possessed the corporate right to settle the right of the interpretation of the Bible. ... Religious authority was transferred from the pope or local bishop to elected representatives of the people."[62] Questions of religion were thus to be settled by the state. As if it were not enough that Copernicus and Galileo had set the world spinning through space; this decision turned it on its head. The Protestant Revolution made the church subordinate to the state.

Diversity

To be nobody but yourself—
in a world which is doing its best, night and day,
to make you everybody else—
means to fight the hardest battle
which any human being can fight.
Never stop fighting.

—ee cummings

As explorers discovered new lands, they came to appreciate the vast diversity of human life. The world was full of different customs, costumes, institutions, and even races. "It was immediately obvious to Montaigne, looking around him at the newly-gathered material from the New World and elsewhere, that men and women had devised many ways of adapting to their environment. It was therefore self-evident that God favored diversity over uniformity."63 This exposure to diversity proved a challenge to the church's one true way.

---

[62] McGrath, *Christianity's Dangerous Idea*,70–71.

Peter Watson, *Ideas*, 516.

It is really just in the last generation that we've become aware of how diverse the world of Christianity was in the three to four centuries after Christ's death. The Dead Sea Scrolls and the Nag Hammadi Library, among other finds, have revealed a number of gospels and epistles that never made it into what we know as the Bible. Most of these were obviously not written by any of Christ's original disciples or by Paul and for this reason alone were omitted from inclusion in the approved canon. (Yet it is worth noting that most serious scholars today think that other forgeries did make it in. For instance, 2 Timothy seems to have been written in the second century after Christ and most certainly not by Paul.)

In the fourth century, the canon was defined and various competing ideas about Christ were consolidated into a (mostly and sort of) uniform view in the form of the Bible. Soon, the church that owned this "true" view even used torture and death to enforce this pure view. Most people look at the Inquisition as evil but I think that the evil originated when the church decided that God could not tolerate diversity of thought and sought to make uniform the theology and teachings that professed to represent his views. Surely God loves uniformity, people thought. This might seem reasonable. It does not, however, seem to be backed up by any real world evidence.

The notion that God's will obviously tends towards the uniform does, I think, miss an important suggestion from nature. (I say suggestion because it may or may not be a "lesson.") Nature suggests that the Creator loves diversity. There are about 1.75 million species on the planet. Some have bones and some do not. Some breathe underwater and some drown in water. Some walk around and some are rooted. Some are really cute and some are hideous. Some are peaceful and some are dangerous. Some are huge and some are too small to see. It's not obvious that you can make many generalizations about nature, other than the fact that nature loves diversity. The life form that works depends on so many things that one would be at a loss to predict them all in advance.

As communities become more developed and free, a similar thing seems to happen with the human population. That is, diversity seems to spring up. We have Goths and hippies, the driven and the laid back, the flirtatious and the prudes, the athletic and the slothful, the intellectuals and the disinterested. The list goes on. It may well be that we have at least 1.75 million *species* of humans among the seven billion people on the planet.

Ultimately, the church had to use force to try to squelch this great diversity of people. To this day, Protestant churches reject Catholicism but tend to accept the central claim that diversity is wrong (although the number of ways that they reject the notion of allowing diversity does, itself, create a fair bit of diversity, from Mormons to Baptists to Presbyterians to Anglicans to Jehovah's Witnesses, and so on). It could be that they are right. It could be. But then how do we explain the motives of the creative force behind the massive diversity of nature? And how do we explain how attempts to make human life all believe one way led to one of the darkest and most violent periods of history, when the church largely ruled the West, between the collapse of the Roman Empire and the rise of the modern, secular nation-state?

The more I look across time and communities, the more convinced I am that one of the simplest measures of advancement is how many kinds of people can make their place in the world. It seems to me that diversity is not just a wonderful thing in nature—it works in communities too. This suggests to me that the church's attempt to go against this trend meant it was destined to become evil. The next time someone says that they know what is best, ask them what is best for whom. Some things that make people feel alive really are universal: oxygen, for instance. Others work for just a minority of folks: live jazz, for instance. Reality is diverse. It seems to me that any explanation of it ought to accommodate rather than deny this.

This shows us a common theme for the first economy: diversity. Trade depends on both excess and diversity. If everyone has exactly the same things, there is nothing to trade. If you have excess salmon and I have excess furs, we have something to trade; if we both have excess furs, trade is of no use. Trade made the world richer because communities were diverse in their natural resources and industries.

A diversity of thought does more than produce nine thousand different denominations. It produces a society that allows individuals to create lives that give them personal happiness or public value that can be shared through markets in the form of jobs, services, or products. An undeveloped economy or society offers little variety when it comes to roles. Medieval Europe offered young men essentially three options: they could farm, fight, or pray. Even a century or two ago, women had very few options: they could become housewives, nurses, or teachers. A child born today is likely to enter a profession that didn't exist when she was born. Today's world has massive diversity and is so much richer than the medieval world of farmers, soldiers, and priests. Not only does specialization create the diversity that makes trade and markets so profitable, but it gives more ways of being, a wider variety of personalities, the opportunity to find expression. The computer programmer who sells a program for millions might have been too scrawny to fight or farm and too inquisitive and questioning of authority to have been a priest. In a less developed world, individuality has less opportunity for expression and individuals have fewer options for realizing their potential. Progress seems to breed diversity and vice versa.

The first economy gradually brought the West out of the Dark Ages. Maybe the simplest reason for this is the shift from treating diversity as bad to treating it as something desirable. Emergent markets and trade all depended on diversity; there is no incentive to trade if the other guy has exactly what you have. A post-Gutenberg world of printing made it easier for diverse minds to find and influence one another, and books became a marketplace for new ideas. And with the Protestant Revolution, even the diversity of conscience and belief began to find expression.

This might be the simplest theme of the first economy: diversity was transformed from deviant to desirable. This meant something profound: it meant that it was no longer a sin to be different. That is, individuals were now allowed to be individuals.

The changes in religion set the stage for something momentous: the eclipse of the church by the state. As religion became something personal, the bonds for communities became political instead of religious. The nation-state became more important as the West become more focused on this world than the next. And the next chapter will offer two stories to illustrate this eclipse.

9 State Trumps the Church

Religion remained important to the West throughout the first economy but it was increasingly something defined by the state rather than the church. One of the most dramatic challenges to the church resulted in a schism that finally resulted in three popes before it was healed. The most defining challenge actually created a new church and – in the process – defined anew the nation-state.

Clay Shirky makes this fascinating comment about revolution. "As with the printing press, if it is really a revolution it does not take us from point A to point B; it takes us from Point A to chaos. The printing press precipitated 200 years of chaos. Moving from a world where the Catholic Church was sort of the organizing political force to the Treaty of Westphalia where we finally knew what the new unit was: the nation-state."[64]

The church was not a particularly good instrument for overcoming the limit of land: a focus on tradition, conformity, and the supernatural was not much help for a community that needed to innovate, encourage diversity and trade, and focus on the question of how best to tame the natural world. So, entrepreneurs invented something better: the nation-state. This put them in conflict with the church, with the church winning this struggle in some communities and losing it in others. Where the nation-state eclipsed the church, communities became rich and powerful. Where the nation-state remained subordinate, communities stagnated.

The same motion that rocks a boat can tip it over. Philip IV of France rocked the boat of state and church about 1300. Henry VIII of England tipped it over in the mid-1500s.

---

64 TED talk, http://www.ted.com/talks/lang/eng/clay_shirky_on_institutions_versus_collaboration.html, at about minute 19.

King vs. Pope: Round One

Because the medieval pope had jurisdiction over kings, kings had to ask his approval to raise taxes. Yet when it came to war, kings didn't want to wait as long as it took to get a pope's permission to raise the needed funds.

When King Philip IV of France went to war with England in 1294, he taxed his subjects without waiting for the pope's approval. Earlier, Philip had excluded clergy from decision-making in his newly emerging nation-state and began to tax them. Pope Boniface VIII denounced him for both actions.

Boniface was a notable character. His contemporaries accused him of being a homosexual and our contemporaries suspect that he was an atheist.[65] Dante so disliked him that he placed Boniface in one of his circles of hell in his *Divine Comedy*. Philip was not particularly happy with him either.

Sometime after the war ended in 1297, Philip arrested a bishop of France. This act so outraged Boniface that he forbade Philip to tax the French clergy and then issued a bull in 1302, "asserting his lordship of the Catholic world."[66] This was essentially his way of asserting that the kings reported to him. He even tried to depose Philip.

Philip was king, not a diplomat. His wrote back to the pope, "Your venerable stupidness may know that we are nobody's vassal in temporal matters." As if that was not insulting enough, he then sent his men to arrest Pope Boniface with the intention to bring the pope to the king's court to face trial in France.

Now you might think that such treatment of God's anointed would generate loud protests from across Europe or even from the king's own subjects. It did not. That right there would make for a remarkable story: a mere king arrests the pope to put him on trial. Yet it gets worse.

Although Philip's men soon released Boniface, the stress of the arrest and the beating they gave him was apparently too much for the pope. Within weeks, Boniface had died of either a stroke or humiliation or injury or some combination.

---

[65] A. N. Wilson, for instance, author of *Dante in Love* makes this suggestion about Boniface being an atheist. If true, it says much about the extent to which the papacy had become a position of power.

[66] William Chester Jordan, *Europe in the High Middle Ages*, 316.

It is probably not much of an exaggeration to say that the king killed the pope.

Now we come to a curious point in the story. A lesser man than Philip might have become apologetic and repentant. Yet one curious characteristic of social inventors is that they don't feel particularly constrained by traditional social conventions. They likely wouldn't be inventing something new if they respected the old. In fact, almost by definition such constraint isn't possible when one is re-inventing society. For good or bad, such entrepreneurs tend to live in their own moral universe. As Saul Alinsky writes, "there are no rules for revolution any more than there are rules for love or rules for happiness."

Philip wasn't the least chagrined by these events. Instead, he pressed ahead with his conviction that in order to create an effective nation-state, the church had to be subordinated to him and not vice versa. (Not that he would have used such language.)

So rather than apologize, he engineered the election of a French pope and then moved the papacy to Avignon, where he could more easily monitor and control it. For more than half a century, from 1314 to 1378, the papacy stayed in Avignon.

As one might guess, Philip's bold move was not easily accepted. Soon, Rome appointed a new pope and the church once ruled by one pope now had two. Before this schism was mended, in 1414, the church would have three popes competing for authority over the West.

Not surprisingly, this schism eroded respect for the church, decreasing its power and increasing the power of the emerging states.

Until French Revolutionaries outlawed religion and made Notre Dame the temple for the Cult of Reason, France was Catholic. Yet this wasn't a Catholicism that saw itself as subordinate to Rome. From the time of Philip, French kings had sovereignty, even over issues of religion.

More than a century later, an English king would do something even bolder than arrest a pope: he made popes irrelevant to his nation-state.

Henry VIII and the Invention of the Nation-State

Like Philip, Henry lived in his own moral universe. What most people know about him is that Henry VIII was a king (from 1509 to 1547) who alternately divorced, beheaded, and outlived five of his six wives. What fewer people know is that perhaps no man did more to invent the modern nation-state.

Henry was the first to monarch to shape trade to accumulate precious metals (something later referred to as mercantilism), building up his treasury. He removed tariffs, moving England towards a free trade zone.[67] This stimulated trade within England at a time when merchants on the Continent might contend with tolls every six miles. Already England had standards for weights and measures that facilitated trade; again, this was in stark contrast to life on the Continent, where across an area the size of a modern country a merchant might be forced to deal with hundreds of different measurement standards and a multitude of currencies. [68]

Henry even introduced surnames—a social invention necessitated by the phenomenon of a William who found himself a member of a nation-state and subsequently one of many Williams rather than a member of a village or family where it might previously have been enough to distinguish himself as the left-handed William or the tall William.

Henry VIII established the Navy Office in 1512 for the purpose of building ships like the *Henry Grace a Dieu*, which carried 186 guns. [69] The British Navy eventually ruled the sea and became instrumental to trade and empire.

Henry furthered England's policy of emphasizing property rights, which encouraged farmers to invest in their lands, thus increasing productivity, nutrition, size and health of soldiers, and even the incentive to defend their own land and crops. [70] The free man fighting for his own land fought harder than the serf.

---

[67] This was no small feat. According to economic historian Eli Heckscher (as quoted in Bernstein, *The Birth of Plenty*, 39), "In the Middles Ages the greatest obstacles to trade were the tolls."

[68] Heilbroner, *The Worldly Philosophers*, 20.

[69] J. M. Roberts, *The Penguin History of the World* (Suffolk: Penguin Books, 1997), 638.

[70] Bernstein, *The Birth of Plenty*, 89.

Yet in a way, Henry's greatest invention was probably less an act of genius than of frustration: he just wanted a divorce. That might seem like a small thing in comparison to the Renaissance or the Protestant Revolts. It was, however, to prove momentous. To get a proper divorce, Henry was dependent on papal approval, but the pope said no. It is hard to think of a more personal affront to a king's sovereignty than someone able to veto his request for a wife who could bear him a male heir.

Henry had married Ferdinand and Isabel's daughter, Catherine. The poor woman suffered numerous miscarriages and provided Henry with a daughter but no son. Childbirth was not easy in the 1500s—even for a queen. Henry thought he deserved a son to inherit the crown and began to look for a new queen.

Henry fell in love with Anne Boleyn and throughout a long courtship in which Anne held out for the position of queen, rather than mistress, Henry continued to petition Pope Clement for a divorce.

Lorenzo Medici raised two boys who would become pope: his son who would become Pope Leo and his nephew who was to become Pope Clement. (Clement had been orphaned when Lorenzo's brother was assassinated in one of the violent attempts to seize control over Florence from the Medici.) Clement had numerous issues to confront, from the violent and intricate Italian politics around him to the Protestant Revolt that was brewing on his watch.

If Pope Clement gave Henry permission to divorce Catherine, he was certain to face the wrath of Charles V. Charles did not just rule over large swaths of Europe, but as the ruler of Spain he also had command over the huge flows of gold and silver that came in from the Spanish holdings in the New World, in Mexico and Peru. Catherine was Charles's aunt. In the midst of everything else, it seemed easier to deny Henry's request than to make an enemy of Emperor Charles.

To be fair, it is doubtful that Clement would have ever imagined that Henry was contemplating something so bold as to make his country independent of Rome.

While the pope resisted Henry's requests, Anne did not: her pregnancy forced the king to act. If she was to bear him a son, she needed to be his wife in order to simplify the inheritance of the crown. So, Henry divorced Catherine and married Anne, without waiting any longer for the pope's permission.

Pope Clement was not amused. He excommunicated Henry. Henry did not call the pope his venerable stupidness or send his men to arrest Clement. He made no attempt to bring the Catholic Church under his control. He presided over a nation-state more defined and fully formed than Philip's France of 1300 and was able to do something even bolder: in 1534, Henry passed the Act of Supremacy, making himself the head of the Church of England. He no longer needed the pope's approval. He no longer even needed a pope.

With this act, the nation-state had officially eclipsed the church as the most powerful institution in England. This shift in relative power was to spread to other parts of Europe. By 1648, the Treaty of Westphalia defined the state as having sovereignty over matters of religion throughout Europe. No longer did the church dictate religion to kings and princes, but instead, monarchs dictated religion to their subjects. (Initially, freedom of religion meant freedom for rulers. It would take about 50 to 150 years—depending upon the country—before freedom of religion in the West meant freedom for the individual under that monarch's rule.) Nation-states still included churches but they were no longer subordinate to them.

The break with Rome gave Henry the freedom to make even more changes. He dissolved Catholic monasteries and partly sold and partly gave their land to the gentry over a period of five years in the largest shift of property ownership in modern history. This generated revenue for his government and made the land more productive. This was also a boost to the goldsmiths, who were to mutate into bankers; it fell on them to dispose of the monasteries' treasuries.

The break with Rome also freed him to turn his back on religious prohibitions against usury. His act of 1545 helped the goldsmiths further by allowing interest charges of up to 10 percent, stimulating credit and economic growth that had been stifled by the church for nearly a millennium.

Henry inherited a very advanced country, but he accelerated its advance. As much as anyone, Henry invented the modern nation-state. And of all his innovations, his break with the church was easily the boldest and most defining for this new institution. Social inventions transform life. Henry's invention arguably did more to change the West than did James Watt's steam engine or Henry Ford's affordable car.[71]

Spain: A Postscript

It's worth contrasting England with Spain. Spain had rights to huge swaths of the Americas and commanded mines whose output dwarfed that of European mines. Pirates able to rob even one Spanish ship on its return from the Americas could be set for life. By all rights, Spain should have leveraged this huge influx of money into a position of dominance in Europe. Instead, Spain was unable to defeat even the tiny Netherlands.

Rather than subordinate the church to the state, Spain seemed to reverse that order. (It is worth remembering that the dreaded Spanish Inquisition was not administered out of Rome; it was a tool of the state.)

Ferdinand and Isabella sent Columbus off to find new trade routes because they knew they were going to need new revenues. After conquering Granada—the last Muslim territory in what is now Spain—these Catholic Monarchs gave Jews and Muslims the choice to convert or leave. This could have made the economy collapse, since so many Jews filled the role of financiers, chief public officers, and artisans. Ferdinand and Isabella knew there could be economic consequences.

"The king and queen always replied that in the first place, they were taking into account the religious benefit to the country, that they had the economic factors well in mind, and that in consequence they were sacrificing it to the spiritual policy which had been decreed."[72]

They sacrificed for God, and God blessed them. In reward for their religious fervor, Spain received a gift from God: her explorers first claimed and then the pope granted rule over the New World. In 1521,

---

[71] By attributing the nation-state to him we are putting a face on an emergent process that, while depending upon the actions of individuals, cannot honestly be attributed to just one person. People like Henry VIII and Henry Ford represent easily digestible simplifications of historical forces and were, themselves, a force in history.

[72] Jaime Vicens Vive, *An Economic History of Spain,* trans. by Frances Lopez-Morillas (Princeton, N.J.: Princeton University Press, 1969), 297.

Cortes conquered Mexico, and by 1533, Pizzaro had conquered Peru. The Americas provided a staggering amount of gold and silver. A ruler who had experienced such unexpected wealth would scoff at Machiavelli's low estimate that Fortune might determine only half of outcomes. Examples like this help to explain communities that resist market forces in favor of religion or tradition: seeming gifts of God—the whim and variability of nature and her resources—are far greater determinants of well-being than sophisticated planning or human intention. Or so it seems. Such perception does little to hasten the embrace of reason over ritual, one key to progress. Columbus's fortuitous discovery of a new world full of gold did little to dissuade Spanish rulers of the notion that God smiled on a policy of religious purity.

Yet the flow of gold seemed to distort Spain's economy. No agricultural advances were made during the prosperity of Charles's reign; with a monopoly on selling supplies to the New World, there was no pressure to improve methods. Commercial techniques in the sixteenth century remained basically unchanged from those imported by Italian merchants during medieval times. Following a century of falling prices, Spain suffered unprecedented inflation. Currency was gold and silver and both poured in from the New World. From 1501 to 1550, prices more than doubled; by the end of the century, they had quadrupled. With prices rising so much faster in Spain than in the rest of Europe, Spain's products soon could not compete with foreign goods. The Genoese "flooded the country with cheap manufactured products, designed especially for the Indies, to the serious detriment of local industry."[73]

The church's policies also distorted commerce. Financing was done covertly or by Jews because the church forbade charging interest. (Though, of course, most Jews had been expelled.) Foreign trade suffered as well. The Catalan (a region of northeastern Spain) merchants lost their North African market because they were afraid of the excommunication decreed by the pope for all who traded with the infidel. Land was the basis of wealth in Spain and in 1500 the king, the nobility, and the church each received about a third of the country's revenues from land. Land revenues supported tradition, not innovation.

In spite of such poor policy decisions, Spain enjoyed unprecedented income streams from its holdings in the Americas. While the flow of gold early in Charles's reign triggered an economic revolution, it was only a tenth of what it would become before his reign had ended.

---

[73] Vicens, *An Economic History of Spain,* 336–37.

Between 1516 and 1520, Spain's average yearly income in gold was 200,000 pesos; between 1551 and 1555 it was nearly 2,000,000.[74] "By 1650, 16,000 tons of silver had come to Europe, to say nothing of 180 tons of gold objects."[75] Yet Spain used this income to buy goods rather than develop its own productive capacity, leading the Venetian ambassador to write, "The gold that comes from the Indies does on Spain as rain does on a roof—it pours on her and it flows away.[76]"

In the end, Spain played by the old rules and England created new ones. Spain may have ruled an unprecedented swath of the globe but it was, in turn, ruled by tradition and religion.

It seems odd to compare English farmers to Spanish conquistadors. Yet it was farming that fueled England's economic progress, bringing it to a point that it could challenge the supremacy of an empire that had conquered huge swaths of two continents even as its emperor ruled a large portion of a third. Leading what could be called a "food-producing revolution," English farmers were a key reason that "In the eighteenth century European agriculture was already capable of obtaining about two and a half times the yield on its seed normal in the Middle Ages. . . .By 1750 the best English agriculture was the best in the world. The most advanced techniques were practiced and the integration of agriculture with a commercial market economy had gone furthest in England, whose lead was to be maintained for another century or so."[77]

England emerged as the new world power because it had best adapted to the new limit to progress. Its ships facilitated the trade that added value to goods moved across oceans. Its laws encouraged the best economic use of land, turning commons and church property into private property into which landholders invested. The creation of the Church of England subordinated the church to the state, allowing Henry and his descendants to pursue policies that supported progress rather than tradition. The pattern of revolutions that had begun with the commercial revolution culminated in a social revolution. In the process,

---

[74] Gertrude von Schwarzenfeld, *Charles V: Father of Europe* (Chicago: Henry Regnery Company, 1957), 261–62.

[75] Roberts, The Penguin History of the World, 620.

[76] Carlo M. Cipolla, *Guns, Sails, and Empires: Technological Innovation and the Early Phases of European Expansion, 1400–1700* (Manhattan, Kans.: Sunflower University Press, 1965, Sixth Printing 2002), 36.

[77] Roberts, *The Penguin History of the World* , 679.

it changed Europeans' notion of intention vs. fate, shifted focus to the secular rather than divine and changed how Europeans defined their major institutions and their place in society.

Land was the limit to progress, and the nation-state was invented to overcome this limit. England, which subordinated the church to its nation-state, emerged from the first economy best positioned for further growth. By contrast, Spain had subordinated the state to the church and would take centuries to catch up.

Yet progress and change did not stop once kings ruled without interference from Rome. The next section, on the second economy, explores what problems the new nation-state faced and the combination of social and technological inventions brought the West out of an agricultural to an industrial economy.

The Second Economy

The second economy did something that hadn't been done since the domestication of crops thousands of years before: it raised incomes and improved lifestyle. The limit to the second economy was capital and by the close of the second economy, the West was awash with new machinery, factories, railroads, new products and millionaires. What it took to move from manual work to automation, from progress based on the trade and conquest of natural resources to progress based on making and selling products is outlined in these chapters.

Chapter 10, Capital, explores and defines the limit to progress in the second economy and how the machinery of industrial capital and the loans and equity of financial capital worked together to change lifestyles and create wealth.

Chapter 11, The Industrial Economy, lists some of the highlights of the industrial economy, some of the major social and technological inventions from the industrial economy

Chapter 12, The Enlightenment, explains what was different about the new philosophy that emphasized progress, science, and human rights.

Chapter 13, Inventing the Bank, chronicles the big social inventions that resulted in bond markets, banks, and enough capital to fund wars and railroads that sprawled across all of Europe.

Chapter 14, Democratic Revolution, tells the story of revolutions in England, America, and France, and connects these events to the Enlightenment and the rise of an industrial economy.

Chapter 15, Bank Dictates to the State, tells the story of how bankers came to finance and dictate terms to monarchs, forcing further democratization of governments and enabling modernization.

10 Capital

After you've conquered and explored the world, what do you do for an encore? How about transforming the stuff you found into stuff you can sell? For that you'll need capital—both financial and industrial.

Economy	First	Second	Third	Fourth
Period	1300–1700	1700–1900	1900-2000	2000-2050
Limit to Progress	Land	**Capital**	Knowledge Workers	Entrepreneurship
Type of Economy	Agricultural	Industrial	Information	Entrepreneurial
Intellectual Revolution	Renaissance	Enlightenment	Pragmatism	Systems Thinking
Big Social Invention	Nation-State	Bank	Corporation	Self
Social Revolution	Protestant Revolution	Democratic Revolution	Financial Revolution	Business Revolution

Land remained important through the second economy but it was the nation-states that began to focus on capital that became the most powerful and wealthy. Capital added value to the natural resources, the land that was so important to the first economy.

The first economy was defined by the efforts and inventions that overcame the limit of land. The second was defined by the efforts and inventions required to overcome the limit of capital. The most obvious of these inventions are captured in history books as accounts of new factories, steam engines, and railroads. Yet just as importantly, this new limit of capital provoked a pattern of big social inventions that, once again, transformed the world into something unprecedented, disruptive, wonderful, and appalling.

The Difference Between Tools and Capital

It is not as if people ate mud and wore leaves during the first economy or even medieval times. Many jobs required expertise and special tools and some craftsmen were members of medieval guilds. These craftsmen and others had tools but their tools were not quite the same as capital. The way that they are different does much to define capital.

Medieval guild members who might make glass or iron or flour knew secrets about how to make these products. They used tools for the job, tools that they could not – in many instances – do the work without. These guilds licensed craftsmen and controlled prices, methods, tools, and even prices. The purpose of the guilds was to promote stability and what was fair, not to promote progress. This was a time when economics was a branch of ethics. Adam Smith wrote *The Wealth of Nations,* the book that more than any other came to be associated with capitalism. He was not a professor of economics but of moral philosophy. Until about the time of the second economy, economic activity was judged by what was "fair," not on the basis of what did the most to raise productivity or incomes.

Guild members relied on expertise and tools, but they did not expect either to change much—if at all—during their lifetimes. A typical apprenticeship was 7 years and change that could obsolete current methods was not welcome. Medieval guilds, like the medieval church, were more intent on protecting tradition than spurring innovation. And like the church, they actually squelched innovation, doing what they could to protect their tools and expertise from innovators who might disrupt their living by undercutting them on costs and price. It was not until the late 19th century that the term innovation had a positive connotation: early in the second economy, innovation had the negative connotation of referring to "a new development that threatened existing order in a detrimental way."[78] Change was just assumed to be negative.

Guilds were about protecting the status quo. By contrast, capital is about betting on the future, on making money from what didn't exist before.

Medieval tools were static; the capital of the second economy was dynamic.

We use the term "capital" for two things that often are collapsed because they are so close in practice. "Capital" refers to plants and equipment—stuff that can make products or provide services. "Capital" also refers to the financial claims on such stuff—bonds (or loans) and shares of stock.

A consumer buys a product hoping to get pleasure from it; an investor makes an investment hoping to get profit from it, profit that can be used to purchase a product later. The machine represents a technological invention and the paper that claims ownership (whether as bond or stock) represents a social invention. In a demonstration of the co-dependence of technological and social invention, these two carry the same name: capital. Capital couldn't really exist without capital and vice versa.

Both kinds of capital—financial and industrial—are purchased in the hopes of profit.

Industrial capital makes products for people and financial capital makes money for them. Both kinds of capital make life easier.

Capital was most visible in the factories and railroads that sprawled across the landscape of cities and former farmland. Less visible was the capital in the form of documents that represented ownership in such ventures, whether it was in the form of stocks or bonds. This capital created a new generation of millionaires whose power was to usurp that of aristocrats. In some sense, the overthrow of monarchies and aristocracy was a revolution of capitalists.

---

[78] Steven Johnson, The Invention of Air: A story of science, faith, revolution, and the birth of America [New York, NY, Riverhead Books, 2008] 198.

The Start of the Second Economy

The first economy was a time of as much turmoil as progress, and it took some time before communities worked out the big institutional questions and were then able to overcome the limit of land and begin to shift their attention to capital.

The Gutenberg Bible (1455), Tyndale's English translation (1524), and Luther's German translation (1534) put Bibles into homes and fed independent thought. Kings and princes rose up to claim their stake on land. The battle for authority between various churches and states was often a literal battle. The religious wars up until the Treaty of Westphalia in 1648 killed huge swaths of population (by some estimates, half the male population in Germany and a third of the Czech population[79]). After 1648, the Continent entered a time of relative peace and for the first time since the Protestant Revolutions began, there was again a generally accepted authority in Europe: the sovereign state.

The nation-state was invented to overcome the limit of land and, once past the chaos of religious wars, it did just that. Then as the limit to progress shifted from land to capital, an industrial economy began to supplant the agricultural economy, most obviously in England.

Life in 1700 was largely defined by the tedium of manual work. People would spend hours doing tasks that today are done in seconds by machines. Products were simple and crude and most production was done in the home. Life was better than in 1300 but not by a great deal. Perhaps the most visible change that came from the progress of the first economy had less to do with increases in per capita GDP than in total GDP, and this simply because there were more people. Global population remained roughly steady from the year 1000 to 1300 (rising from 310 million to 360 million). After that, it began to grow, even with the setback from the Black Death. Global population between 1300 and 1700 grew from 360 million to 600 million.[80]

But there is something curious that happens when you have more people living in relationship with each other. As cities get larger, incomes and rates of innovation rise. An increase in the number of people trading goods and ideas changed the rate of innovation. Change

---

[79] http://en.wikipedia.org/wiki/Thirty_Years'_War

[80] From http://en.wikipedia.org/wiki/File:Population_curve.svg

stimulated more change and that dynamic became clear during the second economy.

Essentially, the stage was set for capital—both the machines that did the work for the people and the financial value that made them rich—to transform life between 1700 and 1900.

Capital's Dynamic

Einstein is quoted as saying "Compound interest is the most powerful force in the universe." It seems a little cute for him but the point is a good one.

Or as Benjamin Franklin put it, "Money makes money and the money, money makes, makes more money." Over time, small differences in returns become large as compound interest works its magic, a dynamic that every financial planner has illustrated to prospective customers.

If your money makes 20 percent a year, after ten years your money is making more money each year than you began with. (If you make 10 percent a year, it takes more like a quarter of century to reach this point.) This is a point worth exploring. A family able to save a small fortune could set up their children—or grandchildren—to eventually "earn" that much each year. The magic of compound interest can make the future better.

Capital is a curious thing. You don't invest in financial capital because you want financial capital. You invest in financial capital because you want money that you can use to buy the things you do want.

The other kind of capital—the technological capital—is the same way. You don't make a tool because you want a tool. You make a tool because you want to be able to more easily make shoes (or whatever it is you are making).

With financial capital, you take money out of your spending to save in the hopes of more money in the future. With industrial capital, you take time and effort out of your work to make a tool (or devise a process) that you can use to more readily make more products.

There are at least two reasons that people invest in capital. One has to do with delay of gratification—people giving up what they could buy now in order to have more money to buy with later. The other has to do with sufficiency—people having enough to live on and simply laying aside money to buy something bigger or different in the future. Some people get more satisfaction from buying products and some people get more satisfaction from buying capital, buying stocks or savings accounts and watching them grow. It is partly honorable that people save and invest. It is also, like so many things, partly personality and preference that can't be explained much more readily than the preference for salty rather than sweet snacks. Some people get more satisfaction from watching returns on stocks than they do from watching high-definition movies on a plasma TV.

Whatever the motivations of individuals within them, communities that begin the process of investing in capital do at least two things: they launch themselves onto the path to prosperity and they trigger a dynamic of change.

The Invention of Capital: Accepting Innovation

I believe that we're coming into a time when social invention will become more common. As a contrast, it's worth reviewing a time when technological invention was considered something novel and almost magical rather than something we planned for as a normal course of business. That is, when technological invention was at the same stage of development as social invention is now.

In 1700, people in the West still traveled no faster than a horse or a sail filled with wind. In this sense, life hadn't changed much in thousands of years. People may have argued about the particulars of their beliefs, but among these beliefs was the conviction that the God they worshipped was no different than the one Moses worshipped. They could now choose between bread and potatoes, but time spent simply procuring and preparing food still represented a huge portion of the day. Capital would change all this.

An acceptance of capital is an acceptance of novelty. Capital changes how we see the world. It is not just that accepting capital gives us a new worldview, but capital and equipment can actually change what we see.

Copernicus made calculations that convinced him that the earth orbited around the sun rather than vice versa. Most people could not see what he saw in the numbers, could not conceptualize this.

About sixty years later, Galileo made a telescope that he used to look for things that Copernicus's theory and calculations had suggested. Anyone with access to a telescope could then see what Copernicus saw, even if they couldn't quite "see" the argument he was making.

About four hundred years after Galileo, NASA made a space module that took pictures to show rather explicitly what Galileo and Copernicus had seen more obliquely. Now, billions of people could see the earth hanging in space, orbiting around the sun.

Equipment—capital—can enable people to see what they otherwise could not, to move at speeds they could not approach on foot, and to calculate what they could never before calculate. We now live in a world that is sustained by equipment—from computers and cars to water and electrical utilities. The quality of our lives is propped up by equipment, built on the foundation of capital.

Capital does not just change how we see the world, of course. It changes how we experience it.

Analysis & The Automation of Work

People can do a great many things, from crawling over rocks to running to swimming to gripping things to throwing them. Equipment, typically, can do only one or two things, and for this reason it was fortuitous that tasks were made simpler as a prelude to automation. Europeans began to analyze, to break into pieces, both the things that they were trying to understand and the work they did.

Rene Descartes was one of the great minds of the seventeenth century (yes, the Descartes of "I think, therefore I am" fame). He defined analysis as a means to understand complexity. His rules for analysis were to become the basis for capitalism about a century later. Although it was probably unintentional, Adam Smith's definition of the division of labor was, in a sense, just an application of Rene Descartes's admonition about how to think. Descartes's abstract philosophical rules become Smith's tangible division of labor.

Rene Descartes, building on Francis Bacon's movement towards the inductive method,[81] had published his *Rules for Thinking* about 150 years before Smith published his seminal work on capitalism. Descartes's admonition for analysis or understanding was to

"... reduce involved and **obscure propositions** step by step to those that are simpler ..."

For Smith, we could substitute "complex productions" for Descartes' "obscure propositions," ending up with an admonition to

"... reduce involved and **complex productions** step by step to those that are simpler ..."

This analytic approach showed up as division of labor—the opening proposition in Adam Smith's *Wealth of Nations* and one that helped fuel a productivity explosion during the second economy, one Smith assumed led to productivity gains of thousands of times. The same principle that was to underpin scientific analysis created division of labor in pin manufacturing and hundreds of other industries.

The opening line of Smith's book is oft-quoted.

"The greatest improvement in the productive powers of labour, and the greater part of the skill, dexterity, and judgment with which it is anywhere directed, or applied, seem to have been the effects of the division of labour."

On a grander scale, as trade exploded during the first economy, entire communities could focus on specialties, on dividing labor. It wasn't just factories that had specialists—the world had them. From raising spices to making textiles, from mining to tobacco, colonies and countries around the world increasingly had specialties and the world became wealthier as a result. Specialization within, and of, nations exploited and increased diversity even more than trade; this was a stark contrast to the medieval religion that had earlier tried to squelch diversity.

Division of labor was key to productivity gains. It was also key to automation. Simple tasks could be given to machines, and division of labor helped to spark the imagination about how to replace these simple steps done by people with simple steps done by machines.

---

[81] Francis Bacon was nearly deified by many Enlightenment thinkers. Bacon was instrumental in moving science from the deductive to the inductive method. The inductive method began with observations and sought to extract certain laws from that. This method has since become synonymous with the empirical method and can arguably be looked back on as the foundation for most subsequent scientific progress, a shift from Plato to Aristotle.

By 1779, the weaving process had been fully automated. Within a matter of decades, labor alone could not hope to compete with machinery, and anyone who wanted to be competitive had to have capital. Factory work may have been tedious, but it was not slow. Productivity soared with the addition of capital. Capital made a bigger difference than labor by about 1800, which is to say that capital raised productivity more than labor and a person with capital had an easier time of finding labor than a person offering labor had of finding someone with capital. Factory workers emerged as assistants to equipment, doing the steps that could not easily be done by machines.

Finally, as the world became larger, individuals could focus on a smaller portion of production processes. Trade made it possible for the individual to meet a wide variety of his own needs while focusing on one specialty. The baker could eat meat and vegetables because the poultry farmer and gardener also wanted variety in their diet. Because of trade, the baker could focus on the work and innovation of one task—making baked goods—producing more than three times as much as he would have if he had spent only a third of his time and focus on baking and the balance of his time acquiring produce and poultry. The diversity that made it profitable to trade in the first economy became something that communities manufactured in the second economy.

The Role of Capital in Community Disruption

Capital made communities richer. It also made them poorer. Although life in 1700 was brutish and nasty and people lived without items like nylons or zippers, a person might eke out a living without access to capital. He could do manual work. By 1900, even a farmer had to have capital to purchase machinery and even land (something that often necessitated loans, making farmers both resentful of and dependent upon bankers). There was no way that a manual worker could make enough products to compete with a factory. If a worker could not either afford his own capital (not practical when it came to factories) or get work in a factory, he could not make a living. Thus, by 1900, making a living generally depended on getting access to capital, whether through employment in growing organizations or through loans. In a very practical way, power had shifted to capital.

Furthermore, the compound interest of capital exacerbated differences in wealth. Over time, someone who invested became richer and someone who borrowed became poorer.

Once the shift toward dependence on capital began, communities had no choice but to embrace this new dynamic. Communities that had no capital could literally be overrun by those that did. To be without the factories and the wealth and armaments they could produce was to have a state without power. The wealth of nations depended on capital and that alone would have been enough to make it irresistible to communities.

Turning Ideas into Capital[82]

As it turns out, there are some predecessors to an industrial economy. Trade alone might be enough to encourage specialization, but handing off those simplified tasks to machines requires someone with the means and incentive to create such machines. The incentive for inventors turns out to pretty neatly be met by patents that give an inventor a means to take an invention public without losing exclusive income from it.

Initially, royalty in the emerging nation-states turned to patents as simply a means to grant favorites with an exclusive on trade while collecting revenues independent of Parliament. Monarchs had trouble getting money from Parliament (more on this later), and while giving a favorite an exclusive on making paper or selling salt, the monarch could collect a fee. Patents initially referred to these types of monopolies.

But Edward Coke (pronounced Cook) changed the meaning of patents when he drafted the "1623 'Act concerning Monopolies and Dispensations with penall Lawes and the Forfeyture thereof,' or, as it has become known, the Statute on Monopolies." The Act encouraged competition by eliminating monopolies for all but one case: "patents could still be awarded to the person who introduced the invention to the realm – to the 'first and true inventor.[83]'"

---

[82] William Rosen, *The Most Powerful Idea in the World: A Story of Steam, Industry, and Invention* [Random House, New York, NY, 2010]

[83] Rosen, The Most Powerful Idea, 50.

With this law, invention was no longer left to those who had the money and means to tinker on their own. Now, bright working class lads could invent something that they hoped would make them rich.

It would take decades before this patent law was to encourage a steady stream of innovations, but one could argue that no law did more to make Britain home to the industrial revolution that would create an economy unlike any before it. If technological invention is important to progress, how much more important is the social invention that encouraged it? Patent law represented a huge advance and laid the foundation for the industrial economy.

An Excess of Capital Leading to Bubbles

Our ancestors living at the dawn of the second economy would be flabbergasted at the amount of capital we have. One might think that our ability to steadily increase the amount of capital would obviously make ours a better world. That assumes, of course, that capital is still the limit to progress. Remember our simple diagram showing how much time it took to process a part?

If we accelerate the time it takes to make a part at the first station, we don't change the products we can make per hour.

The first work station does not limit our output. It is the second workstation, in this example. What happens when we do accelerate the speed of a work station that is not the limit? We get a build up of inventory stacked waiting for the second work station that takes 5 minutes to process each part. There is no revenue that comes from building up inventory after the step of the first workstation. There is only cost of inventory.

A similar thing seems to have happened here at the close of the third economy.

As I write this, the West seems to move from financial bubble to financial bubble. Booms and busts seem to occur with some regularity, the cycle of business expansion, over-expansion, and then busts seeming to define modern economies even more assuredly than progress. But bubbles of particular kinds of assets seemingly occur with greater regularity. This might have something to do with the huge sums of capital sloshing about the planet in search of returns. It could be that our ability to create financial capital has improved more rapidly than our ability to create profitable investments. That is, our great progress at overcoming the limit of progress has continued even as we've come into an economy that seems limited instead by entrepreneurship. The result? All this capital bids up the price of existing assets, at turns creating bubbles in asset markets as varied as real estate, stocks, and gold.

How much capital is out there?

It's hard to tell for sure.

Just before the global financial meltdown of 2008, in late 2007, Alan Greenspan estimated that "hedgeable assets" worldwide were worth about $100 trillion. In mid-2007, hedge funds deployed about $2 to $2.5 trillion of equity capital. Yet given that they leverage, the amount they were actually investing was probably a multiple of that—something more like $20 or even $100 trillion.[84] Keep in mind that the entire world's GDP is only about $50 trillion.

If the value of these markets is staggering, so was the cost when they faltered. If you make a down payment of $10,000 on a $100,000 house, you can double your original investment in the first year if house prices rise 10%. That's the good news and one reason that banks and hedge funds have done so much to leverage investments. They've become masters at "creating" financial capital in order to leverage returns. The bad news, of course, is that if - and when - house prices fall 10% in the first year, you can lose everything. Worse, if house prices fall 20%, you can owe more than you have in the house. You now have to sell "good" assets in order to raise money to pay down your debt, selling your silverware and cars, for example. The problem is, if everyone in the neighborhood suddenly has to come up with $10,000 to cover the drop of 20%, it is hard to get much money for the cars and silverware. A drop in prices in one asset can spread like a virus to infect other markets.

That dynamic was at work in the 2008 financial meltdown. When markets fell, assets as varied as real estate and stocks dropped tens of trillions. About 30 million people around the world lost their jobs. Millions lost their homes.

There are ways to smooth out the effects of the inevitable ups and downs of financial markets. The West has learned this lesson (more on this later) but apparently has to re-learn it every time an extended boom makes regulators and investors alike more lax.

But there is something more at work here, I think. Our ability to create financial capital can actually be seen as an extraordinary ... well, asset, once we learn more about entrepreneurship and creating investment-worthy opportunities. Think of what an advantage it will be to have trillions in capital in a world of startups from within and without companies, to say nothing of the various possibilities for capital consumption that will come from schools and government agencies. Entrepreneurship often (but not always) takes capital. The good news is that our world has it.

---

[84] Charles Morris, The Trillion Dollar Meltdown: Easy Money, High Rollers, and the Great Credit Crash [Public Affairs, New York, NY, 2008]

Back to 1700

But in 1700, the notion of trillions of dollars would have seemed like the wildest kind of science fiction. They still faced the very real limit of capital but overcoming this limit was to transform the world. Most obviously, it created a new, industrial economy that shifted brute effort from people to machines, allowing huge increases in productivity, income, and the number of goods households bought and used. For the first time in about seven thousand years, real income was to increase[85]. Dramatically.

The next chapter in this section on the second economy highlights some of the big technological and social inventions and events that would define the industrial revolution that largely played out in the period from 1700 to 1900.

---

[85] Rosen, *The Most Powerful Idea*, 104.

11 The Industrial Economy

A new economy emerged, centered on the factories and finances of capital.

Economy	First	Second	Third	Fourth
Period	1300–1700	1700–1900	1900-2000	2000-2050
Limit to Progress	Land	Capital	Knowledge Workers	Entrepreneurship
Type of Economy	Agricultural	**Industrial**	Information	Entrepreneurial
Intellectual Revolution	Renaissance	Enlightenment	Pragmatism	Systems Thinking
Big Social Invention	Nation-State	Bank	Corporation	Self
Social Revolution	Protestant Revolution	Democratic Revolution	Financial Revolution	Business Revolution

While economies after 1700 consumed more resources than any in history, it was the British who had money and power enough to easily command those resources. The British encouraged capital formation most obviously with patent law that extended their notion of property rights to ideas, and they led the world into a new, industrial economy.

A curious thing happened during the second economy. The West moved away from superstition and magic and when it did, something magical happened. Inventors built machines that automatically built products and enabled people to travel faster than any living thing had traveled before. A schoolboy was said to have explained the industrial revolution as, "A wave of gadgets swept over England about 1760." These gadgets created an even larger wave of products. And for the first time in thousands of years, incomes began to rise.

If the idea of private property was one of the keys to the progress of the first economy, the idea that ideas could become property was one of the keys to the second economy.

Obstacles to Innovation

People did not own property during medieval times so much as rule it. This meant that their efforts were as likely to go into protecting their land as investing in it. During the first economy, the new nation-state took on the task of protecting property through a combination of force and a legal system. Once this was in place, landholders could invest in their land, feeling secure that their property rights would be honored.

Medieval times also meant that innovation was frowned on. Breakthroughs were a threat to the status quo and it was not only the church that resisted heretical thinking; even the guilds sought to protect the income of members by regulating – and often squelching – product invention. The first economy, with its challenge to the church, introduced innovative thinking.

Finally, during medieval times literacy rates were low, books were expensive, and hamlets were far apart – practically impossible to connect through any regular trade and travel. So, even if someone made a breakthrough and put it into practice, their invention could easily die out before getting reported or shared widely.

The British Invent Invention

Patents turned ideas into property. Patents gave inventors an incentive to sacrifice wages and even invest capital (their own money or, more typically, that of backers) in the development of a new machine. Patents could make an inventor rich. And then, even after the patent had expired, they could make a country rich.

Patents proved to be a powerful social invention.

Edward Coke's legislation for patent protection passed in 1623. It was not until the end of the century that an inventor taking advantage of this law would arguably begin the industrial revolution that would prove catalyst for the industrial economy.

In June of 1699, Thomas Savery demonstrated a steam engine that could be used to drain mines. (This act alone is as good a reason as any to date the second economy from 1700.) The steam engine mattered because before its invention, all work was done by humans or animals. The speed of travel – like per capita income – had hardly changed in thousands of years. Little was automated and the work of water wheels or windmills to power mills for grinding grain, for instance, was limited and dependent on variables that could not be managed. (An excess or shortage of running water or wind could make it difficult to harness the energy of a water wheel or windmill.) It took later inventors to Savery's machine first effective and then efficient. Made effective, the steam engine could be used in any coal mine. Made efficient, it could be used anywhere.

The need for the steam engine traced back to the need for alternative fuel. It was not long into the first economy before England exhausted its supply of trees. Wood was needed for homes, carts, ships, and heating. As the population and economy grew, demand for wood depleted forests. In addition, forests were often cleared to create farmland. Even at the beginning of the first economy, England was importing timber from Scandinavia but even that was not enough.

As the supply of wood dwindled, the English turned to alternative energy: coal. Coal, though, was not just dirty. It was difficult to mine. One of the biggest problems with coal mines is that they tended to fill with water and needed to be drained. If a coal deposit was thoughtful enough to be located close to a river, it was possible to harness energy from the river by a water wheel, energy that could be used to pump water out of the mines. But of course, coal mines are indifferent about whether or not they could be conveniently drained by pumps powered by water wheels. Savery built his engine to solve this problem.

A series of inventors helped Savery's steam engine to evolve.

Thomas Newcomen debuted a more powerful steam engine in 1712. The problem with Savery's engine is that it could not work for mines much deeper than 20 feet. Some of the most important mines were – of course – considerably deeper than this. Newcomen's advance built on Savery's invention (Newcomen received only ¼ of the returns from his patent, the rest going to Savery and his partners). But it was not just that Newcomen had a brilliant insight: he experimented for a decade before he could make his insights practical. Patent law promised him returns that could justify this investment. And it paid off: his steam engine could pump water from mines much deeper than Savery's engine, making his the engine of choice.

Newcomen had invented a steam engine that could pump water out of the coal mines and it – rather conveniently - used coal for fuel. Sadly, it was not fuel efficient; about the only place it made sense to use his engine was in a coal mine.

James Watt was one of many who were fascinated by Newcomen's engine. He was one of a few who was able to improve it. He soon formed a partnership with Matthew Boulton, who saw the potential for a steam engine that was more fuel efficient. Boulton may have been the first to realize that such an engine could be ubiquitous, applied everywhere that work needed to be done, not just coal mines.

1776 was one of the most defining years of the second economy. Not only did the American colonialists declare their independence from the biggest, richest, and most powerful empire in the world, but the first engineering text book was written, Adam Smith defined capitalism with *The Wealth of Nations,* and James Watt introduced an engine that made Newcomen's obsolete.

Matthew Boulton's vision to apply the steam engine elsewhere led him to imagine and manage the construction of London's first factory. James Watt invented the general purpose steam engine. His partner Matthew Boulton invented the automated factory.

"The Albion Mills ... was built on a scale hitherto unimagined. The largest flour mill in London in 1783 used four pairs of grinding stones; Albion was to have thirty, driven by three steam engines, each with a 34-inch cylinder. Within months after its completion, in 1786, those engines were driving mills that produced six thousand bushels of flour every week.[86]"

Savery, Newcomen, and Watt were not the only inventors inspired by the times. Even a century after Edward Coke passed his legislation to protect patents, there were few patents awarded. From 1700 to 1740, Britain issued fewer than five patents a year; from 1740 to 1780, the

---

[86] Rosen, *The Most Powerful Idea in the World*, 187.

annual number had quadrupled, to nearly nineteen, and from 1780 to 1800, it was up to fifty-two,[87] 10X what it had been at the century's start. Throughout the eighteenth century in Britain, the number of patents grew each year by nearly 4%. In the US, the number of awarded patents grew more than 6% a year from 1790 (only 3 that year) to 1900 (when there was a total 24,656). Patents made ideas property and this – as much as anything – helped to create capital, the key to the second economy.

Trade Profits Become Capital to Invest

Industrial capital required financial capital. Put simply, if you were going to create a factory that made six thousand bushels of flour every week you needed a serious amount of money to invest.

The first economy made the world bigger, connecting more people and turning the whole world (well, most of it anyway) into one market. Globalization began long before the twentieth century. Bigger markets promised more profits but also drove demand for more capital. If you are going to become the provider of rum to the world, you need something bigger than a kitchen sink. You will instead need equipment enough to make lots of rum which, in turn, requires lots of money. Industrial capital required financial capital.

One of the chief sources of financial capital was from successful merchants. Successful merchants might have more profits than they could use in their trading, so they made informal loans to the people they buy from or sell to.[88] In time, what was done informally became institutionalized; social interactions lead to social invention. In one generation, a trade merchant extends credit to a store that sells its goods; in the next generation, a bank formally extends a loan with interest.

To see one example of how this worked, we have only to look at the

---

[87] William Rosen, *The Most Powerful Idea in the World,* 184.

[88] Given the numerous steps between harvest, intermediary brokers, factories, and stores, credit lines evolved simultaneously with trade as merchants created a de facto credit system.

wildly successful Dutch, whose relative economic standing seemed to have peaked in about 1700, right about the time of the transition from the first to the second economy. In their economy's evolution, we can see the evolution from trade to manufacturing.

Dutch Trade Becomes Dutch Manufacturing

As previously mentioned, the Dutch were great traders. Soon, they parlayed profits from trade into making thing that they could trade.

When their population grew faster than their farming capacity, they had to import Baltic grain. In order to get this grain, they needed to make something to trade in return. Initially, they made floor tiles, roof tiles, and bricks.[89] They also made ships to trade these goods and found that the ships were, themselves, yet another good they could trade and sell; Dutch shipbuilding and shipping became huge industries. This, in turn, gave them even more ability to trade.

"Contemporaries guessed that the Dutch possessed sixteen thousand merchant vessels in the mid-seventeenth century, something like half the European total. . . . At times there were more Dutch than Spanish ships off Spanish America and more Dutch than English ships off English America."[90] The shipping industry gave the Netherlands access to more raw materials and was yet another way to generate profits, profits invested to make the Netherlands a center for making textiles and processing sugar.

This investment of profits into new industrial capital was partially driven by necessity. As more traders from Spain, Italy, England, and the Netherlands took to the sea, there was more competition for trade. This drove down prices for simple trade and created a need to manufacture or process goods into something of higher value in order to regain profits.

Trade at the beginning of the first economy tended to be for lightweight and expensive items like silk and spices. By the eighteenth century – the start of the second economy – trade had evolved from

---

[89] http://eh.net/encyclopedia/article/Harreld.Dutch

[90] Dunn, *The Age of Religious Wars*, 102.

just focusing on medieval luxury goods, "into the modern mass trade of new bulky necessities—hence the flourishing triangular trade of rum, cloth, guns, and other metal products from Europe to Africa, slaves from Africa to the New World, and sugar, tobacco, and bullion from the New World to Europe."[91]

If a country could find some way to make goods instead of merely trade them, though, it had the potential to become very rich. The capital that allowed a country to manufacture goods rather than just trade them could be, as Adam Smith explained, the basis for *The Wealth of Nations.*

Trade introduced new products and at least one was to stimulate conversations and thinking that led to a social invention that seemed to defy God's will.

Innovations of the Second Economy: Coffee and Insurance

Among the exotic new foods brought to Europe was coffee. Remember the European reliance on beer and wine as a source of calories second only to bread before the first economy. Now suddenly imagine Europe recovering from a hangover in a coffee house, where the new beverage stimulated conversation and ideas. By 1715, there were two thousand coffee houses in London alone,[92] and these coffee shops, along with newspapers, were the medium for sharing culture in the same way that radio and TV were centuries later.

The link between coffee and capitalism is little appreciated. It's worth remembering that water couldn't be trusted until fairly recently. In 1900, life expectancy in the United States was forty-seven years. By 2000 it had raised to seventy-seven, a gain that, by some calculations, had as much to do with improvements in access to potable water as anything. Tea and coffee were a great way to make water safe in the centuries between the time when urban centers became so crowded and when

---

[91] Geoffrey Barraclough, ed., *Times Atlas of World History* (London: Times Books, 1980), 155.

[92] Watson, *Ideas*, 531.

officials were able to provide utilities that could guarantee safe water to so many through public water works. Beer and wine allowed for urbanization by providing safe hydration to people who couldn't depend on clean rivers. Coffee and tea might have been the original economic stimulus, a stimulating alternative to alcohol.

Productivity gains did come from trade, improvements in agriculture, and nascent capitalism, but caffeine helped. You may want to compare your productivity by drinking three liters of beer a day in one week and three cups of coffee a day the next. Now imagine an entire continent making such a change and it's easy to imagine how important coffee's contribution to capitalism was.

Venture capitalists who had financed, well, *ventures* of ships traveling between Britain and the Americas were understandably anxious for news. Ships heading to foreign ports faced risks like foreign currency devaluation, a drop in demand for the goods they carried, embezzlement by ship captains, shipwreck, and even pirates. Investors could easily be ruined. Then, as now, venture capital was profitable but risky. Investors were eager for information about when, and whether, their ship would come in. In 1688, Edward Lloyd opened a shop that offered coffee with a side of information about the status of ships. It was here that one of the pillars of modern finance was founded.

The caffeine-fueled conversation at Lloyd's about how to deal with risk led to a new social invention: an insurance market called Lloyd's of London. Essentially, by forgoing a portion of one's cargo one was insured against losing the whole of it, and investors willing to insure the load could negotiate a fee with the venture capitalists. The coffee that sobered Europe thus also stimulated a conversation that led to Lloyd's of London, the world's most prestigious insurance market.

How does insurance help to overcome the limit of capital? Well, if you think that your life savings might literally become shipwrecked, you'll hesitate to put your money into venture capital, not wanting to risk it on a ship and its cargo. The problem with this strategy is that as fewer people invest in shipping, there are fewer goods in the community. This means that everyone has fewer items to trade, there is less money to be made, and thus there is a lower quality of life. If there is no trade with the Orient, there is no pepper for the steak. So communities that make it easier for people to invest will enjoy more goods and higher incomes. Insurance is one way to make it easier to invest. The communities that more quickly find a way to insure investments will get more investments and therefore more returns and all the unpredictable consequences of new products and services in the community. (Really, what genius could have ever predicted that coffee would stimulate insurance? And yet capitalism—as with all social change—is full of such unintended consequences, for both good and bad.)

Now insurance might seem an obvious thing to buy, but that just shows how positively modern is your mindset. In the seventeenth century there was still a persistent view of misfortune as God's will, something to be accepted like spankings from the headmaster. Heilbroner gives a succinct account of a man who, in 1644, was on trial for excess profit, a man facing excommunication because of his greed. The minister uses his repentance to "thunder forth in his Sunday sermon on some false principles of trade. Among them are these:

'I. That a man might sell as dear as he can, and buy as cheap as he can.

II. If a man lose by casualty of sea, etc., in some of his commodities, he may raise the price of the rest.

III. That he may sell as he bought, though he paid too dear ...'

All false, false, false, cries the minister; to seek riches for riches' sake is to fall into the sin of avarice."[93]

It is odd to think of actuaries as cultural outlaws, but there you have it. Even the idea of insuring against God's will seemed wrong to many. As is so often the case with social invention,[94] the biggest obstacle is the prevailing notion of what's proper.

Textiles – Those Proper British Try to Clothe the World

While men like Newcomen and Watt were making advances to the steam engine, other inventors were working to automate the steps to make textiles and clothing. Once Watt gave the world a general

---

[93] Heilbroner, *The Worldly Philosophers*, 21.

[94] To be clear, back in the 1400s Italians had invented insurance policies and these had expanded within the growing economy of Europe. What Lloyd's coffee shop did was create a market, like a bourse, for insurance policies to be drawn up and exchanged.

purpose steam engine, innovators in textiles were ready for it. The steam engine was first used to make flour and then fashion.

The textile industry was Britain's most important industry through most of the second economy. Between 1700 and 1800, Britain's export of textiles tripled, "and with two-thirds of the total generated by cotton goods, British manufactured exports amounted to 40 percent of national income – the largest percentage ever enjoyed by any nation before or since.[95]"

In the first economy, goods weren't altered much: wool was spun, grain ground, wood cut, and potatoes boiled. In the second economy, manufacturing made all of this more involved and complex. In the first economy, a manufacturer could be competitive by simply making bolts of cloth; by the second economy, they competed by making clothing

At the beginning of the first economy, international trade was an activity reserved for the rich. At the beginning of the second economy, it was the same with manufactured goods. Such goods really were *manu*-factured. That is, they were made by hand. If it took a week for the average worker to make a shirt, than a shirt cost at least one week's wages. If a producer hoped to sell to larger markets, he had to find a way to automate this work. If shirts could be made in just minutes, everyone could afford one. Or more. Making more meant making big improvements in more than just one step, though.

To process raw cotton into finished cloth required three steps. Carding cleaned the raw cotton. Spinning turned clean cotton into yarn. And finally weaving turned yarn into finished cloth.

In 1733, John Kay invented a flying shuttle that weaved yarn into finished cloth. This would have greatly increased the production of cloth if only carding and spinning had also been automated. In 1748, Lewis Paul invented machines to card raw cotton. Now, the step of spinning was clearly the limit to producing cotton, but that was the most difficult and delicate of the steps. It still had to be done by hand. About the time that James Watt was developing his general purpose steam engine, a series of inventors solved the problem of automating this last step. By the 1780s, factory owners had coupled the automation of spinning with James Watt and Matthew Boulton's steam engine.

Meanwhile, across the Atlantic, in 1793, Eli Whitney's cotton gin

---

[95] Rosen, *The Most Powerful Idea in the World*, 219.

automated the removal of seeds from cotton. Exports from the United States exploded. "Between 1790 and 1810 American cotton production increased from 1.5 million pounds to 85 million pounds per year.[96]"

Between 1760 and 1837, England's imports of raw cotton rose from 2.5 million pounds to 360 million pounds.[97] More raw material required more machinery, and more machinery required more raw material. So as the imports of cotton grew, so did the number of machines. "The number of power looms in English textile mills increased 100-fold between 1813 and 1850."[98] And this automation made cloth more affordable; "cotton cloth fell in price from thirty-eight shillings per pound in 1786 to less than ten shillings by 1800." Again, as with coffee, this sort of progress affected the world in ways obvious and not so obvious. Affordable cotton made underwear affordable and more common. After 1850, there was a dramatic falloff in infectious diseases. The most deadly diseases of that time - cholera and typhoid - are spread by fecal-oral contamination[99]. Given that it mitigated this sort of spread, underwear saved lives. Again, who could have predicted?

More Industry

The industrial economy was not just limited to flour and fashion. The power of patents affected production everywhere in Britain. In 1701, Jethro Tull invented the seed-planting drill (although it took decades to become widely used and centuries before he would inspire the name of a rock band) and followed this with numerous other agricultural innovations. In 1709, Abraham Darby invented iron smelting with coke, allowing the replacement of more expensive charcoal by cheaper coal in foundries. He was the first to mass-produce brass and iron goods, turning Britain into an exporter of brass goods. By 1784, Henry Cort had patented the process for mill-rolled iron, weaning Britain of its reliance on iron imports and ushering in a new stage of production.

---

[96] Bernstein, *The Birth of Plenty,* 219

[97] Roberts, *The Penguin History of the World*, 647.

[98] Bernstein, *The Birth of Plenty*, 156.

[99] Bernstein, *The Birth of Plenty,* 220

Farming, textiles, mining, and iron production were among the industries first transformed by this early stage of the industrial revolution. And all of those were to seem mere prelude to the transformative force of the railroad.

Railroads

The first communities to be transformed by trade had ports along the sea. First the Italians along the Mediterranean and then the Dutch and British along the Atlantic benefited from the trade of the first economy. Ports were transformative, but it is worth remembering what they are. "Port was originally an Anglo-Saxon word that meant 'market.'"[100] The railroad would do for regions like Bavaria, Russia, and Prussia what the compass and shipping had earlier done for Dutch and English seaports—exposing the average person to new products and competition through trade with regions from which they'd previously been shielded. It wasn't ports, exactly, that were so transformative. It was markets and the railroad had the potential to make any town a port.

The railroad was capital intensive, harnessed the inventions of steam engines and steel production, and exposed inland countries and cities to trade patterns more disruptive than the trade that first transformed the Venetian, Dutch, and English communities situated beside the sea. Railway mileage grew exponentially during the nineteenth century, transforming landscapes and markets. "By 1875 the world possessed 62,000 locomotives, 112,000 carriages and almost half a million goods wagons, carrying between them, so it was estimated, 1,371 million passengers and 715 million tons of goods, or about nine times as much as was carried by sea each year (on average) during this decade."[101] It was the Internet of its time, offering alluring investment opportunities directly and disrupting and expanding companies seemingly having nothing to do with railroads. And this stimulated trade. "The world's trade between 1800 and 1840 had not quite

[100] Lacey and Danziger, *The Year 1000*, 93.

[101] Eric Hobsbawm, *The Age of Capital: 1848–1875* (New York: Vintage Books, 1996), 55.

doubled. Between 1850 and 1870 it increased by 260 percent."[102]

Railway Mileage Open (000 miles)[103]

	1840	1850	1860	1870	1880
Europe	1.7	14.5	31.9	63.3	101.7
North America	2.8	9.1	32.7	56.0	100.6
India	--	--	0.8	4.8	9.3
Rest of Asia	--	--	--	--	*
Australasia	--	--	*	1.2	5.4
Latin America	--	--	*	2.2	6.3
Africa (inc. Egypt)	--	--	*	0.6	2.9

* Less than 500 miles

Napoleon and his republican troops had been on a mission to spread liberty throughout Europe, challenging the aristocracy that still ruled serfs in places like Prussia, Russia, and Austria. Even after Napoleon was stopped at Waterloo, the railroad continued to bring the outside world's influence into these regions, furthering the pressure on the rulers of these regions to defend against ideas such as democracy and representative government. Yet in order to defend themselves from this threat, they had to adopt elements of it. The central European states

102 Hobsbawm, *The Age of Capital*, 34.

103 Hobsbawm, *The Age of Capital*, 54.

of Germany began to foster industry, knowing that unless they could match the productive capacity and sophistication of the British and French military they would be unable to defend their way of life. Ironically, these very forces of industry, perhaps even more effectively than invading armies, transformed the way of life that the German aristocracy sought so desperately to defend.

The progress of the industrial revolution and enlightenment thinking forced changes in countries other than England, but no other country was as defined by these two forces as the United States. Timing was serendipitous for the United States. As land was being settled in the "west"—a vast region that first meant anything off of the Atlantic seaboard and eventually referred to places as remote from the Atlantic Ocean as Oregon or California—the railroad and telegraph emerged as new technologies. These technologies helped to link the vast regions of land from coast to coast into one huge market, making it possible to build huge factories.

A Dark Side of the Factory: Child Labor

Capital had a dark side, however, one most obviously seen in child labor.

Alexander Hamilton, Washington's Secretary of Treasury, wrote favorably of how manufacturing made children more productive: "Of the number of persons employed in the cotton manufactories of Great Britain, it is computed that 4/7 nearly are women and children; of whom the greatest proportion are children and many of them of a very tender age."[104]

Life had never been easy for children. Famine, disease, and war don't require a minimum age for their victims. It is hard to imagine a world harder for children than the lawless world of medieval Europe or growing up in the midst of the brutal battles of the religious wars that devastated towns, fields, and families. So it is not as though the industrial revolution brought with it something novel in its disregard for the lives of children. Still, there is something that seems systemically

---

[104] http://american_almanac.tripod.com/hammanuf.htm Excerpt from "Report on the Subject of Manufactures," by Alexander Hamilton, December 5, 1791.

barbaric about work that put children on assembly lines for twelve or more hours per day. And child labor was widespread at the height of untrammeled capitalism in the late nineteenth century. The first textile factory to use the Arkwright machinery employed "nine children, seven boys and two girls ages seven to twelve."[105] In 1820, "children comprised more than two thirds of the Pawtucket textile work force."[106] . The following account does not, sadly, report something exceptional but instead, something sadly typical of the time.

"Here an Anglican curate describes the typical fate of a young boy in an English textile factory during the heyday of the Industrial Revolution, in the middle of the 1800s:

'He ... had been found standing asleep with his arms full of wood and had been beaten awake. This day he had worked seventeen hours; he was carried home by his father, was unable to eat his supper, awoke at 4 A.M. the next morning, and asked his brothers if they could see the lights of the mill as he was afraid of being late, and then died. (His younger brother, aged nine, had died previously. ...)'"[107]

According to one 1833 report, 40 percent of the employees in New England factories were children between the ages of seven to sixteen who worked from daylight to 8:00 p.m..[108]

Anyone who does not understand this utter disregard for the life even of innocents would fail to understand the resistance to capitalism that came in the form of everything from romanticism and Communism to labor movements and anarchy. Capital was a wonderful tool but was a harsh task master.

An Economy Focused on Capital

No economic force transformed the world like the industrial economy. It

---

[105] Beatty, *Colossus*, 65.

[106] Beatty, *Colossus*, 68.

[107] Mihalyi Csikzentmihalyi, *The Evolving Self: A Psychology for the Third Millennium* (New York: Harper Perennial, 1993), 96.

[108] Beatty, *Colossus*, 72.

rearranged landscapes, cities, and the daily experience of life with a disruptive impact previously limited to war and other disasters. The time from 1700 to 1900 was disruptive and noisy and brought us more products than we'd ever had before. Wealth exploded. Population exploded. The diversity of products exploded. Too often, even machines exploded. These machines, though, changed what was possible.

From the time of Homer to the time of Shakespeare, incomes had barely changed. Measured in "constant 1990 U.S. dollars, incomes fluctuated between $400 and $550 for seven thousand years." The fact of a sudden growth in income would have been enough to change life. But it was more than that. In order to overcome the limit of capital, people had to change their thinking, their education, their careers, their habits of production and consumption, where they lived and how they lived.

A person who had fallen asleep in 1700 to be awakened in 1900 would be far more disoriented than someone from 1900 awakened in 2000. The person from 1700 would have to make sense of inventions as varied as trains and cars, photography and telephones, Coca-Cola and the striptease. There is little about the world of 1900 that would make much sense to this poor soul.

A new worldview did help to make sense of this new world and also helped to make this new world. This new world limited by capital required more than just new technology. It required a change in how one thought about the world. And as had happened during the Renaissance, the leading minds of the time provided the most subtle but important social invention: an intellectual revolution we now call the Enlightenment. You can read some about it in the next chapter.

12 The Enlightenment

The Enlightenment that fed and was fed by capitalism and democracy was more obviously an intellectual revolution than the Renaissance. For the first time in history, people expected progress, and worked to define natural laws rather than relying on divine intervention.

Economy	First	Second	Third	Fourth
Period	1300–1700	1700–1900	1900-2000	2000-2050
Limit to Progress	Land	Capital	Knowledge Workers	Entrepreneurship
Type of Economy	Agricultural	Industrial	Information	Entrepreneurial
Intellectual Revolution	Renaissance	**Enlightenment**	Pragmatism	Systems Thinking
Big Social Invention	Nation-State	Bank	Corporation	Self
Social Revolution	Protestant Revolution	Democratic Revolution	Financial Revolution	Business Revolution

The first great assault upon the traditional social system occurred in England's thirteen colonies. They were comparatively free and prosperous and subject to rather generous, progressive government. The assault was not led by the oppressed, but by those *who had little to gain except the fulfillment of certain ideals rooted in the spirit of the Enlightenment.*

—Walther Kirchner

The Enlightenment introduced the idea of progress and laws in place of deference to authority (whether that authority came from priest or monarch). While it might be thought of as merely a philosophy, its most notable practitioners were directly involved in inventing a new world through both technological and social inventions.

The Inescapable Simplification of Reality

Some model of the world is inescapable. The world is too complex to make sense of without some simplification of it. No matter how hard we try to just "be realistic," we are always dealing with some simplification of reality.

According to Tor Norretranders's fascinating book, *The User Illusion: Cutting Consciousness Down to Size*, your brain is tasked with an amazing responsibility. Your senses bombard it with about eleven million bits per second. Consciousness, however, can process only about ten to forty bits per second (estimates vary). So, the challenge of your brain is to process eleven million bits into eleven bits in way that accurately represents, or maps back to, the eleven million bits. The million-plus bits flowing in from your eyes, for instance, have to be processed into familiar shapes ("Hey—that's my buddy Bill!") that show up in consciousness as one bit rather than millions of disparate bits indicating colors, shapes, and spatial location. Cognitive processes below the surface of consciousness, processes that by definition we are unaware of, translate the millions into the few.

As if that were not amazing enough, there is more. The brain takes about half a second to perform this feat—a remarkably rapid rate of calculation for processes so complex. Yet a half second is a really long time when it comes to awareness and sensations. This creates a challenge: how does consciousness stay in the now when, in fact, it is lagging reality by half a second?

Well, as it turns out, consciousness does not keep up with reality.

Consciousness, however, is all that we're conscious of. So the brain merely slips into our perception of reality a little lie about when we were conscious of it. The brain performs an amazing feat: once it has processed the eleven million bits into the twenty bits to be comprehended by consciousness, it back-dates this reality. And of course, since we're conscious of only what we are conscious of, if the brain informs our consciousness that there was no delay, we will believe that there is no delay.

Let me repeat that. Tests indicate that although it takes a half second to process the *sensations* of reality into the *perception* of reality, consciousness basically tells us that it is instantaneous. It tricks us.

So, here's the real kicker. If consciousness lags reality and we don't, for instance, take a half second to decide to flex a finger or look up, what is the role of consciousness, or awareness? How is it that we interact with reality in real time even though our consciousness lags it by half a second?

It almost seems as though consciousness does not make decisions so much as trail after the cognitive processes that make such decisions—processes that are not even at the level of awareness—and explain, apologize, or rationalize what has just happened. The role of consciousness may be less that of the driver of the car than that of the insurance agent who follows after the car, leaving claim forms in its wake. Someone has quipped that we don't so much have a rational brain as a rationalizing brain.

Given that our perceptions are so subtly distorted at the personal level, it ought not to seem incredible that this distortion also occurs at the social level. That is, whatever models of reality a community embraces, they are invariably incomplete, simple, and mistaken for the realty they model. Still, communities adopt worldviews because they are inescapable. We need coherent, shared views of the world. As with any social invention, though, these worldviews are powerful for some things and inadequate for others.

The Enlightenment

A worldview is the most subtle but also the most influential of social inventions. It changes how people explain the world and what they expect of life. The Enlightenment did more than any other philosophy to undermine faith in authority and shift reliance on revelation to reason. Perhaps most importantly, it defined a world of causation and predictability rather than of miracles and confusion.

Priests used the pulpit to spread the word; Enlightenment thinkers used books and classrooms. The eighteenth century is peppered with social milestones, such as Prussia making school attendance compulsory in 1717 and Scotland establishing the first circulating library in 1726. One of the big ideas of the Enlightenment was educating people on the ideas of the Enlightenment. Through the eighteenth century, an "enlightened" public gradually came to trust science and reason more than superstition and dogma; such a public could be trusted with a vote—but that gets us slightly ahead of the story.

One could do worse than explain the Enlightenment as stemming from the minds of Isaac Newton and John Locke, probably the two greatest minds to ever regularly dine together. Newton applied his powerful intellect to developing laws for the physical world and John Locke applied his to the social world. To this day their ideas define much of our physical and social world. Newton's was a philosophy that applied to the movement of planets and machinery, the language of "for every action there is an opposite and equal reaction." Locke's applied to people and governments, the language of "life, liberty, and property," as an entitlement that described the freedom of movement of people and the quest for pleasure and products that defined the markets of this industrial age. Newton's laws represented the biggest transformation of God since the advent of monotheism. After Newton, God was no longer viewed as a being who interfered by miracles into the daily course of events but was, instead, viewed as one who had defined the world by immutable laws; not an agent of caprice but rather of order. Locke's laws represented the biggest transformation of government authority since the days of early Greece. After Locke, monarchs were no longer the ultimate authority, who could impose their will, but were, instead, subject to constitutional laws just like everyone else, not agents of caprice but of rather of order.

Among other things, these laws created a world conducive to capital. Investors who know the future will be safe from whim are more likely to invest, more likely to act in anticipation of returns. One of the big obstacles to capital formation is uncertainty. Laws helped to lessen the uncertainty of the future. The Enlightenment, by encouraging reliance on proof rather than authority, encouraged invention and experimentation, which helped to trigger the further development of capital. Communities that aligned themselves around Enlightenment principles were the most developed, advanced, and capital-rich. Capital was the limit to the Industrial Economy, and capital in the form of machinery required a new physics of cause and effect, while capital in the form of finances required a new government based in law rather than individual whimsy or judgment. The Enlightenment thus provided a way of thinking that helped to overcome the limit of capital.

Theories for Facts: Newton Explains What Copernicus Saw

The leading Renaissance thinkers were willing to adapt their minds to the facts but weren't sure how to fully explain them. Although it took decades for most scientists to accept Copernicus's revolutionary claims, those scientists were not stupid. In addition to Scripture and their own senses (it was obvious even to the casual observer that the sun rose and the earth was stationary), they had a fairly reasonable, scientific objection. Copernicus could accept facts as he observed them, but didn't really have a cogent explanation of why the solar system worked as it did. Imagine this conversation.

Copernicus's debate opponent says, "So, Nicoli, let me grant you your silly premise for a moment. Let's assume that we do, indeed, circle the sun. You claim that we're spinning about a thousand miles an hour while hurtling in some kind of orbit around the sun. Okay. What about centrifugal force? Spin a rock at the end of a string and see how many seconds it takes the ant on that rock to fly into space. Why doesn't this happen to us? Why don't cows slip out of the grip of milkmaids and fly over the moon?"

"I don't know," says our hero Copernicus. "I just know what the data suggests. We are orbiting around the sun. I can't explain it. I just know it is so."

"So," continues his opponent, "you have no explanation? You make no attempt to account for the simple fact of centrifugal force? You just want us to believe something that even you don't understand?"

"Yes."

Not much of a debate. On the one hand, we have ants without

opposable thumbs obviously unable to keep their grip on a rock in orbit, a phenomenon that would suggest that we should be observing panicked cows floating off into space if Copernicus was right. On the other hand, we have someone arguing that the data on the movement of planets fits better if we assume that it is the sun and not the earth that is stationary, if we assume that we're hurtling through space thousands of miles an hour. Preposterous.

It took an Enlightenment thinker—*the* Enlightenment thinker—to explain why. Isaac Newton solved two problems with one universal law. It is tempting to think—reasonable to suspect—that the explanation for our circling the sun would be different from the explanation of why it is not impossible to find our car in the morning, uncertain as to where it has spun off to in the Milky Way through centrifugal force. Newton sees a falling apple and realizes that it is pulled by the same force as the earth is. Gravity is the universal force that explains why cows don't fly and the earth does. Newton added laws—a theory—to observations and facts.

Newton gave the lovers of facts a set of laws that made sense of their facts. In 1687, Newton published his "Philosophiae naturalis principia mathematica," in which he stated the laws governing the universe (e.g., "To every action there is always opposed an equal reaction"), including the law of gravity, and formed the foundation for other sciences. This occurred two years before Locke wrote his *A Letter Concerning Toleration* arguing for religious freedom.

A Reliance on Reason Rather than Revelation

In 1712, England executed its last witch and just a couple of years later, Prussia abolished witch trials altogether. The realization that it made no sense to bring someone to trial for witchcraft (where is the proof of magical causation?) might be the simplest example of the progress of reason in the West. It was an attempt to use proof as the basis for decisions in the public realm. As with so much progress, though, this change had its adversaries. What seems obvious to us now was for the times controversial. John Wesley (1703–91), who founded the Methodist faith, spoke for many when he said that to not believe in witches was to not believe in the Bible.

The Enlightenment popularized the notion of proof as having more authority than, well, authority.

In some ways, the Enlightenment was a break with Plato's ideals. Plato's allegory of the cave remains a powerful story about "truth," suggesting that what we observed was not the "real" truth but was merely shadow. Ideals outside of observation were real. Thus truth was not the product of observation but was, instead, the product of revelation.

Christianity and its claims of spiritual truths and a reality that were not of this world buttressed this notion of Platonic ideals. This Platonic notion of reality was the dominant one for much of the medieval period and even into the Renaissance, although the Renaissance, with its emphasis on the sensual, was to erode this. The Enlightenment, by contrast, embraced what could be proven and not merely asserted or "revealed."

Common people, though, were less likely to discuss Platonic ideals or even spiritual truths. The way they might express their belief in reality as something other than what we see was by telling stories that today we'd refer to as superstition or myth. They relied on authority. For them, magic was real and the miracles reported in the Bible had not stopped but continued into the present day. Theirs was a world where witches lived in the woods and had the power to wreck crops or inexplicably kill your pig or even force you to miscarry by use of the evil eye. Giving up a belief in mystery and magic as causation for daily events is a slow process, and, to be fair, we still don't "see" causation—we merely infer. Newton's wonderfully mathematical and scientific gravity is as invisible as the witch's spell. It is, however, predictable.

As a reminder that progress is rarely linear, it is worth pointing out that the great Enlightenment thinker Newton was fascinated by the possibility of alchemy and essentially devoted the last third of his life to decoding the mysteries of the Book of Daniel and Revelation to learn the truth about Armageddon and the end of the world. [109] It is true that the Enlightenment made the world more rational, but it is not true that it has—even to this day—freed us of all that eludes proof.

In the thirteenth century, Roger Bacon advocated the empirical method, and about a decade later—presumably when lesser minds finally figured out the implications of what he meant—they jailed him for heresy. Roger Bacon was a hero to Enlightenment thinkers. We don't

[109] Barzun, *From Dawn to Decadence*, 197.

normally think of the empirical method as heretical, but it is. A person who can trust his own senses and reason doesn't need authorities to explain his world. He can, in fact, defy authorities when the facts and his reasoning lead him there. And worse, he is trading revelation for observation.

The Enlightenment included dozens of great thinkers. By the late eighteenth century, the matter of trust in self was made explicit. In 1784, Immanuel Kant published "What Is Enlightenment?" and wrote, "'Have courage to use your own reason!'—that is the motto of enlightenment." And of course even Kant, champion of freedom, looked over his shoulder, seeming to curry favor from Frederick the Great of Prussia (ruler of Kant's realm) eager that his call for change not threaten a man who could threaten Kant. By that point many Enlightenment thinkers were taking the individual away from the dictates of church and state and into the arms of reason. Earlier, in 1733, Alexander Pope defined the new focus of this Enlightenment period in his "Essay on Man," writing, "Know then thyself, presume not God to scan, the proper study of mankind is Man." It was not just that we were to trust our own senses; we weren't even supposed to be interested in things that evaded our senses. Such things were, in fact, considered to be nonsensical.

Reason wasn't the only thing that made Enlightenment thinkers tend to reject religious claims. Fatigue and disgust also played a part. Religious wars and persecutions persisted through the seventeenth century, religious battles that were violent conflicts over propositions that could not be proven. Religious wars made Enlightenment thinkers—indeed, made most Europeans—wary of claims of faith, and particularly faith so keenly felt that it could be the basis for war.

The Enlightenment's emphasis on proof was to change government. Proof became a predecessor to democracy. Whereas religion and authority were once the basis for laws, reason and democracy became the new basis. Many believed in divine rights of kings—that is, that God had ordained kings. God's favor could not be proven, however, whereas ballots could be counted. The Enlightenment was thus the philosophy that would lay the foundation for democracy and capitalism.

By undermining the certainty about religion, the Enlightenment also helped to promote religious freedom. Many of the Enlightenment thinkers were deists, which essentially meant that they believed in a God but did not really believe in church authority. Many deists were anticlerical. Few expressed this as starkly as Denis Diderot, who championed (and wrote most of) the first encyclopedia. He said, "Man will never be free until the last king is strangled with the entrails of the last priest." Immanuel Kant was typical of many in his acceptance of the basic tenets of Christianity as a loving religion but rejection of supernatural prophecy and miracles as evil. Rousseau wanted deism adopted as France's civil religion, and Ben Franklin, Thomas Jefferson, and George Washington were all deists.[110] Jefferson composed his own Bible, extracting the supernatural from his version. Thomas Hobbes dismissed religion as a product of ignorance. From thinkers like this, the notion emerged that morality need not depend on religion. The state could be a vehicle for protecting and advancing the general welfare, without resort to religious authority. Individuals could believe but could not impose their beliefs – not even if they were rulers.

Question Authority

Enlightenment philosophers arrived at a different idea about authority. For them, individuals had "inalienable" rights that they only partially yielded to a ruler in order to enjoy the social order that came from living under good government, protected from life under lawless brutes. This authority did not come from the king but, rather, originated with the people. John Locke did the most to articulate this idea of rights.

Locke, in his *A Letter Concerning Toleration*, clearly addressed the need to abandon religious government. To appreciate how different his thinking was, note that "when John Locke attended Oxford, there were sixty senior student berths: one in moral philosophy, two each in law and medicine, and fifty-five in theology."[111] He defined the modern position that most religious people living in the West now hold and saw no reason to impose his faith on his fellow citizen:

"I esteem it above all things necessary to distinguish exactly the business of civil government from that of religion and to settle the just bounds that lie between the one and the other. If this not be done, there can be no end put to the controversies that will be always arising between those that have, or at least pretend to have, on the one side, a concernment for the interest of men's souls and, on the

---

[110] Watson, *Ideas*, 521.

[111] Bernstein, *The Birth of Plenty*, 102.

other side, a care for the commonwealth."

Locke also demonstrated bravery in criticizing the practice of religious coercion, standing up to the zealots on both sides of the religious debate in England:

"That any man should think fit to cause another man—whose salvation he heartily desires—to expire in torment, and that even in an unconverted state, would, I confess, seem very strange to me, and, I think, to any other also."

Additionally, Locke made the point that religion itself was corrupted when it gained converts through the force of the state.

"The care of souls cannot belong to the civil magistrate, because his power consists only in outward force; but true and saving religion consists in the inward persuasion of the mind, without which nothing can be acceptable to God."[112]

Locke's reasoning was largely secular, as distinct from his opponents who argued for the divine rights of kings. Locke relied on things that could be proven and left the subjective to individual conscience.

Even this was a difficult departure from the prevailing mindset in most of Europe. When Denis Diderot was teaching Catherine the Great of Russia, he was confronted by "loutish courtiers [who] burst in on him in front of the court and one said, 'Sir, a + b / z = x. Therefore God exists. Reply!' According to the report ... Diderot was struck speechless."[113]

What distinguished the Enlightenment philosophers was not that they all believed in the veracity of the Bible (as did Newton) or that they were all Deists like Jefferson who believed that the Bible reflected core truths (for instance, that God created the earth) but was wrong when it contradicted science (for instance, that God created the earth in six days). Neither were Enlightenment philosophers necessarily agnostic, like Thomas Paine and probably more of his peers than would admit it. Rather, Enlightenment thinkers were characterized by reliance upon reason, the empirical method, and freedom to believe or not as data and their conscience led them. Enlightenment thinkers did not all reject religious truth. Instead, they rejected the ability of one group or person to impose revelation upon another.

---

112 This point was inspirational to the Virginia Declaration of Religious Freedom and foundational to the new American government.

113 Barzun, *From Dawn to Decadence*, 373.

During Martin Luther's lifetime, freedom of religion referred to the right of the prince to choose the faith for his realm. According to Locke's revolutionary philosophy, freedom of religion referred to the right of the individual to choose for himself regardless of what the prince of his realm may choose. If this philosophy could be translated into law, it meant that the rights of individuals were to be considered just as important as the rights of princes. Such a notion was not just at the heart of religious freedom, it was at the heart of a new kind of political system.

Property Rights and the Right to Happiness

John Locke did more than argue for toleration. He claimed that the individual had the right to life, liberty, and property,[114] and that government did not grant these rights. Indeed, these rights were not granted at all, but were innate. Property rights were essential to the next innovation in economics: the industrial economy. The act of inviting monarchs to rule England, as if they were being hired on as employees, signaled that the real power in England had shifted from Crown to Parliament. This shift also signaled a transfer in power from the individual who governed the land to the individual who owned it.

Of course, royalists clinging to the notion of divine rights of kings were not the only ones who challenged this claim. Jeremy Bentham (1748–1832), who argued even for equal rights for women and the decriminalization of homosexuality, quipped, "The idea that people have natural rights is nonsense on stilts." According to Bentham, the basis for governance ought to be maximization of utility—essentially the greatest good for the greatest number. This was a distinctly economic idea as well, one that led to policies that were—at best—loosely correlated with what a theocracy might prescribe.

What Locke and Bentham and so many Enlightenment thinkers did agree on was that the pursuit of individual happiness was the right of

---

[114] Thomas Jefferson later changed this to life, liberty, and happiness, seeing property rights as just a smaller set of rights that allowed the individual to be happy. This confusion of property with happiness might account for the acres of shopping malls that have since developed within the United States.

citizens. The state in their formulation was still powerful, but it was not a vehicle for the pleasure of the monarch who answered only to God. It was, instead, a tool for the masses. Again, what seems so obvious to us now in a world so much designed upon the principles of the Enlightenment was truly revolutionary at the time.

Progress Rather than a Fall From Grace

The Enlightenment challenged medieval thinking in a way that built upon the optimism of Erasmus: Enlightenment thinkers believed in progress. For them it was simply not true that since man's fall from grace in the Garden of Eden he could hope only for spiritual salvation and expect little or nothing from this life. It was, perhaps, little wonder that economic growth, as best we can measure it, began during the Enlightenment. Voltaire, for instance, believed that man ought not to spend his life atoning for original sin but instead working to improve things here and now—mostly by reforming the big institutions like church, state, and education.[115]

This notion of progress was rooted in the notion that the self could be developed. The discovery of different tribes and peoples around the world during the age of exploration made it clear that people adapt to their history and circumstances, suggesting that the self could be changed.

Tied to this notion was the idea that the individual could be given license to pursue his own self-interest. The basis for society was no longer common religious belief but, instead, a shared economic well-being, with improvement seen as the product of institutional change and individual initiative rather than spiritual salvation or miracles.

This flew in the face of the notion that one ought to be prepared for a good death and instead suggested rather persuasively that people could instead be educated and prepared to live more productively and happily right here on earth.

Again, Locke was a pioneer in this area. "The man mainly responsible for this approach was John Locke (1632–1704), in his "Essay

---

[115] Watson, *Ideas*, 528.

Concerning Human Understanding," published in 1690. In this book, prepared in draft as early as 1671, Locke himself used the word 'mind' not 'soul,' and referred to experience and observation as the source of ideas, rather than some 'innate' or religious (revelatory) origin. . . .Arguably the most important of all, [Locke] said that the self, the 'I,' was not some mystical entity relating to the soul, but an 'assemblage of sensations and passions that constitutes experience.'"[116] He emphasized what could be sensed and measured, even in an arena of life as personal as the definition of self.

Locke wrote about the mind rather than the soul. It was during the Enlightenment that the human sciences were born, the study of economics, language, sociology, and history. The word "psychology," for instance, was not commonly used in English until the 1830s.[117] By the end of the second economy, the study of self had become secular, based on what could be proven and measured: William James's and Sigmund Freud's writings on psychology were to define a new area of study by 1900.

Benjamin Franklin: Embodiment of the Enlightenment

Perhaps no one person better embodied the various elements of the Enlightenment in action than Benjamin Franklin. He alone signed all four documents that founded the United States (the Declaration of Independence, the Treaty that made France an ally with the revolutionaries fighting for their freedom, the treaty with England and France that ended the war and the Constitution that established the new nation). He was also an inventor, successful publisher, and international celebrity who had wealth, wisdom, and no need for wigs. (Although this author is only wildly speculating, it would seem that the popularity of powdered wigs from this time traces back to a desire to imitate the fabulous hair of Newton and Locke.)

Franklin knew about money. "A penny saved is a penny earned," is the kind of maxim that helps to popularize new behaviors of saving, and helps to move a community into a new economy based on money

---

[116] Watson, *Ideas,* 533.

[117] Watson, *Ideas*, 532

rather than barter. He knew about publishing. Between 1753 and 1775, the daily sales of newspapers roughly doubled; Franklin used this new medium first to create wealth and then to help to create a nation. This was an age in which pamphlets spread ideas and changed minds. Thomas Paine's *Common Sense,* published in 1776, sold more copies per capita than any American book since and helped to justify the revolution. Ben Franklin made his wealth by publishing "Poor Richard Almanack," which sold as well as any book but the Bible in its time. And Ben knew about invention. His lightning rod alone has probably saved billions since its invention. Before it, whether one considered lightning an act of God or an act of nature, it was something that regularly happened and could rapidly destroy property. His lightning rod was one more way that Enlightenment thinkers were wresting control from fate.

The Enlightenment shaped Ben Franklin's mind, which, in turn, did so much to shape the New World. He, like all the other founding fathers, was heavily steeped in this exciting new philosophy.

The social invention that changes minds is the social invention that changes all others. Like the Renaissance, the Enlightenment provided the philosophical principles referenced in the design and transformation of the really big institutions: the bank, which was largely invented during the second economy, and the nation-state, which was radically transformed.

The Enlightenment was suited to the industrial economy, which focused on overcoming the limit of capital. Industrial capital requires experimentation and an understanding of the principles of motion—two phenomena that the Enlightenment as defined by Newton was perfectly suited to provide. Financial capital requires individuals able to make their own judgment and openness and free flow of information to investors (helped as well by the growing number of periodicals and encyclopedias and an emphasis on freedom of the press), something that the Enlightenment as defined by Locke was perfectly suited to provide.

It was not enough to simply have abstract notions about capital, though. The social invention that would do so much to create the industrial economy was the bank. The story of its origins and forms is told in the next chapter.

13 Inventing the Bank

The handoff was made from God's invisible hand to the market's. While the hands were invisible, the social inventions that purported to do the will of God and market were visible; what the church had been to medieval Europe, the bank became to the second economy.

Economy	First	Second	Third	Fourth
Period	1300–1700	1700–1900	1900-2000	2000-2050
Limit to Progress	Land	Capital	Knowledge Workers	Entrepreneurship
Type of Economy	Agricultural	Industrial	Information	Entrepreneurial
Intellectual Revolution	Renaissance	Enlightenment	Pragmatism	Systems Thinking
Big Social Invention	Nation-State	**Bank**	Corporation	Self
Social Revolution	Protestant Revolution	Democratic Revolution	Financial Revolution	Business Revolution

While the state continued to exercise legal authority over the bank, it became more dependent on it. The bank was better suited to overcoming the limit of capital than was the nation-state and as capital became more important to progress, the bank became more powerful. As capital markets became international, the nation-state's influence over the bank became even weaker: the invisible hand controlled even the state.

Serious About Money

The English took money seriously. So seriously, in fact, that they appointed the most celebrated mind of the time to be their Master of the Mint. From 1699 until he died, Isaac Newton held this position. Imagine Stephen Hawking as Federal Reserve Chairman to get some sense of how much esteem and—in a way—how much naiveté the English had for the topic of money.

John Locke, too, got involved in at least one project with Newton, helping him with the recoinage of the British currency. As we might expect from these great minds, they did well. Newton set a mint price of gold in 1717 that would hold (save for a few wartime interruptions) for two hundred years.[118]

Money is funny. Isaac Newton, when he wasn't decoding the movement of planets or puzzling over apocalyptic predictions, played with alchemy. He thought it possible to turn lead into gold. Curiously, if he had succeeded, far from making him rich, this breakthrough would have just made gold as common as—and hence no more precious than—lead. In spite of the dreams of anarchists and communists, we have yet to make market economies work without money, and money has its own dynamic.

Even as Master of the Mint, Newton lost money in the South Sea bubble, an investment fiasco that was one of those periodic investment schemes that replace clear explanations with great hype and confusion. This one cost the English millions. For him, investment markets were more difficult to comprehend than the mysteries of the universe. Anyone who has groaned at the sight of a 401(k) statement could take comfort at being in good company. After the South Sea Bubble Newton said, "I can calculate the motions of the heavenly bodies, but not the madness of people."[119]

The bank was invented to deal with the limit of capital and it gradually

---

[118] Kindleberger, *A Financial History of Western Europe*, 23.

[119] Bernstein, *The Birth of Plenty*, 155.

wrested control away from the nation-state. During the second economy banks emerged as a force able to create and control capital.

Inventing the Modern Bank

The word "bank" comes from the Italian word for bench, *banca*, and referred to a place where moneychangers exchanged one foreign currency for another. As trade around the Mediterranean Sea grew, traders had to be able to change monies from one currency to another as they traded goods from one city-state or empire to another. During the early days of the first economy, currency exchange and coinage were the main services offered by these *bancas*. The banking we know today—banks as a service that allowed the creation of capital—was to evolve slowly.[120]

Governments—even the church—required financial services, but representative government did the most to stimulate the development of financial markets. A certain threshold of economic development seems to have been necessary as well: the financial market innovations of the Venetians, the Dutch, and the English were each preceded by first economy gains from trade and made by relatively prosperous communities. The English financial system represented the culmination of centuries of development. The Bank of England came to define many of the practices that determined how capital was made and managed in industrialized nations.

The first step towards the modern bank came during the first economy. As bankers and emerging states began to finance new ventures, they pushed against early church prohibitions. Later, the progression of increasingly complex states—from city-state to league of city-states to nation-states—became a catalyst for innovations in finance. The most financially powerful communities were the ones that emerged from communities with the most mature governments.

---

[120] Michael Prestwich, *The Dawn of Modern Banking* (New Haven: Yale University Press, 1979), 80.

Overcoming Church Prohibitions

Before exploring how finance overcame church prohibitions, it is worth pointing out the difference in finance between a traditional and a market economy.

Remember that a traditional economy is static. Roles are prescribed, and rather than being moved by markets, economic activity is moved by ethics, by what is "right." If you borrow money this year that you have to pay back next year, you've merely deferred your problem. And if you don't have enough this year and you have to pay back a loan next year—a loan you have to pay back with interest—you will be even worse off. In a traditional, static economy, prohibitions against "usury" are actually a sort of kindness. People who don't have enough now will just be in worse shape later in a world with loans and interest. In this static world, there is no excess in the future to trade for the shortage now. Life is zero-sum and all interest on loans does is shift money to bankers, who don't so much create wealth as merely rent it out.

In a dynamic and growing market economy, however, loans with interest are a very different thing. If you borrow money to invest in improving your farm, it really is reasonable to suspect that you might get 10 percent more from next year's harvest than this year's and be able to pay back half of that 10 percent extra in the form of 5 percent interest. In such a world, loans really can help to create wealth—and not just for bankers. A market economy can grow with the right investments, creating more in the future to pay for a lack now.

Religion is about tradition. It is not about change. And it is about respecting the poor. With that in mind, it is no real wonder that the medieval church had prohibitions against money lending. For the West, this ban on usury was the first hurdle to overcoming the limit of capital.

Constantine's Council in Nicaea in 325 AD established Christianity as the official religion of the Roman Empire. That same council banned lending by clerics. This was not so unreasonable. It made sense to prohibit the exploitation of the poor, particularly by clerics who would have likely been using church funds. Yet as tends to happen with religious things, if a little is good than more is better. This "a little more is a little better" approach evolves from something simple like modesty into something excessive like the burka. In the West, prohibitions evolved from forbidding clerics to lend money to excommunicating any moneylenders by 850 AD.

It was only gradually during the first economy that communities began to trust the profit motive. Aristotle thought it was unfair to make money from money, and St. Augustine thought that "business is itself an evil,"[121] and he lumped together three principal sins: lasciviousness, the lust for power, and the lust for financial gain.[122] To want more than God gave was a sin.

A Renaissance pope changed church prohibitions. Pope Leo had spent the surplus left to him by Pope Julius within just a couple of years. If anyone could blast through the budget, it would be a Medici. Leo pawned "palace furniture, table plate, jewels, even statues of the apostles."[123] Then, in 1517, he lifted the ban on usury. It is hard to ban what you need, and Leo needed to borrow.

From this point forward, church prohibitions became less of an issue in finance, but the stigma remained, particularly within Protestant countries. For centuries after Leo, Jews were still disproportionately represented in banking for the simple reason that Jews with ambition were generally banned from positions in state, church, or military but had—for years—been able to negotiate and make loans that Christians were officially banned from making.

As the church became less of an obstacle to loans, finance began to emerge. The first real innovations came from Venice, a city-state. The next came from the Netherlands, which was a league of city-states. Finally, in England the modern bank and bond markets as we know them were invented.

A Series of Serious Social Inventions

If you owned the government (which is to say, if you were a king or queen), you would most certainly rather tax people than borrow from them. If you tax them, their $100 is yours to spend and the transaction is done. By contrast, if you borrow from them you have to pay them

121 Bernstein *The Birth of Plenty*, 38.

122 B. Mark Smith, *The History of the Global Stock Market from Ancient Rome to Silicon Valley* (Chicago: University of Chicago Press, 2003).

123 http://en.wikipedia.org/wiki/Pope_Leo_X

back, with interest.

Of course, if you are someone likely to be taxed, you'd obviously prefer to loan the government money and be paid back.

So, as governments became more representative, they became more prone to borrowing rather than taxing. As people – through Parliaments or other representative bodies – had more choice in the matter, governments were more prone to issue bonds than taxing citizens. The first example of this comes from Marco Polo's Venice.

Venetian Bonds

Venice was neatly situated along the Adriatic Sea in waterways that made it both accessible to trade and difficult to attack. It was rich even before Marco Polo's trade routes made Venice a conduit between the Orient and Europe. It may seem obvious, but it is worth mentioning that the first people to loan money had money to spare. Profits from trade financed finance in Venice.

In 1167, the city-state of Venice needed money, and rather than tax their citizenry, they resorted to a forced loan to raise money. The wealthy provided the money and received, thereafter, 5 percent on their invested capital. Given the stability of their government, this proved a safe investment. Even popes subscribed to Venetian bonds. (That's right. The heads of the same church that prohibited usury were buying bonds. Reality is always messier than pronouncements about it.) Yet one problem with these bonds was that they tied up one's capital. There wasn't really a formal way to retrieve your money other than through the periodic payments.

So, by the 1300s, Venetians had devised a new social invention that was to have a huge impact on the evolution of finance. They created secondary markets that allowed these claims on interest payments (what we now call bonds) to be sold between individuals. This gave investors liquidity.[124] Investors didn't have to wait ten or thirty years to get their money back; they could sell the bond for its remaining value at any time. Because this made bonds more liquid, this lowered the

---

124 James McDonald, *A Free Nation Deep in Debt: The Financial Roots of Democracy* (New York: Farrar, Straus and Giroux, 2003), 72–73.

Venetian government's cost of borrowing. This secondary market made bonds even more valuable to investors. This provided investors with a new source of liquidity and a new source of capital for private ventures. The bond market that emerged then helped to stimulate Venice's economy, leveraging her great wealth to even more productive levels. The bond market gave people a safe and productive place to put their money, and once money begins making money, the community has more money. Venice got rich from trade. It became even richer when it added this innovative financial market to the mix

However two things began to erode the relative power of Venice. One was that Mediterranean trade gave way in importance to global sea trade (initially shifting to the Atlantic as the triangular trade between Europe, Africa, and the Americas emerged). The other was that, during the 1500s, the city-state began losing place to emerging nation-states that were larger, eclipsing growth in government revenues. As you can see in the table, Venice's revenues were comparable to France's in 1500, but by 1600 the revenues of France, a nation-state, dwarfed those of Venice, a city-state.

Government Revenues, 1500 - 1600[125]

(Tons of Silver)

	1500	1600
Castile	51	423
France	60	372
Venice	41	68

Yet before the nation-state completely eclipsed the city-state, an odd hybrid between the two was to host the next wave of financial inventions that would carry into the modern age.

[125]McDonald, *A Free Nation Deep in Debt,* 148.

A Republic of City-States

The Netherlands gradually won the majority of Asian trade in its contest with the Portuguese. Like the Venetians before them, the Dutch soon translated their trading profits into financial innovations.

The Dutch also furthered the move towards participatory government. This, as it turns out, was a boon to public finance and the development of bond markets. As members of a republic, the Dutch were both the beneficiaries of loans to the state and the makers of such loans. This was their government—not some elevated monarch's. Money raised by the government benefited them by becoming a vehicle for their policies. And the government representatives were also the merchants who bought the bonds, who provided the money. By contrast, an absolute monarch borrowing from his subjects or foreign bankers might default on loans with little compunction. (Well, beyond the concern about what it did to their credit ranking.)

For example, Charles V (emperor of large swaths of Europe and the New World but, for simplicity, someone we'll simply refer to as the King of Spain) quickly began borrowing from the Fuggers, a family who began as weavers and then made fortunes in mining and money lending. The Fuggers not only financed Magellan's circumnavigation of the globe but became the Vatican's biggest creditor during its period of military aggression and Leo's extravagant spending. (The Fifth Lateran Council, which met from 1512–1517, overlapping with Julius's and Leo's papal rule, removed most limitations against collecting interest on loans. Such changes did not just make it simpler for the church, but for anyone, to borrow from people like the Fuggers.)

The Spanish monarchs continued to borrow from the Fuggers but, on five separate occasions between 1557 and 1627, they defaulted on their loans. After the bankruptcy of 1575, the Fuggers began to withdraw from such business.[126] It was, for them, not worth it to deal with monarchs.

The Dutch, by contrast, were a good bet for investors. Again, given that the government was essentially ruled by the very merchants who

---

[126] Barraclough, *Times Atlas of World History*, 145.

bought some of the government bonds, there was far less chance that this government would default on its bonds. Participatory government was thus a boon to finance.

It didn't much matter that Charles had one of the largest empires in the history of the world or even that his regime created the annuity, a financial instrument of lasting popularity that committed the state to make fixed interest payments to any person designated by the purchaser for the life of the designee.[127] Charles (and his descendants who sat on the throne) was a bad credit risk.

The Netherlands, by contrast, had thriving trade, representative government, and financial markets that allowed it to borrow heavily during its war with Spain. In 1568, Charles's son Phillip fought against the Netherlands in an attempt to impose financial and religious discipline. The Netherlands wanted religious independence (this was a Protestant revolt against distant, Catholic rule) and did not want to be subject to Phillip's financial demands either. By the war's conclusion eighty years later in 1648,

"The Netherlands had transformed themselves into an independent and extraordinarily wealthy republic. Spain, however, was in precipitous decline, and many Spaniards agreed that 'the war in the Netherlands has been the total ruin of this Monarchy.'"[128]

Through war the Dutch came to realize the potential of their system of finance and how trade helped to finance the realization of that potential. To finance their defense, they borrowed more than they likely would have in other circumstances, but this borrowing actually did a great deal to stimulate innovation in financial markets. The Dutch had a much smaller population than Spain, but were nonetheless able to raise sums that rivaled those of the larger empire. "The special genius of Dutch finance was getting everybody into the act. Anyone with a few extra guilders was as liable to purchase government securities as someone today would be to plow savings into a money-market or stock mutual fund."[129] "By the year 1700, the Dutch were by far the world's wealthiest people, with a per capita GDP that was almost twice that of the nearest competitor, the English."[130] And this came about not so

---

127 Smith, *The History of the Global Stock Market*, 14.

128 McDonald, A Free Nation Deep in Debt, 151.

129 Bernstein, *The Birth of Plenty*, 143.

130 Bernstein *The Birth of Plenty*, 202.

much in spite of debt as because of debt, debt that helped to promote the development of financial markets.

Public Debt in Holland, Castile, and France, c. 1650[131]

	Population Millions	Public Debt in Local Currency Millions	Public Debt Per Capita Grams of Silver
Holland, c. 1650	0.8	133 (guilders)	1,663
Castile, c. 1650	5.0	150 (ducats)	607
France, 1661	18.0	870 (livres)	376

What emerged from the Dutch struggling for their independence and King Phillip struggling to control them was the revelation that population had become a less important determinant for winning wars than money.[132] The Dutch, by broadening the portion of their population purchasing bonds, became formidable.

During the 1600s, the Dutch government offered investors a *Losrenten.* Investors who gave the government an initial amount would collect payments in perpetuity. This was not a bond that matured in fifteen or thirty years. This bond paid indefinitely and the Dutch took this promise seriously. William Bernstein offers this story.

---

[131] McDonald, *A Free Nation Deep in Debt*, 152.

[132] And it may, as well, have illustrated that the group fighting for freedom will always have an edge over the group fighting for control, a lesson that imperial powers and the parents of teenagers alike have been slow to learn.

In 1624 a woman named Elsken Jorisdochter invested twelve hundred florins in a bond paying 6.25 percent that was issued to finance dike repair. Free of all taxes (similar to a modern municipal bond), she handed it down to her descendants. ... In 1938, the bond came into the hands of the New York Stock Exchange, and as late as 1957, the exchange presented it for payment of interest at Utrecht.[133]

More than three hundred years later, the Dutch were still honoring their obligation on the bond. Creating such confidence in investors means that a government is able to finance debt for far less than someone like the Spanish, who had a history of defaulting on their debt. If you trust a government's promise to pay back, you won't demand as much interest. But if you suspect the government might default—as investors in the seventeenth century would have with Spain—you want higher interest payments. You don't expect to be paid back for as long a period, so you want to be paid back more while you can.

Growth of Per Capita GDP

in the Sixteenth and Seventeenth Centuries[134]

	Per Capita GDP, 1500	Per Capita GDP, 1700	Growth Rate 1500–1700
Holland	$ 754	$ 2,110	0.52%
England	$ 714	$ 1,250	0.28%
France	$ 727	$ 986	0.15%
Italy	$1,100	$1,100	0.00%
China	$ 600	$ 600	0.00%

[133] Bernstein, *The Birth of Plenty*, 143.

[134] Bernstein The Birth of Plenty, 196.

A brief intermission in which the author points out something curious about what happens when capital eclipses land as the limit to progress

Venice is the most curiously unique and beautiful city I've visited (although to be fair, the list is hardly comprehensive). A large part of its charm lies in the fact that it is intersected by canals rather than roads. The city is built on water. The Venetians don't seem to honor the typical requirements for dry land as a prerequisite for building a city.

The Dutch showed even less respect for the convention of needing land to build on, not merely bridging a cluster of islands as did the Venetians but actually claiming land from the sea. The dikes used to drain the land (and periodically flood it when enemy troops occupied the fields) have roughly doubled the land on which the Dutch can live.

Land was the limit to progress in the first economy. But as it turns out, with enough capital, communities can create land. I don't think it's any coincidence that two of the primary pioneers of financing in the West didn't just conquer land but literally created it. This little phenomenon is worth remembering today, as the developed nations struggle so to create jobs, even for knowledge workers. By becoming more entrepreneurial, these communities will be able to create jobs, just as these early financial innovators created land. Mastery of the new limit allows you to create more of the old limit.

The Founding of the Bank of England

From the city-state of Venice to the confederation of city-states of the Netherlands, our story of social invention brings us to one of the first nation-states. The transfer of financial power from the Netherlands to England was made personal by the passengers in just a couple of ships.

Just before the Glorious Revolution, in 1688, "laws were enacted that created what has been termed by historians the Financial Revolution in England, parallel to the Industrial Revolution. A parliamentary guarantee of the government debt was established, making that debt no longer simply a personal obligation of the monarch. A Promissory Notes Act passed, making all debts negotiable and hence transferable."[135] Simply put, this meant that England, and not the monarch, stood behind the debt, and the debt could be bought and sold in secondary markets. This essentially laid the foundation for the bond market in England.

After the Glorious Revolution in 1689, Parliament sort of "hired" William and Mary from the Netherlands to become their new monarchs. (More about that in the next chapter on democratic revolution).

John Locke sailed to England with Queen Mary. King William came over on an earlier ship, and he arrived with a passenger who may well have had nearly as much influence on England's future as did Locke: political economist Sir William Petty.

Petty knew and trusted the Dutch financial institutions. Along with Petty came a number of Amsterdam's financial elite, including the Barings and David Ricardo's father. In 1694, five years after he took the throne, King William authorized the founding of the Bank of England. William was Dutch, and his transplantation of so many of the Dutch financial inventions atop a nation-state gave him—and finance—even more power.

The Bank of England differed from its predecessors in Venice and the Netherlands in more than scope: it sat atop the bureaucracy of a nation-state. In the wake of the Glorious Revolution, Parliament established means to ensure the collection of revenue to pay interest on the bonds that many of its members held. The Bank of England was given a monopoly on handling England's debt, and as such, it became a source of both financing for the government and steady income for investors. The merger of the Dutch financial institutions with the British political institutions created the industrial economy—or at least the foundation for financing the capital that such an economy required. The inventors who were to define the technology of the industrial economy did not just benefit from patent laws: they benefited from additional sources of capital that could finance their investments.

Shortly after establishing the Bank of England, the government mimicked the hugely successful Dutch East India Company, establishing the New East India Company (1698), the United East India Company (1708), and the South Sea Company (1710). Stock was sold and dividends were paid from the profits made from the trading monopoly held by these companies; this become another source of income for

---

[135] Smith, The History of the Global Stock Market, 19.

investors and furthered English investment habits. (More about these later, but it is worth pointing out that these companies were less multinational corporations than corporations that were a tool of national policy.) Coupled with greater British national power (especially in the form of the Navy that was begun by Henry VIII), the British soon surpassed the Dutch, using evolved forms of the Dutch's own social inventions. From 1500 to 1700, no country's economy grew as rapidly as the Dutch; after 1700, the British economy began to grow at a rate that the world had never before seen.

British Finance: Loans Rather than Taxes

In the eighteenth century, the British Parliament was largely comprised of landowners and merchants who were profiting from the new economy. As Parliament gained power, British monarchs were forced to gain the approval of Parliament to finance their spending. Like the Venetians and the Dutch before them, Parliament members preferred to make a loan rather than pay a tax.

Given Parliament members that supported payments on bonds often held those bonds, they were fairly secure. One of the truisms of investment is that risk and return are linked. If the risk of loss is higher, the potential return must be higher.[136] Given that investors saw little risk of default on British bonds, Britain, (as the kingdom was called after England's union with Scotland in 1707) paid less to finance its debt than did France or Spain. Investors soon learned that parliamentary government meant a lower risk of default, and this was just one of the reasons that capital grew less certainly and more slowly under absolute monarchs. But in this sense, Britain's situation was little different than that of the Netherlands. What was to make an even bigger difference was the various pieces of this new government we call a nation-state.

---

[136] For example, imagine there are two games people would pay $1 to play. The first offers a 50 percent chance of a $2 reward, making its probable value equal to $1. The second offers a 25 percent chance of a $4 reward, also making its probable value equal to $1. The second game has both more risk and more reward.

Niall Ferguson's Square of Power

Tax Bureaucracy Parliament

National Debt Central Bank

Niall Ferguson argues that the invention of modern financial markets came out of the confluence of four earlier inventions, all combined for the first time in Britain in the eighteenth century. He illustrates it in this square of power[137]. One way to think about it is that the area enclosed by the line connecting these four points covers much more than the area that could be covered by only three (or, obviously and to the point of straining the metaphor, more than could be "covered" with the line between just two) points.

One corner of Ferguson's square is the bureaucracy for raising taxes. France was reliant on agents who promised the crown a certain amount and then would collect taxes on behalf of the government, keeping the difference. The English, by putting in place a bureaucracy, were able to keep a higher percentage of the tax revenues for the

---

[137] Taken from Niall Ferguson's The Cash Nexus: Money and Power in the Modern World, 1700 - 2000.

government. Parliament—or a representative government—made government budgets more transparent and legitimate for people, who could see that the taxes collected were being used for their government. A national debt made it easier to cover sudden big expenses, like war. Finally, a central bank meant that the government had some way to manage this debt and to extract a premium from issuing paper money. These four elements were combined for the first time in Britain at the dawn of the second economy.

Almost better than the direct effects of these four social inventions was the emergent effect of the four in combination. As Ferguson argues, the need for a tax-gathering bureaucracy suggested a need for a system of formal education to create literate and numerate civil servants. Parliaments did even more to ensure the rights of private property owners, themselves so often property owners. The need for a financial system able to buy and sell bonds helped to create a bond market that could be used for more than just government debt. And the central bank—a role played in the United States by our Federal Reserve—tended to stabilize the credit system, making financial crises less frequent and intense.

As Niall Ferguson summarizes it,

> These [four] institutions also fostered the development of the economy as a whole. Better secondary and higher education, the rule of law (especially with respect to property), the expansion of financial markets and the stabilization of the credit system: these were vital institutional preconditions for the industrial revolution.
>
> Individual rights, too, influenced returns. A strong Parliament that protected the rights of the individual against a king's whim created a climate in which people were more likely to invest. Confident that neither their assets nor returns would be seized, they were more likely to sink money into farms and factories. After the Glorious Revolution, Britain had created such an investment climate. [138]

It is simpler to speak of social inventions like the nation-state then to speak of the myriad pieces that go into it. These four social inventions all contributed to Britain's ability to create and manage capital and were just a few of the social inventions that went into the complex we call the nation-state.

---

[138] Niall Ferguson, The Cash Nexus: Money and Power in the Modern World, 1700 - 2000, (Basic Books, New York, NY, 2002) 15–16.

And while the early states were so defined by war and battle for land, England was less distracted by this. War was expensive. Throughout the 1600s, the English monarch's attempt to get involved in European hostilities was resisted by the House of Commons, which was unwilling to squander money just to become a great power. [139] Charles II lived for a time in France, where the aristocracy took warfare seriously. His attempts at warfare in the seventeenth century frustrated, he complained to his sister that, "The thing that is nearest to the heart of this nation is trade, and all that belongs to it." [140] He did not write this admiringly.

England was focused on a different kind of greatness than that sought by the warring powers on the Continent. In 1797, the French implemented military conscription ("the draft") and the British implemented income tax. The British were, as always, mindful of revenues.

The difference between France and England (or earlier, England and Spain) was not one of resources. France's population was considerably greater than England's, as was its total GDP. The difference was one of social inventions: British institutions were better at creating, protecting, and using capital.

A more succinct comparison of England and France would simply point to this: The Bank of England was formed in 1694 and the Bank of France in 1800.[141]

Just as the Dutch were able to incur more debt than their Spanish foes, the English were able to outspend the French in their repeated wars, for much the same reason. King Louis XIV and his kin were much stronger monarchs than were their counterparts in England, and for this reason France was a much weaker nation. (A relatively stronger monarchy meant a relatively weaker Parliament.) Ultimately, it is the dispersion of power rather than the concentration of power that results in the greatest strength.

---

[139] John Brewer, *The Sinews of Power: War, Money and the English State, 1688–1783,* (New York: Alfred A. Knopf, 1989), 137.

[140] Will and Ariel Durant, *Age of Louis XIV: A History of European Civilization in the Period of Pascal, Moliere, Cromwell, Milton, Peter the Great, Newton, and Spinoza: 1648–1715* (New York: Simon and Schuster, 1963), 259.

[141] Kindleberger *A Financial History of Western Europe*, 114.

Fractional Reserves

In retrospect, capital had clearly become the limit to the economy by about 1700. The British did not just merge the Dutch financial institutions with their own political institutions. They made a modification to the banking system that was to have huge consequences and greatly increase the amount of capital they had. The British began the practice of fractional reserves.

Fractional reserves don't sound sexy, but this is sort of a cool way to create capital, and one of the more clever ways to overcome the limit of capital.

Imagine that you have ten people each deposit £100. Your bank now has £1,000. The question is, how much money should you keep on hand to cover deposit withdrawals? Strictly speaking, you might keep the full £1,000, just to be able to cover the withdrawals that might be made. Yet it is doubtful that everyone with £100 will demand their money at the same time. You could instead reserve just a fraction of the £1,000 and be prepared to provide money to the one or two people who want to withdraw their £100 in any given week. The difference between what you could keep on reserve and what you have could be loaned out. What that means is that for every £1,000 deposited and officially on the books as money on hand, the bank might loan out £800 to £900. While the depositors have a total of £1,000 in assets deposited in your bank, your bank has another £800 in assets in the form of loans that borrowers will pay back.

This means that banks can effectively create money. Fractional reserves multiply money.

To this day, setting the fractional reserve requirement is a big part of defining monetary policy because it makes such a huge difference in the amount of capital available for loans and purchases. Fractional reserves are just one example of how banking and monetary policy can influence an economy. The British led in such social inventions, most obviously through the Bank of England.

By means of the Bank of England, the British probably did more than any other people to define the modern world of finance. John Kenneth Galbraith waxes elegant (as he was wont to do) in describing its impact:

The pioneering instrument of reform was the Bank of England. Of all institutions concerned with economics none has for so long enjoyed such prestige. It is, in all respects to money as St. Peter's is to the Faith. And the reputation is deserved, for most of the art as well as much of the mystery associated with the management of money originated there. The pride of other central banks has been either in their faithful imitation of the Bank of England or in the small variations from its method which were thought to show originality of mind or culture.[142]

Risk, Return, and Post-Renaissance Thinking

One way to look at finance is as a trade between risk and return. Any merchant will tell you that pricing goods is tricky. It is even trickier to price financial products trade your money today for more money tomorrow. The biggest variable in determining the price premium is the amount of risk.

For instance, the insurance that covered shipments between continents was a way to trade risk for return. If you bought an insurance policy for your ship, your return would be lower by the amount of the insurance premium. But your risk, too, would be lower, as you were now insured against loss. Insurance lowers your risk at the price of a lower return.

Markets trade what you have in excess for what you don't have. The farmer with more wheat can trade with the manufacturer who has more textiles. The investor who wants more return can insure a shipment for the venture capitalist who wants less risk. Financial markets trade something more abstract than goods: they trade risk and return. Financial markets have been allowing investors to make tradeoffs between those two ever since their creation, and as financial markets have matured, the measures of risk and return have depended on increasingly sophisticated notions of probability calculated through increasingly sophisticated equations. In today's world, about 80 percent of stock market trades are made automatically by algorithms reacting to market movements, algorithms that most of us would not understand.

---

142 John Kenneth Galbraith, *Money: Whence it Came, Where it Went* (Boston: Houghton Mifflin Company, 1975).

Risk changes the probability of getting paid tomorrow, and probability is not easy to calculate.

Leonardo da Vinci might have been the greatest mind of the Renaissance. No one since has matched his range of abilities, from painting masterpieces to sketching machine guns and designing dredging equipment and other new gears and machines. The man was not just a genius; he was the epitome of genius.

Yet his correspondence with one of the pioneers of probability suggests that Da Vinci would have struggled with the math taught in a fourth-grade classroom today. This new world of finance required a new kind of thinking.

More and Bigger Banks

Once the foundation was laid, the practice of banking spread. In the fifty-eight years between 1855 and 1913, the number of bank offices in England grew six fold. Each office was able to protect and create capital by taking deposits and making loans. As the bank became more dominant, capital became more defining.

Banks in England and Wales[143]

Year	Banks	Offices	Offices per Bank
1855	405	1,185	2.9
1870	365	1,628	4.5
1885	319	2,460	7.7
1900	164	4,570	27.9
1913	70	6,573	93.9

By the late 1800s, the British had emerged as the community with the most capital and, not coincidentally, the most power in the world. By 1873, economist and journalist Walter Bagehot reported these

---

143 Kindleberger, *A Financial History of Western Europe*, 88.

differences in deposit amounts in the major financial centers:

London £120,000,000

New York £40,000,000

Paris...£13,000,000

German Empire .... £8,000,000[144]

British social inventions created real capital and this gave the British a real advantage in economic strength and global influence. Only as the West reached the point at which capital no longer limited did Germany become a serious economic contender to Britain. When the limit shifts, the lead shifts to the community best able to invent their way past the new limit, but that is the story of the third economy. Before telling that story, we need to tell the story of what happened to the nation-state when the limit shifted from land to capital. The result was revolution and the transformation of politics and government. That story of democratic revolution began in Britain then created a new kind of nation-state in its former colony. And, it is told in the next chapter, another tale of how social invention forced institutional revolution, an echo of how the newly invented nation-state forced the Protestant Revolution. The monarchy that so benefited from the eclipse of the first economy was dethroned the second time it played out.

---

144 Bernstein, *The Birth of Plenty*, 157.

14 Democratic Revolution

In 1689, the British "hired" monarchs to run the country, subject to the laws rooted in their constitutional documents. About a century later, the British colonists in America decided to do away with monarchs and rely only on a constitution. This invention caught on.

Economy	First	Second	Third	Fourth
Period	1300–1700	1700–1900	1900-2000	2000-2050
Limit to Progress	Land	Capital	Knowledge Workers	Entrepreneurship
Type of Economy	Agricultural	Industrial	Information	Entrepreneurial
Intellectual Revolution	Renaissance	Enlightenment	Pragmatism	Systems Thinking
Big Social Invention	Nation-State	Bank	Corporation	Self
Social Revolution	Protestant Revolution	**Democratic Revolution**	Financial Revolution	Business Revolution

When it came to attracting capital, democracies had a number of advantages over absolute monarchies. For one thing, they could be better trusted so were able to attract capital at lower rates. For another, their reliance on laws rather than potentially arbitrary pronouncements by monarchs made them a safer place for investments of any kind, made them more trusted for their respect for property. A government did not have to necessarily get rid of its monarch, just make even him or her subject to laws along with the rest of the population.

As the modern bank emerged, it fed and was fed by the big institutional transformation of the second economy: democratic revolution.

There seem to be two stages to social invention. In the first, elites invent a new, powerful institution that makes them rich and powerful. In the second stage, revolutionaries grab control of the institution and make it a tool of the masses. In the first economy, revolutionaries wrested control of the church away from the popes; in the second economy, they battled kings and queens for control of the state.

The transformation of the church revolved around the issue of who was right. When people suddenly able to read the Bible for themselves became aware that many of the things they'd been taught were nowhere to be found in the Bible, many rebelled against the authority of the church. They made up a new church. (They, of course, would not have seen it this way. From their perspective, they were simply following the dictates of conscience and revelation. They would not have said that they were engaged in an act of social invention but would have described it instead as doing God's will.)

The transformation of the next big institution—the revolutions that changed the nation-states from monarchies to representative democracies—was less about who was right than about who had rights. Whereas the Protestant may not have seen the Catholic Church as "his" church, the patriot rebels who fought to overthrow the rule of monarchs did see the nation-states as "their" countries, and they wanted control over them. This was clearly a fight about who got to dictate policy and govern, about ownership of an institution that had already been invented. If Louis XIV and Henry VIII were among the inventors of the modern nation-state, then Ben Franklin and Thomas Jefferson were among the radicals who thought that a nation-state should become public property and no longer just rest in the hands of the aristocratic elites.

The Benefits of Monarchies: Patriotism Personified

The concept of a nation-state is more abstract and harder to grasp than is the notion of a monarch. A king or queen is a person and can be seen and understood as someone—or something—real. Pledging allegiance to a king was not so very different from pledging allegiance to the lord of feudal times, meaning that the monarch offered some continuity from life before the nation-state, and this helped the fledgling nation-states to gain acceptance among the populace.

A monarch gives personality to something that might otherwise be too legalistic and vague. Whether a people tolerate or adore their king, this shared sentiment is one more reason for a sense of unity. Even today, in a time of democracies, the press and people seem to more readily grasp and respond to the personality of a president than his policies. A lot of people didn't really know what George W. Bush was getting us into when we invaded Afghanistan and Iraq, but they did know that they would rather drink a beer with him than with John Kerry. (Given George's antipathy towards alcohol, one hardly knows whether to attribute this to affection or spite, though.) A monarch gives a face to the state, and a strong-willed, visionary, and long-ruling king can do a great deal to define a country. King Louis XIV was all that. Well, at least long ruling; no European monarch has ever reigned longer than his seventy-two years.

King Louis XIV became king at age five (in 1643). His opponents, seeing an opportunity in his youth, twice tried to overthrow this boy king. The first time he was able to beat back their attack with an appeal to national identity. The second time he prevailed by the promise of prosperity that came from a national, as opposed to a regional, economy.

In 1648, the French Parliament threatened Louis (and his mother, who was, in reality, the monarch until he came of age) and demanded lower taxes and a move from an absolute to a constitutional monarchy, among other things. Louis's mother refused these demands, but before this quasi-revolution was over, she had to pawn her jewelry for food.

French parliament members were not elected, so the people weren't naturally disposed to support the demands of Parliament as inherently any more representative of their wishes than those of monarchs. Then parliament made a strategic mistake by appealing to the Habsburg

Empire and Spain for help in their struggle against the boy king.[145] The French people by this point felt more French than oppressed, their sense of national identity stronger than their sense of class. The French people thus sided with the boy king, and this attempted revolution was essentially ended.

A second rebellion was tried after Louis, at the ripe age of thirteen, asserted his sense of independence not by getting a tattoo or quarreling with his mother but, instead, by announcing that he was king. (I'm sure that he was not the last teenager to make such an assertion, but he was probably the last to be taken so seriously.) Soon, his foes again tried to wrest control from him. This time, the old feudal aristocrats, who wanted to steal back the power that the king (or more accurately, the lineage of French kings) had taken from them, backed the rebellion. The chaos that ensued disrupted the economy and even food supplies, and soon the people again decided that life under a king was better. Life under a king seemed more stable and economically secure than life under a still poorly defined parliament.

In this we see one benefit of monarchies. A king helps to define a national identity and gives a face to a national economy. This was particularly important early in the development of the nation-state, and the France that King Louis XIV inherited was not yet fully formed. The feudal aristocrats almost succeeded in performing what would have essentially been an act of devolution, undermining the power of the nation-state at the expense of returning power to the principalities that had been consolidated under previous French kings. This easily could have stunted economic development, as each little region did its bit to tax the exchange of goods and to protect their local businesses.

Trade was difficult within France at this time. Had the feudal aristocrats won, they likely would have returned to their policies of sub optimization, each doing what made sense in his or her little manor or province, with little concern for the country as a whole. Merchants moving goods from Paris to the Channel during the feudal period, or from Switzerland to Paris, had to pay tolls at sixteen points; between Orleans and Nantes it was even worse, with twenty-six separate tolls.[146] The king, with the interests of the entire nation at heart, was eventually able to champion policies that made the nation as a whole wealthier, even if the competition that came from freedom to trade across

[145] Durant and Durant, *The Age of Louis XIV*, 5.

[146] Durant and Durant, *The Age of Louis XIV*, 25.

regions might threaten a particular business or industry within a region. With this in mind, King Louis's finance minister, Jean-Baptiste Colbert, lowered and removed local tariffs in order to encourage trade. This made the nation more prosperous.

Monarchs were able to pursue policies that were good for the nation, even if other political powers were less interested in such abstractions.

It's probably true that the monarchy was an unavoidable stage in the development of the nation-state, but it was certainly not an ideal one.

How Monarchs Became Oppressive

Yet absolute monarchies became oppressive because they simply gave too much power to the ruler and made the state the instrument of a monarch rather than the people. Worse, the early monarchies saw themselves as inheriting the role of the church: that is, they took responsibility for the souls of their subjects, ensuring that everyone had the benefit of the "right" religion by outlawing all but the state church. The monarch dictated the religion in the realm.

For example, in France the Protestants (known as Huguenots) were at turns tolerated, persecuted, killed, and driven out of the country. The worst of it took place in 1572, when the Catholics decided to attack Protestants, killing more than twenty-five thousand in Paris alone. This event was remarkable but not unique.

Centuries elapsed between the time when the state wrested control over religion from the church and the time when it gave this control to the individual. This matter of dictating religion was reason enough to label any monarchy oppressive.

Yet there were other reasons as well. Monarchs became oppressive because they were given absolute power. This may sound ridiculous now, but it is worth remembering that the early monarchs were just making things up as they went along. We can call it social invention or creativity or an exercise of power, but the fact is that there was a great deal about politics, governing, and creating a sense of national identity that no one—including the monarchs—knew until they actually tried to rule. In such an environment, it is hard to imagine how any monarch creating a new nation-state could have been subordinate to a constitution and a code of laws. In fact, by definition, the creation of any new government entails breaking the laws as they existed when the creation began. As Saul Alinsky puts it, there are no successful traitors: one is either a founding father or a failure.[147]

In practice, the king's absolute power meant that he—like the Renaissance popes before him—lived a life divorced from that of his subjects. Even if his people suffered famine or poverty, the king lived a life of luxury of a sort previously unknown. Given that everyone was making things up as they went along, even the monarchs did not, at first, realize how much wealth and power could be theirs. Only after he was invited to a banquet put on by the finance minister he had inherited from his father were Louis's eyes opened to how much revenue was streaming in from the taxes on his subjects.

This finance minister, who was taking a portion of the taxes for personal gain, had commissioned the construction of a chateau that, at its peak, employed eighteen thousand men and covered the area of three villages. King Louis XIV thought that the man was "stealing beyond his station," and, after being invited to a dinner at this minister's chateau that served six thousand guests dinner on plates of silver or gold, would have arrested the man that very evening, "but his mother convinced him that it would spoil an enchanting evening."[148]

After he'd removed the finance minister from his position, Louis took the man's wealth and added it to his own. Suffice to say, Louis lived well. And in this we see another problem with absolute monarchies: they make the state a tool for the few.

Louis and his finance minister, for instance, intentionally kept wages low (making it illegal for workers to unionize, among other things), so as to make France more competitive. Spurring the export of goods with low wages meant spurring the import of gold and silver. The new nation-state created a great deal of wealth, but not much of it seemed to enter the pocket of the common person. By some estimates, the French peasant under Louis lived no better than did the medieval serf before the first economy.

Meanwhile, in England, the story of the succession of monarchs illustrates another problem with these early nation-states. An absolute monarchy is too dependent on the personality and policies of individual monarchs to offer stability and continuity.

---

[147] Saul D. Alinsky, *Rules for Radicals*, 34.

[148] Durant and Durant, *The Age of Louis XIV*,19.

The Problem of Royal Instability

Henry VIII fathered two queens by two very different wives.

Henry's first wife, Catherine of Aragon, was fiercely Catholic. His creation of the Church of England enabled him to divorce her. It seems safe to assume that this did little to dissuade her from her faith. Henry and Catherine were parents to Mary.

Henry's second wife, Anne Boleyn, was Protestant. His creation of the Church of England enabled him to marry her. It seems safe to assume that this did a great deal to persuade her of how right her new faith was. Henry and Anne were parents to Elizabeth.

Unsurprisingly, Mary and Elizabeth each inherited their mother's faith. While this wasn't surprising, it did make things complicated when first Mary and then Elizabeth inherited the throne.

When the Catholic Mary became queen in 1553, most of England was alarmed. They did not want to again be subject to Rome. Their alarm was made worse when Mary married the very Catholic Phillip, the son of the Emperor Charles, who had inherited rule over Spain and the Netherlands. As England's populace had feared, Mary soon began to persecute Protestants. In her attempt to steer England back into the fold of Catholicism, she executed hundreds of Protestants. Perhaps if she had not died only five years into her reign, she might have succeeded in her efforts to lead the country to repentance. As it was, she was left with the title "Bloody Mary."

When Elizabeth inherited the throne, she again made the Church of England the official state religion. It seemed that the matter of religion was settled. While the Continent was convulsed with religious wars, England enjoyed a creative period. The most famous of Elizabeth's subjects, born in the same year that Michelangelo died, was at the height of his craft under her reign: Elizabethan England is probably best known for Shakespeare. In a testament to England's progress, Shakespeare helped to define the individual as someone other than priest, soldier, or farmer. Progress meant that individuals had to wrestle with questions of identity and could not just accept the identity given by one's role. Shakespeare—first among the post-medieval dramatists—gave us individuals.

Authority of Rule

Henry VIII chose not to be subject to Rome, but for centuries afterwards England wrestled with the implications of this break. The key question for this new nation-state was that of authority: what was the source of authority for legitimate rulers? Henry broke the supposedly divine chain of authority that extended from God to pope, pope to monarch, and monarch to people.

At one level, the question was a simple one. Monarchs inherited thrones the way that children in the present inherit estates: upon the death of a parent, the child took the throne. Yet this posed a serious problem for England. What if the child who inherited the throne had not inherited the parent's religion? What if the child was Catholic and threatened to return the nation to the subjection of the pope? Under what authority could a nation replace its ruler in order to keep its religion?

Virginia was named after Queen Elizabeth. Now the alert reader will note that it would make more sense if the colony had been named Beth or Liz. But Elizabeth died childless, and the state in the new world was named for her state of virginity.

And thus, with Elizabeth's death, inheritance bounced over to Scottish[149] relatives, and in 1603 James I took over as the English king. (Yes, this was the King James who was to give his name to a new version of the Bible.)

During the time of James I of England and King Louis XIV of France, monarchs, it was argued, were divinely ordained and their subjects were to obey them as if they were "God's image on earth."[150] Note that they weren't citizens but, rather, subjects. A king was subject to God, and the people in the kingdom were subject to him. Yet the issue of how God ordained kings was a little problematic as long as the English were

---

[149] About a hundred years later, in 1707, England and Scotland were unified to become Britain.

[150] Mark Kishlansky, Patrick Geary, and Patricia O'Brien *Civilization in the West, Fifth Edition*: *Volume II, Since 1555* (New York: Longman, 2003), 509.

debating religious issues.

The England that James I inherited was home to more than one version of the Bible. One popular version, the Geneva Bible, was printed in Geneva, Switzerland, home of the Calvinists. For these Protestants, many of them religious refugees from France, their faith was an act of political defiance. They sought scripture that would reconcile their need for rebellion with the need for obedience. These Calvinists believed that the common person needed a commentary to help decipher the mysteries of scripture, and the commentary they had inserted into the Bible highlighted a number of instances in which the people were justified in rebelling against a "bad" king.

King James I did not particularly care to have such political commentary mixed in with his people's religion. He stated, "As it is atheism and blasphemy to dispute what God can do, so it is presumption and high contempt in a subject to dispute what a king can do, or say that a king cannot do this or that." Rather than rely on scriptures that challenged the authority of kings, James authorized a group of translators to create the King James Version of the Bible, a text free of political commentary. The works of Shakespeare under Elizabeth and the King James Bible did much to solidify England's sense of itself as a nation—a people bound by a common language, culture, and history. And just as Shakespeare's works eclipsed the reign of Elizabeth, so did the King James Bible eclipse the reign of King James I. But the real intention of King James' Bible was to remove from the Bible suggestions that a people could challenge their king.

Ironically, James's Bible actually furthered the erosion of authority figures in England by making the written word, rather than the clergy, the reliable authority. It became a model for political reforms that would continue throughout the century, as the English decided to subject even their rulers to the written word. His authorized version was a masterpiece of literature almost by accident, focused as it was on simply making the Bible accessible to the common man. Although Protestants argued about the interpretations of different passages, they did agree on one thing: the Bible was the authority to which religious leaders should conform and not vice versa. Protestants had done away with the pope and embraced the Bible. Before the end of the century, they would adapt this model to government, forcing even their monarchs to conform to the Constitution and not vice versa.

It was the religious reformers who did the most to challenge political institutions. It is hard to conceive of a more revolutionary worldview than theirs. The Puritans seemed clear that the state was a social invention that could be changed:

"The Puritans who appealed to reason in support of popular rights pointed out that human institutions were a matter of choice designed for a purpose and maintained by custom. They should be changed when the purpose was no longer served. Mere length of time—custom—is arbitrary, not in itself a reason."[151]

As it turns out, authority figures have about as much authority as people give them. In spite of James's attempts to create a Bible that would support rather than challenge the monarchy, his own son became a victim of regicide. Regardless of their exact religious positions, most of the English were devout Protestants, and while they were discomfited by James's apparent homosexuality, they were even more troubled by his son's condition: Charles I was Catholic.

Oliver Cromwell: Puritan Rule

When Charles I abrogated Parliament,[152] he said, "I owe an account of my actions to God alone."[153] His subjects were less clear on this point, eventually beheading him because of his impudence. By this point, Parliament was too serious a force to so casually dismiss. The opposition to Charles I was led by Oliver Cromwell, a Puritan.

The Church of England that Henry VIII founded was, in many respects, the Catholic Church without ties to Rome. The Anglican Church, as the Church of England is also known, retained many of the ceremonies, ornaments, buildings, and hierarchy of the Catholic Church. The Puritans, however, wanted to purify the church of what they saw as residual errors—doing away with rituals that seemingly had no basis in accounts recorded in their new King James Bible.

England was roughly divided in two. There were Parliamentarians who

---

151 Barzun, *From Dawn to Decadence*, 266.

152 This act basically dismissed the landowners and merchants who were also parliament members so that Charles could run the government without their input or oversight.

153 Maurice Ashley, *Magna Carta in the Seventeenth Century* (Charlottesville: University Press of Virginia, 1965), 25–27.

supported both a stronger Parliament and the Puritan church and there were Royalists[154] who supported the Crown and the Anglican Church as it presently stood. This was a division between progressives (the Parliamentarians) who wanted more change and defenders of the status quo (the Royalists) who resisted further change. Parliamentarians felt as though the church was only half reformed and that monarchs needed a check on their power. For them, it was key to limit the power of a monarch who might turn the country back to Catholicism, threatening the salvation of good Englishmen.

Charles I ruled without Parliament for years, but eventually had to call a parliamentary session to approve additional financing. It was the "House of Commons which represented the dominant social class, the landowning classes,"[155] and Charles was forced to turn to them for revenues. He had tried to tax the people, but without Parliament there was no real mechanism for collecting these taxes. Once convened in 1628, parliament drew up a "Petition of Rights" that stipulated no taxation without an act of Parliament and no imprisonment without trial. Charles grudgingly agreed, but a short time later he abrogated Parliament yet again.

The clash between Parliamentarians and Royalists became a Civil War from 1642 to 1649. King Charles's increasing reliance on foreign soldiers buttressed Parliamentarian claims that theirs was the more "English" cause, and eventually a critical mass of the people sided with them, leading to the trial that resulted in Charles's overthrow and eventual beheading.

Oliver Cromwell became the head of England at this point, calling himself Lord Protector rather than King, but ruling with as much self-assurance as any monarch. He led raids into Ireland's Catholic districts, outlawed dancing and theater (a true tragedy for the country that had buried Shakespeare only thirty-three years before Cromwell's reign began), and made the Puritan religion England's one true religion. Like Charles I before him, Cromwell eventually lost patience with legislature and abrogated Parliament to rule unencumbered, without the oversight of any but God. (It seems that legislative bodies never do well at gaining popular approval. We love the idea of representative government but in practice, given the many people they have to represent, such government inevitably appears clumsy and inefficient.)

---

[154] These two groups are also referred to as Roundheads and Cavaliers.

[155] Roberts, *Penguin History of the World*, 569.

Cromwell continued the tradition of theocracy in England, although under rule of a Puritan rather than an Anglican or a Catholic.

After Oliver Cromwell's death, his son, Richard Cromwell, came to power. Richard, however, was not as forceful as his father, and within a short time the English replaced him with Charles I's son, Charles II. Once again, the English had dancing, gambling, theater, and a king.

More Royal Turmoil: The Reigns of Charles II and James II

As tends to be the case, a lot happened under Charles II. For our purposes, it is enough to point out that he tried to move Britain back towards Catholicism. Parliament was able to force him to retreat from his policies, and Charles II eventually ended up again at court in Versailles, supported in his "retirement" by King Louis XIV. Another Catholic king ruled and an illegitimate son of an earlier monarch contended for the throne. Each real or threatened reign brought with it a threat to at least one group's religion.

What became obvious in the turmoil of the seventeenth century is that if Britain had to change religion and policies each time a new ruler ascended, it would be in continual turmoil.

The Glorious Revolution

At this point, Parliament decided that it no longer wanted to have its religion, finances, or rights threatened every time a new king or rebel or even product of a royal affair rose to power. They invited William and Mary (James II's daughter and her husband) to rule; their reign was to be markedly different.

One might have hoped that Protestants with political power would use it more graciously than the Catholics who opposed them. Sadly, they did not. The Catholics burned heretics at the stake, drove Jews from their homes, and confiscated Protestant property. The Puritans were no better. Cromwell led savage forays into Ireland that had precedent in Old Testament massacres: entire towns were leveled and every citizen killed. In eleven years of Puritan-inflicted misery, the Irish population declined from 1.5 million to just over six hundred thousand. Catholic children were even taken from their parents to be raised as Protestants in England, an act of kindness in the eyes of Protestants convinced that Catholics were bound for eternal damnation. Cromwell's oppression of Ireland did more than make portions of that country fiercely Catholic and opposed to English rule; it proved that attempts to create a heavenly kingdom on earth necessitated that rulers must first create a hell.

The question that plagued England for centuries regarded which religion to impose on the people: Catholic, Anglican, Puritan, or some other variant. Rather than answer this question, Enlightenment thinkers posed a new one: what right did any civil authority have to dictate beliefs to any individual? The dilemma of choosing the "right" religion was shifted from the community to the individual, and the objective of government was focused on the common welfare rather than individual souls. In order to separate the issue of authority from religion, however, they had to devise a new notion of rights, one that would arise out of a new philosophy.

The Rise of the Constitution

Here in the United States, we often overlook the importance of the Glorious Revolution. Yet once the English Parliament overthrew the monarch they feared would bring back Catholicism, they brought in William (from Holland) and Mary as a new kind of monarchs. They made clear to William and Mary that their ability to reign would be subordinated to the constitution[156]. The ultimate power no longer would reside in the monarch but, instead, in law. (A shift very much like the shift Protestants made from ultimate authority in the person of a pope to ultimate authority in the Bible.) From this point it was probably

[156] To be clear, the British had no single constitution as did the Americans about a century later. Their constitution is actually a set of documents, the most obvious being the Bill of Rights of 1689 that limited the power of the monarch. The set of documents that form the U.K.'s "constitution" include the Magna Carta and the Habeas Corpus Act of 1679.

inevitable that some would eventually do away with the monarch altogether, as the American colonialists did about a century later.

Parliament was an institution common to Europe. It had earlier served two purposes: to give landholders an opportunity to complain to the king, and to give the king an opportunity to tax the landholders once they were done complaining, the king like an impatient lover who puts up with the obligatory small talk before the sex. As the historian Arnold Toynbee put it, the English carried Parliament across the gulf that separates the criticism of government from its conduct.

This was key, because the emergence of a nation-state—in both England and France—meant that the monarch held a monopoly on "war, justice, taxation, and coinage. ... Monarchy implies centralization. Without it, the well-defined region called nation could not be a nation-*state*."[157] With such a monopoly on power, countries needed a countervailing force to represent interests beyond those of the aristocracy.

Before William and Mary were crowned,

"Parliament was careful to impose certain conditions, specified in the 'Bill of Rights,' to which the new rulers and their successors would have to submit. Parliament was to decide all matters of taxation, to control the army, and to supervise legislation."[158]

William and Mary's ascent to the throne in 1689 was hailed as the "Glorious Revolution" because it ushered in a new era in which individual rights were protected from the whims of monarchs, and because it was bloodless—not counting the battles in Ireland. (England itself would have been completely free of bloodshed had not James II, in the stress of being deposed, suffered a nose bleed.)

John Locke

Newton explained Copernicus's revolution, shifting the center of the

---

[157] Barzun, *From Dawn to Decadence*, 241.

[158] Walther Kirchner, *Western Civilization from 1500* (New York: Perennial, 1991), 94.

solar system from earth to sun. John Locked explained the constitutional monarchy that shifted the ultimate source of government from monarch to constitution. As apologist for the constitutional monarchy of William and Mary, Locke began an idea that would spill into the next century as a fabulous experiment in governance. The American revolutionaries were students of Locke.

John Locke was born during the reign of Charles I and witnessed civil war, regicide, and myriad abuses by Puritan and Catholic rulers alike. "As a young man, Locke wrote, 'From the time that I knew anything, I found myself in the storm, which has continued to this time.'"[159] It is no wonder that this thoughtful man was to become famous for writings that included *A Letter Concerning Toleration*. He accompanied Queen Mary on her voyage from the Netherlands to England to take the crown from her father, James II, but his ideas preceded Parliament's offer of the throne to Mary and her Dutch husband.

Locke's idea of a social contract fit well with England's earlier product of social reform, the Magna Carta. To Locke, the just government received its authority from the people, authority that was neither inherited nor granted by God. Locke, in a sense, updated the sentiments expressed in the Magna Carta to contemporary times.

The Magna Carta was a demand from feudal rulers who did not want their power absorbed by ambitious kings. In 1215, when King John of England needed money for war, the feudal powers essentially got him to sign an agreement to give up powers in return for his revenue (their taxes). The Magna Carta was written in 1215 but not published until 1499, and not translated into English until 1534. Although the idea existed very early, it was not until after the Guttenberg press that the idea began to revolutionize thoughts and then institutions. It had real impact once Enlightenment thinkers like John Locke who articulated ideas about inalienable rights that originated in the people—not the state. In a sense, this meant that the state was a tool of the people's will. To fully realize the potential of this perspective, a community would completely rid itself of monarchs.

---

[159] Bernstein *The Birth of Plenty*, 79.

The Founding Fathers

The American Revolution was dramatic. It seized the attention of the world and has inspired groups ever since. A group of brilliant commoners took the principles of the Enlightenment seriously enough to create a society, a grand experiment that would prove this new philosophy. Once when John F. Kennedy hosted a group of American Nobel Prize winners, he quipped, "There has never been so much brainpower here all at once in the White House since Jefferson dined alone." And Jefferson was simply *one* of the great minds who helped to build the nation. He did not create the Declaration of Independence alone; not only did he benefit from the wisdom of a collection of geniuses, but he also had Locke from whom to borrow. Locke wrote, "life, liberty, and private property," which Jefferson turned into "life, liberty, and the pursuit of happiness." (With such phrases in the DNA of the country, it was perhaps inevitable that the United States would pioneer consumer credit and the use of shopping as therapy.) This country would be shaped by the pursuit of happiness and the will of the individual, not a monarch.

England subordinated monarchs to a constitution. The Americans would go a step further and eliminate monarchs altogether.

The Americans did away with the notion that wealth was something to which only aristocrats could aspire and created a country where aspiration for more, what would come to be named the "American Dream," would eventually be a promise for anyone. And James Watt's invention—and the nascent field of engineering—promised to liberate humanity from the limits of its own strength, giving substance to the hope of those optimistic Americans who would have been properly dismissed as deluded utopians had it not been for the technological advances of the second economy. Human potential had been transformed, and the American revolutionaries did more than anyone else to define the government that could best realize this potential.

Why Not France?

The French were the first to prove that a nation-state needn't be on a new (to the West) continent to become democratic. The French, of course, were working with far more baggage than the Americans, who literally had a brand new continent on which to build, and felt none of the compunction for respecting Indian culture that many of the French felt for the culture they'd inherited from their rich and varied past. In 1789, George Washington was elected the first president of a nation in the history of the world. Think about that: the first elected president in the history of the world. As if that were not enough accomplishment for the West for one year, the French Revolution sent King Louis XVI and his Austrian bride Marie Antoinette to trial and then to the guillotine. It is hard to think of a more stark illustration of how much democratic revolution changed things around than this: commoners could become kings and kings could be tried and sentenced to death as if they were mere commoners. Social invention changes what is true. A former land surveyor now ruled a nation larger than any in Europe, and the rule of Louis XV's grandson and a daughter of Habsburg royalty were usurped by Enlightenment philosophers.

Those crazy French were not the only ones who were inspired by the American experiment to the point of killing a despot and putting in place some form of democracy in the hopes of creating a new country; the Americans themselves did this with their invasion of Iraq early in the twenty-first century. The French and Iraq experiments both seem to point to the importance of proper sequence in social invention and change. For this reason, it is more interesting to look at the French Revolution than the American.

As the younger Bush learned by invading Iraq with the intention of creating an example of democracy in the Middle East, it's difficult to get a people to respect popular will expressed through vote when they still trust religious leaders who speak for God. At a certain stage of government, even the masses feel that God's one vote counts more than the votes of the masses. Or, put differently, at a certain stage the masses actually trust an elite group to speak on behalf of that one God, and trust that elite more than the opinion of their own neighbors. Until people have come to question the authority of religious leaders, democracy struggles to gain credibility. Who cares what is popular if you know what is right?

The French realized that religion was an obstacle to a republic. For a time, they even outlawed religion; the Notre Dame cathedral was renamed the Temple for the Cult of Reason in the years after the Revolution, and then was essentially turned into a barn for some time. Yet this sentiment reflected the beliefs of the elite, not the masses. The average person wanted his religion. Although quite a number of the founding fathers of the United States were deists (who generally believed in a God but not the divinity of Christ or the inerrancy of the Bible), most of the revolutionaries and average people were religious. When Thomas Paine, who had done as much as anyone to articulate and inspire the revolution with his pamphlet "Common Sense," wrote a pamphlet mocking the Bible, he was essentially excommunicated from American society. The United States did not renounce religion but, rather, made it less relevant to political affairs for the simple reason that no *one* religion had a monopoly on beliefs. There is a big difference between religious diversity that takes away the political power of religion and outlawing religion entirely in order to take away its political influence. Sadly, for the French, their revolution did not build atop the foundation of religious freedom that the American's revolution did. The French, in a sense, were jumping straight past the first economy's social revolution and into the second economy's. They had not created diversity in religion before trying to create a democracy. This unstable foundation was to prove insufficient for a republic and about fifteen years after the Revolution, Napoleon was Emperor—crowned in the gorgeous building that was again a cathedral, again called Notre Dame rather than the Temple for the Cult of Reason.

For all the amazing things they did in their democratic revolution, the French had not done a very good job with the two previous revolutions: the transformation of the church and the creation of the bank. So while they transformed France from monarchy to republic for a time, they soon morphed into an empire and then lapsed back into a monarchy. For all their genius and great intentions, they still had some unfinished work to do. In terms of social invention, they were building the walls before laying the foundation.

While England wavered between persecuting Anglicans, persecuting Catholics, and persecuting Puritans before finally deciding to tolerate nearly all religions, France remained steadfastly Catholic. This not only cost France in terms of a foundation of religious diversity but it literally cost them money. French religious intolerance provoked capital flight in the early and formative stages of capitalism.

The Cost of French Religious Intolerance

In 1598, with the Edict of Nantes, French Protestants were given religious freedom, but as sworn defender of the Catholic faith, Louis only reluctantly tolerated Protestants. In 1685, he revoked the Edict of Nantes and the persecution of Protestants escalated. Of the 1.5 million Protestants living in France, about four hundred thousand fled. They took with them their silk looms, paper mills, shops, and tanneries. [160]

In the late seventeenth century, some of the Protestants in Britain who had fled French religious persecution established silk manufacturing. This helped diversify the British textile industry while weakening that in France.

While England was creating a constitutional monarchy, France was creating religious refugees who spread across Europe, representing the loss of French civil liberties and economic strength. By one estimate, these religious refugees transferred about £3 million of capital to England. [161] The income that could have helped to finance Napoleon was to finance his British enemies instead.

France's Bad Luck at Investing

It wasn't just that France had largely skipped the big revolution of the first economy, trying to build a republic atop a foundation of religious intolerance. France had struggled with capitalism as well. Its early experiences with banking had not gone well. Knowing that they were missing out on the economic progress of England, the French made a bold—but in the end disastrous—leap into modern finance in 1718.

John Law was part visionary genius and part madman. Sadly, the French didn't know which part was which. Law created the Banque Royale and blended control of the currency, the national debt, and tradable shares representing profits from his Mississippi Company operating out of the North American French territory. His scheme began well. Share prices rose twenty times; even more amazing, his issues of bank notes from the Banque Royale rose from 18 million to 2.6 billion livres. The spectacular rise in stock price and that in the volume of currency were both related and unsustainable. All that new money was raising the prices of shares. The word "millionaire" was coined to

[160] Durant and Durant, *Age of Louis XIV*,74.

[161] Smith, *The History of the Global Stock Market*, 19.

describe the winners in this intoxicating game, but it was the concept of bankruptcy that was to leave an indelible mark on the French consciousness. The "Mississippi Bubble" burst and so did French trust in banks, a further setback in France's development of financial institutions during the eighteenth century. After this event, "There was hesitation even in pronouncing the word 'bank' for 150 years."[162]

The result was that France, in spite of her many potential advantages, offered a lower standard of living than Britain by the time of the French Revolution in 1789. The state was subordinated to the will of kings, who blissfully ignored the plight of peasants even as their rivals on the throne of England were forced to respond to the demands of merchants and landowners. England and France were the first two modern nation-states. France, however, had been less successful at building the financial markets and religious diversity that were so key to success in the second economy.

Democratic Revolution: A Revolution in Increments

The democratic revolution is often described as a dramatic tale of brave revolutionaries who overthrew the tyranny of a distant empire or nearby monarch (depending on what country's history you're reading). In the United States, we have a wonderful story about brave and wise men who gave us our modern democracy. And the story is true. Yet it is not complete. The revolution declared in 1776 was radical, but it was, in the larger scheme of things, an incremental thing.

It had its start about a hundred years before, when the English made the monarchs William and Mary subject to the constitution.

Furthermore, while the Revolution of 1776 was a beautiful thing, it didn't really change the rights of most Americans. It took 34 more years before people (well, property-owning white males) of any religion could vote. It took another 74 years before even white males who didn't own property could vote. It was 144 years after 1776 before women could vote and 148 years before Native Americans were considered real Americans and able to vote as well. Not until 189

[162] Smith, *The History of the Global Stock Market*, 46.

years later were minorities' voting rights ensured. And it took nearly 200 years – in 1971 - before the eighteen-year-olds considered old enough to die for their country were considered old enough to vote for their leaders. (And it is probably no coincidence that since then we've not had a military draft.)

The real limit to change is always the collective imagination. For all of their vision, it is not the least obvious that our founding fathers could conceive of an eighteen-year-old black female without property casting the vote that might elect the next president.

Social progress is often a bet on the person who has yet to prove himself. By definition, it almost has to be. Before 1920, women could not prove that their vote mattered, for the simple reason that it did not.

A couple of centuries later, the American Revolution is still inspiring the spread of democracy. Right here within our borders.

Once the nation-state became a tool for the individual, it was subject to the newly emergent financial markets and their agent: the banker. The next chapter tells the dramatic story of how a man from the ghetto grew up to command kings.

15 Bank Dictates to the State

Once the Rothschilds had created an international capital market, the state was subject to its terms. While political power was limited to national elections, capital could skip across borders and the new nation-states had to compete for capital.

The Rothschilds and the Creation of Modern Financial Markets

Before the second economy, ghettoes were a section of town reserved for Jews. Jews could live nowhere else, and as the population of Jews grew, the squalor and congestion in these ghettoes was enough to be its own kind of persecution.

Whether Jews were rich or poor, they had few rights. Yet the periodic violence against Jews made even this denial of rights seem tolerable. Pogroms—attacks on Jews—might be sparked by any number of events, from real or perceived crimes by Jews to a renewed outbreak of the plague in a nearby area.

Although life inside the ghetto was hard, to step outside the ghetto meant a trip into dangerous and humiliating territory. Jews were subordinate to any and everyone else. It wasn't just that they had to bow to the wishes of the Christians in town. A prosperous Jewish merchant or banker might find himself bossed around by even a child. For sport, children walking down the lane could holler, "Step aside, Jew," and any Jew would be forced to obey, stepping out into whatever muck or traffic was in the road.

Jews had no place in church or state, but given the peculiarities of Catholic law, Jews were often able to fill roles as bankers, roles that would make a good Christian either an outlaw or a social pariah. Because they could work as traders and bankers, they sometimes had wealth; rarely, though, did this translate into any kind of social power.

Mayer Rothschild was a successful merchant and banker who helped the aristocracy (and others) with investments. Mayer saw the importance of trade and realized that the ability to have trusted agents in various parts of Europe would give an organization certain advantages in trade. Mayer sent his five sons to four cities (one stayed in Frankfurt with him), giving his sons branch offices in Frankfurt, London, Vienna, Naples, and Paris.

One in particular was to emerge as a banking genius: Nathan Rothschild, in London, was to become one of those historical figures whose potential was perfectly suited for his time. In concert with his brothers in the various corners of Europe, he was to plunge into the great act of social invention that so defined the second economy: he helped to create modern financial markets. Nathan was a banker.

Napoleon created a great opportunity for bankers when he drove the British to debt in defense of Europe. Nathan did the most to exploit this opportunity.

Overthrowing Tyrannies and Exporting the Republic

The French Revolution was precipitated as much by financial crisis as anything else. In 1787, the French finance minister declared the monarchy bankrupt, triggering a meeting the following year of the Estates General (a legislative body similar to the British Parliament), which had not met since 1614.[163] Once assembled, the Estates General did not readily cede power. A revolution ensued and the new French Republic that emerged did not trigger a new era just for France, but for all of Europe. Like the Americans they had earlier helped, the French overthrew the monarchy and created a republic.

Yet the French were not satisfied simply to do away with their own monarchy. They had a sense of destiny. Napoleon led the French on a military campaign. The intention of these French who were newly converted to the gospel of democracy was to overthrow monarchies throughout Europe and to liberate people from the old ways. Napoleon and his troops brought Enlightenment by artillery. The British rallied to oppose Napoleon, not eager to see the entire continent fall under the control of their long-time adversary, who had most recently offended British sensibilities by siding with the rebellious Americans. Soon, Britain was united with most of the Continent in defense against Napoleon.

---

[163] H. G. Wells, *The Outline of History: Being a Plain History of Life and Mankind by H.G. Wells, Revised and Brought up to the End of the Second World War by Raymond Postgate, Volume II* (Garden City, NY: Garden City Books, 1956) ,710.

The British sent a large force to the Continent, but it was difficult to feed, clothe, and equip these troops who were so far away. One option was that the British troops on the Continent could be fed by pillaging the locals. This, however, had the tendency to turn the local populace against an army, which could prove problematic. Alternatively British troops could be fed with supplies from home, but this, too, was problematic, creating vulnerable supply lines that were hard to manage and protect. A third option was to simply send money to the troops to use to purchase what they needed from the locals. This, by contrast to pillaging, had the tendency to win the locals over to the invading army's side, as the troops became a source of income and potential prosperity.

But of course, this solution raised the problem of how to raise enough money to finance such an army.

Fighting Napoleon With Bonds in Britain

Opposing Napoleon proved hugely expensive. The British spent about £830 million on the war, with government spending rising sharply from about £18 million to around £100 million between 1793 and 1815. Although the Parliament created new taxes (including the income tax), they still had to finance a huge amount of this expense through debt. "National debt soared from £240 million in 1793 to £900 million in 1815, close to 200 percent of national income."[164]

Nathan Rothschild was able to capitalize on Napoleon's ventures by being bold enough to buy bonds from the British government and then, in turn, sell them not just to the British but, through his brothers in Vienna, Paris, Frankfurt, and Naples, in the international bond market. Brokering the sale of these bonds earned the Rothschilds large sums and made them rich. Very rich. It was not obvious at the beginning of the 1800s, though, that the Rothschild brothers would be the bankers to most benefit from this sudden surge in national debt.

Early in the rise of the banking system, the Baring Brothers had obvious advantages over Nathan and his brothers. Lutherans, the Baring

[164] Niall Ferguson, *The House of Rothschild: Money's Prophets, 1798—1848* (New York: Penguin Books, 1999), 84.

Brothers were more readily accepted into British society than the Jewish Rothschilds. While Nathan was making money trading in textiles, two members of the Baring family (who had also made their initial fortune in the textiles business) were already members of Parliament. It would not have seemed a particularly good bet to predict that the Rothschilds would emerge in the 1820s as the dominant bankers in Europe. The Barings financed the Louisiana Purchase and the French indemnity payments after Waterloo. The French finance minister in the early 1800s was widely quoted as saying: "There are six great powers in Europe—England, France, Russia, Austria, Prussia and the Baring Brothers."[165] Perhaps no quote could better capture the rise of the banker during the second economy.

Yet the Rothschilds outmaneuvered their rivals because of risk taking, luck, and connections. They were bold, quickly agreeing to tasks that other bankers hesitated to accept. For instance, while Britain was financing its armies and its allies in the war against Napoleon, the Rothschilds readily agreed to transport money to troops on the Continent.

During this time, the elder Baring died and the Dutch Baring brother was unable to act in his stead after Napoleon invaded the Netherlands. This gave the Rothschilds an advantage.

Friendships and kickbacks provided the Rothschilds connections within various European governments, directing deals to them worth millions.

Yet perhaps the most important distinction was that the Rothschilds had offices and contacts throughout Europe in a market that had truly become international. At this early stage of capitalism, information was at a premium. News about events, and their impact on bond prices, was scarce and slow to arrive. This meant that credit was as likely to be determined by personal acquaintance and word-of-mouth endorsements as any objectively reported financial data. In such a world, personal networks and trusted sources were enormously important. Writing about Wall Street in the early 1900s (a time with even more information to process than the early 1800s, when the Rothschilds rose to prominence), Ron Chernow claims that

At bottom, the real power of old-line bankers lay in their monopoly over information, a commodity even rarer than capital in those days. ... Wall Street bankers profited from the gross imbalance between what

---

165 Ron Chernow, *The House of Morgan: An American Banking Dynasty and the Rise of Modern Finance* (New York: Atlantic Monthly Press, 1990), 26.

they knew about these companies and what the poor, benighted masses did.[166]

The Rothschilds—particularly Nathan, who was based in London—seemed to have a real genius for these early investment markets. Being scattered about Europe, collecting and distributing information, was key to the brothers' success in the markets. Although they did not have the Internet or even phones, they used the most advanced form of rapid communication available at the time:

A fleet of carrier pigeons ... sped news of major events to the Rothschilds, accounting for some of their early killings. ... In a famous lament, Talleyrand sighed, "The English Ministry is always informed of everything by Rothschilds ten to twelve hours before Lord Stuart's dispatches arrive."[167]

As they became better acquainted with various policy makers, their information advantage was extended to include knowledge of upcoming decisions about the fiscal policy of governments. The Rothschilds and their carrier pigeons constituted, if not a worldwide web, then at least a European-wide nest of information.

The Napoleonic wars made the Rothschilds wealthy. After the war, it became clear just how powerful this made them.

The story of Napoleon's victories and defeats deserves its own book. (The curious reader can probably find one or two.) Suffice to say that this military genius and political conundrum (a man who became emperor in order to spread democracy?) transformed Europe.

Royalty throughout Europe were left shaken by Napoleon, who had toppled many thrones and threatened them all. Royalty who had previously felt happily secure in their wealth and privilege now felt the sudden urge to modernize, or at least to modernize their armies. But this was, of course, expensive, and hasty modernization meant that they would need debt financing. Through his experience in helping the British to finance unprecedented levels of debt, Nathan Rothschild had proven himself the global expert in bond financing. This expertise was to create a curious reversal of fortune for a Jew from the ghetto and for German royalty from the castle. It was also to prove illustrative of

[166] Ron Chernow, *The Death of the Banker: The Decline and Fall of the Great Financial Dynasties and the Triumph of the Small Investor* (New York: Vintage Books, 1997), 33.

the bank's eclipse of the state.

The King of Prussia Bows to Nathan Rothschild

Investors had a bad track record with absolute monarchs. Monarchs were too likely to spend money on unproductive causes (like huge palaces, for instance) and to default rather than submit themselves to moneylenders. Investors soon realized that parliamentary governments were more reliable than monarchs in terms of repayment. They therefore charged absolute monarchies higher interest rates. Often during the eighteenth century, Britain was able to borrow money at half the rate that investors demanded of the more frequently defaulting French.

In 1815, Napoleon was defeated at Waterloo and a king once again took the French throne.[168] Nonetheless, France had created an arms race among Europeans and unease among royalty, and this put a great strain on some of the more traditional economies, like those of Prussia and Russia. These countries were forced to seek financing for both modernization and armaments.

After the war, the Prussian king, Friedrich Wilhelm III, turned to the Rothschilds for a loan. Prussia was a great power. It was the country that would eventually bring about the union of Germany, and Prussia was home to the city of Berlin, which would become the German capital. The King of Prussia was no petty aristocrat when he came to Nathan Rothschild in the wake of the Napoleonic wars, asking for financing to modernize his country and army. Prussia was one of the great powers in Europe.

Yet Nathan Rothschild's response to Wilhelm's request for a loan was symbolic of the great shift in power that had occurred. In a letter dated 1818, Nathan Rothschild explained to the Prussian King:

...the late investments by British subjects in the French funds have proceeded upon the general belief that in consequence of the representative system now established in that Country, the sanction of

[168] Nathan Rothschild, who knew before other investors that Napoleon had been defeated at Waterloo, used information about Napoleon's defeat to play the markets and to quickly make a small fortune, enlarging his capital and influence.

the Chamber to the national debt incurred by the Government affords a guarantee to the Public Creditor which could not be found in a Contract with any Sovereign uncontrolled in the exercise of the executive powers.[169]

Rothschild basically said that investors preferred parliaments to absolute monarchies, and he was defining terms for the loan in this initial negotiation, as any lender might do. What was highly unusual and completely remarkable was that a mere banker could dictate the terms of the loan to a king in this stage of negotiations. And these were not just any terms. He was requesting that Friedrich Wilhelm III submit to a parliamentary form of government in order to qualify for the loan he had requested. Through negotiations this clause was modified, but not by much. The finalized contract included a clause that basically demanded constitutional reform as a precondition for any further borrowing. This, perhaps more than any other act, signaled a watershed moment: a banker was now dictating terms to a king. Before the King of Prussia could borrow his next round of financing, he would have to share power with parliament. Just consider what this says about the rise of the banker in relation to the state. Nathan Rothschild, member of a group who in one generation could be forced off of the sidewalk by children, was now ordering one of Europe's most powerful kings to give up power to Parliament. Step off the sidewalk indeed. The French armies wanted to topple kings and institute republics in their place. What the great General Napoleon was unable to do in Prussia with military force, Nathan Rothschild the banker was able to do with capital.

London as Financial Center

The loan also helped to further London's role as the capital of capital. "[The loan to Prussia] was the first time a large loan for a foreign country was denominated not in the currency of that country, but in pounds sterling. Britons could now invest in foreign securities without fear of adverse swings in the value of foreign exchange. ... Rothschild

169 Ferguson, *The House of Rothschild*, 270.

in quick succession underwrote sterling loans for Russia, Austria, and Spain."[170]

By the late nineteenth century in the United States, capitalists literally bought congressmen, paying for legislation that would allow them to buy land for railroads for little or no money in return for stock in those railroad companies. After democratic revolutions that transferred power from monarchs to representatives, financial markets had increasing influence over governments' options. By the close of the nineteenth century, financial markets did more to dictate events than did governments. By the beginning of the twentieth century, capitalism was perhaps at its peak of power and the West had fully adapted to capital.

Capital was scarce during this second economy and bankers knew who had it and who needed it. They could consolidate deposits of tens of dollars each from thousands of depositors into million-dollar investments out of reach of any one depositor (or divide the debt of millions into ten-dollar bonds within the reach of any investor). Bankers were able to grant or refuse loans to anyone, and this made them very powerful—powerful enough even to dictate terms to kings. This power over the state was to continue throughout the twentieth century. In 1993, Bill Clinton reportedly asked Alan Greenspan, "You mean to tell me that the success of the program and my reelection hinges on the Federal Reserve and a bunch of f___ing bond traders?"[171]

Conclusion

In the two hundred years between the end of William's reign in 1702 and the end of Victoria's reign in 1901, the world was transformed as never before. Across the American and European continents, revolutionaries threw off the tyranny of monarchs and submitted instead to the tyranny of factory rhythms. By the last half of the nineteenth century, railroads and telegraphs crisscrossed Europe and America, and British exports of machinery were doubling every decade. Writing in 1848, de Tocqueville opined that beginning with the eleventh century,

---

[170] Smith, *The History of the Global Stock Market*, 50.

[171] Bernstein, *The Birth of Plenty*, 44.

every half-century brought nobility and commoner closer together on the social scale. By 1900, the common person could enjoy a variety of foods and choice of products that royalty from 1500 might have envied. During the Christmas holiday of 1843, Charles Dickens introduced Ebenezer Scrooge and the modern idea of Christmas to the world; from the time of Shakespeare and Queen Elizabeth to the time of Dickens and Queen Victoria, a new world had been created. This was the second economy, a world in which institutions, attitudes, beliefs, and habits adapted to the era's new limit to progress. Capital rose to prominence, and the Western world reinvented itself to adapt to its demands and overcome its limit.

Progress doesn't stop just because the turntable has reached a new pinnacle, though. The CD still gets invented and adopted. Social invention is similar.

The next section begins the story of the third economy, the economy into which you were born and learned about how the world works. When the limit shifted from capital to knowledge work, the wave of change began anew. The third economy is outlined from about 30,000 feet in the next introductory section.

The Third Economy

IV The Third Economy: Minds & Money, 1900 to 2000

The third economy is the one that still defines so much of what we expect of progress. The limit to the third economy was knowledge workers and the percentage of people engaged in formal education each decade in the West steadily trended upwards. It was the corporation, though, that rose to prominence in this economy, and just as it was in earlier times with church, state, and bank, the corporation has become the West's dominant institution. The story of the origins and emergence of the information economy is told in these chapters.

Chapter 16, Knowledge Workers, explains why people manipulating symbols of things rather than actual things can create so much value.

Chapter 17, The Information Economy, lists some of the highlights of the information economy, and some of the major social and technological inventions from the information economy

Chapter 18, Pragmatism, explains the origins of the philosophy adopted by so many knowledge workers and why such a philosophy would appeal to, and benefit, this new kind of worker.

Chapter 19, Inventing the Corporation, goes through the history of the invention of the modern, multinational corporation, arguing that it was invented as a way to manage and coordinate knowledge workers.

Chapter 20, Financial Revolution, chronicles the major change in attitude towards credit, and the rise of financial products as varied as the credit card and junk bonds.

Chapter 21, The Corporation Eclipses the Bank, gives two examples of how the corporation that was largely started and expanded by the bank came to usurp it in power and influence.

16 Knowledge Workers

Capital took the work out of work. Or, rather, changed it from the product of brawn to the product of brains.

Economy	First	Second	Third	Fourth
Period	1300–1700	1700–1900	1900-2000	2000-2050
Limit to Progress	Land	Capital	**Knowledge Workers**	Entrepreneurship
Type of Economy	Agricultural	Industrial	Information	Entrepreneurial
Intellectual Revolution	Renaissance	Enlightenment	Pragmatism	Systems Thinking
Big Social Invention	Nation-State	Bank	Corporation	Self
Social Revolution	Protestant Revolution	Democratic Revolution	Financial Revolution	Business Revolution

While at first glance it would seem that capital in the form of huge factories and growing financial markets was more important than ever in the twentieth century, it was increasingly led by knowledge workers who created the products, machinery, and markets of the third economy. Once the West had overcome the limit of capital and was able to make more products than ever, the limit shifted to knowledge workers who could manipulate the symbol of the things that machines make and move.

By the late nineteenth century, the work of inventing the roles, tools, and organizations for knowledge workers was to become the most important work for advancing industrial economies. By the late twentieth century, even the least developed countries were well aware that knowledge workers were the limit to progress and found ways to invest in education and research and development and to attract corporations as a means to economic progress.

That's Symbolic

Knowledge work is different from manual—or manufacturing—work, in that knowledge workers manipulate symbols rather than objects. A knowledge worker might draw a blueprint but never actually move a wall.

Knowledge work is a sloppy term that covers a wide range of activities. To be precise, every activity involves some degree of knowledge, but it is not true that every worker manipulates symbols of things instead of actual things. Former U.S. Labor Secretary Robert Reich labels such professionals symbolic analysts.

Symbolic analysts solve, identify, and broker problems by manipulating symbols. They simplify reality into abstract images that can be rearranged, juggled, experimented with, communicated to other specialists, and then, eventually, transformed back into reality.[172]

Management guru Peter Drucker puts it more simply, referring to the knowledge worker as "the man who puts to work what he has between his ears rather than the brawn of his muscles or the skill of his hands." He further describes knowledge workers as "people who have been schooled to use knowledge, theory, and concept rather than physical force or manual skill. ..."[173]

James Beniger, perhaps the writer with the best understanding of the evolution and dynamics of the information economy and the knowledge worker central to it writes,

"This use of human beings, not for their strength or agility, nor for

---

[172] Robert Reich, *The Work of Nations* (New York: Vintage Books, 1992), 178.

[173] Peter Drucker, *The Executive in Action* (New York: Harper Business, 1996), 527.

their knowledge or intelligence, but for the more objective capacity of their brains to store and process information, would become over the next century [the twentieth century] a dominant feature of employment in the Information Society."[174]

Reich, Drucker, and Beniger were all writing in the late twentieth century. Drucker coined the term "knowledge worker" around 1959. Although the terms and concepts used to describe knowledge workers were to emerge only in the last half of the twentieth century, knowledge workers themselves became increasingly important to economies within the developed nations by the end of the nineteenth century. Much of the social invention that would transform the West in the twentieth century was work done with the purpose of creating these knowledge workers and then making them productive.

As with each limit before it, knowledge work required the invention of a new institution through which to be effective, new tools, and a new philosophy. Its rise would transform the previously dominant institution. The modern corporation—invented for the third economy—gained much of its power from its ability to manage knowledge workers and make them more productive. The information technology that made men like Tom Watson of IBM, Gordon Moore of Intel, and Bill Gates of Microsoft rich was the tool set that made knowledge workers more productive. A philosophy that was so much more pragmatic than Enlightenment thinking that it was labeled Pragmatism came to define knowledge workers' thinking. And the bank that had been so central to the rise of capital was forced to change and to become subordinate to this new limit to progress.

Knowledge is the only meaningful resource today. The traditional "factors of production"—land (i.e., natural resources), labor, and capital—have not disappeared, but they have become secondary.

—Peter Drucker

---

[174] James Beniger, *The Control Revolution: Technological and Economic Origins of the Information Society* (Harvard University Press, Cambridge, MA 1989) 225.

The Emergence of the Third Economy

The developments of the industrial revolution drove a wedge between work and physical exertion. No longer was it a given that the average person would add value by doing rather feebly what a machine could do with more force than a horse. It was to take more than a century for society to realize how fundamentally life, work, and value would change as the industrial revolution's new machinery liberated a growing number of workers from physical labor.[175]

Yet the success of the industrial revolution created a new problem: the tools, products, processes, markets, and even organizations that workers confronted were increasingly complex and large. Accordingly, the demands placed on the average worker involved more problem solving than sweating, and jobs began to require knowledge of principles as taught in the fields like engineering, science, and psychology.

Increased complexity and scope made the manipulation of the symbols of things rather than actual things more valuable. As projects put more capital at risk, the cost of error became high enough that planning became more important. As investments began to represent more and more money, it was increasingly important to get the plans right before even starting a new venture.

Imagine that you are building a porch out back. You plan the construction and then—all by yourself—you get to work on it. You buy lumber, maybe a new tool or two. Planning is helpful, but it is not essential that you get your initial plans just right. You have some latitude to change as you build.

Contrast that with building a skyscraper. You can't afford to have a crew of three hundred standing around after you suddenly realize that you don't have the right tools or enough material and you have to run off to buy more. Nor can you afford to get the building up twelve stories before you realize that you need a different foundation. You have to plan properly—that is, you have to manipulate the symbols of the construction, from budget to blueprints to schedules—before you begin. The cost and complexity of the project make it prohibitive to "just do it."

---

[175] It was not immediately clear to what they had been freed, and the threat of automation initially was very real. People did lose their jobs to machines.

Whether the work at hand was more complex factories, bigger infrastructure projects, or product launches, demand grew for knowledge workers able to simulate and plan the "real" work before it even began, and then to manage and coordinate that work once it was underway.

Yet demand for people who could manipulate symbols of things was not just a consequence of increased scope and complexity. It was also due to the fact that as change became more rapid, experience was of less help; theory that enabled knowledge workers to generalize from one situation to another, new situation became more important. In this, knowledge workers were generally more adept. Education on principles made it easier to deal with constant change.

Demand for knowledge workers was also driven by a need to understand, respond to, and shape market demand.

Before someone built a factory to make a particular kind of watch or washing machine, it was helpful to know that there might be some demand for that product. It didn't do much good to build a big factory that made more product than people wanted. If you were more successful at making things than selling them, you could go bankrupt. Capital no longer limited and the question was not whether you'd be able to make enough; the question was whether you could make the right product. Demand for products had to be predicted before capitalists would make investments. Businesses needed to understand the market. Yet knowledge workers who manipulate symbols do not just predict demand. They also try to change it, through marketing and advertising. A great advertiser can be worth millions—manipulating symbols like models and actors and iconic figures to, in turn, manipulate the consumer into buying the product. Advertising, branding, and marketing are all examples of knowledge work that addresses demand-side considerations.

Knowledge workers were thus in demand for everything from the conceptualization and design of products to the packaging and distribution of them; from managing supply chains to creating demand and managing all points in between. As the economy became more complex, knowledge workers became more important to success.

It is simpler to change the design of products than to change products already made. It might cost about one hundred dollars to make a simple design change. It might cost a million to change that design once you'd already set up machinery in a factory to make the product. And it might cost hundreds of millions to put out a recall to change the product once it was already out in the field and in use by your customers. In the modern economy, it is probably true that knowledge work doesn't just save money; without knowledge workers, a company can't even make money.

Education and the Invention of Knowledge Workers

The economies that prospered in the twentieth century went beyond industrialization. Among other things, they adopted a variety of policy measures to raise the percentage of young adults enrolled in school. In the United States, for example, the percentage of fourteen- to seventeen-year-olds in school rose from just over 10 percent in 1900 to about 94 percent in 2000.[176]

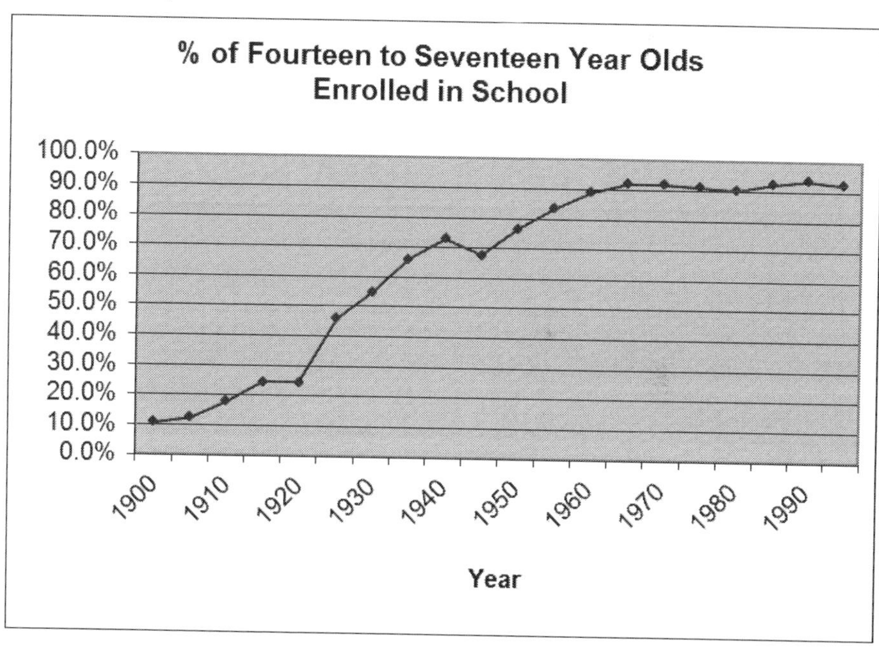

With this extraordinary rise in education rates came an astounding rise in incomes. Per capita income rose about ten times during the twentieth century. Life expectancy also rose, from forty-seven to

[176]No. HS-20. Education Summary – Enrollment 1900 to 2000, and Projections, 2001. http://www.census.gov/statab/hist/HS-20.pdf, 9 July 2011.

seventy-seven years between 1900 and 2000[177]. No era in history had brought such dramatic rises in real income or such improvements in health. Indeed, only a couple of previous *centuries* could compete with the progress made in a single decade during this century of dramatic progress.

Germany pioneered much of modern education. In the U.S., few seem to realize that the word kindergarten has German origins. Its universities, too, produced knowledge workers at the leading edge of ability. After World War I, for instance, the Allies could not even decode the patents they stole from the Germans and had to hire away German engineers and scientists in order to use them.

Germany's educational system produced iconic philosophers and industrialists. Karl Marx proved history's most persuasive critic of capitalism. Karl Benz, a product of Karlruhe Polytechnic School, invented the first car to be powered by an internal combustion engine, and founded what would be, by 1900, the world's largest automobile company. Rudolf Diesel, graduate of Munich Polytechnic, invented the engine that bore his name. The British led innovation in the industrial economy, largely by such social inventions as patent law. The Germans were early leaders in the information economy, largely on the strength of innovations in education, particularly the invention of the modern university. As with the British patents, the positive impact of this social invention could have hardly been foreseen.

During the twelfth century, Cambridge, Oxford, Bologna, and Paris all had universities. These were different from what we know today, in that they were institutions designed to teach what was known. To be sure, there was problem solving (particularly as academia wrestled with the problems of law created by changes in states and their relationship to the church), but the general thrust of the university was less about creating new knowledge than passing along old wisdom.

The Enlightenment changed that. Enlightenment philosophers were intent on experimentation and tinkering. They were in search of principles that could describe swaths of phenomena and predict things that hadn't yet happened.

It is less true than convenient to label someone like Henry VIII an inventor of the modern nation-state. Many monarchs, ministers, and philosophers were involved in this big act of invention. Yet Henry did play a big role, and his is an easier story to tell than the nuanced

---

[177] These numbers are for the U.S., but similar trends held throughout the West.

story of the many who contributed bits and pieces in various regions. In a similar way, Wilhelm Humboldt can be called the inventor of the modern university and may be a big reason that so many of the innovators in thought and technology emerged from Germany in the late nineteenths and early twentieth centuries.

Wilhelm Humboldt was the equivalent of the Prussian ambassador to London when Nathan Rothschild was negotiating his loan with the King of Prussia. His intervention on behalf of the Rothschilds helped them to secure the loan that would be so instrumental in the creation of the international bond market. He was a philosopher and wrote a book that helped to establish linguistics as a field of study and to define semiotics. Linguistics and semiotics are probably the areas that best epitomize the problems of the information age—the question of how meaning is created and how it is conveyed through symbols. In a sense, Humboldt laid the foundation for the transition into the digital age, where reality would eventually be made virtual.

Wilhelm's brother, Alexander von Humboldt, is even more famous. He is credited with helping to found climatology, oceanography, and geography and as being an inspiration to Charles Darwin. Alexander explored Central and South America and today has more geographic spots around the globe named after him than does anyone else. One can only speculate that if their parents had penned a guidebook on parenting it would have sold well.

Yet the accomplishment of Wilhelm's that would impact the world like no other was this: as minister of education, Wilhelm Humboldt established what could arguably be called the first modern university.

This university differed considerably from those in the past because its members did not seek just to disperse knowledge but to actually create it. This not only taught students the scientific method, it made the university the source of new methods and processes that could steadily (and at times radically) improve industry. Like capitalism and the bank before it, research and the university began a process of systemic innovation.

Like Thomas Jefferson, Humboldt understood the importance of education that focused on developing the individual. His intention as minister of education was to open education to all social classes. "The grand, leading principle, towards which every argument unfolded in these pages directly converges, is the absolute and essential importance of human development in its richest diversity," he wrote in his book *Sphere and Duties of Government*. The development of knowledge workers was hard to separate from the development of the individual, and among other things, this put pressure on governments to place more emphasis on the education and development of everyone.

As the third economy began to emerge, Germany was well positioned for it. By 1887, Germany (in keeping with the tradition established by Humboldt's research universities decades earlier) had established a university that "was devoted to research in the new field of electrical engineering" and

with its focus on industrial applications, was a center of excellence, a playground for the best scientists and engineers, ... The private industrial research laboratories which emerged in Germany's chemical and electrical industries of the late nineteenth century also acquired a high status and established a new pattern of applied research which in turn influenced the organization of research in the university ...

Prussia took the lead in devising a science policy which used private sector funds but remained under the influence of the state with respect to its strategic orientation. In line with these policies, the Kaiser-Wilhelm-Gesellschaft zur Forderun der Wissenschaften was founded in 1911 as a private association controlled by the government. Within its first three years, the Kaiser-Wilhelm-Gesellschaft established five research institutes, devoted to chemistry, physical chemistry, coal, biology and medical science, which were directed by powerful representatives of their respective discipline who were chosen for their academic reputation. Many of the activities of the Kaiser-Wilhelm-Gesellschaft were directed not towards basic research but towards applied research which proved extremely useful in the chemical and electrical industries.[178]

One of the clear results of superior education was that Germany passed Great Britain in productivity. As can be seen in the table below, England had eight times as many illiterates as did Germany. German universities were systematically turning out chemists, engineers, and managers while the United Kingdom continued to rely on policies that focused on the development and performance of financial markets and benignly neglected its labor market. For the United Kingdom, capital was still the thing. The Germans seemed to be the first to realize that knowledge workers were beginning to matter even more.

---

[178] Benn Steil, David G. Victor, and Richard R. Nelson,editors, *Technological Innovation and Economic Performance*, (Princeton University Press, Princeton, New Jersey, 2002) 142.

Illiteracy Rate of Males in Selected European Countries[179]

Country	Year	Illiteracy Rate
Sweden	1875	1%
Germany	1875	2%
Denmark	1860	3%
Switzerland	1879	6%
Scotland	1875	9%
England	1875	17%
France	1875	18%
Belgium	1875	23%
Austria	1875	42%
Italy	1875	52%
Spain	1877	63%
Russia	1875	79%

Creating the Institutions for Knowledge Workers: Universities and Corporations

Coordinating the activities of knowledge workers drove demand for a new kind of knowledge worker: managers. This, in turn, drove demand

[179] Hobsbawm, The Age of Capital 43

for a new kind of education.

In 1904, Edward Mead (Margaret Mead's father) "created the prestigious Evening School of Accounts and Finance at Wharton. "[180] Harvard went a step further than Wharton: "In 1908 it created its Harvard School of Business, the first independent professional school with a full-time faculty anywhere to offer master's degrees in business administration (M.B.A.s). 'We take men without regard to what they have studied in college,' wrote Dean A. Lawrence Lowell, 'and we must teach them business, not political economy.'"[181]

"'The one-man ownership stage' in capitalism was dying, wrote one of the original Business School faculty. What was needed was training in management, 'administrative organization,' 'large investment banking,' and 'large scale organizations'—in short, all those institutions and activities that formed the bedrock of the new corporate industrial order."[182]

Knowledge work had always existed in some form, but it was not until the late 1800s that it became institutionalized into lasting roles. It took coordination between schools and corporations to create the new knowledge workers. The following graph of the U.S. workforce through the twentieth century shows the dramatic rise in the percentage of workers engaged in knowledge work. (For our purposes, the portion engaged in "Information" work is a reasonable proxy for the professionals engaged in knowledge work.)

---

[180]William Leach, Land of Desire: Merchants, Power, and the Rise of a New American Culture (New York: Vintage Books, 1993), 160.

[181] Leach, *Land of Desire*, 161.

[182] Leach, *Land of Desire*.

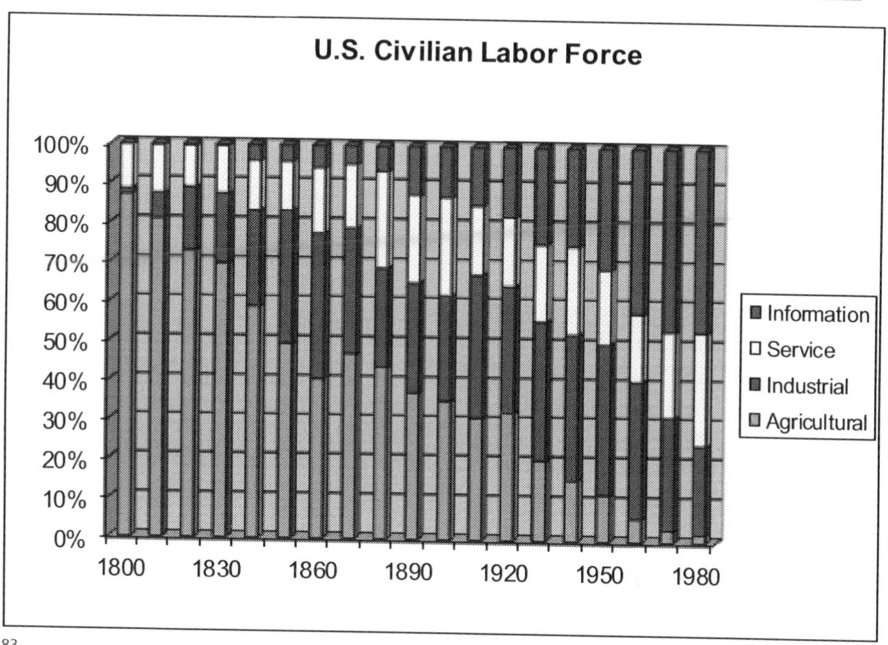

183

This growing number of knowledge workers tended to work within large bureaucracies—government or corporate organizations. Specialists who created value only in coordination with other workers, they needed an organization to add value to their efforts. These bureaucracies did more than create a role for the knowledge worker—they had the effect of putting even more emphasis on specialization and coordination. Knowledge workers are rarely effective on their own. Rather than produce a physical product like "a ditch, a pair of shoes, a machine part, [a knowledge worker} produces knowledge, ideas, information. By themselves these 'products' are useless. Somebody else, another man of knowledge, has to take them as his input and convert them into his output before they have any reality."[184]

Blueprints have no value without a team of people able to turn them into a building. A knowledge worker can make this team more effective

---

[183] Beniger, *The Control Revolution*, 24.

[184] Drucker, *Executive in Action: Managing for Results, Innovation and Entrepreneurship, the Effective Executive* (HarperBusiness, New York, NY, 2004) 529.

by creating a blueprint of a house that people will bid for and using technologies and materials that save money. A knowledge worker could save and/or make lots of money for the organization. Yet the knowledge worker could not do this alone. She needed others for this, and those others had an increasing tendency to show up as fellow employees within corporations. During the third economy, the number and size of corporations grew rapidly.

Knowledge workers affected every industry. Even industries that were not obviously dependent on the manipulation of symbols benefited from knowledge workers.

The nineteenth-century steel industry was the first to make routine use of researchers who continually monitored the relationship between ore quality and the final product. Steel baron Andrew Carnegie exulted in the advantage his lab gave him over the competition. 'Years after we had taken chemistry to guide us [competitors] said they could not afford to employ a chemist. Had they known the truth then, they would have known that they could not afford to be without one,' he said.[185]

There was no escaping the need for knowledge workers. Ignoring the importance of knowledge workers in the twentieth century was akin to ignoring the importance of capital in the nineteenth century: it guaranteed stunted economic development.

Conclusion

In 1810, when Wilhelm Humboldt founded the University of Berlin, there would have been no way for him to predict the advances that would come from the creation of generations of knowledge workers. And the number of knowledge workers continues to rise: today, there are more scientists alive on the earth than have lived in all of history up until now. Advances in biotech, nanotech, computing, pharmaceuticals, and a host of other fields promise to transform our world in unpredictable ways. Just as Humboldt could have never predicted the plethora of advances that occurred between his time and ours, so could we never hope to predict what knowledge workers will create next.

---

[185] Bernstein, *The Birth of Plenty*, 123.

We do know that knowledge workers drove demand for technology able to process, store, analyze, and communicate information, helping to create a new information economy. They also drove the need for a new philosophy that would allow them to solve problems less sweeping than the universal problem Newton solved with his theory of gravity, and they would find this in Pragmatism. These new kinds of workers required a new kind of institution through which to coordinate their efforts, and they found this in the corporation. Finally, all of this would require a transformation of the bank, of financing, as befits a world no longer limited by capital, but instead needing copious amounts of capital to create knowledge workers and keep them profitably employed. As had previously happened with land and capital, the social inventions required to overcome the new limit of knowledge workers brought sweeping changes, and this is the story of the third economy. Overcoming this limit is what defined the information economy, the economy described in the next chapter.

17 The Information Economy

The manipulation of symbols became to the new economy what the manipulation of goods had become to the last. The changes this wrought were more than symbolic.

Economy	First	Second	Third	Fourth
Period	1300–1700	1700–1900	1900-2000	2000-2050
Limit to Progress	Land	Capital	Knowledge Workers	Entrepreneurship
Type of Economy	Agricultural	Industrial	**Information**	Entrepreneurial
Intellectual Revolution	Renaissance	Enlightenment	Pragmatism	Systems Thinking
Big Social Invention	Nation-State	Bank	Corporation	Self
Social Revolution	Protestant Revolution	Democratic Revolution	Financial Revolution	Business Revolution

The information economy seemed most obviously to be about developing information technology but this technology was mostly important simply because it did so much to enable and make knowledge workers productive. Communities most focused on creating and making productive knowledge workers gained the most wealth and power in this new economy. The information economy can most easily be understood as the rise of the knowledge worker.

If we increased the level of education in this century as much as we did in the last, we'd be keeping people in school until the age of fifty.

That's not likely to happen. As we did with the industrial economy in about 1900, we may be reaching a point of diminishing returns for this information economy. While it worked, however, the information economy was the most extraordinary economy yet.

Communities creating more capital—both industrial and financial—defined the industrial economy. Communities creating more knowledge workers and the tools and institutions to make them more productive have defined the information economy.

We're reaching the limits of the information age and, in the developed nations, the policies and strategies of the information economy are becoming less effective. We can't continue to make productivity gains through more education or by giving more power to the corporation or by taking on more debt. A new strategy will need to emerge.

Yet first it is worth exploring why those strategies were so effective before we examine what role knowledge workers will play in the next economy. I think it is clear that knowledge workers will continue to be a part of the next economy, but in a slightly different role, in the same way that capital continued to be an important part of this information economy. That is to say, the knowledge workers that were so key to creating the information economy will be necessary but no longer sufficient factors in the creation of the fourth economy. Still, for about a century knowledge workers led development.

Two social inventions were particularly notable during the third economy. The modern university created knowledge workers. The corporation gave them a place to work and to become productive. The university gave them knowledge. The corporation translated that knowledge into market value.

The defining technological inventions of the information economy were tools for knowledge workers. From the typewriter and the telegraph at the very dawn of the information economy to the smart phone and the Internet of the early twenty-first century, information technology transformed and then defined this economy in the same way that powerful engines and assembly lines transformed and then defined the industrial economy.

These social and technological inventions first made the knowledge worker and then made him or her more productive. The confluence of these inventions has created the most advanced economy yet.

The information economy changed what was meant by "labor productivity." The defining figure in an agricultural economy is the farmer with a hoe. The defining figure in an industrial economy is the factory worker helping to manufacture hoes. The defining figure in an information economy is the engineer who works on design plans for a backhoe.

Expanding Markets Lead into the New Economy

The bond markets that made it possible for parliament members to avoid taxes made it possible to finance railroads. Laying down rails across a continent proved even more capital intensive than war and the financial markets that had matured to finance the Napoleonic Wars were later ready to finance this new industry.

The idea behind a railroad is an interesting one. Railroads essentially connect consumers and suppliers, connect town to town, and connect factories and stores. Railroads gave inland areas access to products and ideas they hadn't had before. This is part of what enabled Germany—a largely landlocked country—to catch up to and surpass the island of England in trade and industry. Suddenly, seaports did not automatically confer an insurmountable advantage in economic development. As it turns out, an economy is kind of like the brain: the value of the connections *between* the parts is at least as high as the value of the parts that are being connected. Brain cells get smart when they are part of a web of dendrites that connect them. Communities get rich when they are part of a web of trade patterns that connect them. Railroads, even more effectively than ships, were able to connect communities and create wealth.

Yet railroads required enormous investment. Nothing previous had ever been quite so expensive. It was possible to build a factory and then gradually increase its size and market. With railroads, the bigger the market connected, the bigger the value. But bigger markets meant more railroad line, and this required more money to invest. Very quickly, the railroads became the property of the parties most willing to take on debt. No one person had money enough to build cross-continental railroad lines with the money in his or her safe.

Bond markets first emerged to finance countries, and then to finance railroads, and then factories. As railroads expanded markets, factories could be made bigger. Instead of having a production capacity large enough to supply just Boston, a factory might expand to provide for all of Massachusetts, or to provide for all of the northeast, or even the nation. Railroads greatly expanded the size of the market that could be served by a single factory.

Capitalists who could build factories and processes that lowered costs enough could find themselves providing goods to the entire country. Local producers could be forced out of business by more efficient competition. The competitive dynamic resulted in a new methodology for factories that was to hugely increase the productive capacity of the West.

The railroad was nominally about moving stuff. Very quickly, though, the telegraph evolved beside it, as a system designed to move information. Advances in the second economy quickly brought demand for the advances of the third: rapid transportation and distribution drove a need for communication. So did the increased output of production.

Continuous Production Technology: Catalyst for the New Economy

Continuous production technology after the American Civil War was the method that represented not just the best in new processes but a radical improvement on what came before. It was the culmination of two centuries of progress in overcoming the limit of capital.

Henry Crowell was one of the first to apply continuous production methodology to a factory that brought raw materials into one end and sent packaged goods out the other. His factory coalesced all of the production steps into one facility. Before this, production was not continuous but instead generally required that the product being made move from one factory to another as it moved along in the process of transformation from raw materials to finished goods.

Yet, successfully finding a way to make lots of a product could backfire. If demand for your product was at one hundred units a month and you are suddenly flooding the market with one thousand units each month, you could actually drive down prices enough to turn your profit margins negative. At first, it seemed that Crowell had made such a mistake.

By the time he completed his factory, it had capacity enough to supply double the number of oats that Americans consumed each year. Americans generally thought of oats as horse food or something that only dour Scotsmen would eat, and demand for them was fairly low. To flood the market with so many oats could easily drive down prices so much that Crowell could never hope to recoup his initial investment, much less make a profit from his amazing new factory.

So Crowell shifted his attention from the problem of how to make more to the problem of how to sell more. The task of making more was a problem of overcoming the limits of capital, of manipulating things and machines to stimulate more production. The task of selling more was a problem of knowledge work, of manipulating symbols to stimulate more consumption and open up new markets.

Crowell may have been the first to use scientific endorsements about the health benefits of his product; he advertised on the side of trains. He was probably the first to send samples to households, sending packages of oatmeal to homes throughout Portland, Oregon (turning his excess productive capacity into a marketing advantage.) Furthermore, he created an image that "branded" his product into the American consciousness: the symbol on the side of his Quaker Oats products became synonymous with oats.

Soon, Crowell had stimulated demand enough to meet the incredible capacity of his factory. As he pioneered the process of managing demand, he created breakfast cereal.[186] Eventually, Kellogg, Post, and others were to duplicate—and even surpass—his enormous success.

As an affable-looking Quaker led America into mass consumption, the problem of increased production began to take second place to the problem of increasing sales through advertising, distribution, brand management, and consumer credit. These new problems created a demand for communication and information technologies, and knowledge workers capable of understanding and using them. The limit to progress was shifting from capital to knowledge workers. It was this shift that fueled the demand for office equipment and computers that would eventually make companies like IBM and Microsoft household names.

Crowell's success was to become an example for a wave of new companies. Ford was the most popular figure in the American imagination when we think of assembly lines, and to be fair, assembling a car is more impressive than assembling a box of cereal. Yet in

[186] Beniger, *The Control Revolution*, 265–66.

between the simplicity of oats and the complexity of cars were a host of products of varying degrees of complexity. Many of these products used continuous production technology, and product by product, industry by industry, the limit to the economy shifted from the productivity of capital to the productivity of knowledge workers.

Making a lot of product without good information was dangerous. Sears got his start working in a telegraph office. A company delivered a shipment of watches to Sears's railroad stop, only to find that demand was not nearly enough to pay for the shipment. Sears ended up with the product for very cheap. (You don't make money by making a product. You make money by selling it. If the product you make doesn't sell, the inventory of very real goods has no real value.) Sears figured out how to sell the watches through a very simple prototype of his catalog. This catalog did at least two things. One, it helped to stimulate demand simply by making consumers aware of products they couldn't have otherwise known about. Children weren't the only one who could hopefully circle dozens of items in the new catalog. Two, it enabled Sears to sell products before they were made—or at least before they were shipped. Products ordered through a catalog did not have to be made in advance, which lowered costs by minimizing the production of goods that didn't sell. This did so much to define American consumerism that Franklin Delano Roosevelt said that the book that he'd like to send to the Soviet Union was the Sears Catalog. This was the beginning of sales through information, and there was little that Amazon and other websites did later that the Sears catalog had not done earlier in a simpler form. (The Sears catalog enabled products to be represented virtually on the printed page; Amazon's website enabled the printed page itself to be represented virtually, a second layer of abstraction. Wilhelm Humboldt, the man who originated semiotics, or the study of symbols, would have been impressed.)

Continuous production factories represented the culmination of centuries of effort to overcome the limit of capital. Yet the success of these factories shifted the limit of the economy from capital to knowledge work. Capital was so advanced that meeting demand was not a problem; knowledge work was so little advanced, however, that stimulating demand was a problem. Retail stores were one way to help solve it.

Retail: The Limit Shifts to Consumption

It took concerted effort to keep up with these factories. In 1899, Thorstein Veblen wrote *The Theory of the Leisure Class* and introduced the term "conspicuous consumption" to explain the West's seemingly insatiable desire for goods. His book was popular and became one more item people just had to buy. Shopping became serious recreation during the twentieth century.

Marshall Fields and Macy's were the smiling faces of the factories that could easily make more than consumers would buy. The limit to profits no longer came from how much manufacturers could make but, rather, how much retailers could sell. Consumption had to be stimulated so that stores could keep up with factories.

It took the collusion of a great many organizations to stimulate demand, but the retail store was perhaps the most important of these organizations. It is here that we see the attempt to create a utopian world that could be had through easy credit. These stores became gateways to the American Dream.

Department stores had to stimulate interest. One way they did this was through store window displays, but such seemingly innocuous social inventions required behavioral change. Even seemingly obvious things for one generation are not so very obvious to the preceding generation. In the late nineteenth century, it was considered rude to stare into windows, so stores hired professional gawkers whose job it was to stare into store display windows and induce others to do the same. A pioneer in store window displays was L. Frank Baum (1856 to 1919)—better known as the author of *The Wizard of Oz* (1900). Both his books and his window displays invited observers into a magical world that promised to satisfy profound longings. And indeed, the average person from the first economy would have likely found the goods in these department stores as incredible as a tin man or a talking lion. The Marshall Field store in Chicago even had a stained-glass ceiling as beautiful as any cathedral of the first economy. People will aggressively seek out food, shelter, and probably clothing without prompting from any advertising. After that, they need to be made aware of needs as varied as an extra pair of shoes or a smart phone. These stores did just that.

One of the more curious social inventions of this time was Santa Claus. Santa did not just make children happy. He made store owners happy. Santa as we know him—the gift-giving saint who holds court in department stores—did not exist before the factories of the time began to produce more products than the old habits of consumption could keep pace with. Like the display windows, Santa was part of an attempt to create a fairy tale land where consumers were made happy by nearly magical gifts. He also helped to clear out products just before it was time to perform year-end inventory. He did not just give gifts to children. He was a gift to the stores.

Christmas gift giving helped to stimulate sales after the American Civil War. In 1867, "Macy's department store remain[ed] open until midnight Christmas Eve, set[ting] a one-day record of $6,000 in receipts."[187] Around 1870, Christmas made "December retail sales more than twice those of any other month."[188] The fact that stores could sell so many products merely one week before year-end inventories must have truly seemed divine.

In that same year, 1870,

"The United States had the largest economy in the world, and its best years still lay ahead. ... This American system of manufacture had created, for better or worse, a new world of insatiable consumerism, much decried by critics who feared for the souls and manners of common people. The world had long learned to live with the lavishness and indulgences of the rich and genteel; but now, for the first time in history, even ordinary folks could aspire to ownership of those hard goods—watches, clocks, bicycles, telephones, radios, domestic machines, above all the automobile—that were seen in traditional societies as the appropriate privilege of the few. All of this was facilitated in turn by innovations in marketing: installment buying, consumer credit, catalogue sales of big as well as small items; rights of return and exchange. These were not unknown in Europe, which pioneered in some of these areas. It was the synergy that made America so productive. Mass consumption made mass production feasible and profitable; and vice versa."[189]

Other, less obvious inventions, made retail possible. Up until about 1830—again, the time of the railroad—products were essentially sold for whatever prices the market could bear. Yet one innovator, Reuben Vose,

---

[187] Beniger, *The Control Revolution*, 260.

[188] Beniger, *The Control Revolution*,

[189] David S. Landes, The Wealth and Poverty of Nations: Why Some Are So Rich and Some So Poor (New York: Norton, 1999). 307.

who specialized in hats and shoes, introduced a one-price system and listed items in catalogs. Buyers were now dealing with a standard price they could accept or ignore. Not only did Vose win business from the competition, he was able to conduct his business with cash sales rather than through granting credit.[190] People liked set prices over which they didn't have to haggle or puzzle. In a world awash in information, one price for one good—rather than a number of prices that various people might negotiate—made life easier and less stressful.

Advertising, too, helped stimulate consumption while also stimulating advances in information technology.

The Rise of the Media

The viewer tunes in to watch her program and finds the advertising a necessary evil; the advertiser funds the program and makes it possible. For the advertiser, the point is not to entertain the viewer. The advertiser's purpose is to move the viewer to buy. Advertisers are trying to change behavior. Is it any coincidence that in this information age, the medium for advertising is called "programming"?

The audience thinks that it is viewing programming; the advertiser thinks that it is programming viewers. Everyone knows that in this information economy, programming is important. Few stop to realize that consumers were being programmed long before computers existed. As Eli Pariser puts it, "If you are not paying for the service, you are the product being sold."

The media—from newspapers to radio to TV—have been instrumental in creating demand for new products. Like the telegraph that quickly came on the heels of the railroad, one could argue that the initial demand for broadcasting to the masses was driven by advances in manufacturing that required companies to sell more. But of course, these new media drove their own advances in technology that were to further transform the experience of living. They became key to the information economy.

The Nazis used the new technologies of mass media and propaganda

[190] Beniger, The Control Revolution, 159.

for political madness. Specifically, they applied these principles to propaganda and the manipulation of mass media as a tool to create a consensus trance, to define national opinion. Used as a tool for stimulating delusions of world domination, the Nazis caused Germany to self-destruct, killing more than sixty million people before they were done.

The Allies—the United Kingdom and even more so, the United States—used this newfound power of mass psychology for something better. Rather than focus the masses on world domination, they focused the masses on consumption. Advertising, branding, and admonitions to "go shopping" kept the populace focused on the importance of making and spending more money. It was still manipulation of the masses, but it was far more benign.[191]

Other evidence that a new information economy was emerging in the late nineteenth century was the emergence of trademarks and brands. The first trademark legislation was not enacted until the 1870s, and it took three months before anyone availed himself of it. However, the new products that were being generated at unprecedented rates by continuous production needed national markets. "Many of today's best-known brand names—Gold Medal and Pillsbury flour, Kellogg's cornflakes, ..., Borden and Carnation condensed milk, Campbell Soup, Heinz 57 Varieties, Proctor & Gamble soap ... began as trademarks for the fruits of new continuous-processing technology in the 1880s. As a result of massive national advertising campaigns, all had become household words by 1900.[192]

The Availability of Credit

Credit was also a key piece of the puzzle to stimulating consumption. Credit meant that the consumer didn't have to wait to buy something and the retailer did not have to wait to sell it. This new economy depended on credit to stimulate sales to the levels that helped

[191] This contrast in the use of psychology and propaganda is covered in the BBC documentary "The Century of Self."

[192] Beniger, *The Control Revolution*, 269

consumption keep pace with production. Credit fueled expansion, and without credit, the entire system could grind to a halt.

Consumers were engulfed in a sea of easy credit after 1922, with installment buying, charge accounts, and a range of small loans adding up to a multibillion-dollar business. The most liberal credit policies "tended to become the rule."

By the end of the twenties, Marshall Field's charge business had risen to 180,000 accounts—almost double the 1920 figure. In such New York stores as Lord & Taylor, Best's, Abraham & Straus, and Arnold Constable, charge operations made up 45 to 70 percent of their total business. Personal consumer loan departments in city banks opened for the first time, and between 1913 and 1929, the number of regulated small-loan offices increased from 600 to 3,500, with loan balances up six fold. ...[193]

After World War Two, this trend accelerated:

Installment credit [purchasing goods through ongoing payments] fueled the great American consumer engine; it grew from $2.6 billion in 1945 to $45 billion in 1960 and then to $103.9 billion in 1970.[194]

During the second economy, capital had been scarce and bankers derived power from this fact. They did not lightly grant credit or make loans. Through the course of the third economy, credit became abundant and bankers, eager to make loans in order to capture a share of this new market in consumer credit, increasingly had to compete for "sales" of credit just as the retail merchants they financed had to compete for the sales of goods. By the end of the twentieth century consumers were less likely to suffer from bankers' refusal to grant credit than the consequence of having taken on too much credit.

Man is a social being. We can never explain demand by looking only at the physical properties of goods. Man needs goods for communicating with others and for making sense of what is going on around him. The two needs are but one, for communication can only be formed in a system of meanings. His overriding objective as a consumer, put at its most general, is a concern for information about

---

[193] Leach, *Land of Desire*, 299–300.

[194] Robert Manning, *Credit Card Nation: The Consequences of America's Addiction to Credit* (New York: Basic Books, 2000), 38.

the changing cultural scene.

—Mary Douglas

Fashion – An Obvious Social Invention

The purpose of fashion is to stimulate demand. It's a pretty brilliant ploy, really, to compel people who have a perfectly good product to replace it.

The new production methods worked very well for making clothes. In the decades after Crowell's success with continuous production, the textile and garment industry grew about two or three times as rapidly as any other industry. By 1915, in terms of sales, only steel and oil were larger industries than the clothing trade.[195]

"'The way out of overproduction,' wrote one fashion expert, 'must lie in finding out what the woman at the counter is going to want; *make it*, *then* promptly drop it and go on to something else to which fickle fashion is turning her attention.'" Constant change was essential to the prosperity of manufacturers and retailers.[196]

The information economy was rich in symbols used for communication and computing. The genius of fashion is that it made the consumer's goods themselves a symbol, one they would pay dearly to enhance and maintain. In an age that was—at least politically—increasingly democratic, fashion was an important symbol of status, signaling rank. Fashion became fashionable just as aristocracies faded.

The Rise of Information Technology

Computers and the Internet are just the latest version of information technology that began with the telegraph, telephone, and typewriter in

[195] Leach, *Land of Desire*, 93.

[196] Leach, *Land of Desire*, 94.

the nineteenth century.

During medieval times, "A letter sent by the emperor from Aachen to Rome would take two months on the way, and a reply would take just as long."[197] (This trip from Aachen, Germany to Rome is a journey of about 1,500 km and now takes about 14 hours by car, and about 14 nanoseconds by email.) By the end of the third economy, a person in Rome could instantly send a video to anyone in the world. As the symbols that represented the world became more advanced, it was easier to experience the world.

The information age technology that first helped to transform the economic landscape was the railroad's companion, the telegraph. In 1831, the first practical, coal-burning locomotive was introduced. In 1837, the telegraph was first demonstrated and patented, and within about a decade was essential to the railroad.

While experimenting with methods to transmit multiple messages through a telegraph line using tones, Alexander Graham Bell (1847 to 1922) discovered in 1875 that he could transmit voices over wires and used this insight to invent the telephone. Within decades, the telephone displaced the telegraph as the preferred means of business and personal communication.

The railroad, telegraph, and telephone were instrumental in uniting a country as broad and sprawling as the United States without resorting to an imperial government. California, now the largest state in terms of population and economic activity, did not become a part of the United States until 1850, after the railroad and telegraph were already spreading across the continent.

By the 1850s, "railroads [had] come to employ more accountants and auditors than any government, federal or state."[198] In 1868, the "Type-Writer" was patented, and the earliest patent for carbon paper was issued the following year. By 1886, the desk telephone was introduced, and by 1887, a calculating machine was being marketed. Although the present generation of office workers might look at this equipment and these roles as antiquated, they would all be recognizable in form and function. Scott Adams could easily pen a recognizable Dilbert cartoon for this period. In many ways, office equipment developments of the early twentieth century were just improvements of the basic functionality

---

[197] Schulze, *States, Nations and Nationalism*, 5,

[198] Leach, *Land of Desire*, 282, for this and all other facts in the paragraph.

of this early equipment. But then came the computer.

The Invention of the Computer and the Spread of Knowledge

As the world was recovering from World War Two in 1948, Bell Labs announced a product that it thought might "have far-reaching significance in electronics and electrical communication."[199] Three of its employees would eventually share a Nobel Prize for inventing this transistor, a small piece of technology that replaced bulky vacuum tubes and laid the foundation for the world's most rapid increase in technological ability. Perhaps no single invention did more to overcome the limit of information than the transistor.

Of course, turning information from something that limited the economy into something that the economy seemingly slid atop like dress shoes on ice was to take more than this single invention. Most obviously, this transistor was to become a part of a computer chip, where transistors were bundled into many on-off switches that could be used to represent numbers, letters, and, eventually, even pictures and videos.

Furthermore, this hardware was of little consequence without programming—a means to manipulate the transistors into an encoded array that could be used to represent, store, and process information. In that same year, 1948, Claude Shannon coined the word "bit" to begin quantifying information as prelude to it being processed by a machine.

By the 1960s, the transistor was part of a computer chip. The chip was embedded in a sea of information theory that was advancing its design and use in myriad ways. Computer programming was changing how people thought and what it was possible to do with this new chip. And it was this set of technologies – more than typewriters and telephones – that would come to define the information economy. Yet even with the advent of this new technology, something was missing. Technological invention alone is rarely enough; to make real gains from the computer chip required social invention, a change in corporate

---

[199] James Gleick, *The Information* (New York: Pantheon Books, 2011), 3.

culture.

One of the three co-inventors of the transistor began a company to exploit this new technology. He didn't just understand the transistor; he had, after all, helped to create it.

William Shockley was co-inventor of the solid-state transistor and literally wrote the book on semiconductors that would be used by the first generation of inventers and engineers to advance this new technology. He had graduated from the best technical schools in the nation (BS from Cal Tech and PhD from MIT), and was the epitome of the modern knowledge worker.

Shockley hired the best and brightest university graduates to staff his Shockley Semiconductor Laboratory. Yet things were not quite right. It wasn't technology, intelligence, or money that his company was lacking. Something else was missing.

To answer what it was leads us to the question of why information has so much value.

One of the beliefs of pragmatism is that knowledge has meaning only in its consequences. This suggests that information has value only if it is acted upon. That is, information that is stored in secret has no consequences. By contrast, information that informs action—knowledge or belief, as a pragmatist would see it—needs to be both known *and* acted upon. This is information that needs to be distributed. Imagine a stock market with lots of information about companies and the economy but only a handful of people who buy and sell stocks. As long as only the elites act upon the information, that information doesn't have much value to anyone else. Put another way, distributed information has value only when it drives distributed decision making.

So, in order for information to become important, it has to inform important actions. Furthermore, the more people who act on this information, the more valuable it will be.

What was missing from Shockley's approach to this brand new technology was a management style or culture that would make information processing valuable. Largely because of this, it was not Shockley who would become a billionaire from computer chips, but instead, a few of his employees.

The year 1968 was filled with news. Even then it was obvious that it was a historical year. It was something that happened with little fanfare, however, that might have been the most impactful event. The events that did receive notice were hugely important. In January, the North

Vietnamese launched the Tet offensive, making it all the way to the U.S. Embassy in Saigon; this might have been the first indication that those unbeatable Americans might finally be beaten. In the United States, civil rights demonstrations that devolved into deadly riots were the backdrop for Lyndon Johnson's signing of the Civil Rights Act. Martin Luther King, Jr. and Robert Kennedy—iconic figures even in life—were assassinated within months of each other. The musical *Hair* opened on Broadway and Yale announced that it would begin to admit women. For the first time in history, someone saw the earth from space: astronauts Frank Borman, Jim Lovell, and William Anders became the first humans to see the dark side of the moon and the earth as a whole, an image that dissolved differences of borders and even continents. Any one of these stories would have kept modern, twenty-four-hour TV networks busy for an entire year. Any one of these stories could have been enough to change modern society. Yet in the midst of all these incredible events, two entrepreneurs quietly began a company that would transform technology and business, a company that would do as much to define Silicon Valley as any other.

Gordon Moore and Robert Noyce founded Intel in July 1968. Moore gave his name to "Moore's Law," a prediction that the power of computer chips would double every eighteen months. Here was something akin to the magic of compound interest applied to technology or, more specifically, information processing.

Moore and Noyce had originally worked for Shockley, but they left his laboratory because they didn't like his tyrannical management. They then went to work for Fairchild Semiconductor, but left again, because, "Fairchild was steeped in an East Coast, old-fashioned, hierarchical business structure," Noyce said in a 1988 interview. "I never wanted to be a part of a company like that."[200]

It is worth noting that Moore and Noyce didn't leave their former employers because of technology or funding issues. They left because of differences in management philosophy.

Once when I was at Intel, one of the employees asked if I wanted to see the CEO's cubicle. Note that this was an invitation to see his *cubicle,* not his *office*. We walked over to a wall that was—like every other wall on the floor—about five feet high, and I was able to look over the wall into an office area complete with pictures of the CEO

---

[200] Daniel Gross, ed., *Forbes: Greatest Business Stories of All Time* (New York: John Wiley & Sons, 1996), 251.

with important people, like President Clinton. In most companies, one can tell pretty quickly who is higher up in the organization than others; the level of deference and the ease of winning arguments are pretty clear indicators of who is where in the organizational chart. By contrast, I've never been inside a company where it was more difficult to discern rank than Intel. Depending on the topic, completely different people could be assertive, deferential, or argumentative. One of Intel's values is something like "constructive confrontation," and this certainly played out in more than one meeting I attended. When a company makes investments in the billions, it can't afford to make a mistake simply because people have quaint notions about respect for authority. Intel's culture seems to do everything to drive facts and reasons ahead of position and formal authority. This might have partly been a reaction of its founders to the management style of their former employer, Shockley.

The first company they left, Shockely's Labs, no longer exists. The other, Fairchild Semiconductor, lost money last year and has a market cap of about $2 billion, just a fraction of Intel's market cap of more than $110 billion. Intel's net profit in 2010 was over $11 billion, and it employs more than 82,000 people worldwide. The more open culture created by these founders seems to have made a difference.

Information technology has little value in a culture that holds on to information. Information technology makes sense as a means to store, distribute, and give access to information and has value as tool for problem solving and decision making.

The pioneers of information technology, like Moore and Noyce, understood this and realized—at some level—that it made little or no sense to create hierarchies where information was held and decisions were made at one level and people were merely instructed at another. The knowledge worker needed information technology as a basis for decisions and action. Before 1830, up until the time of the railroad, the information sector of the American workforce was less than 1 percent.[201] By the close of the 20th century, everyone seemed to need technology for storing and processing information.

By paying double typical wages, Henry Ford created a new generation of consumers for his car. Moore and Noyce didn't just create information technology; they helped to popularize a management culture that distributed information and decision making, helping to

[201] Beniger, *The Control Revolution*, 23.

create even more demand for their amazing new technology.

Silicon Valley

Silicon Valley didn't just help to create the technology that gave knowledge workers more information. It helped to create the management style that gave them more autonomy about how to use this information. The behavior and the technology—as so often happens—went together. Ex-Shockley employees went on to start about sixty-five different companies in Silicon Valley—a place that was to become the center of attention of the technological world because of its innovations and success in venture capital, popularization of employee stock ownership, and, of course, developments in computer and software technology.

The information economy was never just about technology. Or rather, its technology, like that of the industrial economy before it, forced changes in how people thought, worked, and lived. That is, technological innovation coincided with social innovation. And some cultures are better prepared for change than others.

Decades ago, the *Economist* quipped that what America is to the rest of the world, California is to America, and what California is to the rest of the world, the Bay Area is to California. There did seem to be something to the culture in California—the Bay Area in particular—that lent itself to the inventions that allowed it to be the epicenter of recent technological and business change.

I may be the only one who thinks it is plausible to draw a line through the free speech movement and counterculture movement in the Bay Area of California in the 1960s, the EST seminars and Esalen Institute consciousness raising in the 1970s and 1980s, and then the tech boom in the 1980s and 1990s. What all of these movements have in common is a ridiculous amount of optimism about the extent to which individuals can change the world in order to realize their own potential and express their own individuality. I believe the line connecting these things starts with a kind of reinvention of self and ends with a reinvention of organizations and markets.

I don't pretend to know any place as intimately as I do California. My children are fifth-generation Californians and I've lived in four distinct regions within the state. That said, I don't know of another place on the planet where people seem so full of possibility. People have historically come to California to reinvent themselves. Captain Sutter did much to define northern California (it was in Sutter's fort that the gold was discovered that triggered the gold rush of 1849) but he was not actually a captain. So far from his home in Switzerland, he presented himself as a captain to other Californians and was accepted as such. Doctor Marsh was one of the early, defining characters in Los Angeles but, as you might guess, was not actually a doctor. Like Sutter, he came out to California and reinvented himself.

California is where Marion Morrison from Iowa could come to become John Wayne, or where Norma Mortenson could grow up to become Marilyn Monroe. It is easy to say that Hollywood traffics in illusion, but it reminds us that symbols that have meaning in a culture are not limited to numbers or the alphabet. Lives, too, are symbols, even if they are fictional.

California is also where—for a time in the final decade of the twentieth century, at the end of the third economy—a person could come to invent a new technology, new company, and new market and in the process transform lives everywhere a little bit and transform one's own life incredibly. At the end of the continent, it is a place of invention, and before the stock market bubble burst in 2000, California was "inventing" millionaires at a rate never before seen in history.

What happened in the 1990s in Silicon Valley was not just a perfect storm of technological and social invention: it was a culmination of the forces of the third economy, from financial innovations that treated capital as abundant rather than scarce, to changes in how corporations were founded and run.

The inventions of the third economy include recreational shopping and employee stock options, the MBA degree, and the personal computer. The social inventions that were the most defining, though, were actually part of larger sets of inventions, and each gets its own chapter. This third economy, and the rise of the knowledge worker within it, fed and were fed by the invention of the modern corporation, the transformation of finance, and a change in thinking. A new, American philosophy of pragmatism was to define the world of the third economy, and it, described in the next chapter, would make sense of all of these twentieth-century changes in ways that Enlightenment thinkers never could.

18 Pragmatism

The rise of the third economy meant growing diversity in population and professions. The population within nation-states became more varied in religion, race, and culture. The workforce became more diverse and specialized. These trends demanded a worldview that focused on local and diverse truths rather than universals.

Economy	First	Second	Third	Fourth
Period	1300–1700	1700–1900	1900-2000	2000-2050
Limit to Progress	Land	Capital	Knowledge Workers	Entrepreneurship
Type of Economy	Agricultural	Industrial	Information	Entrepreneurial
Intellectual Revolution	Renaissance	Enlightenment	**Pragmatism**	Systems Thinking
Big Social Invention	Nation-State	Bank	Corporation	Self
Social Revolution	Protestant Revolution	Democratic Revolution	Financial Revolution	Business Revolution

Pragmatism was not adopted in every sector of life, but most politicians and business leaders who make policy and would confess to a philosophy, generally confess to this. Pragmatism is a philosophy better suited to work and challenges of knowledge workers than is Enlightenment philosophy. Its emphasis on specific solutions to specific problems and disregard for universals made it a natural fit for these new specialists.

Introduction

Carl Jung once claimed that a myth is not a myth if it is known to be a myth. To the ancient Greeks, the stories about Zeus and his cohorts weren't beliefs. To them, their gods were real. Only once anthropologists come along from another time or culture could the Greek gods be studied as myths.

When the modern politician or businessman says that he's pragmatic, this is offered as evidence that he is not beholden to some outdated philosophy, is not ideological. To the ancient Greeks, the stories of Zeus and Aphrodite were not myths or literature: they were scriptures that explained why the world was the way it was. In a similar way, throughout the third economy, pragmatism was less often considered a philosophy than simply the way that things were. Pragmatists are generally philosophers who are dismissive of philosophy.

Like glasses we wear, we don't so much see pragmatism as see the world through its lens, to borrow a metaphor from Stephen Covey. Pragmatism is both invisible and obvious, the way that most policy makers and knowledge workers see the world. It's worth reviewing how this came to be.

The four men who seemed to do the most to define pragmatism were Charles Peirce, Oliver Wendell Holmes, William James, and John Dewey. Peirce was the philosopher who inspired the other three, who first laid out the ideas behind Pragmatism. But it was Holmes, Dewey, and James who would redefine law, education, and psychology through the process of furthering Peirce's early work on the philosophy of Pragmatism. Before touching on their contributions, though, it is worth reviewing what their time was like through the life of the man who would show his respect for Pragmatism by granting his most important appointment to one of Pragmatism's founders: Teddy Roosevelt made Oliver Wendell Holmes Chief Justice of the Supreme Court.

"Throughout history, every great expansion of the human mind has revealed to the individual new powers to perceive and change reality." —William James (paraphrased)

Teddy Roosevelt Wrestles with Capitalism

The turn of the twentieth century was an ugly time for the working man. Workplaces were notoriously unsafe. The powerful capital machinery that made so many products could easily tear off a limb or kill a man; this machinery was designed for productivity, not safety. Households sent their children to work instead of school in order to earn enough to pay the bills; given that adults worked six twelve-hour days a week, children seemed to get off easy having to work only nine-hour days. It was not unusual for factories employing young women to require them to live on the factory grounds, and while the constitution may have granted them freedom to easily come and go, their bosses did not. Life was not just harsh. It was ugly. The rapid construction of towns and factories was transforming beautiful, natural landscapes into ugly and polluted scenes. The world was still subordinate to the limit of capital, even though capital was no longer limited. Teddy Roosevelt, however, was not the kind of man to simply acquiesce to these realities.

After Roosevelt had served two terms as president, he retired. One of the first things he did after retiring was to take a hunting trip to Africa, where, in a typical display of Roosevelt energy, he seemed intent on shooting at every animal he saw. He and his son killed about five hundred animals, including seventeen lions, eleven elephants, and twenty rhinos.[202] After the slaughter, he swung by Norway to collect a Nobel Peace Prize and then came back home.

Roosevelt had essentially appointed William Howard Taft as his successor, and when Roosevelt returned he was outraged to see that President Taft had reversed many of his hard-earned gains for labor. Thus, Roosevelt decided to run for president once again.

He actually beat Taft in the Republican primaries. In those days, though, the popular vote was not the final vote. Republican Party

---

[202] http://www.eyewitnesstohistory.com/tr.htm

elders, never really comfortable with Roosevelt even when he wasn't running for an unprecedented third term in opposition to a Republican incumbent, nominated Taft for re-election instead. Roosevelt's response was to start his own party. Then he delivered a speech that for context and content was probably unmatched in the history of American politics.

The 1912 campaign was a four-way race between Republicans, Democrats, Socialists, and Roosevelt's progressive, Bull Moose Party. As in any time of great change, there was great debate about what was next; politics had a little more texture back then.

Like presidents before him, Roosevelt wanted to send troops to intervene in labor strikes. Unlike presidents before him, Roosevelt's intention was not to break up the strike but, instead, to socialize the mines in order to protect the workers. Roosevelt wasn't afraid to take on corporations and capitalists. He wasn't anti-capitalist, but he certainly did not see government's role as simply acquiescing to capitalists' oppression of labor. He seemed to intuit that knowledge work was going to become the new limit, and wanted to subordinate capital to labor; at a minimum, his sense of human decency did not let him ignore labor's plight.

He had done all that as president, but as a candidate he was even more impressive. Even bullets couldn't stop him.

On October 14, 1912, Roosevelt, en route to the Milwaukee auditorium to speak, rose to wave at the crowd and was shot in the chest. This created a fair bit of commotion, as you might imagine. (It's worth remembering that this was the man who became president because of an assassination.) His assistants insisted that he go to the hospital. He spit into a handkerchief and, seeing no blood, concluded that he would live long enough to deliver his speech and ordered them to take him to the auditorium instead.

The audience—this was 1912, a time before cell phones, TVs, or even radio—had no idea that Roosevelt had just been shot until he dramatically opened his suit jacket to show the spread of blood. When his aides saw this, they panicked at the sight of so much blood and again insisted that he rush to the hospital, but he again shook them off. (Now that is a called an attention-getting opening and is much more effective than a joke.)

Roosevelt explained to his audience that his speech was more important than his safety. (And, fortunately, it was a long speech. The sheaf of papers, fifty pages folded over, in his breast pocket was so thick that it slowed the bullet. Had he been delivering a speech as succinct as the Gettysburg Address, he might have died. Fortunately for him, he lived in a time of complexity, at the dawn of the information economy.) He stood up for those who could not defend themselves—women, children, minorities, and even nature. Roosevelt's platform continued his defense of natural beauty (as president, Roosevelt had protected huge swaths of land like Yellowstone and Yosemite from development) and argued for progressive taxation, old-age insurance, regulations on business, an end to racist practices, the abolition of child labor, and woman's suffrage.[203] There were probably no issues that better defined the difference between 1900 and 2000 then the ones that he championed. No third-party candidate before or since got more of the vote and perhaps no candidate better defined politics for the coming century. He lost his bid for a third term, but his issues—his ideas about how the world should be—eventually won.

Roosevelt's politics probably had as much to do with the force of his personality as any philosophy, but his appointment of Oliver Wendell Holmes to the Supreme Court suggested a great sympathy with the philosophy of Pragmatism. That a man who so influenced a new century would be influenced by Pragmatism is reason enough to explore it.

Oliver Wendell Holmes and Legal Pragmatism

Oliver Wendell Holmes thought that judges did not reason their way to conclusions in cases but, instead, had conclusions for which they then developed and offered a rationale. Holmes's instincts accorded with what psychology then and cognitive science now seems to suggest: the unconscious or subconscious mind does much to dictate the direction of consciousness. We are not so much rational as rationalizing.

Holmes's disdain for the idea of the law as something that followed from constitutional proofs in the same unerring manner as equations followed from mathematical proofs was to be the bane of conservative jurists for more than a century. Yet this relative, pragmatic approach to

[203] Eric Rauchway, *Murdering McKinley: The Making of Theodore Roosevelt's America* (New York: Hill & Wang, 2003), 189–90.

law did more to define law through the third economy than did Enlightenment thinking. Conservatives may prefer to avoid the apparent legal complexity that comes from acknowledging the nuance and context of specific cases, but universal laws like "Thou shalt not kill" quickly break down in a world where people argue about whether the definition of killing should include warfare, abortion, capital punishment, or turning animals into meat.

Like business, the law and politics of the third economy were at the very least influenced, and very often defined, by pragmatism. The classic model of legal thinking suggests that precedent from earlier cases is key and that a judge has a responsibility to be consistent with earlier cases, creating a coherent stream of legal decisions. By contrast, the legal pragmatist is more ready to question whether the new context of a new case renders the old finding irrelevant. And the pragmatist is fairly skeptical about whether there are any foundational, or universal, truths that ever apply. A legal pragmatist, like any other pragmatist, believes that specific context is more important than universal truths, and worries less about legal precedent than about the consequence of a particular ruling, judging its truth more by its fruits than by its roots.

Education may have done even more than law to define the third economy, and probably no thinker did more to define American education than the pragmatist John Dewey.

Dewey Is For Doing: Education as Action

Education was an essential and important part of the third economy. Around 1900, an average of one new high school opened every day in America.[204] There was an explosion in the number of schools and, of course, the number of teachers, which created a demand for new ways to think about education.

There is perhaps no one more often referenced in American education than John Dewey, even decades after his death. Dewey got involved in education because of his children. He was so captivated by his son's social intelligence and precocious learning that he regularly sent

[204] Richardson, *William James*, 367.

anecdotes about him to family. Yet this child, Morris, died when he was not quite two and a half. Dewey remained fascinated by the development of children and became horrified at the condition of the schools he saw in Chicago. He began a new school that quickly grew in enrollment and in reputation. The emphasis in this school was on doing as an integral part of learning. For him, stimulus and response, thinking and doing, were all part of a greater whole. Knowledge was what informed action. Dewey's approach to education was very much conducive to the thinking of the new generation of knowledge workers: its emphasis was not on what one knew but on what one could produce or do with what one knew.

John Dewey argued that ideas are simply tools, just like forks: they either work or do not work and have no value beyond their efficacy in use. The fact that a fork doesn't work well for eating soup is no indictment of the fork, just feedback about when you do and don't want to use it. Dewey, in criticizing education, argued that, "knowledge is not just something that we are made conscious of,"[205] but is what we use to understand "what now happens." In other words, knowledge of consequence is something that translates into action and outcomes. Knowledge is how we predict what will happen and, by extension, is what we use to make things happen. The pragmatist is fiercely empirical, more interested in verifiable results than in grand theories, immutable truths, or sweeping generalizations. He isn't looking for a set of universal ideas; he waits until life presents him soup or salad before reaching for a spoon or fork. Ideas are proven by the results one achieves in using them.

There is one element of pragmatism that seems terribly abstract, yet would define much of the information technology. This is the notion that communication is less a function of the signal than of its interpretation.[206] This is seen, to comic effect, when an English-speaking tourist speaks more loudly to the native speaker in hopes of being understood. Clarity and volume are not the issue—it is not that one doesn't *receive* the signal but, rather, that one does not *get* the signal. The problem is one of interpretation, of understanding the signal once it arrives.

When symbols are rich in meaning, knowing how to respond is less a matter of communication than interpretation. This means that the

---

[205] Louis Menand, *Pragmatism: A Reader* (New York: Vintage, 1997), 217.

[206] Beniger, *The Control Revolution,* 86–91.

receiver of the signal has to have prior programming.[207] It does little good for the message to clearly arrive in Spanish when the receiver can't speak Spanish. "Prior programming" in such an example would mean that the person who heard the message would have learned Spanish and could make sense of the message clearly received. In the same way, someone who had not had "prior programming" to make sense of an x-ray or blueprint could do little with it. In social terms, this suggests increasing the emphasis on education. Education, the prior programming of specialists, is key to the creation of knowledge workers. Dewey's emphasis on education may have had its initial catalyst in observation of the son whose development so delighted him, but education in an age of increasing specialization was of huge economic value.

William James: Pragmatism and Pluralism

The nation-state that had eclipsed the church was based on a sense of shared nationality. People who shared a common language, history, culture, religion, race, and culture formed a shared government, or state. One nation made one state.

America was to challenge all this. By the time of the pragmatists, it was obvious that the United States was going to be something different. A melting pot. Jews and Catholics joined the Protestants. Blacks became citizens alongside the whites who had once enslaved them. Germans, Italians, and Chinese, among others, formed communities that often kept their own language and culture.

The idea of one nation was, of course, never a complete reality. Even when Isabella and Ferdinand used the Spanish Inquisition to force religious purity onto the nation, there was still some variety in the population, even if it was only the differences between the dreamers who tilted at windmills and those less infused with dreams of adventure. Yet never had the idea of unity been so challenged as it was after the American Civil War. The universal laws of the Enlightenment that seemed to assume sameness in the population were proving inadequate.

---

207 Beniger, *The Control Revolution*, 90.

For this new reality, William James seemed to offer the perfect antidote. His personality and thinking were wonderfully inclusive. He was a boyhood friend of Oliver Wendell Holmes (the two were ten months apart), and shared Holmes' sensibilities in regards to truth. So many of his contemporaries were dismissive of religions other than their own or simply dismissive of all religions. James baffled both groups by taking an unconventional look at religion. Rather than argue about which faith offered access to heaven and which led to hell—propositions for which there was no proof—James judged belief based on what it produced in this life. If a particular faith made someone happier or more compassionate, it was true. It made a difference. James was not interested in the universal truths that were the goals of Enlightenment thinkers and most religious people. Rather than a world of universals, William James's world was "a universe of eaches."[208]

William James became a bit of an activist when the United States followed up its defeat of Spain in the Philippines by rejecting the efforts of Filipino nationalists and imposing on the country an American-sanctioned government. James thought that this approach ignored what was different about the Filipino culture and showed a dangerous blend of arrogance and ignorance, suggesting as it did that there was only one right way to govern. People are different, he noted, and that is not something to struggle to overcome but to accept.

William James's younger brother was the novelist Henry James. Their parents had raised them on both sides of the Atlantic, seemingly making the children's education (there were four boys and a girl in the family) the focus of their lives. James had been exposed to European culture and had lived in a variety of countries and spoke a number of languages. His brother Henry lived in Europe for most of his adult life, and William returned there frequently.

James's embrace of pluralism—whether through a variety of religious experiences, or the defense or embrace of other cultures—was fundamental to his philosophy. He lived in a time when the United States was becoming far more varied and talk of racial purity was not something limited to a fringe group in white robes, but was something discussed openly. The pragmatist's embrace of variety was to become an important part of redefining what was meant by nation-state. It was also an important part of redefining work.

---

[208] Richardson, *William James*, 4.

The Philosophy of the Knowledge Worker: Will Think for Cash

The question for pragmatists was not whether an idea was universally true. The question for them was what approach or idea or tool worked best in the specific situation in which they found themselves.

Less interested in the universal truths that Newton's mind gravitated towards, pragmatists articulated the philosophy of specialists who had specific problems to solve in a particular context. Veterans of a war between opposing worldviews, they were suspicious, if not entirely dismissive, of claims of universal or absolute truths.

It is worth considering how James's insistence upon the nature of reality being something rich, complex, diverse, and even contradictory might play with the information economy that was emerging as he helped to invent pragmatism. James rejected the notion of abstract concepts capturing reality, but in a world before books, simplifications were all one might reliably carry in one's head. James published his book *Pragmatism* in the century that brought the world the Internet; massive amounts of memory and easy access to it made it possible to respect massive diversity in practice. In a sense, pragmatism's embrace of diversity enabled and was enabled by the information technology of the time. This might be one reason that James's former student and fellow professor, George Santayana, said of him that "He had a prophetic sympathy with the dawning sentiments of the age, with the moods of the dumb majority. His scattered words caught fire in many parts of the world. His way of thinking and feeling represented the true America, and represented in a measure the whole ultramodern, radical world."[209]

Even as James' and Holmes were defining pragmatism around 1900, some dismissed pragmatism as a tool for knowledge workers rather than a real philosophy. European critics claimed that pragmatism was "typically American, 'a theory for engineers'—minds limited to action and deaf to ideas."[210]Although James's book sold well when it initially came out, he was surprised by the reaction of the philosophical community, which "ranged from doubtful and grudging partial acceptance to derisive and hostile rejection."[211] Yet these critics seemed

---

[209] Richardson, *William James*, 495.

[210] Barzun, From Dawn to Decadence, 667.

[211] Richardson, *William James*, 493.

to miss the point.

It was no secret that this philosophy was related to the economy, to business. Pragmatism is a progressive philosophy, looking forward to consequences rather than backwards at sources of authority, tradition, or ideology. Disregarding the search for principles that had characterized the work of Enlightenment philosophers, William James felt that the truth or validity of any belief lay in its use. "What is the *cash-value* in terms of practical experience?"[212] James asked, raising a question that has been echoed by corporate scientists and managers perhaps a million times since.

James argued that, "Compared with what we ought to be, [we] are only half awake."[213] He felt that while ideas like "Fatherland," Holy Church," "Science," or "Liberty" might seem vague, they could give people more energy. In a sense, he was arguing that the right social inventions could help to unleash the individual's potential.

For the Enlightenment philosopher, the holy grail of thought might best be represented by the laws of physics as articulated by Newton—the laws of gravity, or "For every action there is an equal and opposite reaction." For the pragmatist, the holy grail of thought might be articulating the legal argument that wins a case before the Supreme Court or writing computer code that becomes a best-selling application. The pragmatist lives in a shifting world and doesn't really expect to trip over any universal or eternal truths. The consequence of an idea, what it allows, is what verifies its truth. This is one of the reasons that pragmatism has become the dominant philosophy in circles where it matters—knowledge workers, like scientists, designers, and policy-makers (whether in government or business) are all pragmatists, and they are the ones who have defined the modern world.

The Third Economy: No Place for Certitude

Oliver Wendell Holmes was a veteran of the American Civil War. Holmes had been shot. More than once. No war killed more Americans, with

[212] Menand, Pragmatism: A Reader, xiv.

[213] Richardson *William James*, 489.

casualties totaling between 600,000 and 700,000.[214] Witnessing this carnage, Holmes, and his friend James had become cynical about ideologies so absolute that they could be resolved only through war. Holmes, in particular, was a "skeptic of doctrines and ideologies. ... He blamed the [Civil] war on the American tendency toward ideological certainty, systematically destroyed all his youthful letters advocating abolition, and for the rest of his life sought to undermine fervent ideologies of all stripes."[215]

Furthermore, conviction that one was right seemed to fail to capture the truth of a world of dynamic change. Late in the nineteenth century, for perhaps the first time in history, people experienced change and progress as a regular occurrence. We talk today about great change and political disagreements, but faster and smaller computers coupled with strident disagreement between conservatives and liberals pales in comparison to the complexity of the world around 1900. In the political sphere, it was not just progressives and conservatives who battled for minds: communists and anarchists were not the marginalized creatures they are today, but actually overthrew and formed governments, assassinated world leaders, and started world wars. Technological innovations, like cars and telephones did more to change thought and behavior than did any computer application we have today. And the sweeping changes affecting society at this time were not limited to the political world or technology. About this time, the ideas of Darwin were gaining credence, suggesting that even species were not stable. This was enough to make one doubt certainty on any topic.

It is no wonder that James would write, "There is no such thing as certitude. What there is is only men who are certain." The philosophy of the third economy had to be as dynamic as the times in which people found themselves.

The masses were less sanguine about a world of such ambiguity and change. Pragmatism may have been useful, but it was not always comforting. It seems hardly surprising that in the midst of this time of tumult, the General Assembly of the Presbyterians declared the Bible to be "without error" in 1892, essentially starting the fundamentalist movement. The Catholic Church had, in 1870, made the claim of papal infallibility. The reaction of many in the face of so much change and uncertainty was to cling more tightly to what they "knew." Pragmatism

---

214 http://www.civilwarhome.com/casualties.htm

215 Nace, *The Gangs of America*, 129.

did not offer comfort; it offered progress.

The engineer and modern professional is neither a Renaissance nor an Enlightenment thinker. By the end of the twentieth century, the dominant way of thinking was pragmatism, a philosophy at one and the same time invisible and obvious, as characterizes any period's dominant philosophy.

These knowledge workers and their new philosophy of pragmatism would find their natural home in the most recent of the big social inventions; the next chapter tells about the invention of the corporation.

19 Inventing the Corporation

The corporation became home to knowledge workers and turned out to be a social invention that facilitates technological invention. On top of this, it proved to be a remarkable new investment.

Economy	First	Second	Third	Fourth
Period	1300–1700	1700–1900	1900-2000	2000-2050
Limit to Progress	Land	Capital	Knowledge Workers	Entrepreneurship
Type of Economy	Agricultural	Industrial	Information	Entrepreneurial
Intellectual Revolution	Renaissance	Enlightenment	Pragmatism	Systems Thinking
Big Social Invention	Nation-State	Bank	**Corporation**	Self
Social Revolution	Protestant Revolution	Democratic Revolution	Financial Revolution	Business Revolution

The bank was made to manage capital, not knowledge workers: for that task, the West invented the modern corporation. While the modern university also emerged in response to the need for knowledge workers, it was the corporation where the efforts of these knowledge workers was translated into new products and wealth, becoming a vehicle for raising economies to a new, unprecedented level of affluence.

Today's Dominant Institution

As I write this in early in the second decade of the twenty-first century, governments everywhere are struggling to stay financed. Riots in Greece, Spain, and France have been triggered by planned budget cuts. Here in California, the state once again faces budget shortfalls of billions, and officials are threatening to cut everything from funding for regional development and mental health, education and health care. Kindergarten teachers and university professors anxiously await layoff notices. The only difference between Democrats, Republicans, and Tea Party candidates is the extent to which they're seriously planning to cut government spending. Once again, experts are projecting a federal government deficit of about $1.5 trillion—an amount greater than the gross domestic product of all but the ten largest countries, and more government spending than in any other country but China, an amount so large that the negotiations to lift the debt limit in D.C. include threats of default.

Meanwhile, the Fortune 500 corporations are holding on to $2 trillion in cash. To put that in perspective, this is an amount roughly equal to the annual gross domestic product of countries like Brazil, the United Kingdom, France, and Italy. While governments struggle, corporations are making record profits and have record dollar reserves.

Business is the animating force in the West, and its high church is the corporation. No institution is more powerful. What the state did to the church centuries ago, the corporation has done to every other institution in the West; it has eclipsed them all in importance. One simply can't understand modern culture or society without understanding the corporation.

What is most remarkable about this is that the modern multinational corporation did not exist 150 years ago. During the third economy, we became organizational men. By 2000, over 90 percent of the work force worked for someone else; in 1800, only 20 percent did. In 2000, over half of employees worked for organizations with 500 or more employees; in 1800, none did.[216]

---

[216] Charles Perrow, Organizing America: Wealth, Power, and the Origins of Corporate Capitalism (Princeton, NJ: Princeton University Press, 2002), 1.

In 1800, the modern corporation did not exist. By 2000, it had transformed the experience and definition of work, shopping, entertainment, investing, ownership, culture, and power.

The corporation was invented to do two things. First, it allowed for a new kind of investment and ownership, a system that had fabulous advantages over traditional partnerships and family businesses. Second, it was a means to create and manage the new limit to progress: like no institution before it, the corporation was made to overcome the limit of knowledge workers. This put the corporation at the center of the new information economy and was to make it—within about a century—the newly dominant institution in the West. No country more fully gave itself over to the singular power of the corporation, and no country prospered more, than the United States.

The Rise of the Corporation

In 1800, the economy was largely the world that Adam Smith described and classical economists to this day imagine: a world in which the invisible hand of the market guides the actions of individuals. Farmers, artisans, and small shops created economic goods. Only the rich "had it made," while most people made their own—from clothes to food to houses.

In 1800, not a single employee anywhere in the country worked for an organization of five hundred or more. By 1900, there were 512,000 factories, each employing thousands; in 1913, Henry Ford employed 12,000 in a single factory. "'The American boy of 1854,' Henry Adams wrote, 'stood nearer the year 1 than the year 1900.' Change on a scale unimaginable to that boy began after the Civil War, and the corporation was its carrier." [217]

There was, until late in the Industrial Revolution, no reason to adopt bureaucracies of any sophistication. "As late as the 1830s, for example, the Bank of the United States, the nation's largest and most complex institution with twenty-two branch offices and profits fifty times those of the largest mercantile house, was managed by just three people."[218]

As communities overcame the limit of capital, however, technological

---

[217] Beatty, *Colossus*, 127.

[218] Beniger, *The Control Revolution*, 14.

invention began to create scope and complexity that outstripped the resources and ability of family businesses or partnerships. The corporation became a preferred means for housing this innovation, and soon it became the breeding ground for a host of new products. The list of innovations from around 1900 includes central heating; the safety razor; stainless steel implements; the electric toaster, iron, and oven; the sewing machine; the dishwasher; the electric elevator; the dial phone; the portable typewriter; radium treatment for breast cancer; heart surgery; the psychiatric clinic; contact lenses; toothpaste in tubes; motion pictures; musical comedy; the gramophone; volleyball and basketball; the Ferris wheel; the jukebox; the striptease; breakfast cereals; milk delivered in bottles; packaged produce; Coca-Cola; margarine; the ice cream cone; the refrigerator; public libraries; the correspondence course; the full-range department store; the chain store; the shopping center; the coin telephone; the traveler's check; fingerprinting; the automatic pistol; the electric chair; the automobile and the airplane; the underground city subway train; the pneumatic tire; color photography; rayon and other artificial textiles; and chewing gum.[219] One hardly knows whether to be empathetic or aghast that in the midst of this explosion of innovation, the commissioner of the Federal Office of Patents would declare, in 1899, "Everything that can be invented has been invented."

If patent law was catalyst to technological invention, the corporation institutionalized it.

The corporation was invented as a means to manage work that was more complex than it had ever been. It was also invented to be an investment as offered by no bank or bond before it. This work of social invention redefined law and society.

Managing (Knowledge) Work

Adam Smith wrote of the invisible hand of the market as the means to direct the actions of individuals. The consumer gravitates towards the cheaper or better bread, the employee towards the better-paying or more gratifying job, the investor towards higher returns or less risk. If plumbers get rich, more people will become plumbers. If people who

[219] Barzun, *From Dawn to Decadence*, 602.

own Qualcomm stock get rich, more people will buy Qualcomm stock. Consumers want products for the cheapest price and producers want to sell them for the highest possible price. Throw in competition between consumers for scarce products and prices go up; throw in competition between producers and prices fall. The tension between supply and demand, between the greed for profits and the greed for bargains, creates market dynamics and occasional equilibriums. We respond to markets. Smith brilliantly described a force that continues to influence communities to this day.

Yet something happened on the way to our current reality. The underlying dynamic of markets became muted by the emergence of complexity, large organizations, and diversity. Adam Smith's invisible hand of markets was—in many instances—replaced by Alfred Chandler's visible hand of management. Observing corporations, Chandler pointed out that, "Much basic economic theory is still grounded on the assumption that the processes of production and distribution are regulated by the invisible hand of the market." [220] The corporation is – within limits – a substitute for the market. The corporation tends to mitigate market forces into something more tempered and controlled. (If you think this is an exaggeration, imagine a world in which your hourly wage or the price you pay for a meal at your favorite restaurant were to change, hour by hour or day by day, as rapidly as do commodity or stock prices.)

The rise of the corporation was transformational for many reasons. From about the time of the Venetians into the 1800s, the family was the most important business unit.[221] However, the family is too small to perform all the work needed in larger corporations, and, of course, the talents, potential, and inclinations of any particular family are unlikely to match those needed to run a modern corporation of any size or sophistication. To create a more sophisticated economy with more specialization and complexity meant that people had to trust strangers. The corporation became one very important means to create such trust. As markets became larger—something for which railroads were most obviously the cause—work became more specialized. This increased specialization created a demand for the type of organizational complexity that the corporation provided.

---

[220] Alfred D. Chandler Jr., *The Visible Hand: the Managerial Revolution in American Business* (Cambridge, Mass.: Harvard University Press, 1977), 4.

[221] Beniger, *The Control Revolution*, 128.

Chandler focused his study on industry in the 1800s, with a particular emphasis on the railroad. To say that the railroad was the Internet of its time might underestimate the extent to which the railroad disrupted and changed the old economy. The railroad was the impetus behind time zones—standardizing time into a few zones rather than leaving each little burg to define its own, local time. The railroad made it possible for one factory to make goods to distribute to many states. One could argue that the railroad, by linking states, made the United States a national market for the first time, and was at least indirectly a catalyst for the Civil War, as the industrialists in the north clashed with the plantation owners in the south over whether it was the "United" or the "States" that had primacy in this new country. For the north, the united mattered most because their rich and powerful were selling, managing, and producing across state lines in regional and national markets. In the south, the states mattered most because their rich were landed, using less-developed technology, and their production was focused locally. Yet Chandler argues that the way that the railroad most transformed society was through the inventions in management and organization that it forced.

There was nothing like a few train wrecks to convince the railroad management that they needed a good way to coordinate work. (This was one reason for the drive towards standardized time zones: "What do *you* mean by 3 o'clock?") The railroad was the first business to force managers to deal with the problem of managing work that they could not *literally* oversee.

A railroad that connected two cities hundreds of miles apart by its very definition had employees spread further apart than line of sight. Among the many inventions of the railroad was the middle manager: a person who managed one group while reporting to yet another manager. Having to manage workers the manager couldn't see—even if it was through a middle manager—did much to drive the information age. Previously, managers could simply see what was being done in the shop or factory. Suddenly, they needed reports—that is, they needed information—to manage work and workers. For them, the representation of work became as important as the work itself.

This need for reporting was a big catalyst for the information economy. (And of course, this far into the information economy we simply don't believe that anything undocumented actually happened. If we don't see the pictures on Facebook, we don't believe that you had a good time. If we don't see the grade, we don't believe you learned the subject. If we don't see the weekly report, we don't believe that you did the task.

Is it any wonder that undocumented workers are the cause of such offense?) As work became more abstract and was coordinated across more and more people, the ability to symbolically represent work—in the form of pictures, words, and data—became more important.

Eventually, tasks became too complex to be done by just one person, and complex projects could involve hundreds. This made something once rare or unknown relatively common.

Distributed Cognition and the Development of the Corporation

Distributed cognition refers to a particular dimension of specialization. Simply put, it means that the knowledge about how to do a task is spread between more than one person or machine. No one person knows how to make a computer, for instance.

One of the pioneers in the field of distributed cognition is Professor Ed Hutchins, at the University of California at San Diego (UCSD). He often articulates the notion of distributed cognition through the example of the observation of a Navy battleship group running war game simulations. No one person can effectively observe, coordinate, or act alone on that ship. And many of the participants in the drill can't even do their tasks without some tool or instrument—for example, the operator is not able to "hear" the objects in the water without the sonar equipment. The cognition that drives decisions and actions is distributed among many people and things.

The modern world is full of such examples. Knowledge workers regularly create "products" that have no value on their own. Think about a junior architect who designs the door trim for a house. Without the workers who actually build the house—not to mention the other designers who design the floor plan that includes the doorways—the value of this junior architect's work is zero. It is only within the context of the rest of the architectural firm and even the construction crew that the junior architect's work has value or even makes sense.

Knowledge work needs—at a minimum—hands or machines to actually turn the knowledge into products or services that ultimately create value. Typically, one knowledge worker needs another. The junior architect needs the drafter, the building engineer, and the inspector—

among others—to collaborate with her.

Before about 1860, the skilled artisan could do all of the work required to make a product, but once industrialists broke the limit of capital, the scope and complexity of work greatly increased. Distributed cognition has become the new norm for modern work.

Work of this nature drove the need for new ways of organizing and the invention of the corporation was a response to this new reality. The corporation was able to coordinate and organize work that was distributed across different people, different skill sets, and different knowledge bases.

As Alfred Chandler points out, the corporation grew in response to the complication of work that came along with the evolution from manufacturing work into knowledge work. Rather than the invisible hand of markets coordinating this work, it was the visible hand of management that now coordinated work.

Ronald Coase won a Nobel Prize in economics for explaining why organizations rather than markets emerged as a means to organize work. Simply put, his theory is that the information costs were too high to justify one-on-one transactions, and it was more efficient to establish companies as a means to organize work instead. Take the example of the guy who wants to buy a burrito. Imagine that each time he wanted to get a burrito for lunch he had to find the guy who made and sold tortillas, then the guy who made and sold beans, and so on for carnitas, guacamole, salsa, and whatever other ingredients he wanted. And then to top it all off, he had to hire someone to assemble all of this into a burrito. Not only would this be a terribly complex task to perform over the course of his lunch break, but the guy who would have to perform the few minutes of burrito assembly would likely charge him for a full hour's work, since it would take him that long to get there and back—and this does not even factor in the place and the tools (the capital) that would be needed to perform all this. A burrito in this scenario might cost hundreds of dollars and take hours to procure. It is much simpler for a customer to just go to the local taco shop, where all the knowledge, the labor, and the capital are pooled into one place, under one manager, and where our hungry hero can buy the burrito for, say, $6 instead. The cost to find each person and item involved in making the burrito is too high. And of course, the average person can actually assemble a burrito (assuming that he doesn't have to raise the chickens, grow the beans and rice, etc.), something he can't do with a really complex product like, say, a number 2 pencil. By about 1900, many products had become too complex for any one person to make. By early in the twenty-first century, many products had become too complex for any one *company* to make, as outsourcing became more and more common. Complexity makes it challenging to coordinate production through one-off market exchanges, or single transactions. It is easier to set up a company and then manage such tasks and transactions (or as they are called within the corporation, process steps). Coase's thesis is that information and transaction costs were higher than the cost of institutionalizing these activities. So, instead of market transactions for each task or project, organizations were formed to turn potentially sporadic transactions into relatively stable processes.

In 1800, individual farmers or artisans conducted most economic activity. By 2000, corporations conducted most economic activity. Rather than being left to markets, work was managed. It was, as shown by Coases's analyses, too expensive to orchestrate all of this by market forces alone.

The corporation did not just rise in prominence along with knowledge work that drove the phenomenon of distributed cognition. The corporation also emerged as an investment uniquely suited to the new realities.

The Corporation as an Investment

To discuss the corporation as an investment is to again return to the railroad.

Prior to the information age, businesses were owned by the managers and managed by the owners. That is, the investors and managers were the same people, a model seen in many small businesses even today. The railroad, by contrast, required too much financial capital to be funded by just one person or even a few partners. Outside investors had to be brought in to provide enough funding to lay down hundreds of miles of track. By necessity, the railroad's owners did not manage the railroad.

Nor did the managers own the railroad. The railroads meant the introduction of a new level of complexity and sophistication—and therefore the introduction of formal reports and layers of management.

Running a railroad required a mix of special skills, focus, talents, and experience that most investors did not have. Professional managers quickly became a necessity.

The railroad thus became the first industry to do what would become the norm within a century: it created a schism between investors and managers. It wasn't just that it was impractical for owners to also manage. The corporation itself had become divorced from the owners. In 1819, Daniel Webster successfully argued for the immortality of the corporation in *Dartmouth College vs. Woodward*. Before Webster moved at least one judge to tears with his eloquence, the identity of corporations had been tied up with individuals. If an owner died, so did the company. In the first economy, the nation-state was made immortal by the cry, "The king is dead! Long live the king!" Daniel Webster did something similar for the corporation. Noah Webster (no relation) may have helped to define American English with his dictionary, but Daniel Webster helped to define what would become the next century's most powerful institution when he persuaded the court that the corporation did not die with any one person.

Limited Liability and Joint Stock

One technical name for the modern corporation is a limited liability / joint stock firm. The combination of these two features did much to contribute to the success of corporations.

Limited liability had previously existed, but the British crown granted it only for public works like colonizing or foreign trade. It was not until the 1820s that the practice became widespread, and it required decades of legal and economic experimentation for this to become common for strictly private companies.[222]

Limited liability matters because it makes it possible for outside investors to put money into a firm that they don't manage. What it means is that you are liable for the expenses or damages of a firm—but only up to the amount that you've invested. An investor is hesitant enough to put money into a business he is not a part of when he

[222] Beatty, *Colossus*, 45.

knows that he can lose all the money he invests. Think of how much more hesitant he would be if he thought that he could be sued for assets he did not invest. Imagine someone buying $10,000 worth of stock in a company and suddenly finding herself liable for millions in the aftermath of a lawsuit on asbestos, for instance. By limiting liability, these big, new, complex businesses could attract outside investors. Although with limited liability one could lose a dollar for every dollar invested, one could never lose $100 for every dollar invested. This feature of the corporation was a huge boon to investment.

The new, complex businesses also required more money than could be provided by a single investor. In fact, they required joint investment. The joint stock clause meant that investors could pool their money into enough capital to build large factories, lay down hundreds of miles of track, or hire tens of thousands of employees. Joint stock firms could do what no single investor could.

Joint stock—or publicly traded—companies were able to achieve a scale never before accomplished. Breaking the limits of capital triggered the creation of ventures with a huge appetite for capital, built on a scale that Adam Smith could hardly have imagined. Adam Smith thought that joint-stock status was justified for only three types of ventures: canals, banks, and insurance companies, and that any other venture could be funded by an individual or partnership. Yet companies producing thousands of *tons* of steel *daily* would have likely been inconceivable to Smith and his contemporaries. Once business had overcome the limit of capital, Smith's special case investments were not the only ones that needed joint investors. Joint investment increasingly became the norm.

In 1862, British Parliament passed the Company Act and invented the limited-liability, joint-stock company. John Micklethwait and Adrian Wooldridge called it "yet another quirky Victorian invention that changed the world." [223] Meanwhile, in the United States, once the south had seceded and the northern industrialists were left to rule congress without interference, they aggressively passed a host of legislation that made the corporation stronger and better defined. Individual states soon began passing legislation that imitated that "quirky Victorian invention." Together, the limited liability / joint stock clauses meant the invention of a completely different kind of institution.

---

[223] John Micklethwait and Adrian Wooldridge, *The Company: A Short History of a Revolutionary Idea* (New York: Modern Library, 2003), xiv.

Going Public

J. P. Morgan became the embodiment of a financier, with his top hat, large vested belly, walking stick that seemed more like a scepter than cane, bulbous nose, and air of someone used to getting his own way. He helped to sell government bonds into European markets after the American Civil War and later got involved in the railroad market. Yet Morgan didn't much care for competition: he saw it as wasteful and as an obstacle to profits. So he helped to establish trusts, which began as agreements between businesses to carve out markets and fix prices, and often resulted in actual mergers.

Through the course of one historic golf game in 1901, Morgan convinced Andrew Carnegie to sell his steel company to him for $480 million. Carnegie apparently had no plans to sell at the outset of this game but could not refuse an offer that would make him the world's richest man. While Carnegie retired to a life of philanthropy, Morgan went on to form US Steel, with Carnegie's steel company at the core. US Steel was the world's first billion-dollar corporation, with a public valuation of $1.4 billion. "A similar deal done today, expressed as the same proportion of GNP, would approach half a trillion dollars."[224] That is roughly the combined market value of Google, Amazon, Apple, and Facebook in 2011. Put into the context of the times, "the federal government, with an annual budget of about $350 million and a debt of slightly more than $1 billion, seemed small by comparison."[225]

Morgan's deal with Carnegie proved to be a turning point. From that point forward, public rather than private ownership would characterize America's notable firms. The conclusion was that "Morgan engineered an extraordinary change. The total amount of capital in publicly traded manufacturing companies increased from $33 million in 1890 to more than $7 billion in 1903."[226] Much of this was the result of consolidation; "1,800 corporations were consolidated into 157 between 1898 and 1904."[227]

---

[224] Micklethwait and Wooldridge, *The Company,* 70.

[225] Smith, *The History of the Global Stock Market*, 92.

[226] Micklethwait and Wooldridge, *The Company*, 69–70.

[227] Joel Bakan, *The Corporation: The Pathological Pursuit of Profit and Power* (New York: Free Press, 2004), 14.

Corporations as a Legal Construct

This British innovation resulted from debate on both sides of the Atlantic and quickly spread to France and Germany, where legislators imitated its form and investors were quick to reward the firms that adopted it. Limited liability was introduced to the United States during the late nineteenth century, at different times in different states.[228]

After 1890, law in the United States began to give corporations even more freedom. Before this time, a corporation would have to apply for each change in business. States had "rules that required businesses to incorporate only for narrowly defined purposes, to exist only for limited durations, and to operate only in particular locations."[229] Delaware and New Jersey were the first states to repeal these rules and give corporations more flexibility. After this point corporations became free and no longer had to subordinate their judgment to government approval. Ted Nace does a nice job of defining the differences between the corporation before 1860 and after 1900, and those differences are captured in this table.

The following table contrasts the classic corporation (before 1860) and the modern corporation (after 1900).[230]

---

[228] Bakan, *The Corporation,* 13.

[229] Bakan, *The Corporation,* 14.

[230] Nace, *Gangs of America*, 71.

Attribute	Classic Corporation	Modern Corporation
Birth	Difficult: required a custom charter issued by a state legislature	Easy: general incorporation allowed automatic chartering
Life Span	Limited terms	No limits
"Shape-shifting"	Corporations not allowed to own stock in other companies; restricted to activities specified in charter	Corporations free to pursue acquisitions and spin-offs and develop new businesses
Mobility	Usually restricted to home state	No restrictions. Not even to the home country.
Adaptability	Restricted to activities specified in charter	Allowed to pursue multiple lines of business and to initiate or acquire new ones at company's discretion
"Will"	Management action hampered by legal status of minority shareholders and of corporate agents	Legal revisions enabled consolidation of management's power

The railroad did more than expand markets and encourage the consolidation of production into larger and larger factories. Because the railroad spanned states, it, in a sense, outgrew the limits of state legislatures to regulate a company. Before we had the multinational corporation, we had the multi-state corporation. And while the railroads seemed to exercise the most influence in changing state laws regulating corporations, companies from a wide variety of industries benefited from the new laws.

The list of companies emerging around the turn of the century to take advantage of these new conditions included "Borden, Heinz, Pillsbury, Coors, Anheuser-Busch, Edison, Gillette, Lipton, Nestle, De Beers, [and] Montgomery Ward."[231]

This gave the modern multinational corporation a different kind of power than the Dutch or British East India Companies.

The East India Companies ruled parts of India. They were, in a sense, a profit-generating arm of the state. They had many of the powers of the state and in a world before messages could quickly move from Europe to Asia, they had authority to act. Today's corporations don't have the kind of power that lets them overthrow governments or fight indigenous people for land (at least, not formally). Yet in the late 1800s, legislation made them independent of the state. In this sense, today's corporations have more autonomy than did the corporations of old.

Previously, corporations were dependent on the state for even something as simple as a change in charter. If you had applied to be a corporation selling apples at the corner of Fifth and Broadway, you couldn't decide to begin selling apples at the corner of Maple and Endicott, or magazines at the same Fifth and Broadway location. Corporations today have far greater autonomy, and are able to change their charter from, say, selling lemonade to selling private jets without needing to create a new corporation. While corporations may not have the same kind of power as they did when the Dutch and British East India Companies conquered and ruled India, they do have freedom to pursue their own goals, independent of any national objectives. The British East India Company was British; BP no longer is.

Their autonomy allows corporations to be responsive. Ford once dominated the auto industry but was surpassed by William Durant at General Motors. Ford *knew* which one car was best for America. Durant was uncertain and instead offered Americans a variety of brands and models. As it turns out, this flexibility was hugely valuable. As William James might have reminded Henry Ford, there is no such thing as certitude, only people who are certain.

It is worth remembering that any form of corporation is just made up, is a social invention. It was not just within the legislature that it was invented. The courts, too, are a place where someone can make a

---

231 Barzun, *From Dawn to Decadence*, 598.

declaration akin to, "this meeting is adjourned" and then judges can determine whether the statement is true or not, whether or not the invention is successful.

Daniel Webster's definition of the corporation held. His argument before the Supreme Court left Chief Justice John Marshall to offer the opinion that the corporation was,

"an artificial being, invisible, intangible, and existing only in contemplation of the law." Among the corporation's properties "are immortality; and if the expression is allowed, individuality; properties by which a perpetual succession of many persons are considered as the same."[232]

Invisible? Immortal? My argument is that the corporation took the place of dominance earlier held by the church; reading this, however, one might think that it, instead, had taken on the powers of a god.

The corporation did not just emerge unchecked. Probably the most famous attempt by American legislators to limit corporate power was the Sherman anti-trust legislation that broke up monopolies of the kind that Morgan liked to create as a means to avoid unprofitable competition. The social inventors who helped to create the modern corporation did not quietly submit to it, and already assumed that they operated outside of state control. John Davison Rockefeller dismissed the legislation, saying "Senator Sherman's bill is of a very radical and destructive character, proposing to fine and imprison all who directly or indirectly participate in organizations *over which it is even doubtful whether Congress holds any jurisdiction.*"[233] [italics added]

Rockefeller saw the autonomy of the corporation as something that transcended not just the laws of states, but even the laws of countries. In this sense, Rockefeller may have been among the first to realize the future possibility of the multinational corporation as an institution that was no longer subject to any state.

---

[232] Beatty, *Colossus*, 83–84.

[233] Ron Chernow, *Titan: The Life of John D. Rockefeller, Sr.* (New York: Random House, 1998), 298.

How the Corporation Defines Our Modern World

No institution defines our world more than the corporation. There are so many signs of the dominance of the corporation that one hardly knows where to begin. It is tempting to simply say, "Look around you." Nobody says, "We should run the government more like a church." If you want to be rich and powerful, you become a CEO, not a president. (Well, unless you live in Africa or the Middle East, where social development is such that the nation-state still is the most dominant institution.)

Corporations define politics. Literally. People get their news from sources like Fox, or MSNBC, or NPR – each a corporation. Corporations own the media, and their hired employees define politicians, inspire hope or despair, and investigate or ignore the true nature of an administration's policies or a political group's platform. They decide what minutia is worth repeatedly broadcasting and which big issues are repeatedly ignored. Our news is not defined by many people; it is defined, packaged, and delivered by a few corporations.

Corporations define what is fashionable and what is obsolete or silly. They entertain us, dress us, feed us, and care for us when we're in preschool, in old age homes, and—increasingly—in K—12 education. The occupations in Iraq and Afghanistan engage more corporate employees than government soldiers.

Corporations create wealth and define how it is shared. They define working conditions, salary, wages, and benefits. Holy days used to be defined by the church, but now it's the corporation that defines for the workforce which days are holidays. Politicians have to win the approval of corporations in the same way that kings, centuries earlier, had to win the blessing of the church.

Depending on your personality and life experience, you may focus on the negatives of corporations. They create massive inequity in wealth. They export jobs to the lowest paid workers in the world, leaving behind unemployment in higher wage regions. They pollute, erode workers' rights, promote shopping as therapy, and lead consumers into debt. They erode government revenues through lobbying and extortion, playing governments off of one another in a bid to host factories that will provide jobs to their constituents. Further, statistics suggest that corporations do as much to perpetuate racism and sexism as to challenge them.

You may also focus on the positives of corporations. They create massive amounts of wealth, not just creating billionaires and millionaires but funding pension funds for millions and millions of the middle class. They create jobs—often great jobs, with benefits, steady pay and promotional opportunities. They provide a tax base for governments, paying taxes on their profits and employee wages and returns to their investors. They create and deploy technology to lower rates of pollution and make life more comfortable and entertaining. They make entrepreneurs and even employees rich. They have challenged and changed racism and sexism, ending policies like don't ask, don't tell long before the government.

What seems lost in the debate about whether the corporation is positive or negative is this seemingly obvious claim: no institution does more to define the modern world.

About a third of the one hundred largest economies in the world are corporations, not countries. Yet this is a ranking that compares corporate sales to the total GDP of nations. Comparing just the size of government spending with corporate sales, the numbers tip in the favor of corporations: by this measure, fifty-two of the largest organizations in the world are corporations, and only forty-eight are governments.

Peter Drucker, by 1946, could write (and boy could he write),

And thus the character of our society is determined and patterned by the structural organization of Big Business, the technology of the mass-production plant, and the degree to which our social beliefs and promises are realized in and by the large corporation.

The emergence of Big Business, i.e., the large integrated industrial unit, as a social reality during the past fifty years is the most important event in the recent social history of the Western world. It is even possible that to future generations the world wars of our time will seem to have been an incident in the rise of big-business society just as to many historians the Napoleonic wars have come to appear incidental to the industrial revolution."[234]

It doesn't seem to matter much, really, whether you're a big fan of the corporation or not. It is, like the church at the dawn of the first economy, the dominant institution. Today, at the dawn of the fourth economy, society is not going to change without changing the corporation. The change that will likely occur within the corporation is a

---

[234] Peter F. Drucker, *Concept of the Corporation*, Revised Edition (New York: John Davy Company, 1972), 9.

story for our discussion of the fourth economy.

But before we tell that story, we have repeat the pattern we've already seen twice. The previously dominant institution was transformed from a tool of elites to a tool of the masses: the story of the transformation of the bank might be the least reported and most important story of the third economy. It's told in the next chapter.

20 Financial Revolution

As had occurred with the church and state before it, the bank and the financial markets it represented became during the third economy a tool for the individuals who had—for more than a century—been its tool.

Economy	First	Second	Third	Fourth
Period	1300–1700	1700–1900	1900-2000	2000-2050
Limit to Progress	Land	Capital	Knowledge Workers	Entrepreneurship
Type of Economy	Agricultural	Industrial	Information	Entrepreneurial
Intellectual Revolution	Renaissance	Enlightenment	Pragmatism	Systems Thinking
Big Social Invention	Nation-State	Bank	Corporation	Self
Social Revolution	Protestant Revolution	Democratic Revolution	**Financial Revolution**	Business Revolution

Financial markets were democratized during the third economy, as bank and government policies were directed at giving the individual increased access to credit and investment markets. While banks remained in private hands, as capital became more abundant, their relationship to it and the markets they served changed. They found themselves selling credit and investment products just like retailers sold any other good.

Introduction

Just like the church and state before it, the bank was democratized. This is most obviously seen in the easy access that the average person had to credit and investments by the close of the third economy, a stark contrast to what they had at the close of the second. Credit cards and mutual funds made the most obvious differences for the masses.

During the first economy, the church was transformed, and during the second, the same thing happened to the nation-state. In each case, the pattern of change was the same: power that had once been closely held by elites was dispersed steadily outward to many. The transformation of the bank and financial markets occurred the same way. The control of credit and access to investments shifted from banks to households.

Like so many things in the information economy, money became increasingly symbolic and abstract, transforming from gold into paper, first, and then into electronic blips. Innovations in financial markets fed and were fed by innovations in information technology. New financial products, like mutual funds you might hope to understand and exotic derivatives you could not, and hedge funds, junk bonds, venture capital, and pension funds all played a part in the transformation of markets. Maybe one of the simplest symbols of the transformation of the bank is that so many of the generic tasks of banking are now conducted by entities that don't even have the name bank. Non-bank financial institutions are, in fact, a huge segment of the financial market.

Government policy changed, too, as governments stimulated the economy with an abundance of capital and spending, through monetary and fiscal policy. In the developed world, government spending rose steadily and dramatically throughout the third economy, and government policy was increasingly directed towards full employment and the development of knowledge workers.

Mutual Funds and Pension Funds

Advances in health meant that people were living longer: life expectancy in the United States rose from forty-seven to seventy-seven between

1900 and 2000. Along with that, birth rates fell. (One of the surest ways to lower birth rates is to raise literacy rates for women. Education raises options.) One drawback to smaller families is that it lowered the probability that parents would have at least one child able to support its parents in their old age. Fewer people farmed or owned their own businesses, unable to sell such things at retirement. These trends conspired to create a large demand for investments from people whose parents and grandparents had never even considered such things. People needed new ways to fund their retirement.

Meanwhile, as governments and corporations grew, they needed capital. Lots of it.

Households' demand for investments to provide for retirement neatly dovetailed with the government and corporations' demand for capital in order to expand. Stocks and bonds became the stuff of everyday conversations at the dawn of the third economy.

Government spending for the First World War made unprecedented demands on financial markets. Between 1913 and 1919, British government debt rose tenfold, from £700 million to £7,100 million. The U.S. federal government spent more on the war than it had spent since its founding in 1789.

In the United States, a campaign to sell bonds ("Liberty Loans") drew in many first-time investors. "The first campaign raised money from 4 million separate individuals. The second was subscribed to by 9.4 million, the third by nearly 18.4 million, and the fourth received support from almost 22.8 million." [235] After the war, many of these new investors switched from war bonds to stocks. Between 1917 and 1921, middle-class investors' share of dividends more than doubled to almost 21 percent.[236]

The new knowledge workers could not help but notice the growth in the stock value of the companies they worked for. This sort of fascination would, of course, spread. When your brother-in-law tells you about the money folks are making on his employers' stock, you might buy a few shares.

"The Americans who were becoming interested in the stock market were, for the most part, members of the new, and newly prosperous,

---

[235] Smith, *The History of the Global Stock Market*, 109–10.

[236] Smith, *The History of the Global Stock Market*, 111.

white-collar class: doctors and lawyers and, most especially, men (and the occasional woman) who staffed the growing middle-management ranks of America's corporations. These same corporations—IBM, Eastman Kodak, Pan American, and dozens of others—were also the growth stocks of the day, which may explain why those who worked for them would begin to get interested in the market."[237]

Choosing individual stocks was confusing and risky, though. Soon, investors who wanted to enter the stock market began to use mutual funds. To buy a share of a mutual fund is to buy a portfolio of stocks that are selected by the mutual fund manager; this is, essentially, a way to hire someone to manage and diversify your investment. After World War Two, there was only a billion dollars in mutual funds in the United States, but in the 1960s, demand for mutual funds exploded. In 1965 alone, $2.4 billion flowed into mutual funds. The growth has abated for only brief intervals since.

By about 1990, the mutual fund industry passed $1 trillion, and it doubled by 1993 to pass the $2 trillion mark. By the end of 2009, a total of about 7,700 mutual funds held about $11 trillion. Worldwide, mutual fund assets were nearly $23 trillion.[238] By 2009, mutual funds—the middle class's door to the market—were more than eleven thousand times bigger than they were at the end of World War Two.

Mutual funds helped to popularize investments, but they were just one of many investment products. Marshall Loeb, *Money* magazine editor in 1980, was one of the fans of the many investment options.

He loved the idea that people had options they hadn't had before. "Just think of all the choices you had by then," he would joyously recall years later. "You had bond funds! You had tax-free bond funds! You had money market funds! You had tax-free money market funds!" He had real insight into the way America was changing; he could talk at great length, for instance, about how the middle class was finally gaining access to all the financial tools that had previously been available only to the rich. He understood the effect of inflation on middle-class behavior. He even liked the way the Age of Inflation had caused the subject of money to come out of the closet; he thought it was healthy for America to talk about its money. He was known to say

---

[237] Joseph Nocera, *A Piece of the Action: How the Middle Class Joined the Money Class* (New York: Simon & Schuster, 1994), 172.

[238] http://en.wikipedia.org/wiki/Mutual_fund

that money was the new sex.[239]

Americans became investors, and their options for investment products—just like the options for consumer products—grew to leave them with a sometimes baffling array of choices. Governments and corporations got their capital; individuals got their retirement accounts. Growing prosperity was in no small part due to middle-class access to capital markets.

Yet another, even more fascinating story, was unfolding in credit markets. This was a story of radical changes in attitudes towards debt, and culminated in something that probably would have seemed as magical to past generations as a smart phone: the credit card.

Building the American Dream

The American Dream defies easy definition. Like a dream, it seems to change all the time. (It's not even uniquely American.) The American Dream for one generation was to be able to have a house with running water and a car. Yet, what one generation aspires to, the next assumes. The American Dream to have a house—any house—was replaced by a dream to have a big house with a pool. The dream of having a radio was replaced by the dream of having a TV, and then a color TV, and then a HD TV, and then ... well, who knows, perhaps a holodeck. As America becomes more prosperous the American Dream becomes more elaborate. This is part of what drives the assumption of debt. Our expectations rise along with rises in productivity and income. Debt is, in part, a vote on the future. We expect a certain level of income that will make it possible for us to sustain payments for today's lifestyle.

The American Dream might be described as "things will be better for the next generation," or even, "things will be better for us in a few years." This kind of hope funds the future. We take out loans to create the future to which we aspire—even if it is merely a loan until the next credit card bill comes.

In the Old World, money was reserved for the elites; retirement

---

[239] Nocera, *A Piece of the Action*, 276.

depended on the kindness of family or charity. The dream of vacation would have seemed like a fantasy to the serfs who never traveled more than five miles from home in their whole life. To freedom of religion and a voice in democracy, the third economy added the hope of affluence and access to investment and credit markets.

It is easy to dismiss the American Dream as petty in comparison to the Western legacy of freedom of religion or democracy. Freedom of religion lets a person define what is most personal—one's own values and beliefs. Democracy allows people to hold their leaders accountable and influence the policy that so influences their lives. Yet the American dream has its own kind of power: it is a story about lifestyle.

The American Dream was partly financed by consumer credit. Before this could happen, however, Americans had to change their attitude about credit. As with so much of progress, this had as much to do with a change in thinking and behavior as with the creation of any specific technology. Social inventions exist in the mind.

The Rise of Consumer Credit

In his book *Financing the American Dream: A Cultural History of Consumer Credit,* Lendol Calder captures the extent to which public opinion resisted the concept of consumer credit. The argument against credit wasn't just the modern indictment that people who went into debt were "mortgaging the future." [240] Debt, its detractors claimed, threatened salvation. [241]

Debt seemed to be a tool of the devil, leading people to buy what they could not afford and to fail to appreciate the true value of things. Consumer credit, of course, encouraged people to seize now what propriety suggested they should wait for, and was evidence of discontent and greed. Those who preached against debt—and many of the most influential preachers of the late nineteenth and early twentieth centuries did—even had a verse clearly advising against it. In Romans 13:8, Paul writes, "Owe no man anything, but to love one another."

---

[240] Lendol Calder, *Financing the American Dream: A Cultural History of Consumer Credit* (Princeton, N.J.: Princeton University Press, 1999), 221.

[241] Calder, *Financing the American Dream,* 224.

Self-denial was key to Christianity[242]: borrowing to buy the latest gadget was the antithesis of that.

These preachers were not particularly sympathetic to the goals of the capitalists, eager to sell their goods. "Credit is the latest ally of the devil. It is the great tempter. It is responsible for half the extravagance of modern life. The two words 'charge it' have done more harm than any others in the language. They have led to a vast amount of unnecessary buying." [243]

Support for consumer credit grew only gradually. Yet as manufacturing became more efficient and less labor intensive (even today, China is losing jobs to manufacturing automation), credit to buy "unnecessary" things helped to finance necessary jobs. Imagine a world in which the volume and variety of products and services purchased did not change through the last two centuries (because the common man could not afford to purchase these things), but where productivity continued to rise as it has. Extrapolate a little and one can further imagine a world where one person is able to produce enough for everyone. In one sense, this would be a world of merit because the one person would—presumably—be best at providing for everyone. Yet it would be an unfair world, in that only that one person would have a source of income. Or would have, if only anyone else had money to pay him. In order for manufacturing productivity to rise without creating more poverty, demand has to rise too. Credit can finance that.

After the Second World War, American consumer debt stood at $5.7 billion. By 1998, that debt had climbed to $1.2 trillion,[244] and in the decade since, it has roughly doubled, to $2.5 trillion.[245]

So, since 1945, consumer debt has grown by four hundred and forty times, whereas GDP has grown by sixty-five times. That is, consumer debt has grown about six to seven times faster than GDP.

Yet here is a little secret about debt: for every dollar of debt, there is an equal dollar of credit. For each dollar that needs to be paid back, there is a dollar that will be paid back. People talk about reckless spending that leads to credit trouble, but one of the biggest things that

---

242 Calder, *Financing the American Dream,* 95.

243 Calder, *Financing the American Dream,* 215.

244 Calder, *Financing the American Dream,* 291.

245 http://www.nytimes.com/2009/08/08/business/08credit.html

debt did was discipline the American worker. Debt worked neatly with the rise of the corporate employee, the person who needed a dependable monthly income to service monthly debt payments.

You've probably heard this wonderful quote of Thoreau's:

"I went to the woods because I wished to live deliberately, to front only the essential facts of life, and see if I could not learn what it had to teach, and not, when I came to die, discover that I had not lived."

You've heard the quote, but probably are not aware of what he means by living in the woods. Not only was it more accurate to say that Thoreau lived on the edge of town rather than in the wilderness (he could walk into town for groceries) but he had financial freedom afforded by his friend Ralph Waldo Emerson. Thoreau didn't have a mortgage to pay; he lived on Emerson's property. Freedom from debt (or even the normal expenses of housing) gave Thoreau a freedom to act as he pleased. The man with a mortgage does not casually walk off the job to spend a few months in the woods.

Knowledge workers working in large organizations were more likely to invest in stocks, bonds, and mutual funds to finance their own retirement. Given their tendency to buy with credit, they were more likely to work within the large organizations that offered them the steady income that enabled them to make regular debt payments.

No tool made it easier for consumers to access credit than the credit card.

The Invention of the Credit Card

Here's a way to win a bet. Give your friends five guesses to name the founding CEO whose company did more in dollars' worth of transactions in one year than any other company. Maybe even go further and say that this company was the first—and so far the only—to do more than one trillion dollars in transactions in a single year.

This CEO's name? Dee Hock.

Dee Hock has probably thought as deeply about organizations, money, and banks as anyone alive. Dee Hock is a philosopher. He's also had a little success in business. In the history of the transformation of finance, the insight he captures here in this quote from his book *Birth of the Chaordic Age*, is perhaps the most important. It gives insight into how deeply a social inventor questions current reality.

"It was necessary to rethink the very nature of the institutional beasts in which we were enmeshed. To examine the most fundamental way the functions of a bank, of money, and of a credit card; even beyond that to the essential nature of each and how it might change with full application of emerging electronic technology. "[246]

His conclusion was that a bank was going to be anything that could guarantee, move, and manipulate data people treated as money. He thought that this might be the basis for a new, global currency. Of course, living in the world he helped to create, it seems obvious that a VISA card could be used just like money. Yet had he tried to explain this idea to the average person when he first had it, he would have likely been met with blank stares. Great ideas are sometimes like that: they meet no resistance because at their inception they make no sense and at their realization they are obvious.

Dee Hock realized that a computer was going to be key to making his vision real, and made a project to create such a computer central to his launch of the VISA card.

An earlier form of the credit card had already come onto the scene in the mid-1960s. The problem was, the system of manually tracking credit, making phone calls to assure a purchase was covered by a client's credit limit, mailing credit card receipts from stores to banks and from bank to bank, all took so long and were so clumsy that the system was ripe for abuse and error. By 1968, the losses were estimated to be in the tens of millions[247]—probably actually much more—and the credit card system was on the verge of collapse.

Hock's team developed a computer that would automate credit card transactions. Today, when you swipe your card at a point of purchase, the retailer instantly gets the money from the bank, which instantly knows your credit limit and how much of it you have used. Hock realized that money was information and that information technology was crucial to this next generation of money.

There are lots of fascinating things about this easy access to credit. For one thing, it lets the average consumer do more to shape the

---

246 Dee Hock, *Birth of the Chaordic Age* (San Francisco: Berrett-Koehler, 1999), 121–23.

247 Hock, *Birth of the Chaordic Age,* 103.

world. The American Dream is not particularly American. Since before the time peasants were day-dreaming about pepper in their stew, we've been able to imagine what we'd do with just a little more money. The miracle of the age of consumer credit is that it gave that peasant money and we got to see what sorts of things he'd buy. It's been fascinating.

Perhaps the biggest shift in credit from the 1800s to the 1900s, though, was the shift in who got to decide who deserved credit. When the consumer made this decision, he would buy what he wanted—no matter how silly it might seem to some staid banker.

After the popularization of the credit card, access to credit was no longer something reserved for the few. One business writer stated, "To have one's credit cards canceled is now something akin to being excommunicated by the medieval church."[248]

It was not just households that changed their relationship with credit markets; governments did too. In the third economy, government policies increasingly treated capital as something abundant, something that could be used to stimulate employment.

Roast Pigs and the Allure of Military Spending

There is a curious story about a little village in China.[249] One day, a family's house burned down. Kicking through the rubble, they discovered that their pig had been roasted to death. To their surprise, this roasted pig was delicious and, given it was more than they could eat, they had a feast and invited everyone in the village. Soon, a plague of house fires broke out, fires whose only casualty was a single pig. It took some time for the villagers to realize that one needn't burn down a house in order to roast a pig.

The United States went through something similar during the third economy, accepting house fires in exchange for roast pig in the form of government military spending and economic growth.

Crowell's problem during the second economy was that he could make

---

[248] Calder, *Financing the American Dream*, 291.

[249] Sadly, I remember the story but not the source.

more breakfast cereal than he could sell. In a sense, this became the problem of the entire U.S. economy at the dawn of the third economy; there was enormous potential for supply but relatively little demand. The First World War and the military-industrial complex it created revealed just how enormous was the potential for production, if only someone could stimulate demand.

The House of Morgan negotiated a contract to manage the Allies' supply line during the First World War. There had never been a war of such magnitude, nor one that stimulated more demand. The House of Morgan purchased about $10 million in products—from corned beef to barbed wire—each day. Total sales of American goods to the Allies were about double that, but even so, this represented a massive sum. How massive? The House of Morgan "presided over purchases equivalent to the world's gross national product a generation before."[250]

It is worth reviewing this. The House of Morgan represented about half of the American sales to the Allies and yet each *month* it purchased as many goods as the whole world had, just one generation earlier. Never had there been such carnage and widespread destruction; and never had so much demand stimulated so much production. The house fire was awful, but the pig tasted wonderful.

The culmination of the second economy was productive capacity that needed special stimulus to be realized. One can talk about how much it cost to wage the war, but that misses a more important point: without the stimulus of the war, it is not obvious that much of this industrial effort would have been made in the first place. Furthermore, goods were not the only things that were made; so were jobs and wealth. There were—economically speaking—huge gains to be had through war. World War One represented the birth of the military industrial complex, a time when Americans began regularly burning down houses to enjoy roast pig. Even now, a century later, American politics and the American economy are dependent on military spending: not even counting the recent occupations in Afghanistan and Iraq, U.S. military spending has gone up about 80 percent in the last decade.

Military spending was not – of course – the only kind of spending that rose during the third economy. In addition to spending, the government managed money – its supply and price (interest rates) – so as to

---

[250] Chernow, *The House of Morgan*, 188–89.

encourage employment.

The Beginnings of the Central Bank

George Washington's first cabinet included Thomas Jefferson as secretary of state and Alexander Hamilton as secretary of the treasury.

Possibly no minds did more to define this new experiment in government than Jefferson's and Hamilton's. Jefferson penned the Declaration of Independence; Hamilton wrote most of the Federalist Papers that explained the constitution. On occasion, geniuses like these two emerge. On occasion, opportunities for transforming something as fundamental as the state emerge. On very, very rare occasions, these two converge into a single time and place. To this day, Americans reap a return from this happy confluence of circumstances and great minds. But great minds don't always think alike: Hamilton and Jefferson had very different ideas about the kind of economy the United States would have.

Jefferson wasn't very impressed with banks. His vision of America seemed to be of a nation of artisans and gentlemen farmers who were educated but who worked the land rather than in factories. It's not obvious that his vision of America's future included big banks and corporations that employed tens of thousands. Nor is it obvious that his own personal experience with credit made him feel predisposed towards banks: when he died, he left his family a debt of what would be—at today's prices—somewhere between one to two million dollars.[251] Jefferson did not want a central bank.

Hamilton's view of the economy was more modern. He argued against Jefferson for a central bank akin to the Bank of England. He saw industry and finance as key to America's future. Washington eventually sided with Hamilton, and the U.S. began with a Central Bank.

Then along came Andrew Jackson, who was not really a fan of institutions, whether legal or financial. He was disdainful of courts, preferring to settle his disputes without lawyers: Jackson fought in fourteen duels. He also destroyed the U.S. Bank, vetoing its charter and

---

[251] http://www.monticello.org/site/research-and-collections/debt

withdrawing government funds. It just so happened that he did this the year that J. P. Morgan was born.

J. P. Morgan: The Last Banker

"Economic historians frequently point out that the United States had no central bank between the expiration of the charter of the Second Bank of the United States in 1837 and the creation of the Federal Reserve System in 1913—coincidentally, the years of Morgan's birth and death. For much of that time, Morgan functioned as the nation's *de facto* central bank, on one occasion even bailing out the U.S. Treasury."[252]

What Nathan Rothschild was to the early part of the nineteenth century, J.P. Morgan was to the latter part. Peter Drucker has a curious explanation of how the Rothschilds lost their place of prominence to Morgan:

"Until 1860 ... the House of Rothschild was the world dominant financial power. The Rothschilds failed, however, to recognize the meaning of the transatlantic migration; only 'riff-raff,' they thought, would leave Europe. As a result, the Rothschilds ceased to be important around 1870. They had become merely rich individuals. It was J. P. Morgan who took over. His 'secret' was to spot the transatlantic migration at its very onset, to understand immediately its significance, and to exploit it as an opportunity by establishing a worldwide bank in New York rather than in Europe, and as the medium for financing the American industries that immigrant labor was making possible."[253]

Morgan's power over industrialists gave him power over markets. As his era's most prominent banker, he was also the one figure able to quell a banking panic.

Banking panics occur when depositors suddenly lose confidence in their bank. Panics have an odd dynamic. When people believe that there is no cause for panic and leave their money in the bank, the bank can almost invariably meet requests for withdrawals. If people believe that there is cause for panic, however, and make a run on the bank, the

---

[252] Bernstein, *The Birth of Plenty*, 126.

[253] Drucker, *The Executive in Action*, 340.

bank will soon find itself unable to meet the overwhelming demand for withdrawals. Since the difference between a bank's viability and closure lies partly in the reality of deposits on hand and partly in the public's trust in the bank, one bank's misery could quickly spread to other banks, as the collapse of one bank might easily erode depositors' confidence in another and another, creating a ripple effect that could turn into a recession or even a depression.

In the days before deposit insurance, when a bank went under, its depositors lost their money. A person did well to be paranoid and be the first in line to withdraw funds at any hint of panic, but such perfectly sensible strategies for the individual were disastrous for the banking system as a whole. Even worse, these strategies were bad for the economy as a whole. As the money supply contracted, less money was spent, and the economy could stall as a result of a banking crisis. The United States suffered from such banking panics in 1873 and 1893.

In 1907, panic hit again. Depositors were running to their banks to get their money before they collapsed. The panic began with Mercantile Nation Bank of New York City, and soon affected other banks and trust companies as nervous depositors withdrew money that, eventually, the banks simply didn't have. With depositors making a run at banks in a growing periphery from the original scene of the crime, J. P. Morgan brought together a group of bankers to shift funds from stronger banks to weaker ones, although he did let the original culprit bank fold. He even convinced John D. Rockefeller to deposit $10 million into one of the affected banks to show his confidence in the bank and the banking system. Such moves gradually restored public confidence, saving the banking industry from claims it could not meet. Eventually, the run on the banks ended and a crisis was averted, or at least mitigated. Yet the event solidified public sentiment that the banking system should be changed.

After a series of Congressional hearings, Harry Davison (a senior partner in Morgan's bank) and Paul Warburg (of the powerful Warburg banking family from Germany) drafted initial recommendations for a new central bank. The economy – indeed the public – needed continued access to capital and did not trust private bankers to provide it.

In 1913, the Sixteenth Amendment created income taxes and the Internal Revenue Service, and the Department of Labor was founded. J.P. Morgan died and the Federal Reserve was created. Americans expected their government to ensure access to capital even in times of crisis.

These tools for economic intervention required some theory. John Maynard Keynes defined that theory, but it was only after the Great Depression that governments were ready for it.

Keynesian Economics: First the Boom ...

The Allies' demand for goods during the First World War had revealed some of the productive potential of the American economy. This unprecedented capacity was directed to the private sector after the war, and the American economy surged. No economy had ever seen anything like the Roaring Twenties. With the war to end all wars behind them, Americans were now busily getting rich. By the 1920s, the groundwork for the third economy was in place. Universities were producing knowledge workers in growing numbers, and corporations were increasing output and stimulating consumption through advertising, marketing, and retail outlets that offered a dizzying array of goods. In 1924, *The Man Nobody Knows* was the bestselling book in the United States; its' central claim was that Christ "'had been the first businessman,' whose parables were 'the most powerful advertisements of all-time.'" It is safe to say that attitudes towards business had changed from medieval times.

Business success made investors bolder. More money to invest, in turn, made businesses bolder. Businesses, investors, and consumers all rose together and for about a decade the results were spectacular.

By 1920, the U.S. population had passed 100 million. During the 1920s, insulin was first given to diabetics; radio became popular with listeners, advertisers, and investors alike; Charlie Chaplin became a star; a copy of the Bible that cost the equivalent of $2,000 in the fourteenth century had dropped to only $3; Duke Ellington made his first records; Babe Ruth hit sixty home runs in one season; Ernest Hemingway and D. H. Lawrence published books that have remained in print ever since; and electricity and running water were introduced into homes that now had cars parked out front. As the limited-liability, joint-stock company (or modern corporation) became more common, more "common" people began to speculate in the stock market. Between 1926 and September 1929, the stock market index rose from 100 to 381. Suddenly, everyone dreamt of living like Rockefeller. The Roaring Twenties were a time of wonderful optimism, great change, and seeming economic miracles.

. . . And Then the Bust

In early September of 1929, the stock market index peaked at 381. By November it had fallen to 145, a 62 percent drop. The market hit its lowest point in June of 1932, falling 91 percent off its peak to a low of 34. Banking panics ensued. Soon, every sector of the economy was affected by this tsunami of financial disaster. The Great Depression was different from any earlier depression in both scale and duration. Between 1929 and 1932, unemployment soared from 3.2 percent to 24.1 percent. During that same time, Gross National Product (GNP) dropped by nearly 30 percent.

During earlier economic busts, drops in sales and employment eventually lowered the price of goods and labor, triggering a fresh round of activity as households snapped up bargain-priced goods and companies snapped up bargain-priced labor. Sometimes within months the downturn was past and the economy was again growing. Yet something was different about this bust. It didn't just destroy wealth and jobs at an unprecedented rate: it lasted far too long.

It is easy to imagine how the Great Depression was perceived at the time. The religious conscience of the nation, never completely comfortable with the Roaring Twenties and its indulgence of consumer desires, saw the Great Depression as an indictment of excess and confirmation that they were right to disprove of consumer credit. Conservative capitalists saw unemployment as a natural consequence of wages and prices rising too high. For them, wealth was something to be reserved for the elites. Keynes, however, reached a different conclusion.

John Maynard Keynes was born in 1883, the same year in which Karl Marx died. He was brilliant and never suffered from undue modesty. When he took his civil service exam his lowest mark was in economics. "I evidently knew more about Economics than my examiners," he concluded. At one point he was director of the Bank of England. He made money speculating on stocks at breakfast before pursuing less lucrative and presumably more interesting, endeavors for the rest of the day.

But his most important accomplishment was the invention of macroeconomics. Treating as central the issues typically left to bankers, his most influential book was called *The General Theory of Employment, Interest and Money.* His basic thesis was that if individuals and companies made rational decisions at the microeconomic level of firms and labor markets, economies might never recover. (Or simply take far too long to recover.) If companies and investors do what is best for them as individuals, they do not do things that are best for the economy as a whole. Rather than hire during a recession, it makes more sense for companies to wait. Rather than buy during a recession, it makes more sense for households to wait. Same with investors. Sadly, when everyone did what seemed best, they collectively just made things worse. The whole economy- or macro economy – floundered.

Keynes's solution seemed counterintuitive: have the government spend money it didn't have to stimulate demand for products. Once they were again selling products, companies would begin to hire. Once households again had jobs, they would start to buy. In case this was not enough, Keynesians advocated stimulating investment by lowering interest rates and even increasing the supply of money.

In the second economy, economic growth was led by capital. In this third economy, Keynes would suggest that the goals of labor should lead capital markets instead: if unemployment went up, investment and credit markets should be artificially boosted by government policy. Capital was now to be plentiful, even if the government had to intervene to make it so. Labor – not capital – was to be the measure of economic progress.

After the Great Depression, governments listened to Keynes's message.

Beginning in 1930, the federal government in the United States began trying to measure unemployment.[254] "America's Employment Act of 1946—the year Keynes died—codified the new wisdom, making it 'the continuing policy and responsibility of the Federal Government ... to promote maximum employment, production, and purchasing power.'"[255] Even "conservative" economists today look to the American Federal Reserve Chairman to stimulate the economy when unemployment rises just a percentage point or two, following the lead of Republican

---

[254] Daniel H. Pink, "The True Measure of Success: Forget GDP. A Better Metric for Prosperity Is Gross National Happiness," *Wired*, December 2004, 29.

[255] Robert Reich, "John Maynard Keynes," *Newsweek*, March 29, 1999, 137, for this and other facts in the article.

President Richard Nixon, who commented, “We are all Keynesians now."[256]

One of the key conclusions of economics is that communities are rewarded when they treat as precious that which is scarce and as cheap that which is abundant. Before Keynes, capital was considered something scarce and labor was considered abundant. Capitalism of the late nineteenth century, the type of capitalism that put Charles Dickens's father in debtors' prison and that worked nine-year-old children nine hours a day, didn't just treat labor poorly, it treated it as disposable. After Keynes, capital was considered abundant and labor valuable. Healthy communities strove to keep people employed and to prepare them for careers that paid well, even if this required public spending. In the third economy, knowledge work was the new limit to progress, and capital was to be made abundant.

Among the transformative social inventions to come out of this time of abundant capital were venture capital and junk bonds.

From Wall Street to Sand Hill: Venture Capital on the Left Coast

In the midst of sweeping changes in financial markets and technology, something new was created. (Well, sort of new: venture capital took its name from the capital used to finance ventures like Columbus's voyage across the Atlantic.)

The traditional bank had been about limiting losses to scarce capital; venture capital was about maximizing returns to abundant capital. Traditional banks treated capital as scarce and business opportunities as abundant (and suspect). Venture capital treated capital as abundant and business opportunities as scarce.

An old-style banker would look at a business plan and decide whether to loan money based on risk. If a banker was getting, say, a 10 percent return, the way he was going to maximize profit was to lose very few loans. He tried to avoid risk.

---

[256] Howard K. Smith, “Nixon Reportedly Says He Is Now a Keynesian.” *New York Times*, January 7, 1971, 19.

Compare that with the strategy of a venture capitalist. A venture capitalist takes an equity share rather than making a loan. He does not avoid risk, because he knows that startups have a very high probability of failure. Yet he also knows that if he invests one million dollars in each of ten companies, it doesn't matter whether nine of the ten fail. It doesn't matter, that is, if the tenth company goes on to be successful and the one million invested turns into $15 million or even billions.

The venture capital industry grew apace with information technology. In 1975, the venture capital industry raised only $10 *million*. By 2006, it raised $25.1 *billion*. This is an increase of 251,000 percent, about 30 percent a year.

Sand Hill Road in Menlo Park, California, became to venture capital what Wall Street had become a century earlier to investment bankers. In 1972, Kleiner, Perkins, Caufield & Byers and Sequoia Capital were founded, helping to finance a different kind of company. The old-style bankers looked at collateral like factories and machinery. These venture capitalists had to assess the value of intellectual capital instead; they were investing in knowledge workers' ideas and their ability to turn possibility into reality. The list of companies just these two venture capitalists have funded reads like a chronology of the personal computer era: it includes Amazon, Apple, YouTube, Cisco, Yahoo!, Electronic Arts, Intuit, AOL, and Google.

Treating capital as abundant made it possible to fund new companies, new technologies, and even new industries. Probably no one, though, treated capital as more abundant than Michael Milken.

Milken's Millions: Junk Bonds and the Run at "Complacent" Management

What Nathan Rothschild was to international bonds, Michael Milken was to junk bonds. His great investment idea was a largely overlooked category of junk—or high-yield—bonds.

About the only certainty in investment is that riskier investments have to promise higher returns than safe ones. In theory, people are indifferent between a 50 percent chance of getting $2 or a 100 percent chance of getting $1. Both have a probable value of $1. Yogi Berra supposedly said that in theory, there is no difference between practice and theory; yet in practice, there is.

In theory, people are indifferent between a 50-50 chance of $2 or $1. In practice, though, they prefer the sure bet. People don't like uncertainty and will pay money to avoid it. This means that in order to get people to play the game of a 50-50 chance of $2, you have to pay them a premium. To get people to play your 50-50 game rather than just take the dollar, you might have to induce them with the possibility of winning $2.10. Or even $2.50. If most people are risk averse enough that you have to pay a big premium to get them to play the risky, 50-50 game, it pays a big premium to play the 50-50 game. Particularly if you play the game repeatedly, you will make more money than if you just took the $1. Over time, you get a risk premium.

That is what Milken observed. The banker mentality of avoiding risk was so systemic that someone willing to play the 50-50 game would make more money. Junk bonds were the 50-50 game that most people were reluctant to play.

Companies in trouble—or unwilling to offer collateral on marginal loans—would sell junk bonds with, say, 20 percent returns when safe bonds might pay 5 percent. These bonds were more likely to fail, but over the long run, research suggested that overall returns in a portfolio of junk bonds were higher than the returns in a portfolio of safe bonds.

Most investors, like traditional bankers, sought to minimize loss. Milken had a more interesting idea: like a venture capitalist, he sought to maximize gains. He got pretty impressive results.

In 1973, Burnham gave Milken $2 million to invest in junk bonds. That year, he made $2 million with it, a return of 100 percent.[257] This did two things: first, it got Burnham's attention, and second, given that he demonstrated expertise in something about which the rest of the firm knew very little, he was given autonomy. As long as he kept making money for the firm, he was free to do as he wanted. Management at Drexel Burnham created an entrepreneurial compensation system that no longer doled out money from a fixed pool but instead gave traders a percentage; this was to have big consequences for Milken.

Within just a few years, Milken had captured huge market share for

---

[257] Connie Bruck, *The Predators' Ball: The Inside Story of Drexel Burnham and the Rise of the Junk Bond Raiders* (New York: Penguin Books, 1989), 31.

Drexel Burnham and had largely defined this new junk bond market. By 1978, profits from Milken's group were equal to the profits from all the rest of Drexel Burnham's business activities. By 1981, Drexel Burnham had issued more than $1 billion of junk bonds in a market of less than $1.5 billion. [258]

Milken bet on businessmen who liked risk. For instance, he turned Steve Wynn's $10 million in equity in a small casino into $100 million Wynn could use for acquisition and expansion. Wynn says, "It was venture capital, masquerading as debt finance."[259] Wynn is now famous for having his name on one of the largest hotels and casinos in Las Vegas and, he claims, the most expensive divorce in history.

Between 1979 and 1986, Drexel's profits rose from $6 million to $545.5 million. In 1986, it was the most profitable investment banking firm in the country. In 1986 someone calculated that the clients Milken had assembled at his annual junk bond conference had net worth that was three times U.S. GNP. [260]

One element of his success was to target what he saw as complacent management, funding hostile takeovers. People like Carl Icahn, who used Milken's financing for takeovers and takeover threats, justified his work as an attempt to shatter ineffectual bureaucracies. In one sense, these takeovers were like a wrestling match between Chandler's visible hand of management and Smith's invisible hand of the market.

Wages rose dramatically during the third economy, but no one had ever had a paycheck like Milken's. In a four-year period in the late 1980s, Milken made more than a billion dollars. Oh, and Milken was sentenced to ten years in prison (he served two) for security and reporting violations. Like so many social inventors, he showed less regard for existing rules than new possibilities.

Milken's philosophy through all of this was that while capital was scarce in an industrial economy, it should be treated as abundant in an information economy.

One reason that I use his example is to illustrate how powerful it can be to stop treating capital as a limit. I also use his story to remind the reader that CEOs can become complacent and that it is the people

---

[258] Bruck, *The Predators' Ball*, 71.

[259] Bruck, *The Predators' Ball*, 58–60.

[260] Bruck, *The Predators' Ball*, 95.

who own stocks who own the company, not the senior management team. Milken seems right to have pointed this out and acted on it. My real qualm with Milken in this regard is that he seemed to simply replaced one set of alpha males who would have been Renaissance popes or Enlightenment-era monarchs in earlier times for another. The point is not to enrich the elites, whether they're entitled CEOs or leveraged financiers; every institution to date has done the most good when it does good for the most people. To me, Milken's financing suggests possibilities for the groups of workers who actually own corporate America through thousands of mutual and pension funds. What if complacent CEOs could be displaced by owners of the company? Milken showed us how that could work. And what if those owners were groups of workers? We haven't seen that yet, but I'd be surprised if something like this doesn't happen in the next decade.

Knowledge Worker as Capitalist: From Creating Products to Creating Equity

During the third economy, two things happened: one, financial innovations as varied as limited liability / joint stock companies and junk bonds created a plethora of investment opportunities and capital; and two, speculative bubbles seemed to move from market to market.

The problem might not be that financial markets are too mature and able to create too much capital and credit. The problem is that the corporation is too immature and unable to create profitable opportunities using that capital and credit. The result? Capital bids up the price of existing assets and we have a series of bubbles. Policy makers looking at financial markets will only see the symptom of this problem. We need to start talking about corporate reform.

James Fallows of the *Atlantic* talked to Nouriel Roubini , who spoke about the danger and increasing severity of economic bubbles.

"These asset bubbles are increasingly frequent, increasingly dangerous, increasingly virulent, and increasingly costly," he said. After the housing bubble of the 1980s came the S&L crisis and the recession of 1991. After the tech bubble of the 1990s came the recession of 2001. "Most likely $10 trillion in household wealth [not just housing value but investments and other assets] has been destroyed in this latest crash [of 2008]. Millions of people have lost their jobs. We will probably add $7 trillion to our public debt. Eventually that debt must be serviced, and that may hamper growth."

After talking about the dynamic of bubbles and how we've been dependent on them for growth, Roubini says, "'The question is, can the U.S. grow in a non-bubble way?'" He asked the question rhetorically, so I [James Fallows] turned it back on him. Can it?"

Perhaps the core problem is that we've created massive potential for financial stimulus but have not created a corresponding potential for translating that into new ventures. So, the financial clout is used to bid up the prices of existing assets rather than create new ones. This can't help but create a series of bubbles, it seems. The problem is not that financial markets are too capable of creating capital. The problem is that business markets are too feeble at using that capital to fund innovation.

Like Crowell able to make more product than he could at first sell, the West can now create more financing than it can profitably use. This alone suggests that the limit has shifted to entrepreneurship.

In spite of what they claim, management within big corporations is not that interested in innovation and creativity. They prefer predictability. Failure is too frightening and failure is inevitable with innovation.

What if companies were to exploit the abundance of capital by – like venture capitalists or even junk bond markets – embracing failure en route to creating new products, business divisions, companies, and even industries? This could be done but it would mean dispersing power to employees, putting in place mechanisms more like markets than bureaucracies, and treating capital as cheap and opportunities as precious. As it is, corporations tend to generate cash rather than find creative ways to invest it. They seem more intent on minimizing risk than maximizing possibilities. It is little wonder that in recent decades, the Fortune 500 have stopped creating jobs.

As long as capital markets are biased towards the purchase of used securities—buying stocks and financial instruments for investments already created—we're likely to see a series of bubbles. Once we get better at making entrepreneurship a normal part of the daily routine of business, we'll still have bubbles but I suspect that they won't be nearly as frequent or pernicious. And the foundational economy upon which financial markets rest will be more diversified and vibrant, offsetting the bubbles that do occur.

Religious freedom from the first economy didn't realize its full potential until the nation-state was transformed through democracy. The fact that the prince or king got to choose whether his realm would be Protestant or Catholic was a form of progress, but the individual still could not make religion a personal choice. Only after the nation-state granted rights to citizens did the individual gain religious freedom.

Religions full transformation did not come until the revolution of the state.

Finance has been transformed but this transformation won't realize its potential until the corporation, too, is transformed to become more entrepreneurial.

Through pension funds, mutual funds, 401(k)s, and direct purchase of stocks and bonds, the typical knowledge worker has become the biggest owner of stocks.

What if Michael Milken's attack on established management is just a hint at what is possible? What if the average person gained greater control over the corporation she owned? What if her investments were less passive and more active, enabling her to change policies and ventures from within the corporation?

Conclusion

During the third economy, the banker lost his relative power over the economy for several reasons. One, the community in which he operated finally decided that it preferred that the head of the Federal Reserve or the elected president steer the economy instead of a private banker. Two, stimulating consumption required the extension of credit, putting the banker in the role more like retailer than staid judge of creditworthiness. Third, the corporation had emerged as an entity capable of generating cash directly from the public via stocks and bonds, allowing it to become less dependent on the banker for its financing. Fourth, the information economy had eroded the banker's monopoly on information, allowing even individual investors armed with a public library or Internet access to investigate investments as thoroughly as could any earlier banker. Finally, the higher paid knowledge worker working in an organization had neither farm nor factory to sell to fund retirement; this new breed of employee became, through pension funds and 401(k) accounts, the new capitalist who fed an enormous surge in the volume and availability of capital. During the second economy, capital had been scarce and the banker who controlled it had power. By the end of third economy, capital was seemingly as plentiful as information. The result was a bank that had more money than ever before but had less power.

"It was a brand new age of banking, one with a less austere image. The stereotypical banker had been a grumpy Scrooge who closely scrutinized loan applications and was congenitally biased toward rejecting them. That befits a historic situation of scarce capital rationed by bankers. But the situation was reversed in the Casino Age, which was characterized by new financial intermediaries and superabundant capital. The banker now evolved into an amiable salesman ...Banking authorities noted certain altered facts of the Casino Age: corporations could now bypass banks and turn to life-insurance companies for capital, raise money through bond issues, or finance expansion from retained earnings. ...banks lost their special position as providers of capital..."[261]

While these changes in the bank were gradual and seemed to come from every angle, they suddenly reached a tipping point in a showdown between IBM and Morgan Stanley. The next chapter gives a story to illustrate how the corporation eclipsed the bank to take its place as the new, dominant institution in the West.

---

[261] Chernow, *The House of Morgan*,530–31, 536.

21 The Corporation Eclipses the Bank

As corporations became larger and more sophisticated, they became more savvy about capital and capital markets, particularly as the relevant capital was less often the traditional industrial capital that could easily be measured and was more often the intellectual capital that knowledge workers within corporations had more experience and expertise in judging. While banks had always had to compete for accounts, by the close of the third economy they were less able to dictate terms to corporations and had to, instead, compete just like other vendors. As capital lost its mystique, bankers lost their power.

Ford Uses Capital to Make Cars and ... More Capital

Henry Ford pioneered assembly line techniques that caused car prices to plunge and sales to soar. His production techniques did as much as any to create the modern automobile. His success made something clear: the corporation could generate its own capital.

On 22 December 1913, the *New York Times* reported that "Money Bill goes to Wilson to-day" in reference to the legislation that would establish the Federal Reserve. Three weeks later, in the magazine section of the *Times* dated 11 January 1914, a story ran with the headline "Henry Ford Explains Why He Gives Away $10,000,000: Declares that he is dividing profits with his employees, not paying them higher wages, and that workers as partners will give increased efficiency."

In retrospect, it seems as though the *Times* had reported a shift in economic power. No longer were bankers deciding who got money: increasingly it was the CEOs of corporations and the federal government that would define the flow of capital. By the 1920s, a growing number of companies financed expansion through retained earnings, paying out less in the form of dividends and relying less on banks for the capital they needed for expansion. Public fascination with bankers like the Rothschilds and J. P. Morgan would increasingly give way to fascination with industrialists who ruled an eight-to-five empire and could never hope to spend their money as quickly as it came in.

In the 1914 *Times* article Ford shared his thoughts on motivating employees. Ford's profit-sharing scheme was labeled utopian, but Ford explained:

"If you expect to get anything out of a man nowadays you must pay him well. If you want the best there is in him, you must make it really worth his while. You must give him something to live for.

"I do not believe in prolonging the conditions which ever since the Civil War have been developing into a curse upon the country, and which in these last few years have caused the Federal Government to step in and make war upon big corporations. You know what I mean—the conditions which have built up a few millionaires and actually pauperized millions or kept them poor. They are out of date."

The article closes as Ford shares more advice:

"'Let me tell you one of our business principles which may explain a lot to some of those who are painfully distressed over the impracticability of our distribution scheme. . . ., We don't borrow money.'

"'When we first started business *we decided we would be our own bankers*. Now, we started last Fall with between $15,000,000 and $20,000,000 of our own money to keep us going through the Winter. And may I tell you that so far we haven't had to draw much on that fund.'"[262] (italics added)

The corporation had begun to surpass the bank in its ability to generate money. "But even after the war, major companies, flush with wartime profits, didn't really need new financing. Increasingly, big business was able to finance itself by means of internally generated funds."[263]

But Ford's success was also just a reminder that capital made capital and successful capitalists did not need bankers to get it. What happened at IBM was more interesting, happening as it did at the iconic knowledge worker employer.

---

[262] Floyd Norris and Christine Bockelmann, *The New York Times: Century of Business* (New York: McGraw-Hill, 2000), 54.

[263] Smith, *The History of the Global Stock Market*, 147.

IBM and Morgan Stanley: The Rise of Transactional Banking

As a biographer of J. P. Morgan, Ron Chernow writes as clearly and as engagingly as anyone on the topic of the transformation of the bank.[264] He depicts the banker as an intermediary between savers and borrowers.

At the start of the third economy, the banker was a towering figure while companies were small and households had little money to save and even less information to guide their savings. Everyone needed the bank.

By the end of the third economy, money from households had flown into pension and 401(k) funds, making households more powerful relative to bankers, and companies had grown to the size of entire countries. On top of this, information technology meant that bankers no longer had exclusive knowledge about who had money and who needed it. The information economy had made financial markets more transparent.

The bankers who were clearly powerful intermediaries between savers and borrowers at the start of the third economy were disinter mediated by the end of the third economy. Customers began to go around them, no longer needing their services. This was dramatically illustrated when IBM reached a tipping point that led them to change their relationship with their banker.

IBM's bank was Morgan Stanley, a firm founded by J. P. Morgan's grandson when legislation forced the split between commercial banking and securities underwriting. Morgan Stanley was, in a sense, the firm that banking legend J. P. Morgan had founded. There was, of course, no person who did more to define American banking.

Saying that J. P. Morgan was a banker is a bit misleading. It would be like saying that Martin Luther was a minister or Thomas Jefferson was a politician. Morgan defined the role of banker in ways that those who followed could never quite imitate. Monarchs traveled to him for financial advice or to request loans. He advised even the papacy on the purchase of American stocks. His powers of persuasion were legendary and could both calm investors and terrify industrialists.

---

264 This account of IBM comes mostly from Chernow, *The Death of the Banker*, 48–51.

Morgan and his partners held directorships in 112 corporations, and in order to limit their competition, they could and did refuse loans to new entrants to the market. Ultimately, however, his power rested on something that the information economy would erode: control of scarce information. The triumphs of the information economy both fed financial markets and eroded the relative power of bankers.

It was Morgan's bank that played underwriter for IBM, helping it to raise money through stock and bond issues.

For a long time, no corporation was a better symbol of the importance of the knowledge worker than IBM. Even the dress code—suit, tie, and white shirt—served to emphasize the fact that these were knowledge workers who were not expected to make their living through physical exertion. Tom Watson—the leader who did so much to define IBM's culture—had the simplest and most telling admonition of the new information economy: "THINK" defined expectations of the new knowledge worker. Today, IBM holds more patents than any other U.S.-based company, and its employees have won five Nobel Prizes. IBM was home to the new knowledge worker and produced technology that made it a household name even before households could afford the personal computer that IBM helped to invent and popularize.

The relationship between Morgan Stanley and IBM was natural in many ways. These were two companies that had done so much to define their respective industry, both led by iconic men who had passed on leadership to their sons. Both companies were incredibly successful. Yet this long-standing relationship was based on underlying realities that had slowly, but fundamentally, shifted.

When banks were relatively strong compared to savers and borrowers, they could dictate terms. Chief among these terms was the requirement of a monogamous relationship with companies. IBM and other blue-chip firms knew not to antagonize their Wall Street bankers. Financial markets were arcane, and small companies needed the expertise of these bankers, even after these small companies became big companies. Or at least that was the case until 1979, when IBM was one of the first to realize it had options to kick free of its bankers' dictates.

"The seventies ... had seen a revolution on Wall Street. The end of fixed commissions in 1975 incited free-for-all competition, and traditional long-standing investment-banking relationships came to an abrupt end. Relationship banking, in which corporations gave their business to investment banking firms they had known for years, gave way to 'transactional banking,' in which investment banks competed anew on every deal. At the same time, wildly fluctuating interest rates caused tremendous volatility in the market. As new financial products were introduced, what became crucial was the ability to perform transactions, and to do it instantly before the opportunity passed."[265]

Between 1975 and 1980, IBM's sales nearly doubled, to $26 billion. Between 1960 and 1980, the number of its employees tripled, reaching 341,000. The information economy created huge demand for computing power and no company was better positioned to meet this demand than IBM. (Imagine that IBM had kept the CPU and operating system in-house rather than subcontracting them to Intel and Microsoft. As I write this, IBM, Intel, and Microsoft combined employ about 600,000 and generate annual profits of nearly $50 billion.) IBM was huge, growing, and redefining the modern office. Its executives must have felt powerful enough to risk a relationship with their banker.

IBM told Morgan Stanley that it would ignore its rule of dealing exclusively with them and would bring in Salomon Brothers to help with a billion-dollar bond issue. Upset, the directors from Morgan Stanley refused to cooperate with IBM and Salomon. They thought that IBM, intimidated, would back down. Instead, IBM went ahead without Morgan Stanley. As Morgan Stanley feared, this did indeed set a precedent.

Most people know that IBM helped to popularize the personal computer, giving households and small businesses confidence in a technology in a way that lesser known brands—like Apple, Commodore, Osborne, and Tandy—could not. Fewer realize that IBM helped to usher in a world of transactional banking to replace relationship banking. There might have been no more obvious sign that the corporation had eclipsed the bank.

Chernow explains what happened in the aftermath of IBM's deal with Salomon:

As the world of relationship banking faded, it was replaced by the fast, anonymous, much less comfortable world of transactional banking. ... Free of the old monogamous relationships, corporate clients promiscuously flirted with many financial-service firms. They turned to different bankers for different services and played one off against another to negotiate the best possible terms. With all major companies now operating in a global arena, they also entertained foreign bankers and developed separate networks of oversea advisers. No longer was it unusual for a blue-chip company to enlist ten different bankers in the

---

[265] Bruck, *The Predators' Ball*, 63.

space of a year. Still more troubling for the bankers, more and more companies placed their debt directly with institutional investors, eliminating the banker's role altogether. The strength of the middleman was rapidly declining, while the power of the providers and consumers of capital continued to grow exponentially, tightening the squeeze on Wall Street.

Manufacturing was to thrive in the third economy, but was never again to lead. A similar thing happened to banks in relationship to corporations. Banks made record profits but they no longer dictated terms. The multinational corporation was simply too big and too powerful to any longer follow the dictates of old-school bankers.

Financing of every kind had never been so important as it was by the end of the third economy. Yet now corporations, rather than traditional banks, provided much of this financing. Icons of manufacturing, like Ford and General Motors, were to make more profit from their financing divisions than from their manufacturing divisions. Bankers no longer had a monopoly on information; they no longer even had a monopoly on banking.

While this story closes the section on the third economy, the world created by the major inventions and revolutions of this economy continue to define us. The problem is, this configuration of social inventions now seems to be addressing an old limit. The next section, on the fourth economy, explores what it would mean to start this anew this pattern of invention and revolution if, indeed, the limit to progress has shifted from knowledge work to entrepreneurship.

The Fourth Economy

The limit to progress has already shifted but the wave of changes to follow has barely begun. The limit to this new economy is entrepreneurship, or social invention. That entrepreneurship would become more common suggests that the self will be less defined by our major institutions than work to define those. This section predicts the emergence of a new economy that will follow the same pattern of progress of the first three.

Chapter 22, Entrepreneurship, explores how it is that entrepreneurs are rewarded more than ever before and what entrepreneurship and its popularization will mean.

Chapter 23, Imagining the Entrepreneurial Economy, speculates about a few technological inventions and then gives examples of what social inventions in business, finance, and education might look like.

Chapter 24, Systems Thinking, gives some of the key characteristics of systems and argues that without a better understanding of systems and their dynamics we might not just economically stagnate but regress.

Chapter 25, Inventing Self, explains why the author might make such a curious claim as this: this new economy will result in a new definition of self and the rise of the individual.

Chapter 26, Business Revolution, speculation about how the examples of the transformation of a few corporations could become just the beginning of a new kind of corporation, one that – like church, state and bank before it – no longer treats the individual as a tool but instead becomes a tool for the individual.

Chapter 27, The Rise of the Individual, leaves the reader with the responsibility to write the next chapter of history.

22 Entrepreneurship

Entrepreneurship – an act of social invention – involves bringing together some combination of land, capital, and labor to create a profitable enterprise.

Economy	First	Second	Third	Fourth
Period	1300–1700	1700–1900	1900-2000	2000-2050
Limit to Progress	Land	Capital	Knowledge Workers	**Entrepreneurship**
Type of Economy	Agricultural	Industrial	Information	Entrepreneurial
Intellectual Revolution	Renaissance	Enlightenment	Pragmatism	Systems Thinking
Big Social Invention	Nation-State	Bank	Corporation	Self
Social Revolution	Protestant Revolution	Democratic Revolution	Financial Revolution	Business Revolution

The limit to progress has seemingly shifted to entrepreneurship. Knowledge workers will remain important – just as capital remained important in the third economy – but will no longer be sufficient as a means to lead growth. To say that entrepreneurship will need to be popularized in this new economy the way that knowledge work was in the last is to say that the act of social invention that has defined every major turning point in the history of Western Civilization will become a regular, rather than exceptional, part of progress. Persistently higher rates of unemployment and erosion in incomes in countries throughout the West, in countries as varied as Japan, Spain, and the US, suggest that we're reaching the limits of our old strategies.

Joel Barker had popularized the idea of paradigm shift back in the 1980s. One frequently quoted remark of his is that "When the paradigm shifts, everyone goes back to zero." In that vein, I would argue that when the limit to progress shifts, a community has to be prepared to reinvent everything that defines it. If indeed the limit has again shifted, we'll soon see how ably we reinvent.

The Returns to Entrepreneurship

At the dawn of the fourth economy, entrepreneurs have become the new celebrities. Bill Gates and Richard Branson, Steve Jobs and Oprah Winfrey certainly deserve fame for creating distinct and successful companies. And they get it. Steve Jobs changed our notions of wealth when—as what seemed like just a kid—he reached a net worth of a million one year, ten million the next, and then one hundred million the year after that. Lately, Gates became the youngest to hit a billion, at thirty-one, and then about two decades later, Mark Zuckerberg hit a billion in his twenties. The rewards for entrepreneurship have never been so high.

Higher prices are the markets tugging at the sleeve of society to say, "Hey! We'd like more of this." Entrepreneurship pays more than it ever has before because there is more demand for it then there has ever been before.

But What Do Entrepreneurs Do?

There is something a little obsessive about the really successful entrepreneurs. Zuckerberg is committed to not charging people for Facebook. Jobs works for a dollar a year. Almost by definition, the entrepreneurs we hear about reach huge success financially, but there seems to be a bit of a paradox in their approach. Most of us think of money as something that would let us do whatever we want. I don't suppose that entrepreneurs are much different in that respect. Probably the real difference is that if they had money enough to do whatever they wanted, they would build successful products and businesses. Social invention is a game of seemingly infinite complexity, and one that entrepreneurs are playing rather than watching. Branson says that some of his friends thought that he should retire to have fun when his Virgin brand became so successful; the thing is, he was already having fun entering new markets with the brand. Money means that these entrepreneurs never have to worry about what they'll pay for a meal or even a private jet, but those sorts of things are actually peripheral to what most engages them.

Michael Gerber's book *E-Myth* distinguishes between the skills needed to make a pie and the skills needed to make a business that makes pies. The notion that being a good baker has much to do with running a successful bakery is what Gerber calls the entrepreneurial myth. One of his points is that entrepreneurship is still little understood, for all the press and adulation that it receives. His more important point is that successful entrepreneurship is about creating a sustainable system and not just being self-employed. An entrepreneur does not just buy himself a job by starting a business. Entrepreneurs don't just break away from one organization but also create a new one.

Economists list four factors of production: land (natural resources), labor, capital, and entrepreneurship. It was only in about the mid-twentieth century that economists began to regularly include entrepreneurship on the list of factors of production. "Economists and 'new economic historians' are skeptical of entrepreneurship as explanation, because it is hard to pin down and does not lend itself to measurement or prediction."[266] Entrepreneurship is the least tangible and certainly the most advanced of all of these factors. Each of the factors gets a return. Labor gets wages. Land—or resources—gets a price. Capital gets interest or dividend payments. After all the other factors are paid, entrepreneurship gets its profit, or takes a loss.

An entrepreneur has to create a system that is more than the sum of its parts. Literally. If the business that an entrepreneur starts and operates makes only enough revenue to pay labor its wages, pay for supplies, and pay back the banker, it will make no profit. Eventually, that means that the entrepreneur has no business. Profits are proof that the entrepreneur has created a business—that is, has created a system—that is more than the sum of its parts.

---

[266] Landes, *The Wealth and Poverty of Nations*, 447.

Entrepreneurship comes in many flavors. Henry Crowell was an entrepreneur who started a business, but he was a big-time entrepreneur. He didn't just found Quaker Oats; he invented breakfast cereal. A person who buys a franchise for a chain is another kind of entrepreneur, but one who has a formula to follow. Crowell had to make up recipes and cook well; a franchisee mostly has to cook well, using someone else's proven recipes.

Yet what these various kinds of entrepreneurs share is the fact that their success or failure is very much a product of their own vision and execution. A factory worker on the line at Ford has to work well to keep his job, but the company's ability to keep him on or lay him off is not really something for which he's responsible. The factory workers who could buy summer homes in the seventies and the ones who were laid off in the eighties and nineties weren't much different from one another. Often, they were exactly the same people. Yet they were working in systems that were mostly defined for them and that faced very different levels of success at different times.

By contrast, entrepreneurs are the ones who define the business with which they'll succeed or fail. The main limits to his success are the entrepreneur's imagination, ability, and read of the market.

Social Invention Is Bigger Than Business

Entrepreneurship is not about becoming a good Christian, a good citizen, or a good employee. It is about creating a new church, a new state, or a new business. Entrepreneurs don't accept the confines of the old institutions but instead create new ones that better align with their own values and potential and—just as importantly—the values and potential of their time.

And, of course, entrepreneurs create new businesses.

Everyone—from the least empowered employee to the most creative entrepreneur—is likely more defined by their times than they'd ever care to admit or even be able to consider. Yet the entrepreneur makes some attempt to define society and not just be defined by it. The most passive among us hear the dictates of society as non-negotiable. Entrepreneurs, by contrast, are engaged in a dialogue with their times, negotiating to close the gap between possibility and current reality.

Entrepreneurs are social inventors. Richard Branson wants to make space a tourist destination. Bill Gates has shifted his attention (mostly) from software development to global development. The Gates Foundation—a non-governmental organization (NGO)—provides about 30 to 40 percent of the Global Health Organization's annual budget.[267] After selling his company to J. P. Morgan, Andrew Carnegie went on to fund libraries and great venues like, well, Carnegie Hall. Business entrepreneurs often shift their focus outside of business to other areas of society. For them social invention is not always synonymous with business creation.

One way to understand systems is by studying their information flows. Entrepreneurs, who create systems, have a different relationship with information and attention than most.

The Third Economy's Rich, Middle-Class, and Poor

Joseph Campbell once quipped that we meditate all the time. The only question is on what we are meditating. Is it our doomed relationship? Our money or lack of it? The prospect of climate change or a takeover of "our" culture by those whose values are different than ours? What we'll have for lunch?

Consciousness will find a stream. The question is whether we will structure our consciousness or if someone else will. For social inventors, the challenge is even greater: their task is to structure the consciousness of others. It is not just a curious saying to claim that social change begins with a change in consciousness. What people are unaware of, they cannot choose. Some people are aware only of what lies before them; some are aware of possibilities that can't yet be seen.

In an information economy, we could distinguish between three groups simply by their relationship to the structuring of consciousness.

---

267 http://www.booktv.org/Watch/12237/How+to+Run+the+World+Charting+a+Course+to+the+Next+Renaissance.aspx, Parag Khanna, "How to Run the World" on C-SPAN BookTV.

Those who are least powerful and least rich are those whose consciousness is structured for them. "Stay tuned" they are told, and they do. They rely on popular media for information and entertainment. At work, they are given defined tasks and processes. They depend on others to direct their attention.

The middle class have created some independence of thought at work and in leisure. What they think about at home is more likely to be related to their own lives, to their own family and hobbies, than to what the media defines for them. What they think about at work requires more problem-solving and task definition than is required of those who are paid less. Their consciousness is largely directed by their own goals and realities.

Finally, the rich and powerful are those who structure consciousness for others. They write the software that defines the processes used to work or even (nowadays) socialize. They write the books and screenplays that hold people's attention and define conversations.

Whether you are rich or poor in this information economy is at least partly determined by whether you structure consciousness for yourself or have it structured for you.

The question of whether you are defining society or being defined by it is at least partly answered by the same distinction.

One result of the shift from mass media broadcasting to Internet multicasting is a shift in consciousness. Or, more accurately, a shift in the structuring of consciousness. What used to come from elites and spread outwards as a monologue has become a dialogue—or multilogue—between many. One side effect of this shift will likely be more ready acceptance of—and willingness to experiment with—social invention.

One last note on the structuring of consciousness: As we near the limits of the third economy, there seems to be even more pressure to work hard to make the old systems work as well as they used to. Some schools have cut back PE classes to once a week for forty-five minutes. (We've obviously abandoned the old Greek notions of developing the whole person and simply become more focused on the individual as a potential knowledge worker.) Work hours are creeping back up after being pruned back by labor unions earlier in the third economy. All this means that there is less time for daydreaming, play, and the fantasies that exercise the imagination. Such acts are wildly unproductive in the short run, but it is essential to be practiced in such things in order to engage the imagination in the act of generating and choosing among possibilities. No one plays, or appears to waste time, more than children, and yet no one learns or changes more.

New Limit

Throughout the West, a few things seem constant. One, never has a workforce been better educated. Two, never have financial markets had more credit or investments to offer. Three, never have governments been more uniformly aligned behind the goals of full employment and economic growth, and never have they pumped more money into the economy to create jobs and stimulate growth. Sadly, not since the Great Depression has the ratio of job creation to layoffs been worse for longer. During the tech boom and rise of venture capital in the nineties, the ratio of job creation to job loss in the United States was wonderfully high. Since the tech bubble burst, the ratio of job creation to job loss has been much lower and, of course, worsened in the wake of the Great Recession of 2009. Today about one in five Spaniards are unemployed, and the rate in of unemployment in the United States seems to persistently stay about double or triple what it was in the 1990s.

It is distinctly possible that the tools that worked so well in the third economy are falling into the category of necessary but no longer sufficient. Something more, it seems, is needed.

If the limit to growth has shifted to the most advanced of the four factors of production, this would explain—and promise—much.

The bad news about the limit shifting from capital to knowledge workers was that it meant disruptive changes in everything from the dominant way of thinking to which institution did the most to define our economy and society. The good news about the shift was that it led to advances the world had never before seen, improving both quality of life and levels of autonomy. The shift from the limit of knowledge workers to the limit of entrepreneurship seems to promise a similar level of disruption and improvement.

This means that we need to popularize entrepreneurship, get a broader swath of people involved in the act of creating new systems, and provide value and structure consciousness in ways that improve quality of life. This is no mean feat. Even the task of sustaining innovation within an organization is one that Drucker described as daunting:

It has become almost a cliché for historians of technology that one of the great achievements of the nineteenth century was the "invention of invention." Before 1880 or so, invention was mysterious; early nineteenth-century books talk incessantly of the "flash of genius." The inventor himself was a half-romantic, half-ridiculous figure, tinkering away in a lonely garret. By 1914, the time World War I broke out, "invention" had become "research," a systematic, purposeful activity, which is planned and organized with high predictability both of the results aimed at and likely to be achieved.

Something similar now has to be done with respect to innovation. Entrepreneurs will have to learn to practice *systematic innovation*.[268]

Imagine taking on the even bigger task of making a form of entrepreneurship, or sustained social innovation, the new task of modern corporations. Obviously, cultivating such ability will require some very big changes to the corporation and to all of society. There is no way that a change this significant can occur within the dominant institution and not ripple across all of the institutions in a community. This will change schools, governments, churches, and non-profits.

Successful entrepreneurs create a new enterprise, a mini-institution that lives at the intersection of their personal values and what society values. They shape it—as much as they can—to their vision. Entrepreneurship involves the same ability to create or redefine organizations that has characterized the great steps of progress throughout Western Civilization, from the acts of Martin Luther and Henry VIII to those of Wilhelm Humboldt and Nathan Rothschild. If more people were made more entrepreneurial, it could empower communities to make progress that impressive a regular part of the social landscape. To predict a world with widespread entrepreneurship is to say that the world will evolve and transform in unpredictable ways. It is, to say something either inane or profound, to predict the unpredictable.

Entrepreneurs bring together land, labor, and capital to create profit. The old limits are not discarded: they become vital elements of this new orchestra. The value that entrepreneurs create emerges out of the interaction of the old limits.

---

[268] Drucker, *The Executive in Action*, 284.

Creating Systems

Entrepreneurs sit outside of society in the same way that entrepreneurship sits outside of the other factors of production.

Given that entrepreneurship involves arranging land, capital, and labor into the production of value, it necessitates control over those factors. This has historically been accomplished when a person starts a business, hires employees, invests in physical capital (through loans, sharing equity, or using his own money), and buys the goods and resources needed to start providing goods or services. This owner, or entrepreneur, has the political and legal power to command these factors.

Successful entrepreneurs can design a corporation that outlasts their careers and even their lives. To stay alive, a company has to undertake entrepreneurial efforts to evolve its products, processes, and markets. This is, in a sense, an entrepreneurial endeavor most clearly performed by a founder or owner. Yet companies that outlast their founders are typically publicly owned, leaving only employees in charge. As a result, companies are basically left with the task of granting to special employees political power over the company's factors of production. Traditionally, the employee to whom that power is entrusted is the CEO and a relatively small number of senior managers with "chief" in their title.

What we've seen in the emergence of every previous economy, though, is that there is enormous value in dispersing power over the old institution to a broader swath of people. Entrepreneurship is rewarded more than ever; it is in demand. Wise companies will do what they can to make more employees more entrepreneurial, dispersing the power to manipulate the other factors into value to those well beyond the ranks of the senior executives and division heads.

It will be enormously difficult to do this within the bureaucratic structures that are still so prevalent. Given that bureaucracies effectively obscure the impact of the individual's effort, management drives work by rewarding behavior that aligns with organizational goals. Such central planning works about as well within corporations as it did within the former Soviet Union.

The popularization of entrepreneurship will require the adoption of tools and organizational structures that give the individual autonomy to act as he or she sees best, provide clarity about system dynamics within the organization and how individual performance maps to group performance, and allow natural consequences for success or failure. In a sense, the corporation needs to recreate some of the dynamic of markets within their operations. Given that some corporations have become the size of countries, this admonition for internal "markets" is not so far-fetched.[269]

Employees Creating Equity & Not Just Products

In the fourth economy, rather than make and design products as they did in the second and third economies, employees will create businesses.

At some point, the horse's trot becomes a gallop. It's not exactly clear at what speed that happens. At some point, employee research and development and project work will become an intentional act of equity creation. At what point this will segue from normal product development to something more akin to a business incubator is unclear. But corporations are already moving in this direction.

Popularization of Entrepreneurship

Perhaps the biggest difference between the education of knowledge workers in 1900 and that in 2000 lies in its popularization. In 1900, only a small fraction of the American population between the age of thirteen and seventeen was engaged in formal education; by 2000, only a small fraction was *not* engaged in formal education. Students read books, listen to lectures, take tests, and earn degrees just as they did a century ago, but do so in numbers that would have certainly boggled the imagination of college administrators of a century earlier. Knowledge work has become popular, and because of that its benefits have spread to a wider group of employees, encompassing a larger

---

[269] Russell L. Ackoff, *The Democratic Corporation: A Radical Prescription for Recreating Corporate America and Rediscovering Success* (New York: Oxford University Press, 1994),142–67.

percentage and number of workers than ever in history. Imagine a similar increase in entrepreneurship during the next fifty years.

What society has done for knowledge work in the last century, it now gets to do for entrepreneurship in this one. Entrepreneurial responsibilities are too important to be limited to a select few within any organization or community.

The popularization of entrepreneurship will be gradual. We talk fondly of democratic revolutions and forget about all the hard work of social progress that occurred between the time that white males who owned property were first given voting rights and the time that female minorities who rent could join them at the polls. The most obvious candidates for taking on more entrepreneurial responsibilities will be the senior scientists, engineers, and project managers within organizations. Indeed, their roles increasingly resemble those of entrepreneurs already. The transformation of the role of employee to something more like that of entrepreneur has already begun. Within the next few decades, the companies that succeed will be those that have determined how to most quickly spread entrepreneurial skills, thinking, and responsibilities to a larger percentage of their workforce. It's unlikely that the percentage of employees who become internal entrepreneurs will ever approach anything close to 100 percent, or even 25 percent. Yet if the average entrepreneur could create four jobs, we'd only need 20 percent of the workforce to be entrepreneurial to make unemployment like hunger – moved from a regular epidemic to something pushed to the margins of society. The point is to create the option of entrepreneurship for any employee and to regularly increase the portion of those who do choose that option.

The employees who choose entrepreneurial roles will need freedom to create. Entrepreneurs do not do well in environments of central planning, something nearly all communist countries have acknowledged in the last quarter of a century. Lest it sound as though my advice is to create an environment free of any rules or imposed consequences, it is worth noting that communities have fallen into at least three categories through history: lawless, law-abiding, and police state. Freedom for the individual does not mean freedom from consequences or freedom from any rules. Police officers patrol areas in every "free" nation. Yet living with police officers in the neighborhood is very different from living in a police state.

Within the developed nations, there is a large gap between starting one's own business and working as compliant employee, subject to (and at turns beneficiary of or suppressed by) other people's judgment.

There is an enormous gulf between traditional employee and entrepreneur – between enjoying relative security while being forced into compliance or facing probable failure (the majority of small businesses fail within a few years) while having the freedom to innovate. This huge gap offers great potential for companies. To the extent that companies can even incrementally move individuals from compliance to creativity, letting each person gradually find his or her own sweet spot in this range, the potential for progress is huge. Forced to choose between a bureaucratic role and role of a traditional entrepreneur, most workers would rather not be forced to make such a stark choice. A community able to make the choice less stark can only benefit. Imagine letting people retain some of the income stability of the employee role and gain some of the risk and return of the entrepreneurial role.

And for all the talk of controlling senior executives who don't allow employees freedom, there is another culprit worth mentioning—the controlled worker. I once heard Peter Block call the myth of leadership a collusion between control freaks and people who want to avoid responsibility. There is a certain freedom from responsibility in letting one's priest or minister define right and wrong, letting the king worry about which wars and budgets are just, letting the banker define return on investment and one's boss define one's job and even career. Such compliance has its origins in the medieval conception of true religion, when obedience seemed like the true measure of righteousness.

While dependency on others may end in disappointment, it does leave one feeling absolved of responsibility. There is nothing unique to monks in this embrace of submission to authority rather than reliance on one's own judgment and choices.

The big problems won't be solved, nor possibilities exploited, by people focused on succeeding within the current social institutions. Rather, as at every major inflection point in history, they will be solved by people who create new social institutions—that is, social entrepreneurs. Progress in the West has not followed from the best efforts of those who struggled to rise up through the Catholic Church or to gain the favor of monarch. Rather, it followed from people who struggled to create new ways of worship and new forms of government, dispersing the power once held by elites.

Here's something that elites have known for centuries: the individual can do the most for the community only by changing that community so that it better conforms to the individual. The point is not to conform the individual to society but to conform society to the individual. That's an easier proposition when the individual is just one person: the king or CEO. It is trickier but much more gratifying when everyone is invited to play this role.

The next chapter takes a different approach. It is a history of the future, speculating about the sorts of social inventions that might define the next economy in a world in which the West works to overcome this new limit of entrepreneurship.

23 Imagining the Entrepreneurial Economy

What would happen if the West shifted from focusing knowledge work and capital to overcoming the limit of entrepreneurship? Probably every institution we know would be recreated again and again in a variety of new forms.

Economy	First	Second	Third	Fourth
Period	1300–1700	1700–1900	1900-2000	2000-2050
Limit to Progress	Land	Capital	Knowledge Workers	Entrepreneurship
Type of Economy	Agricultural	Industrial	Information	**Entrepreneurial**
Intellectual Revolution	Renaissance	Enlightenment	Pragmatism	Systems Thinking
Big Social Invention	Nation-State	Bank	Corporation	Self
Social Revolution	Protestant Revolution	Democratic Revolution	Financial Revolution	Business Revolution

What will most distinguish the fourth economy will be social invention and, specifically, giving more employees a more entrepreneurial role. The result will not only be more innovation within corporations but within all organizations, including schools and government. The cumulative effect of each employee making his own change to the corporation will result in a host of new organizational forms. Corporations will remain important but will come in a wider variety of forms, from the traditional business to business incubators to forms we've yet to see. For instance, Ricardo Semler, one of the pioneers of organizational innovation, offers employees 11 different ways to get paid.[270] As happens in every domain in which human creativity is allowed to express itself, the result will be great and growing diversity.

During the third economy, the economy and wages grew faster than at any time in history. Between 1900 and 1999, average wages in the U.S. grew from $4,200 (in 1999 dollars) to $33,700. Not only that, but the average work week fell from fifty-three hours to forty-two: people could afford more products and more leisure. Work was also safer. In 1900, 1,500 coal miners and 2,550 railroad workers were killed; by 1999, those figures had dropped to 35 and 56. Much of this had to do with a greater emphasis on knowledge work. In 1900, only 14 percent of Americans had graduated from high school, a number that had increased to 83 percent by 1999. Between 1910 and 1999, the percentage of Americans graduating from a school of higher learning rose from less than 3 percent to 25 percent. Child labor dropped from 6 percent of the workforce to zero.271

Yet something seems amiss early in the twenty-first century. The strategies that proved so effective in the twentieth century are less so now.

Wages grew phenomenally during the third economy, yet their growth slowed near the end of the century. Between 1900 and 1980, average U.S. wages grew at an annual rate of 2.2 percent. In the 1980s, the growth rate fell to 1.8 percent; in the roaring 1990s, it fell again, to 1.6 percent, and in the first decade of the twenty-first century, it fell into the negative range, at -0.3 percent. These might sound like small differences, but percentages have a way of quickly compounding. By 2009 (in 1999 dollars) wages were just under $33,000. Had wages continued to grow from 1980 to 2009 at the same rate that they'd

---

[270] Ricardo Semler is the author of *Maverick*, but this tidbit was shared at the 2011 WorldBlu conference on organizational democracy.

[271]Donald M. Fisk, *American Labor in the 20th Century*, http://www.bls.gov/opub/cwc/cm20030124ar02p1.htm.

grown from 1900 to 1979, wages would have been $45,500. To repeat: wages were $12,500 less than they would have been at the old rate of growth. This is a difference of nearly 40 percent.

You could make the case that politicians have been giving tax cuts because the workplace is no longer giving raises. The pressure to sustain take-home salary has led to astronomical deficits and an increasing polarization about how to deal with diminishing salaries that shows up in the public sector as a nasty confluence of increased social needs and diminished resources with which to address these needs. As people make less, there is more need for social services like unemployment and health care. As people make less, there is less tax revenue available to pay for social services. Conservatives want to cut taxes to make up for less pay; liberals want to increase or sustain social services to make up for less pay. For all the stress caused by this conflict, little attention seems to be paid to why pay is no longer growing and why we now have to make such hard choices.

So what if the reason for this drop in wage growth is that the old limit no longer limits? Knowledge work less obviously seems like a limit these days: recent college graduates are suffering from unemployment and underemployment at stubborn rates and white-collar employees are often among the long-term unemployed. A college education still improves your odds of being employed and making more money, but it seems to less obviously guarantee such things.

It is distinctly possible that the information economy is past. At the dawn of the industrial economy, we had more capital than ever; the limit shifted to knowledge work because we had a glut of capital, not a shortage. Maybe one simple bit of evidence that we're past the information economy is that information no longer limits. We have a glut of it.

It would be tough to predict what sorts of technological inventions would follow from Coke's patent law in the early seventeenth century, just as it would be tough to predict what sorts of social inventions will follow from people taking seriously this notion of a shift in limit from knowledge work to entrepreneurship. Foolishly, I'll try to describe a little of what sorts of changes might occur.

Longevity

There's no reason to think that the rate of technological invention will slow. Out of a slew of advances that I could never hope to predict, I do think it is worth predicting two things.

One, biotech seems to be about where information technology was about 1970. That is to say, the most amazing advances are still ahead and will change the world greatly in the next few decades. This suggests some fascinating possibilities in regard to health and longevity.

Aubrey de Grey, a researcher at Cambridge, has a concept he calls the "longevity escape velocity."[272] He points out that science need not make us immortal to dramatically increase life spans. We can escape from inevitable death by simply getting to the point that we increase life expectancy by twenty-four hours every twenty-four hours. Last century, life expectancy rose about 30 years, from 47 to 77. This works out to a nearly 8 hour increase in longevity every 24 hours. If that rate of increase tripled to 24 hours, we'd have reached what de Grey calls the longevity escape velocity. Every twenty-four hours, life expectancies would rise another twenty-four hours.

It's a fascinating possibility, but we don't even have to go that far for people to seriously reconsider their lives. I think that the prospect of living even 100 to 120 years would be enough to prompt a variety of life changes.

I've given groups the exercise of imagining that life expectancy has doubled to 150 years. I've asked them to discuss how this might change how they approach their lives. What I did not expect the first few times I gave this thought experiment was the percentage of people who said that they simply did not want to live that long. Life was long enough, said about 15 to 40 percent of each group.

If people face the prospect of living considerably longer, I suspect that they'll demand even more of life. We often say, live like you'll die tomorrow but there is little that you can do in a day and little that you can't endure for that long. The more interesting question to ask is what would you do if you had another century? What would you simply no longer endure and insist on changing and what kind of work or projects would you want to do to accomplish something that did justice

---

272 Jonathon Weiner, *Long For This World: The Strange Science of Immortality* (Ecco, New York, NY, 2010)

to such a grand timeline? Faced with the prospect of another century, it is hard to believe that people would endure conditions at work, for instance, that so many endure.

Longevity alone could be enough to stimulate a wave of social invention.

Inventing New Systems

One difference between a great employee and a great entrepreneur is how they relate to the company. A great employee gives a great performance within the company; by contrast, the great entrepreneur creates a great company. One works within the system, and the other creates a new system.

Entrepreneurship is about creating systems. Systems thinking will become more common and its application won't be limited to social invention. It will do more to impact all areas of life, including technological invention.

Invention will increasingly be about inventing new systems and not just new products. Of course, this is not new. The car was invented in parallel with a thousand other things as varied as radios and gas pumps, repair shops and roads. What will be new is the degree to which inventors will attempt whole system change.

New energy systems, for instance, will be required to replace oil and coal, lest we revert to life standards from before the second economy. It is possible that productivity will drop because we'll be unable to find alternatives as cheap as oil and coal. It is also possible that we'll do for energy what we have done for information, making its unit cost drop to absurdly low levels. The latter suggests that we'd create new energy systems, not merely a new machine or single technology for energy.

A systems approach to invention suggests that technological invention will look more like social invention. That is, rather than invent in the lab and then debut a new product, inventors will have to engage various players in the system from the point of inception. This alone suggests changes in property laws (how do you protect inventions that don't yet exist?) and blurring the boundaries between the traditional domains of business and government. To solve these problems is going to require – surprise! – some clever acts of social invention.

This, of course, implies another prediction. It suggests that we'll be able to invent sustainable systems, systems as varied as our food, energy, transportation, and utility systems. There is, of course, no guarantee that we will learn how to invent new systems successfully, like we do today with new products. Failure is always an option. No one has ever guaranteed that so many of us could live so well for long. But even just a continuation of our current lifestyle requires this scale of invention. That, alone, will necessitate a wave of social invention.

Reaching the End of the Third Economy

As I write this, unemployment rates are only slowly falling in response to the biggest stimulus package since World War Two. To be fair, the stimulus seems to have given us a return by averting a catastrophe of Great Depression magnitude. The stimulus package did not, however, manage to actually avert what has proven to be the worst recession and slowest recovery of the third economy. We avoided the Great Depression but ran smack into the Great Recession.

This year (2011) the United States has a projected deficit of $1.5 trillion. This is the difference between taxes collected and money spent in just a single year. Outside of the United States there are only six countries with GDPs bigger than our *deficit*. It's a big deficit. Of course there are countries that have it worse: per capita deficits are huge, and many in the West are bigger than that in the United States—places as varied in culture and economic strengths as Japan and Spain. This set of financial issues and sluggish economic indicators seems to show as little regard for national borders as did industrialization or the spread of information technology.

We're spending all of this money in the hopes of a multiplier effect—that is, in the hopes that the money spent by the government will trigger spending by businesses and households and that will jumpstart the economy. Yet if that is the goal, why not go after it more directly? What if it is not enough to simply create more knowledge workers and assume more debt to stimulate production and consumption?

Maybe it would be better to have a policy to fund new businesses that would be to our time what the GI bill was to the explosion of knowledge workers after World War Two.

We want jobs. Why not use the stimulus money to create companies that would provide these jobs? Why give trillions to banks in the hopes that they will give it to companies in the hope that they will create jobs? Why not fund start-ups whose business plans include immediately hiring new workers?

After World War Two, the American government funded education for returning soldiers. This GI Bill really was instrumental in helping to create a new economy where professionals with advanced degrees did more to stimulate GDP growth than did capitalists and factory workers. People who would not have otherwise gone to college—who could not have afforded it—got degrees and pursued careers that their parents could not have imagined. By creating so many knowledge workers, the GI Bill helped to make the United States successful in the information economy. This was legislation that helped to overcome the limit of knowledge workers. What about legislation to overcome the limit of entrepreneurship?

Why not create a program that will allow us to look back in thirty years at the amazing companies that were started by the infusion of start-up capital? It is distinctly possible that these companies could found new industries and create wealth. Just as the GI Bill put people through college who would not have otherwise gone, this new bill could help people who would not otherwise be able to start a company do just that. Policy like this could increase the number of entrepreneurs in a time when—based on obvious indicators like the number of new businesses and jobs created—we do not have enough entrepreneurs. This would not be such a big change from what Keynes recommended and FDR did. In the thirties and forties, the banks weren't loaning enough and households and businesses weren't spending enough, so government policy did more of both. Since the bust, venture capitalists have stopped venturing capital to start-ups at the same rate as before and job creation has fallen; one can almost trace a direct correlation between the rate of growth of venture capital financing and job creation. Keynesian policy stimulated the economy when traditional banks didn't; why not create a modern policy that stimulates start-ups when venture capitalists don't?

Some portion of those funded by this policy could become the next generation of defining entrepreneurs. This would stimulate not just consumption but also two other things vital to a sustained economic solution to our current plight: new jobs and wealth. By creating more entrepreneurs, this new stimulus package could help to create an entrepreneurial age.

Ultimately, our twin deficits (trade deficits and government deficits) will not shrink until we begin to produce more and begin to create wealth faster than we deplete it. Why not replace deficit spending with investment in our one of great economic strengths: innovation and entrepreneurship?

If entrepreneurship limits, create more entrepreneurs. Yet given the dominance of corporations, it is not enough to limit the effort to create more entrepreneurs to just government efforts. It is not even obvious that government agencies will be more than salve (albeit badly needed salve) on a wound. We'll have to go inside the corporation to properly address this new limit. As it turns out, this won't be such a bad thing for employees or stockholders. (And in any case, it is getting harder and harder to tell the difference between those groups.)

The Corporation Now

You go to work inside of a corporation. Senior managers formulate the corporation's policies. Goals are set for your department for the year. Your department head translates those goals into your goals. It may well be that you and your peers can see a number of problems with the overall plan as it applies to you, but your attempts to point that out are largely ineffectual. You have little control over the direction of the company. You can leave the company if you are unhappy with its direction, but you would have to find a company run differently or start your own, both uncertain and difficult prospects.

Meanwhile, you contribute money each year to a pension fund. Some of you might have millions in retirement accounts and some of you might have only hundreds. But collectively, you and your fellow American workers "control" $6 trillion in stocks through pension and 401(k) funds. Although you and your peers own the companies in which you invest, you aren't particularly happy with their policies. The companies' policies seem to most obviously benefit senior managers. You can take your money out of the company, but you would have to find a company run differently.

You are pleased that your employer has created jobs in your

community. This generally helps. You also know, however, that these jobs and your potential are not the aim of your company. If and when these jobs can be done for less in places like the Ukraine or Mumbai, they will be.

It is not just your community's jobs you are concerned for: you are also worried about your planet and don't really know what, if anything, your employer is doing about climate change and other environmental issues. Even if you care deeply about environmental issues, you're not quite sure how to map that concern into the policies at the very company where you work.

What is the quip? It's like a fly riding an elephant who thinks he is steering the elephant. The elephant doesn't mind and it makes the ride more interesting for the fly. Many within the corporation share a feeling similar to that of the fly. The influence of the individual seems minimal.

The Corporation of the Future

Sometime in the next ten to twenty years, our concept of corporations will be transformed. Corporations will become a tool for individuals, a real departure from today, when the individual is the tool for the corporation.

You will go to work inside a corporation. Just like inside of a national economy, there will be regulations, opportunities, and natural consequences. But no one will define your goals. What you will do will be a product of some intersection of where you see opportunity for making money, what you enjoy doing, and what you think would best realize your potential. This is not the clergy sharing their divine revelation with you to dictate your life; this is you struggling to define that yourself. Opportunities inside of the corporation will arise organically. Employees—maybe 1 percent or maybe 50 percent—within the corporation will act like entrepreneurs, putting forth business plans that capitalize on connections, technology, markets, or capital and know-how within the corporation and without (the walls of the corporation will be porous).

Fellow employees will vote on these ventures in two ways. One will be by signing on to an entrepreneurial venture that they see as promising. This will take advantage of two things—widespread expertise and natural markets. (If employees are uninterested in a particular venture, it suggests serious flaws with it—flaws that might never come to light until after the fact in the world of traditional corporate management or financing from bankers or venture capitalists.)

The second way in which employees will vote will be through their pension funds. Employees will have the opportunity to invest in ventures at the ground-floor level, helping to fund their own projects or the projects of fellow employees. Employee money can be invested in company stock or in the start-ups underway within the company. This, too, will be a market signal about where experts familiar with the market, technology, and people involved think it best to direct resources. And it will be a chance for employees to get in on the ground floor of some very lucrative opportunities.

Given that they'll have the option to invest their labor or capital, employees will much greater influence over the company. More importantly, they'll have much greater influence over their own work and lives.

The community will benefit as well. In this new economy, policies will organically emerge from the actions of dozens, hundreds, or thousands of employees. They will no longer be top-down directed. People making policy rarely choose to put the smokestacks upwind from their houses. Communities will make choices for the company that are good for the community; just as importantly, individuals will make choices for the company that are good for the individual.

Imagine teams of employees presenting various business plans. They will present these plans not to management, but to their peers. These plans would represent potential equity creation and the peers who would vote yea or nay on the plans would be the very people who provide the capital to fund these ventures. Employees must invest their money for retirement, and already some portion of that often goes to the very company in which they are employed. Imagine this going further and employees actually deciding on the business ventures, the teams, and the project managers in which to invest. This promises all the excitement and energy of a fantasy league but for something other than a fantasy.

This could not only give employees more control over their retirement, but it would give a company a way to become "a land of opportunity," where employees could hope to get rich. Not only would employees have a stake in the ventures, but, done properly, the employee-led teams and project managers could have a disproportionate stake in the venture. Compared with what a team might make outside of a company, the possibility for wealth would be less. Given that the company is providing the infrastructure and employment as teams pursue new ventures, the company would take a share that would be even greater than that taken by venture capitalists. Compared with what a team could make as traditional employees, though, the possibility for wealth would be greatly enhanced. Such activities within companies would exploit the huge gap that now exists between the extremely high risk and return of traditional entrepreneurship and the low risk and low return of traditional employment.

This is not all speculation about what might happen in the future. There are companies that have already taken steps in this direction. Bill Gross, founder of Idealab, and Jack Stack of SRC Holdings come to mind (more on these two later). People like Gross and Stack are pioneering new ways to redefine the company as a business incubator—a company that makes companies and not just products.

It took decades for the steam engine to become a general purpose machine and centuries before parliament was foundational to government rather than something that could be dissolved each time a monarch grew impatient with its ineffectuality. There is still a great deal to learn about how to make employees more entrepreneurial. But new economies are not so much defined by new knowledge as new questions. The question of how to make corporations more entrepreneurial is one that raises a thousand more questions and opens up thousands of new possibilities.

Such internal ventures might require a redefinition of ownership, but certainly not on the scale of what Henry VIII did when he took property from the church or when England even earlier began the enclosure movement, making communal property private. Just as communities worked to define intellectual property, savvy companies will find ways to reward employee entrepreneurship while still creating wealth for traditional stockholders. Still it is easier to solve these problems than it is to solve the problems that arise from ignoring them.

If the corporation changes in such fundamental ways, so will schools and governments.

Education & Entrepreneurship

Education is perhaps one of the more exciting arenas for social invention. Even to the casual observer, the failure of a system that assumes every child has the same potential, same goals and same interests is obvious. The school system works reasonably well for producing the next generation of academics, but it doesn't do such a great job for people who are interested in making money, finding spiritual peace, creating and sustaining healthy relationships, gaining mastery of plumbing, or any of a number of other pursuits that communities deem important.

We in the United States keep talking about a failing school system and then do even more to reinforce the same system, same goals, and same approach. If we could find an export market for standardized test scores, the emphasis on them would make more sense. As it stands, this emphasis is just baffling. Not only are children vastly different in their approaches to learning and their potential but they are on widely varying paths. As the world becomes more advanced, it becomes more diverse. Generations ago, a woman in higher education was probably going to be a nurse or a teacher; today, she is just as likely preparing for a career that didn't exist when she started kindergarten. It is not obvious how emphasizing standardized anything is preparation for that reality. Schools as they are now constructed simply were not invented to keep up with our rapidly evolving society.

One of the ways that schools may become more entrepreneurial is through the increasing emphasis on the use of video and computer programs that will free millions of teachers across the country from repeating the same instruction over and over to the average child in the class. This will radically decrease the amount of time needed for the generic kind of instruction that really is inescapable and important—things like math and grammar that are the building blocks for so much knowledge. Imagine what would happen if such videos and programs could free up even 10 percent of teachers' time—or what might happen if it could free up 50 percent of their time.

The teachers could then focus on customizing education for students by using that 10 to 50 percent more time for new tasks that are now largely ignored. Tasks like working through misunderstandings and finding ways to apply what is learned to the student's life—all the hard work of customization that so often gets short changed because teachers are so busy teaching what could be, in a sense, automated—could be the teachers' new focus. Such a change in how our schools work would, of course, be a great trigger for technological innovations: not just more learning videos and games, but even simulation exercises (not necessarily computer based) that help students to gradually and regularly map the gap between academics and their personal future. The emphasis in this educational system would be on diversity and realizing the potential of individuals, not on standardized test scores and performance within a group.

Within corporations, at least two things will be going on that could easily be adapted to education. Systems thinking will help to blur the boundaries between institutions, blur the boundaries between work and learning, for instance. Corporations will also be putting more emphasis on entrepreneurship which includes projects to launch new businesses.

Students too could use systems thinking to look outside the boundaries of their schools for possibilities for learning. And they could use projects to change their world rather than just study it. Learning could take place through community projects.

Imagine that students needed to define and execute projects that took them out into the community. Poverty. Transportation issues. Drug use. Health problems. There is no shortage of issues that communities face. What if teachers and professors and their students had to define and execute projects that would—worst case—result in new knowledge about how to deal with these issues and—best case—result in better outcomes in these domains? Why couldn't architecture and building trade students get their experience from real-world projects that also lower the rate of homelessness? What if students actually helped local businesses to become more productive, helping to solve problems in marketing, sales, design, manufacturing, intellectual property, or training?

Before the third economy, universities were generally expected to simply teach knowledge. After, they were expected to create it. The admonition to "publish or perish" was an admonition to continue adding to knowledge.

What if we now go a step further? What if schools were not just a place for social research and technological experimentation but for social experimentation? What if students were engaged in projects to study and minimize homelessness, drug abuse, and pollution, and to enhance the creation of jobs and public spheres where people gathered to exchange goods and information? What if schools didn't just teach the history of social invention but gave students the chance to practice of social invention?

Education Adapts to the Child

Not only could schools blur the boundary between work and learning, between social study and social invention, they could be adapted more to the realities of real human beings. Institutions like schools are just made up: people, by contrast, are real. Schools can better adapt to real human beings by designing education to accord with some of the more interesting theories about who people are rather than who we think they should be. One of the reasons that love is so intoxicating and desired is that being loved means being fully embraced for who we are. Institutions that insist we should become someone we are not seem to be the opposite of that. Love opens up a person; institutions, too often, shut them down.

One of the more interesting theories of who we are is Howard Gardner's theory of multiple intelligences. Someone quipped that after Howard Gardner defined these various kinds of intelligence, the question shifted from *whether* your child was smart to *how* your child was smart. Gardner writes[273] and talks to the various ways that people learn, think, create careers, and change communities. He lists eight kinds of intelligence.

Multiple Intelligences:

- Spatial: the artist or architect with the ability to see and manipulate objects in three dimensions;
- Linguistic— poets and speakers who use words and language as their tools;
- Logical-mathematical: the computer programmer or math professor who can reason and manipulate numbers;
- Bodily-kinesthetic: the dancers and athletes whose control over their bodies lets them do with precision and strength what others are left to admire;

[273] Howard E. Gardner, *Frames of Mind: The Theory of Multiple Intelligences* (Basic Books, New York, NY, Third Edition 2011).

- Musical: performers, songwriters, and composers;
- Interpersonal: the leaders, salespeople, and politicians who sense what others are feeling and know how to influence others' emotions, reasoning, and actions;
- Intrapersonal: the psychologists and theologians who are introspective enough to understand the inner life;
- Naturalistic: the farmers and ecologists who understand and work with the rhythms and dynamics of nature.

Additionally, fairly popular notions of learning suggest that people have at least three kinds of learning styles: some are visual, some auditory, and some kinesthetic learners.

If we assume that any one of the eight kinds of intelligence could mix with any one of the three kinds of learning styles, we have a fairly complex menu of minds. In theory, we'd have three times eight, or twenty-four, different kinds of learners. We'd have auditory learners who are most gifted with interpersonal intelligence and visual learners whose greatest gift is logical-mathematical kind of intelligence and so on.

This suggests that in a time of entrepreneurship and social invention, we might create at least twenty-four kinds of learning experiences, if not even twenty-four different learning institutions. This customization of learning for different types of students would be just one example of how institutions could be made into tools for the individual

In this context, thinking of developing an educational system that would work best for a particular kind of learner, one gets a better appreciation of W. Edwards Deming's disdain for grades. Imagine grading a visual learner whose potential intelligence was intrapersonal—a person who might be brilliant at reading facial expressions, gestures, and body language for clues about another's emotions and thoughts. Now imagine that this person was struggling to learn within a school designed for auditory learners, where the types of intelligence that are emphasized are language and math. This child would get a low grade. In this system, he or she would be made to (unfairly) look stupid or inept or lazy. This would almost be excusable if it were really the case that the only way to make a living was to be good at math or language. In fact, a person who can read and influence others might make more money in sales or management than anyone who pursued a career in literature or algebra.

Deming said that if we know a student got a 92, say, or a 58, we know nothing about the student. The amount of learning a student gains is a function of an equation of X * Y = student score. X is the system and Y is the student. You can't solve for Y (the student's ability) without knowing X (the system's contribution). And of course, for one child the system is a perfect complement to her potential whereas for another it is a miserable clash. For one student, the system works. For another, it does not. For the intrapersonal, visual learner, the interaction of the educational system and the student produces a 58, a grade of D. For the logical- mathematical, auditory learner, the interaction of the system and student produces a 92, or an A. The question is not whether the student is smart, but how. In a time of rampant social invention, there is no reason that new systems can't be created that better suit the individual. School should be a means for a student to discover and develop his own potential, not be ranked against other students on criteria that may or may not have anything to do with his—or even his community's—future.

Another domain that might change because of social invention is finance.

Banking on Your Friends

Banking revenues in the United States alone are hundreds of billions per year. Banks, though, are just intermediaries between people. One person has, say, $20,000 to save for future use and another person has $20,000 they need to borrow to use now. The person who puts $20,000 in a savings account in the bank may get a 1 percent return. The person who borrows $20,000 for, say, a car loan may have to pay 11 percent interest. The bank takes the $20,000 from the saver, paying her 1%, and then gives it to the borrower, charging him 11%. The bank gets the 10% difference to finance operations and generate a profit. Banks make trillions from this difference in savings and borrowing rates.

Curiously, the bank might provide this service for two people who are neighbors, friends, or fellow employees. What if new social networks could be used to bring these two together, letting them split the 10% might otherwise go to the bank? What if the person needing the loan could borrow it at 5% from the person who would otherwise make only 1%?

Obviously there are other factors involved, but still the potential shift from banking institutions into households is huge.

Banks get to be intermediaries because they know who has money and who needs it, who is a credit risk and who is trustworthy. These are information advantages and there is nothing uniquely about banks that suggest that they are the only ones who should have or be able to respond to such information. Sometimes social invention like patent laws changes technology by stimulating invention of things like steam engines. Sometimes technological inventions like the internet and social networks change society by stimulating the inventions of things like new means to invest and borrow.

More important than this type of possibility for changing finance is the reminder that the internet has changed the information costs for transactions. This could easily change and even obsolete a variety of organizations.

Work

Fill your bowl to the brim
and it will spill.
Keep sharpening your knife
and it will blunt.
Chase after money and security
and your heart will never unclench.
Care about people's approval
and you will be their prisoner.

Do your work, then step back.
The only path to serenity.

—Lao-Tzu

Work matters. Profoundly. It has the potential to define us as much as anything else in our life. Think of the people who stand out in history, people as different as Picasso, da Vinci, Marie Curie, Maria Montessori, Bob Dylan, Beethoven, and Kurt Vonnegut. We know them through their work.

So what does it mean to be defined by work that is defined by someone else? What does it mean to conform to processes defined by management teams who know little of our potential or unique skills?

Perhaps the greatest gift to quality of life will be treating work as a good in and of itself and not just as a means to produce goods. For now, this goal of good to do is little considered within the corporation. The point of the company is to please consumers or to provide a return to stockholders. This could change as employees become more entrepreneurial.

The goal of an entrepreneur is not just to make money. Entrepreneurs are seeking autonomy. "Being my own boss," is what many say motivates them, and a successful entrepreneur does not just have money enough to often what the rest of do rarely, if at all. The successful entrepreneur has created a business that works without him, giving him time and discretion about how to use it. His work does not always produce flow, but as long as it supports what he's creating, even taking out the trash can feel meaningful. A successful entrepreneur is not just seeking to maximize profit. He considers more variables than that in his approach to work. It is "his" business and he can use it to try to create more money or more leisure or more engaging tasks.

As employees become more entrepreneurial, they may well focus at first on making more money. Eventually, they may their ability to create equity the way past generations created products to become richer. Eventually, they may use this new-found ability to create more leisure and more gratifying task as well.

Timothy Ferris advocates a regular examination of one's work in light of the 80/20 rule. Look for the 20 percent of your activities that produce 80 percent of the profits or return. Work to minimize the 80 percent of the work that doesn't contribute quite so much and amplify the 20 percent that contributes more. By systematically doing this, he argues that you can move towards a 4 hour work week. His real argument is to design work the way you would design products: to maximize satisfaction. He is, of course, not talking about just satisfaction with a product but satisfaction with a lifestyle. His ideas are popular and – it seems to me – rightly so. This design of work is stupidly overlooked in the emphasis on designing products that are, by contrast, so ephemeral and marginal to our happiness with life.

Beyond the Idea that Only Elites are Social Inventors

This suggests a few ways in which social invention might change this entrepreneurial economy from the information economy. It is an exercise worth trying at home. You might just define an entrepreneurial opportunity that will come to define you.

The thing to remember is this: all of this is just made up. Every institution that defines you is a social invention. Every institution. From church and family to school and work, from media to financial markets.

What is not just made up? People and their vast differences. Nature and its gifts and demands. Systems and their dynamics. Our need for a society in which we can live and realize our potential.

Perhaps I'm the only one who thinks it is a fascinating prospect to imagine a world where what is made up is adapted to what is real, but I doubt it. You would not have read this far if you thought that the individual needed to do more to adapt to social inventions rather than vice versa. Daydream a little. In a few years, you might just wake up to live that daydream.

Entrepreneurship is about bringing together land, labor, and capital into some venture that makes a profit. Put differently, entrepreneurship is about creating a system that is more than the sum of its parts. While Pragmatism helped generations of knowledge workers to solve problems, a more entrepreneurial approach suggests a better appreciation for systems and systems dynamics. It suggests that systems thinking become to this next economy what the Enlightenment was to the second economy, and key elements of this worldview are explained in the next chapter.

24 Systems Thinking

Our world is defined by systems and yet most of the players and policy makers in these systems still define their thinking by pragmatism. It might be time to change this.

Economy	First	Second	Third	Fourth
Period	1300–1700	1700–1900	1900-2000	2000-2050
Limit to Progress	Land	Capital	Knowledge Workers	Entrepreneurship
Type of Economy	Agricultural	Industrial	Information	Entrepreneurial
Intellectual Revolution	Renaissance	Enlightenment	Pragmatism	**Systems Thinking**
Big Social Invention	Nation-State	Bank	Corporation	Self
Social Revolution	Protestant Revolution	Democratic Revolution	Financial Revolution	Business Revolution

Systems thinking is better suited to entrepreneurship than is pragmatism, focused as it is on relationships and emergent phenomenon. After all, entrepreneurship is about creating a new system. We will still need pragmatic specialists – even more than ever. But the context of their work will be at least as important as the work itself, the context defined by the venture they are a part of creating, a context that systems thinking will help to create.

Living at the Corner of Sustainability & Collapse

Two things have happened to create a need for systems thinking. One is that the knowledge workers of the third economy have created systems of increasing complexity. Two, these systems are often at odds with natural ecosystems and human psychology—the two givens to which any social and technological systems eventually must adapt.

Modern systems are enormously complex. The dynamics of financial systems, transportation systems, and energy systems as varied as underwater oil drills and nuclear power plants are all examples of systems that we've discovered our limits to manage or control in times of crisis. The good news is that we've created some wonderfully powerful systems. The bad news is that we've created some incredibly difficult systems. They show their fragility from time to time, in problems like blackouts, traffic jams, oil spills, market crashes, meltdowns, plane crashes, bankruptcies, and wars.

As *Black Swan* author Nasim Taleb points out, it is in the time of crisis that systems are defined—or, more precisely—redefined. The treatment that the turkey gets every day leading up to Thanksgiving does not ultimately defines how he was treated; that one, exceptional, day just before Thanksgiving does this. The days in which the nuclear power plant safely generates energy do not define it nearly so much as the day it goes radioactive.

It is also increasingly apparent that our economic system is at odds with nature, itself a system with its own dynamics and requirements. There is nothing unique about this. Many of our institutions are at odds with our own nature, with who we are.

Climate change is probably the most obvious symptom of the clash with nature, but the depletion of life in the ocean, the diminishing levels of fresh water, and the destruction of small ecosystems are all evidence of a clash.

Less obvious is the extent to which our inventions—particularly our social systems—clash with human psychology, and are at odds with who we are. Corporations are pretty good about conforming to psychology when it comes to products: the intuitive feel of the iPhone and its appeal as a product is just one of many bits of evidence of how seriously corporations take human psychology when it comes to humans as consumers. Corporations seem less able to engage the human when it comes to our roles as producers, though. As previously mentioned, the design of work is something rarely considered much less done intentionally. We too often brute force learning and work within our social systems with carrots and sticks (or, in an attempt to stay positive, using carrots as sticks). Generally speaking, corporations are less sensitive to human psychology when it comes to the design of work than in the design of products.

We live in a world of systems. Systems are defined by the interaction of their parts and interventions in them often have unintended consequences. A pharmacist prescribing Lupron for cancer can trigger a diabetic reaction. A new business process introduced to lower costs can end up raising costs. Budget cuts for preschool in one decade can raise crime in the next. Bodies, businesses, and society are all examples of systems. One option for dealing with such systems is to ignore their properties and confusing interactions. A better option is to apply systems thinking to them, trying to better understand their defining relationships and dynamics.

Systems thinking is not a luxury of philosophical indulgence, as if we as a generation had decided to sit in sidewalk cafes discussing existential philosophy while smoking unfiltered cigarettes. We live among and depend upon systems that are growing ever more complex; failure to understand systems leads to a growing sense of helplessness. It makes us feel angry even with those most curiously complex and obstinate systems we call institutions.

Americans' confidence in institutions has steadily declined in the last couple of decades. The most obvious drop has probably been in Congress, where approval ratings that were in the low 40s in the early 1970s have dropped into the teens more recently. Yet it is not just in politics where Americans have become distrustful. The Great Recession has exacerbated a steady downwards trend in our confidence in banks (60 percent confidence in 1979 became 22 percent confidence in 2009). Furthermore, Americans are even less confident in big business than in small business (16 percent vs. 67 percent), and while confidence in small business has gone up slightly, confidence in big business has dropped about 40 percent in just the last few years.

Americans have seemed to lose confidence in nearly all institutions.[274] Even marriage is suffering from a lack of confidence: fewer people get married, those who do are more likely to divorce, and 44 percent of Americans under thirty think that marriage is headed for extinction (although, curiously, 95 percent of this age group want to get married).[275] All of these institutions are systems, and all seem to be faltering in the modern world.

I would argue that one reason we've so lost confidence in our institutions is that they don't seem to have adapted to the modern world. The reason for that may simply be that these institutions—defined by relationships—are subject to system dynamics that have not held together well with the glue of Enlightenment and pragmatic thinking. Understanding systems dynamics requires, well, systems thinking.

Defining Systems: Emergent Phenomenon and Relationships

Like dogs watching television, we participate in systems that we vaguely understand and can predict only within fairly narrow boundaries. We still have so much to learn about systems and systems thinking but as with all of life, we start with what we know rather than what we don't.

Systems are characterized by emergent phenomena, properties of the whole that emerge out of the interaction of the parts. Hydrogen is a gas. So is oxygen. Yet combining two atoms of hydrogen with one atom of oxygen gives you water, a liquid. Sometimes emergent properties are intuitive and sometimes—as with H_2O—they are not.

W. Edwards Deming offered an interesting example of emergent phenomenon. He made the point that when assessing a team made up of three people it is easy to think that we'll know how the group will

---

[274]Lydia Saad, "Americans' Confidence in Military Up, Banks Down," June 24, 2009, http://www.gallup.com/poll/121214/americans-confidence-military-banks-down.aspx

[275]Belinda Luscombe, "Who Needs Marriage?" *Time*, November 18, 2010, http://www.time.com/time/nation/article/0,8599,2031962-2,00.html

perform if we simply look at the performance of each individual. The team performance of Tom, Carmen, and Jin could look like this:

Tom's performance [T] + Carmen's performance [C] + Jin's performance [J] = team performance [x]

In fact, that might well be the least of the equation. The team's performance is also a function of:

Tom's working relationship with Carmen [T~C] + Carmen's working relationship with Jin [C~J] + Jin's working relationship with Tom [J~T] + the dynamic that emerges between all three [T~C~J]

An equation that at first blush looks like

T + C + J = x

is actually

T + C + J + [T~C] + [C~J] + [J~T] + [T~C~J] = x

This is not a problem of simple addition. This is a problem of relationships and emergent phenomenon. Jin could be a great guy but cause the other two team members to perform poorly. Carmen might be a poor performer on her own but might make the team work better. The symbol ~ sometimes adds and sometimes multiplies as team members bring out what is better in each other; it sometimes subtracts and sometimes divides as they, at other times, undermine each other or leave each other feeling lessened. What emerges out of relationships is not simple and cannot be reduced to its parts. Systems are defined by emergent properties, not just their parts. The proverb, "In an avalanche, each snowflake pleads its innocence," captures the fact of emergent phenomenon transcending any one agent.

It gets more complex. The world in which we live is defined by dynamics within systems, dynamics across systems, and the dynamics of systems within systems. Like Russian dolls, our world is not only composed of systems but has layers of systems. Your respiratory system can perform in ways that allow you to run a marathon or be unable to rise out of bed; if you are a king, this difference can ripple across a kingdom to shatter a fragile peace, your body's system affecting the political system.

Sometimes the butterfly stirs up a storm and sometimes it gets pinned inertly into the collection. It's hard to predict which it will do just by looking at the butterfly.

Spilling across Traditional and Institutional Boundaries

Individuals get made heads of departments within organization. Carla is the vice president of engineering and Kumar is the vice president of manufacturing. At one level, responsibility in such an organization is amazingly clear. At another—at the level of interactions and unintended consequences—nothing could be more confusing. For instance, if engineering is designing a product to use eighty-seven different-sized bolts and the purchasing agent in manufacturing is finding it nearly impossible to keep such a variety of bolts in inventory without blowing his budget for parts, who is "responsible" for that? Carla or Kumar? Is that a manufacturing problem or an engineering problem?

At a community level, responsibilities are even harder to assign. Imagine that companies complain that schools are unable to properly prepare students for work. Are schools responsible for this problem?

What if teachers complain that parents are not sending children to school properly prepared for learning? Are families responsible for this problem?

What if parents complain that their company works them such long hours that they haven't got the time or energy to help their children with schoolwork? Are companies responsible for this problem?

For the most pernicious problems of communities, organizational responsibility breaks down. Our analytic perspective and the organizations structured in accord with that perspective promise little help with the significant problems that have emerged. In the words of the systems thinker Dee Hock, "The nature of our organizations, management, and scientific expertise is not only increasingly irrelevant to pressing societal and environmental needs, it is a primary cause of them."[276] Many of our problems are not just difficult to solve using analytic thinking but are the result of organizing our world to conform with analytic thinking.

It is hard to believe that adopting a systems perspective won't cause us to rethink our institutions at the most fundamental level. This is to say, it is hard to believe that the social invention of this new worldview of systems thinking won't cascade into even more social inventions. One of the surest ways to change reality is to change how people define reality.

---

[276] Hock, *Birth of the Chaordic Age*, 57.

Rediscovering What Pragmatists Discarded

William James and the pragmatists were trying to get past abstractions to reality on its own terms. Pragmatists seemed acutely aware of the fact that systems of thought that sought to idealize or define reality were too often impositions upon reality, impositions that did as much to distort and ignore reality as they did to actually reveal it. Throwing off these old philosophical systems was a great and necessary step in the progression of thought.

Yet James's critics accused pragmatists of dividing the world into the Harvard curriculum, and there is some truth in it. Just as the Harvard curriculum was divided into different areas of study, focusing one on politics, say, with little or no regard for literature or economics, the pragmatist allowed a person to focus on one problem or domain with little or no regard for another. Pragmatism helped give birth to generations of specialists whose disdain for ill-fitting generalizations also tended to keep them from considering other specialties or issues that exist in larger systems. These specialists didn't think that attempts to change the larger system were very pragmatic, and they were right.

The good news is that pragmatism freed specialists from systems of thought that too often ignored the specific peculiarities of reality. The bad news is that pragmatism helped to further fragmentation, and helped specialists to ignore systems of thought or, really, any kind of system.

There is, of course, at least one problem with this: in a world full of pragmatists all focused on specific solutions to specific problems in a specific context, the system as a whole is neglected. Some intelligent experts are hard at work trying to understand how to sell cars, some at how to sell political candidates, others at how to understand climate change, but few are at work trying understand how all these (and other) pieces come to together to inexorably move us towards a calamitous collision of products, politics, and climate—that is, how our habits threaten our habitat. Working towards a solution to this problem is terribly un-pragmatic, suggesting a course of action that is both improbable and implausible. Problems like climate change are not just, as Al Gore points out, an inconvenient truth, but ones for which our social inventions have left us ill-equipped.

Here at the dawn of the fourth economy, pragmatism is no longer terribly pragmatic.

Reaching the Limits of Analysis

In the twentieth century, knowledge became more fragmented and knowledge work became more specialized as scientists and practitioners generated more knowledge. This is perhaps one reason that the systems thinking revolution emerged in a number of areas. Biologists, urban planners, and rocket scientists all found themselves developing vocabulary and methods for understanding complex interactions that exceeded the scope of their language. Mathematical (and eventually computer) models came into vogue and were used to better understand dynamics over time. Elements of systems thinking emerged from various disciplines, and thinkers using labels as diverse as cybernetics, urban planning, biological thinking, adaptive complexity, self-organizing systems, economics, and ecosystems were all developing similar tools and methodologies.

You can discover one problem with these approaches just by listening to a discussion of the deficit on C-SPAN. The numbers and projections quickly make the eyes glaze over. Listening to conversations about systems dynamics can be like trying to follow a preschooler's description of a cartoon. Fortunately, the information economy has brought us computers able to run complex simulations that teach us systems dynamics. We may have options for dealing with systems that don't fully depend on narratives.

Talk seems like a bad way to explore or explain systems dynamics. Fortunately, some folks are focusing on adapting experts' simulations into something that can help to facilitate learning and decisions.

In a simulation of a small community named Greenvale, researchers studied participants' ability to effectively change policies that would, for instance, balance such goals as air quality and employment. Traditionally, the pro-environment folks would debate the pro-business folks and likely no one would change their mind about anything.

The good and bad participants did not differ ... in the frequency with which they developed hypotheses about the interrelation of variables in

Greenvale. Both the good and bad participants proposed with the same frequency hypotheses on what effects higher taxes, say, or an advertising campaign to promote tourism in Greenvale would have. The good participants differed from the bad ones, however, in how often they tested their hypotheses. The bad participants failed to do this. For them, to propose a hypothesis was to understand reality; testing that hypothesis was unnecessary. Instead of generating hypotheses, they generated 'truths.'"[277]

Further, the simulations helped everyone to learn and to converge on some useful policies. Pro-environment folks learned that it didn't do too much good to protect the environment through such onerous legislation that it drove out businesses. In this scenario, no one could live in the town because there were no jobs, so the healthy environment was merely a consolation prize. Also, the pro-business folks learned that disregard for the environment made the place unfit as a place to raise families. Jobs were irrelevant because no one would live there. The simulation helped the two groups to converge on policies that would balance two really important goals – jobs and environment.

Systems thinking has the potential to change the twenty-first century as much as the Enlightenment changed the second economy or pragmatism changed the third. (And for those of you who have not been paying attention through earlier chapters that would be a lot.)

Systems thinking reveals flaws in the analytic perspective that has so pervaded science and policy. The analytic perspective would lead one to conclude that a fertilizer that greens one's lawn is good, even if the ocean downstream is harmed by it. The analytic perspective would conclude that a rise in GDP is a good indicator of progress, even if such a rise was the result of spending too much on food, which triggers obesity and excessive spending on health care (and, oddly enough, further rises in GDP). The systems perspective does not allow us to conclude that an economic system that consumes its habitat in the process of creating goods *is* good.

It seems overwhelming to deal with systems interactions and unintended consequences. Key to reaching our objectives without destroying ourselves is the development of systems technology—tools and policies—to complement the sophisticated analytic technology that has

---

[277] Dietrich Dorner, *The Logic of Failure: Recognizing and Avoiding Error in Complex Situations*, trans. Rita and Robert Kimber (Reading, Mass.: Addison-Wesley, 1996), 23–24.

evolved since the dawn of the first economy.

Technology at the Dawn of the Fourth Economy

Technology is a means for achieving goals. As the environment or goals evolve, so must technology. This is just as true of social technology like voting and brainstorming, as it is of "hard" technology, like cars and airplanes.

If a person wants to cross the room, she walks. If a person wants to cross town, she drives. If she wants to cross the continent, she flies. The scope of the goal determines the choice of technology, from house slippers to jet airplane.

If a policy maker passing legislation or making decisions affecting a corporation wants to plan a meeting for that afternoon, he talks. If he wants to put in place a budget for the next year, he talks. If he wants to create rules or legislation that will shape the next generation, he talks. Even as our world becomes more complex, the tools popularly used to make decisions and policy are little evolved from what we've used since the dawn of the first economy.

Policy-makers worked to create tools for full employment and education in the third economy, and ways to measure returns on capital and track profits in the second. It's time that we did more to develop and popularize the use of systems thinking technologies. If we were to immerse students in such technologies, it could greatly influence the intuition of voters and employees as they struggle to change and succeed within the systems that so define their lives.

Policy Making and Systems Thinking

The three people who have perhaps done the most to translate systems thinking considerations into business practices are W. Edwards Deming, Russell Ackoff, and Peter Senge. In the midst of a plethora of business books that perpetuate many of the same ideas first put into practice a century ago, these three represent a focus, instead, on significant change to corporations, change rooted in systems thinking. W. Edwards Deming gained fame as the consultant to whom the Japanese gave great credit for their advances in quality and market share. Ackoff had a close following of students who loved his ability to articulate the differences between analytic and systems thinking. Senge has been associated with MIT for decades, gaining fame with his *Fifth Discipline* book that advocated the use of systems thinking to create learning organizations.

"By and large, [managers and policy makers] don't learn from their experience because the most important consequences of their actions occur elsewhere in the system, eventually coming back to create the very problems they blame on others," claims Peter Senge. One of the challenges to formulating policy is that changes to the system that seem to help one area or constituency may hurt another, and the cause and effect may be hidden from policy makers. Without technologies to capture this, such effects may never be addressed at their point of origin. For instance, here in San Diego, budget cuts have resulted in more and bigger potholes. Friends have complained about the expense of blown tires and bent wheels caused by these potholes. Yet, on paper, this cut in government spending could be shown to stimulate businesses – at least local tire shops.

Senge's point goes right to the heart of the institutional challenge posed by systems thinking: system dynamics almost invariably bring one across the borders of traditional institutions. For me, this alone suggests that a shift to systems thinking will trigger an unprecedented wave of social invention.

Perhaps the most difficult dimension of dealing with systems is that their complexity can be a challenge to autonomy. Early in the 1900's, efficiency expert Frederick Taylor stated that, "the system must come first." Taylor's answer to growing complexity was to subordinate the autonomy of the individual to that of the organization. Yet history indicates that autonomy is what animates progress and to ignore the individual in the midst of establishing systems, jobs, and processes is to deny the presumed reason for such systems.

One of the chief challenges to policy makers is balancing, or perhaps more accurately integrating, the needs of the individual and those of the system. Nobel-prize-winning economist Amartya Sen views the expansion of freedom "as both (1) the primary end and (2) the principal means of development."[278] That is, autonomy of individuals is both the means and the end of economic progress and any solution to dealing with complex systems that subordinates this autonomy of individuals to systems is a dead end, whether it is subordination to the tyranny of kings, communists, or corporate planners.

It is key, then, to provide individuals with tools, models, and theories about the dynamics of the systems in which they find themselves in order to allow them to both improve those systems and become engaged in their work. Given the complexity of modern organizations and projects, individuals are often unclear about how their work impacts market success or even how it interacts with that of others on their team. Without making the dynamics and the context of the individual's work more visible, management cannot expect to do more than elicit conformity to standards.

Anyone who argues that our technology and thinking is good enough already to deal with the issues of systems is probably not paying much attention to systems. There is a lot that can be said about systems and systems thinking, but probably the most important thing we can say is that we seriously need to learn more about how to manage and live with them.

It may be no coincidence that the world's richest man is a computer programmer. Programmers have "theories" about how software will behave once they've inserted a new line of software or altered an existing one. As this new code interacts with hardware, other software programs, and even other lines of code within the same program, unexpected results ensue. It is not surprising that programmers spend a great deal of time debugging code, basically analyzing and correcting unintended consequences of even simple changes. Such a profession would quickly wean a person from idealistic notions about how to make a change. Successful programmers soon learn that it is more profitable to challenge their own thinking than to curse their computers when faced with unexpected results. Policy should be formulated in a similar way. One of the reasons that it is not is because of our still rudimentary understanding of system dynamics.

Understanding systems dynamics requires a particular kind of dialogue, a quality of openness that simply isn't present in many cultures. Particularly within politics, policy seems more the product of ideology

---

[278] Amartya Sen, *Development as Freedom* (New York: First Anchor Books, 2000), 36.

than that of honest experimentation.

There is a great deal of literature about getting ahead. I think there is some great advice in this. I also think that it doesn't matter nearly so much who is king as it does whether you have a dictatorship or a democracy. And no matter how many books you sell on how to become king, in that system only one man will. Now that the pay differential between senior executives and average workers is so great, the rational employee focuses on career advancement. A focus on organizational improvement that might not work or might work but never be traced back to the individual who made the improvement is perhaps more risky than simply getting ahead. If all your focus is on winning the race on the obstacle course, you have little time left to actually remove the obstacles. Systems thinking suggest less concern with who is in the upper or lower tail of the distribution than with how to change the distribution, less concern with who is peasant or aristocrat than what is happening to average incomes.

Compare Americans in 1900 and 2000. Americans in 2000 made eight times as much and lived thirty years longer than their counterparts a century ago. This is not because they were more ethical or more conscientious or smarter or harder working. This is because the systems in which they lived, learned, and worked were all better aligned with their own potential. A North American born in the United States will make a multiple of one born in Mexico, not because of any genetic differences, but because of the myriad technological and social systems that improve her potential from the time she is in utero.

It seems to me that if we want to change what is possible for the individual, we'll have to change the systems the individual operates within. You could holler at a bunch of people in 1900 to work harder, but they still wouldn't be as productive as the people in 2000. To do that, they needed new systems or the reinvention of the systems of work and learning and thinking that defined them. Changing dialogues within organizations like schools, corporations, and governments—or even the larger conversation about what is possible across those organizations—will largely start with the kind of social invention that every new economy has begun with: a change in thinking. And once systems thinking begins to define how we see the world and the possibilities within it, this one social invention will ripple to every other, forcing us to redefine our organizations and even how we define ourselves.

Russell Ackoff

Russell Ackoff may have been the most articulate of the systems thinking advocates. He made the distinction between analysis and synthesis and suggested that what was "true" of a problem or situation from the perspective of analysis might not be true from a perspective of synthesis. That is, what made sense from simply looking at the pieces might not make sense when one looked at the whole.

Russell Ackoff rather persuasively argued that analysis has defined our worldview since the Renaissance. If you analyze something, you take it apart. Once you figure out how the pieces work, you then bring those pieces back together into the whole and what you have is knowledge.

Ackoff saw a change in worldview, beginning during World War Two, from analysis to synthesis. (I think that he's right about such a change in regards to thought leaders, but not for the average person. Today politicians can claim to be a pragmatist without making people think they're advocating some odd, new philosophy; it's not obvious that claiming to be a systems thinker would provoke the same benign response in the media and public.) Synthesis is the opposite of analysis. Rather than look at the parts of the thing you want to understand, you look at what it is a part of. You look at the role it plays in that larger whole and then you deconstruct that to understand the parts. Why did cars once seat an average of six passengers and now seat closer to four? You won't figure that out through analysis, by taking cars apart. You have to look at the larger system cars are a part of to understand that. Household size has gone down at the same time that fuel prices have gone up. Cars seat fewer people because families are smaller and smaller cars are generally more fuel efficient—not because there is anything particular about the evolution of car technology that you'd ever decode by dissecting cars.

Systems are defined by their interactions. A happy family is one that gets along. Two great people can be in an awful relationship and two awful people can be in a great relationship. There is no real understanding of good or bad without an understanding of the system the thing is a part of. One community might consider a person wonderful, while another might consider him awful: what you might do to win approval in a violent group would make you an outcast in a peaceful one, and vice versa. The behavior of a knight on a crusade in 1100 that made him seem brave and virtuous would make him an international war criminal in 2000.

Systems are dependent on their parts but are very different from their parts. For instance, two lonely people might come together in a wonderful relationship. What is true of them in isolation ("I'm lonely") is not true when they are together ("You complete me").

Systems Thinking and Entrepreneurship

Entrepreneurship is a matter of building a system. An entrepreneur brings together land, labor, and capital to create a company that he hopes will make a profit.

A central notion behind the fourth economy is the idea that a spate of social inventions that follow from systems thinking—acts of entrepreneurship that transcend (and include) the normal boundaries of business—is what will define this next economy.

A business, though, is just one kind of social system. If the work of the fourth economy will be more focused than ever on the task of entrepreneurship, on inventing and reinventing social systems, it seems as though deeper intuition and better tools for effecting system dynamics is not just nice but necessary.

But systems thinking, entrepreneurship, and the spate of social inventions they might inspire is not, in itself, progress. Progress throughout all four economies does the same thing: it gives more autonomy to the individual. Without some clear sense of what it means to define a life aside from the social programming of our big institutions, read the next chapter on the invention of the individual.

25 Inventing Self

Begin with any institution, perhaps school. Imagine what it would be like if it were perfectly adapted to you: your learning style, your goals or questions about what goals are worth pursuing, your own need for certain type of experience, an educational experience that exposes you to new ideas, new skills, and new people that would inspire you and make you more capable. Imagine it gave you a mix of physical, social - emotional, spiritual, and intellectual experiences that left you feeling like a whole person. Imagine inventing such a school and then discovering that there are others who would thrive in the same place.

You've just imagined what the fourth economy might mean for you.

Economy	First	Second	Third	Fourth
Period	1300–1700	1700–1900	1900-2000	2000-2050
Limit to Progress	Land	Capital	Knowledge Workers	Entrepreneurship
Type of Economy	Agricultural	Industrial	Information	Entrepreneurial
Intellectual Revolution	Renaissance	Enlightenment	Pragmatism	Systems Thinking
Big Social Invention	Nation-State	Bank	Corporation	**Self**
Social Revolution	Protestant Revolution	Democratic Revolution	Financial Revolution	Business Revolution

Social Invention

We will always be social creatures, defined in some inescapable measure by the society we are born into and by its institutions. But if entrepreneurship and social invention are to become more common, it is no longer enough to let this be the default, that our institutions would define us. Instead, the individual has to be the starting point for their reinvention, not merely a tool for them. We know that reading is important and no matter the struggle, it is a skill we expect of every normal, healthy child. The fourth economy will be a place where we work to create adults with a similar expectation of not just defining a life but what that might mean for defining or adapting the institution to who they are or aspire to be. Literacy is too important to leave to mere chance; the same is true of the social invention that begins with a sense of one's own potential and what next needs changing in order to realize that potential.

Within the West, the big social inventions have always been happy to define the individual. At various times and to various degrees, social programming has had a ready answer to the question of what the good life meant: being a good Christian, a good citizen, rich, an A student, or a good boss or employee. Imagine defining yourself instead as something not defined in turn by an institution. Then imagine what sort of social invention you'd have to engage in to create something akin to a school, a church, a government, or a business that would facilitate that person you aspire to be. Or, even more interesting, imagine a new social invention that in the act of creating would create the you that you aspired to be. Because we are inescapably social creatures whose lives emerge out of relationships, we cannot create a life without finding or creating a context for it.

Beyond Imitation & Role Playing

We're working against a natural instinct to learn from and imitate those around us. Much of children's amazing capacity to learn comes from imitation. They quickly know what is fashionable, how to speak (and with what accent), who to love, and who to fear. Put simply, we're born ready to be programmed and culture is that program.

Mihaly Csikszentmihalyi says that when he leads classes through the process of defining a personal mission or life purpose, it takes him considerable time to get them past the notion that their mission ought to somehow be defined by the big institutions.[279] Their first attempts are generally defined in terms of doing a better job at roles they're already in: they express the desire to be a better wife or mother, a better employee or better Buddhist or Mormon. Their goals vary but, often, their initial attempts to define a life are through roles within institutions in which they've found themselves. It takes him considerable time and effort to get past those roles to something more personal.

We have come into consciousness in the shadow of family, church, state, markets, and, more recently, the company. It is little wonder that we define our life goals in their terms. We want to be rich (hurrah for the imprint of the financial markets). We want to be a good dad (kudos to the genetic and social construct of that most persistent institution,

---

[279] Based on a private conversation with him and, over the years since, heavily paraphrased, I'm sure. For one thing, he did not use the phrase “defined by the big institutions.”

the family). We want to be more productive or to get our MBA. We want to be a better Baptist. And, of course, all those are well and good. I have no contempt for these institutions. Nobody should. For all their faults, all of these institutions do seem to make us more human and have—generally speaking—made the experience of being human better.

But what about you? Who are you? Outside of religion and politics? Outside of market valuations and measures of productivity? Who is the you that can dictate to church and state, banks and companies? Because finally, the only other alternative is that they dictate to you.

Choice is one level of freedom, but design is a higher. The question for social invention is, What is the design requirement? What are the design goals for the school or business we're within? It seems to me that our design goals would be our potential. Democracy wasn't created—or designed—to accommodate uneducated peasants; it was designed for educated citizens. Democracy was designed for colonial Americans' potential, not their past. Design suggests inspiration from who we aspire to be, not just who we've been.

It should sound terribly odd to speak of the next big social invention as the individual. It seems the individual predates any of the big social inventions mentioned so far. To say that the individual is the next big invention reveals, I'm sure, something oddly romantic, and by romantic I do mean the nineteenth century movement.

Romantics like Beethoven held the notion that the soul was something unique within you that wasn't you yet. It was your potential. Realizing that potential has at least two parts: discerning what it is and then realizing it. What begins as a vague impulse becomes clearer as we listen to it and respond, what Joseph Campbell would have called following your bliss. The soul is what we discover through some odd combination of existential angst and eureka moments found in doing or being. I rather like this notion and think it is as useful a description of the soul as any. I do think that the world and flesh can destroy the soul. Both represent programming, one cultural and the other genetic. The biological imperative and social conventions are, to a degree, inescapable. Yet they also ought to be kept in their place. "What has a man profited if he has gained the world but lost his own soul?" The question is not whether you'll dance to the beat of cultural or genetic programming: that is inescapable. The question is whether you'll create your own music or dance over the top of that rhythm.

I do believe that there are things common between souls. I don't believe that anyone else can know your soul, know what is important to you. Phillip Pullman said that one's life begins when he is born and one's life story begins when he realizes that he was born into the wrong family. I would expand that somewhat, to say that anyone paying attention must eventually have a moment in which he wonders if he has been born into the wrong society. I suspect that you'd have to be on some fairly strong drugs to escape those moments when you feel like a Martian. At that moment, when you feel like you were born into the wrong society or culture, you have a few choices: withdraw from others to find your own soul, ignore this persistent call of your own soul, or make an attempt to change society to better accommodate your own potential.

This is not self found through the act of contemplating one's navel. Within the context of social invention or entrepreneurship, this act of inventing self is not just about turning inward and disregarding the world. It is, instead, about creating our place in it. The challenge of self is that it needs to connect with what is most personal and also with the social world "out there." Self, like any system, emerges out of relationships; the two most important are the relationship to what is within us, what we'll call for lack of a better term our soul, and the world in which we find ourselves. To ignore either is to feel disconnected.

Lest this sound overwhelming, it's worth reviewing what is, for me, one of the best examples of how to create an impactful life without feeling like one is banging one's head against a wall.

Buckminster Fuller and a Grand Experiment

In 1927, a thirty-two-year-old man stood on the edge of Lake Michigan, ready to throw himself into the freezing waters. He was bankrupt, the result of his third consecutive business failure. He'd been drinking heavily and was grief-stricken over the death of his first child. He didn't know how he would support his wife and newborn daughter. It wasn't just that he was struggling in business. Years before the bankruptcies, he'd been expelled from Harvard during his freshman year and never did complete his degree. At that moment, his life seemed to him like a pattern of failures.

Fortunately, however, in this moment of drunken grief, Buckminster Fuller[280] had the presence of mind to make an extraordinary decision. He realized the freedom inherent in his decision to kill himself. If he was already prepared for the worst thing that could happen, how could any other fate be any worse? Why not take half a step back from this irreversible extreme and transform his life into a different game instead? Rather than throw away his life, why not instead throw away his old notions of what it meant to be a success? Why not define his life outside of the old notions of goals and achievements as defined by normal social convention or the big institutions?

At that moment, he decided to turn his life into an experiment—an experiment to see how much difference one ordinary person could make.

The difference that Fuller's life made has yet to be fully understood or felt. He was a pioneer of ecological thinking and sustainability—balancing economic and environmental needs. His influence continues to spread as a growing number of people adopt the thinking that he helped to introduce. Although he never did complete his degree at Harvard, Fuller was awarded forty-four honorary doctoral degrees, was granted twenty-five U.S. patents, and authored twenty-eight books.

When Buckminster Fuller turned his life into an experiment (many called him Bucky, but he referred to himself as Guinea Pig B), he created the conditions for an extraordinary life. Perhaps best of all, his failures were feedback for an experiment, not a reflection of who he was, not something to take personally, never a reason to jump. Turning his life into an experiment gave him the best of both worlds: he ended his life even more accomplished than someone driven to achieve or compelled to prove something, and yet he remained more sanguine than someone who avoided risks altogether and remained stoned on the couch.

You may say that on that bridge that night, Fuller saved his own soul. He didn't withdraw from the world or give up on himself. What he did do was give up trying to find happiness by pleasing something as abstract and vague as an institution or the world. It seems to me that his life provides a fascinating example of what it might mean to become an individual.

---

[280]See http://architecture.about.com/library/bl-fuller.htm andhttp://www.bfi.org/introduction_to_bmf.htm for quick biographies of Richard Buckminster Fuller, 1895 to 1983.

The modern world was born when scientists during the Enlightenment began testing hypotheses and conducting experiments rather than blindly quoting Aristotle or church authorities. The modern world—its science, technology, and even social institutions and practices—has emerged from the application of the empirical method to objective reality. Planning, or theorizing, followed by doing, followed by studying the results of doing, and then finally adapting the initial plan or theory, is the cycle of progress.

Consider the possibility of applying the empirical method to one's own personal, subjective reality. Much of the modern world has been about objective proof of shared reality. Wouldn't it be curious to see what might happen if we became empirical about subjective, personal reality? I think it might save souls—or at least help to define them.

The Individual in the System

Joseph Campbell: Darth Vader has not developed his own humanity. He's a robot. He's a bureaucrat, living not in terms of himself but in terms of an imposed system. This is the threat to our lives that we all face today. Is the system going to flatten you out and deny you your humanity, or are you going to be able to make use of the system to the attainment of human purposes? How do you relate to the system so that you are not compulsively serving it? It doesn't help to try to change it to accord with your system of thought. The momentum of history behind it is too great for anything really significant to evolve from that kind of action. The thing to do is learn to live in your period of history as a human being. That's something else, and it can be done.

Bill Moyers: By doing what?

Joseph Campbell: By holding to your own ideals for yourself and like Luke Skywalker, rejecting the system's impersonal claims upon you.[281]

---

281 Joseph Campbell and Bill Moyers, *The Power of Myth* (New York: Doubleday, 1988), 178.

The story of the first three economies is the story of how individuals gradually wrested control over their own lives from the West's defining institutions and the elites who ruled them. The constant theme of progress throughout all four economies is the rise of the individual over the institution. First, from a powerful church the individual gained freedom to worship (or not) in accord with his own conscience, beliefs, understanding, and feelings. Then, from absolute monarchs the individual gained influence over policies—policies as varied as the cleanliness and safety of streets, public works projects, pensions, education, and laws regulating death and divorce. The transformation of the bank in the third economy is the story of how the common person obtained insurance coverage, investment options, and access to credit that once was reserved for only the elite. Financial markets have been democratized; the savings and borrowing of the middle class drives financial markets in developed countries. Each time the pattern of revolution has repeated, it has granted more autonomy to the individual, and in this recurring theme we have the definition of progress.

A person with a car has more choices and autonomy than a person with only shoes. A person with a vote has more autonomy than a person living under tyranny. A person with a roof over his head has more autonomy, more choice about how to focus his attention during the day than the homeless person whose attention is continually diverted towards finding shelter, protection, and privacy. True economic progress results in more autonomy and greater choice about how to live.

Bill Moyers reported[282] on a conversation he'd had with a Chinese-American woman about her freedom to choose between eating chicken feet and going to McDonald's. She explained to Moyers that this choice was not trivial; to her it represented something deeper. "That is the American dream! That I can compose my own life. That I can invent who I want to be," she told him.

The antithesis of this dream is a fundamentalist religious leader coercing the individual to wear, do, or believe certain things; a tyrant able to imprison citizens without trial or to confiscate property at will; a boss whose control over an employee is more important than

---

282 "The Salon Interview: Bill Moyers," <http://archive.salon.com/news/feature/2003/04/07/moyers/index2.html>

measures of productivity or the employees' own quality of life or conviction about how best to work. Progress depends upon the creation of institutions as tools and then, access to—even control over—these institutions becoming a right for everyone in the community.

Progress since the beginning of the first economy, around the time of Marco Polo in 1300, has been remarkable. Nathan Rothschild, the co-creator of the modern bank, probably had more liquid wealth than any man in the world in 1836. He nonetheless died at the age of fifty-nine of an infection that could be cured today with a trip to any drugstore in the developed world. Nathan, the richest man of his time, the man who dictated terms to kings, could not afford antibiotics for the simple reason that they did not yet exist.[283] Genuine progress creates options for better and longer lives for everyone—even the elites who would seem to have everything.

One of the first studies of mortality, conducted with London's population in the early 1600s, documented the brevity of life during the first economy, the time just before industrialization. The following data compares the percentage of the population to survive to sixteen, twenty-six, and so on, at ten-year increments. It compares London in the seventeenth century and the United States at the close of the twentieth. For instance, by age sixteen, 99 percent of Americans were still alive; by contrast, only 40 percent of those born in London survived to celebrate their sixteenth birthday. Only 1 percent of seventeenth-century Londoners lived to seventy-six, as opposed to 70 percent of Americans in 1993, a startling contrast.

[283] Landes, *The Wealth and Poverty of Nations*, xvii–xviii.

Percentage of Population Surviving[284]

Age	London (in the early 1600s)	U.S. (in 1993)
0	100	100
6	64	99
16	40	99
26	25	98
36	16	97
46	10	95
56	6	92
66	3	84
76	1	70

It is not just life expectancies that have improved. So have freedoms. Prior to 1066 (when the conquering Normans introduced the feudal system), "virtually all the documentary sources—wills, land deeds, and

[284] Peter L. Bernstein, *Against the Gods: The Remarkable Story of Risk* (New York: John Wiley & Sons, 1996), 83.

the literature of the day—clearly show that the basic underpinning of the rural economy in several parts of England was a class of workers who can only be described as slaves." Slavery was common throughout Europe at this time, and the very word "slave" was an indirect reference to the Germanic tribes' successful raids of neighboring Slavic populations. "In the year 1000 people could not imagine themselves without a protector. You had a lord in heaven and you needed a lord on earth." In certain regions of Europe, the local rulers did even more to ignore the rights of their subjects, claiming the right to "bed the young brides of the village on their wedding night." Things weren't all bad; slaves would occasionally receive perks. The shepherd, for instance, got "to retain the use of twelve nights' dung at Christmas."[285]

The story of the West since this time is one of increased freedom and steadily improving lives. Still, there are some assumptions we make about human psychology that still devalue autonomy. You might call the emphasis on autonomy one of the design requirements for the next iteration of social inventions.

Skinner vs. Deci

If you were to design a new school or business, you could base it on the psychology of B.F. Skinner or Edward Deci. The choice between these two is stark and is a choice between control and freedom.

Before exploring the differences between them, it helps to define two terms: extrinsic and intrinsic motivation. Extrinsic motivation comes from outside the person and intrinsic comes from within. If you are extrinsically motivated to pick up trash, you do it because you'll get money or because you want other people to think that you're not a slob. If you are intrinsically motivated to pick up trash, you do it because you take pleasure in the feeling of cleaning up the place, of making it look better.

B. F. Skinner pioneered behaviorism. Put simply, his philosophy of psychology was a logical extension of Newton's physics of cause and effect. Skinner basically formalized the notions of carrot and stick, the

---

[285] Lacey and Danziger, *The Year 1000*, quotes in this paragraph taken from pages 45–49.

rewards and punishments that shape behavior. Grades in schools and bonuses at work are usually based on his theories.

What is true of Skinner's philosophy is that it accurately predicts a great deal of behavior. He gave insight into extrinsic behavior, behavior done for rewards outside of the activity. For instance, the behaviorist explains the person who does work that he despises for money that he loves.

Yet the behaviorist's prediction misses the fact that extrinsic rewards have very different impacts than intrinsic rewards in long-term behavior and even short-term results. If you pay children to sample yogurt, they are more likely to taste it for the first time. Skinner would say, "I told you so." But what is curious is that later, when offered yogurt, children who were offered money to eat it the first time are less likely to eat it again. It seems like they learn that this is behavior that is not worth engaging in just for the joy of eating yogurt: without an extrinsic reward, they see no reason to eat the yogurt.[286] A person just watching children's first response to bribes for eating would conclude that bribes promote desirable behavior. Yet the extrinsic rewards of the behaviorist do more to provoke compliance than actually change patterns of behavior, or habits. One of the many reasons that existing systems are so often unsustainable is that they rely on extrinsic rewards. Such rewards are a little bit like heroin; it takes more and more reward to get less and less compliance and even the compliance one does get is rarely a source of creativity or even sustainable change. These behaviors are rarely internalized. Rewards can even distract individuals from the very tasks they're designed to encourage. People who are engaged in a task are the ones who do it best—people lost in the details of an activity without thought of the reward or punishments that lie outside of it. That is, people who experience the work as a good to do during the task, rather than get distracted from the doing with thoughts of the goods to have that come after the task. Extrinsic motivation works, but works poorly.

The behaviorist's use of carrot and stick in the "motivation" of employees confuses manipulation and motivation. The psychologist Edward Deci [287] has clarified the difference between three types of authority that might define the role of parents, teachers, or managers:

---

286 Notes from a talk delivered by Alfie Kohn, author of *Punished by Rewards.*

287 Edward L. Deci, *Why We Do What We Do: The Dynamics of Personal Autonomy* (New York: G. P. Putnam's Sons, 1995).

controlling, permissive, and autonomy supportive. Controlling authorities attempt to dictate behaviors through the use of rewards and punishments. Permissive authorities basically abdicate responsibility. These are the parents, teachers, or managers who simply throw up their hands and say, "do what you want" to those who may not have developed the judgment to choose wisely. Autonomy-supportive authorities practice what Deci advocates: supporting the person's ability freedom to choose. This is supportive because choice suggests an understanding of consequences, which most novices don't have; the manager or parent's job is to clarify – as best they can – causes and effect so that the employee or child can understand their choices. The result of this is development and increased autonomy.

Advocates of behaviorism claim that rewards and punishments work. They are right, in a very narrow sense. Yet the locus of control is in the hand of parent, teacher, or manager rather than child, student, or employee. Extrinsic motivation assumes someone else is in control, is defining what the individual will do. If individual autonomy is unimportant, such control may have benefits like increased predictability, but it rarely results in the unexpected innovations that are the essence of improvements in productivity and quality of life. The issue has to do with more than just productivity, however.

It is through autonomy that the individual finally realizes his or her potential. The individual living under a dictatorship is not able to realize his potential, nor is it the person abandoned by his community. Neither control by others nor lack of self-control seems particularly effective at bringing out the most in people. This suggests something fundamental about the modern worker.

From grading in schools to ranking in the workplace, the dominant social constructs attune individuals to extrinsic rather than intrinsic signals. That is, these institutions condition individuals to respond to outside stimulus without provoking the really hard work of understanding one's own drives and aptitudes. Schools and workplaces can treat knowledge workers as robots who must be programmed, rather than as individuals who need to discover their potential. The result is the antithesis of entrepreneurial impulse.

Releasing the Worker

When he was walking through a General Motors plant in the 1980s, W. Edwards Deming was heard to say, "The worker must be released."

In the 1980s and 1990s, Deming was one of America's most respected management consultants. He got that kind of status in Japan, however, about three decades earlier. In those last couple of decades, he got some credit for Japan's post-World War II economic rise. Many of the Japanese companies adopted his philosophy, with its emphasis on using statistics to understand and manage systems like factories, to raise their quality and continuously improve their products. As he predicted, the rest of the world was soon asking for trade protection from Japanese goods.

His philosophy often clashed with the typical management culture. He said at least once that in the future the mythology of present-day management would seem more curious than the mythology of New Guinea.[288] He also said that he didn't worry about the future: executives would either learn how to manage a system or go out of business. Two of the key elements of his philosophy were an appreciation for a system and an appreciation for human psychology. Specifically, he felt that things like grades and ranking workers replaced intrinsic motivation with extrinsic motivation and took the joy out of learning and work.

Deming saw that too many employees were alienated from their work by poor management structures and systems over which they felt they had little control. For him, the engagement of workers was inextricably linked to the adoption of tools that showed management and worker alike the system in which the individual worked, and began to give workers the power to regularly improve that system.

A constant theme throughout the history of Western civilization has been the rise of the individual, and this matter of giving more autonomy to the individual worker will simply be the next chapter in the story of Western civilization's development:

Martin Luther declared, "We are all priests," and dispersed the power of the pope to the common person, laying the foundation for each individual to exercise freedom of religion and conscience.

"All men are created equal," Thomas Jefferson penned in the document

---

[288] I am sure that I heard him say this. I've never been able to find it in his writings since, nor get confirmation from other folks I've talked to.

that created a democracy—a form of government in which every individual (from the president to the poorest or youngest voter) has exactly one vote.

"Must mankind be hung on a cross of gold?" William Jennings Bryan asked rather melodramatically, questioning the policies that subordinated life to capital and limited the benefits of capitalism to just a few. The reform movements of his time, such as gaining an eight-hour work day and prohibiting child labor, were also key to raising the needs of individuals to a higher level than the needs of capital.

To these cries for individual liberty we can add Deming's: "The worker must be released." Although such a cry might seem laughable when compared to the enormity of release from religious or political tyranny, this sentiment expresses the feeling of any worker struggling to adapt to an irrational manager, impractical process, or impersonal system that demands that the worker approach work as a stifling activity that often does more to frustrate potential and productivity than to express it.

Process Conformity and the Disappearance of the Individual

In the early days of the information economy, railroad engineers had to be "programmed" with very specific instructions regarding speeds, departure times, and procedures. This was key to safety, and their subordination to such prescribed rules was essential. Later, a factory worker who started work thirty minutes late could hold up dozens of co-workers unable to run the assembly line without him at his place on the line. Yet the advances of technology are such that this programming can now be fed into computers, robots, and systems that are both more accurate and more obedient than even the most conscientious person.

Far too many jobs are the information age equivalent of flipping burgers. "Two minutes on side one, ninety seconds on side two—slide onto the bun to serve," we tell the fast-food worker. What do we tell the knowledge worker? "Look at the data from these stores and determine if there are anomalies or trends that are worth analyzing." (The unspoken command is to analyze the data even if nothing significant has occurred, because one doesn't want to appear less than busy.) There is nothing particularly engaging about this work, nor is it sustainable as a means for making a living. If a job can be reduced to a set of instructions, those instructions can be fed to a worker in any country—even one where costs are dramatically lower. (It will be decades before an employee in France or the United Kingdom can hope to compete with employees in India or the Ukraine on the basis of wages alone. Higher wages can be sustained only by working in better systems that make people more productive.)

Jobs ought to be process oriented, but not in ways that can be replicated by robots. In his study of happiness, Csikszentmihalyi has found some common patterns to what most engages the individual. The task that most engages us is one that represents a balance between challenge and skill, when both the skill called upon and the challenge faced are above average for us. One's sense of time becomes distorted in such activities, typically seeming to accelerate. And a paradox emerges from Csikszentmihalyi's study of flow. The more one loses oneself in a task, that is, the less self-conscious one is during its execution, the more able one is at the task's completion. This means that the person who loses herself in a task is more likely to find herself in her work. Thus, the state of mind that Csikszentmihalyi calls flow is not just psychologically rewarding—it is a means for development and growth. Like autonomy, flow is both reward and price for development. The strict adherence to process required in too many jobs precludes the attainment of flow and, by extension, development of the self. To dictate a process to someone without regard for whether they can attain flow is the antithesis of making the employee more entrepreneurial.

As with carrot and stick, forcing process on the individual shifts the locus of control—not only over what is done but also over how the individual develops—to the institution. This is a kind of control over one's life that certainly mocks the notion of freedom.

In his book, *Good Business*, Csikszentmihalyi quotes Robert Shapiro, former CEO of Monsanto. He makes a critical point about how individuals fit into organizations.

"The notion of job implies that there's been some supreme architect who designed this system so that a lot of parts fit together and produce whatever the desired input is. No one in a job can see the whole. When we ask you to join us, we are saying, 'Do you have the skills and the willingness to shape yourself in this way so that you will fit into this big machine? Because somebody did this job before you, somebody who was different from you. Someone will do it after you.

Those parts of you that aren't relevant to that job, please just forget about. Those shortcomings that you have that really don't enable you to fill this job, please at least try to fake, so that we can all have the impression that you're doing this job.'

"It's a Procrustean concept, and it studiously and systematically avoids using the most valuable part of you, the part of you that makes you different from other people, that makes you uniquely you. If we want to be a great institution, that's where we ought to be looking. We ought to be saying, 'What can you bring to this that's going to help?' Not, 'Here's the job, just do it.'"[289]

What does Shapiro mean by "a Procrustean concept?" Procrustes was a figure in Greek mythology who forced travelers to fit into his bed by stretching their bodies when they were too short or cutting off their legs when they were too long. It is probably true that the vast majority of employees are both stretched to the limits of their capacity in some aspects of their job and literally cut off from real and crucial parts of their self in others. In either case, being forced to fit into a job in such a way does little to realize the employee's potential or, by extension, the potential of the organization.

Conclusion

Finally, freedom seems to be about making a bet on the individual, even if she has yet to prove herself.

"[T]he very point of emancipation ... is not to give power to those who have earned the right to it, but to lift the helpless to a level where they are free to learn how to use the right.

"Those who oppose freedom argue that as illiterates, as slaves, as children, they cannot manage the household, which is true though illiberal. The political history of the West has been a running battle between the "realistic" deniers of one freedom after another and the generous ones who gambled on another truth, that capacity is native

---

[289] Mihalyi Csikszentmihalyi, *Good Business: Leadership, Flow, and the Making of Meaning* (New York: Penguin Books, 2004), 103.

to all and depends only on fair conditions for its development."[290]

It may not be realistic to bet on employees becoming more entrepreneurial, but we're not trying to perpetuate current reality, we're trying to realize future potential. Work reminds us that finding one's bliss is not the same as losing one's self in a video game that engages but is – in the end – meaningless. From factory worker to artist, the person who is working ideally is engaged in what she's doing and at the same time creating something of value for others. Whether it is the work of a mother to care for a child or that same mother's work to write a paper that changes a field of study, work is a ligature between people.

Transforming work may sound less grand than winning freedom of worship or fighting democratic revolutions but it is yet another chord in this same orchestra of progress, of increased individual autonomy. And you could even say that work matters more than finance, religion, or politics.

Only the most avid voters head to the polls more than twice a year and only the most devout believers attend church more than twice a week. By contrast, work is the one thing that structures our time and commands our attention for hours and days at a time. And, in the words of VISA's founding CEO, Dee Hock, "Tyranny is tyranny no matter how petty."[291] To transform the experience of work is to transform the experience of life and even one's definition of self.

Of all the social revolutions of history, the revolution in work may be the most personal. It is probably true of all of us that we have little awareness of how great our potential is, and we barely grasp how much work it will take to realize that potential. (Almost by definition, to realize one's life potential takes a lifetime.) The point of life is not to fit ourselves into a series of institutionally defined roles. The challenge is to realize our potential if we have to create new roles or even new institutions in which to do that.

And that's been the real point of progress all along. In that sense, in the midst of all the profound and sweeping changes of the last seven hundred years, nothing has really changed at all.

---

[290] Barzun, *From Dawn to Decadence*, 534.

[291] Hock, *Birth of the Chaordic Age*, 24.

You need the world to realize your own potential. And here's the really amazing thing: the world needs you to do the same.

The individual, though, will not gain autonomy in a social vacuum. The first place in which the individual is likely to become more entrepreneurial, to begin the process of defining institutions based on one's own potential rather than potential based on the big institutions, is within the corporation. The next chapter speculates about what revolution might look like.

26 Business Revolution

The corporation is today's dominant institution. What if, like the church, state, and bank before it, it were to become a tool for the common person rather than simply using the individual as a tool?

Economy	First	Second	Third	Fourth
Period	1300–1700	1700–1900	1900-2000	2000-2050
Limit to Progress	Land	Capital	Knowledge Workers	Entrepreneurship
Type of Economy	Agricultural	Industrial	Information	Entrepreneurial
Intellectual Revolution	Renaissance	Enlightenment	Pragmatism	Systems Thinking
Big Social Invention	Nation-State	Bank	Corporation	Self
Social Revolution	Protestant Revolution	Democratic Revolution	Financial Revolution	**Business Revolution**

While there will always be senior leaders within organizations with more responsibility, their job will change as power is dispersed more broadly. The corporation – like a country – will ultimately be judged by how well it lets its employees create a desirable life, to pursue something akin to the American dream. As it has in every new economy before, power in the dominant institution will be dispersed.

The Recurring Pattern of Dispersing Power and Ownership

Again, the pattern of progress in social invention seems to be this: elites invent an institution able to overcome the new limit. As a result, those elites become rich and powerful. Generations later, the power over and ownership of those institutions are dispersed. Monarchs and their ministers invent the modern nation-state; generations later, democratic revolution makes political policy subject to popular vote rather than the divine rights of kings. One huge wave of social change comes from the invention of a new, effective institution. The next huge wave comes from the democratization of that institution.

I've made my argument for the corporation as the most defining, powerful, and dominant institution of our time. Now I predict that it will be the next institution transformed by a new limit. Control of the corporation's power to do good and bad will fall into the hands of communities. There are a lot of reasons for this, and many implications from it. Perhaps the two most obvious consequences will be the popularization of entrepreneurship and the rise of the individual over the institution yet again.

Simply put, these great institutions of western civilization are powerful and useful. They give meaning and coherence to life. The corporation provides income and wealth and gives us work and a sense of identity, among other things. When more people are able to use corporations as tools, more lives improve. It is one thing for one person to have a car, and it's another for everyone to have a car. It is one thing for a CEO to be able to define the policies in a company to greatly benefit himself, and it is another for everyone in the company to have such power. Our social inventions are tools that make our lives better; the more people who are able to use them, the better.

The corporation is today's most powerful institution. Its pricing policies for drugs literally determine who can afford to live. (And its R&D and investment policies determine which lives it is *possible* to save.) Its employment practices do a great deal to determine whether individuals live below the poverty level or like kings, and how much time parents have with their children. It designs and produces our houses, clothes, cars, entertainment, and working conditions, and between assignments at work and media content at home, even shapes the content of our thoughts. The corporation does wonderful things, like create wealth, products, services, markets, and jobs. It also does awful things, like pollute the environment, erase local cultures, and define and finance political campaigns. There is no institution that more defines our modern world.

The corporation has adapted to globalization, expanding rapidly in this new environment. From 1990 to 1998, the number of transnational companies rose from 37,000 to 60,000 and the number of affiliates from 170,000 to 500,000.[292] No one government regulates such corporations. The transnational corporation in a very real way transcends nations.

It is not just that the corporation is so powerful. It has redefined our expectations of every institution. Politicians promise to run governments more like a business (and with the second Bush administration, for the first time in history the president had an MBA and the vice president was a former CEO). Schools talk about their students and communities as "customers."

Corporations demand free markets in which to operate, generally resisting attempts at regulation and central control. Yet the corporation itself is a centrally managed economy with five-year plans and clearly defined hierarchies and definitions for almost every process. Corporations choose to operate within free markets but rarely use free markets to direct resources within their own operations.

During the last half of the nineteenth century, legislators in the United States, the United Kingdom, Germany, and France created the legal frameworks for modern corporations. One of the key legislative innovations of this time was freeing corporations to practice business outside of the confines of their original charters. No longer did corporations have to apply to governments to make changes in business location or products. This advance helped to usher in a new era of corporations that created wealth, jobs, and innovations unprecedented in human history. In this era of accelerating change, government control over business charters made little sense.

There were, however, problems from the start. One of the fundamental problems of corporations is that they separate ownership and management. The heads of corporations are just employees, yet their positions give them power typically associated with owners.

---

[292] John Micklethwait and Adrian Wooldridge, *A Future Perfect: The Challenge and Hidden Promise of Globalization* (New York: Random House, 2000), *xxi*.

CEOs: The Last of the Monarchs

The CEOs in today's corporations are the last of the monarchs. Within open, democratic societies people can and will malign the president or prime minister. George Carlin can say, "I have as much authority as the pope, only not as many people believe it," and fear no visit from the Spanish Inquisition. Pundits can say vile things about George Bush and Barack Obama without fear of losing their citizenship. Yet a CEO within a company is unlikely to be openly questioned or confronted by his employees, especially those who wish to keep their jobs. For the most part, even the owners (the investors) of the corporations employing these CEOs have little influence over them. CEOs of Fortune 1000 firms make about $500 for every $1 made by their average hourly employee, and even that ratio tends to understate differences between them in terms of influence over policy and direction.

CEOs making millions each year are able to enjoy lifestyles and technologies that Pope Alexander VI or Louis the XIV would have envied. General Electric's former CEO Jack Welch, even in retirement, was showered with perks. GE paid for his New York penthouse, fresh flowers, wine, laundry and dry cleaning services, a cook and wait staff, a housekeeper, country club memberships, tickets to basketball and baseball games, tickets to Wimbledon, and unlimited use of the corporate jet.[293] And the company was subsidizing his life style after already paying him hundreds of millions in salary, stock, and bonuses—nearly $125 million in 2000 alone. The corporate boards presumably charged with oversight of CEO pay and behavior are often populated by fellow CEOs who know that questioning such salaries and perks would only threaten their own privileged positions.

I don't pick on Jack Welch because he was a bad CEO. By all accounts he was great. GE's stock value soared during his long tenure. Yet let's contrast that with Bill Clinton's eight years as president. Under Clinton, the American economy performed well on almost every measure. Welch and Clinton might have been comparable executives in terms of success, but they were paid very differently. Clinton made $200,000 a year. (Clinton's pay was not even 1% of what Welch made; Welch's salary in one year could have paid Clinton for a period of time nearly equal to the centuries covered in this book.) Centuries ago,

---

[293] William G. Flanagan, *Dirty Rotten CEOs: How Business Leaders Are Fleecing America* (New York: Citadel Press, 2004), 49–50.

people simply accepted that a king required enormous income and wealth. Today, we have a similar belief about CEOs, it seems. I suspect that GE could have hired a CEO for less than $125 million a year. For now, the difference between what we think is reasonable pay for CEOs and presidents is baffling.

Worse than the absurd ratios of CEO pay to that of their employees is that CEO prosperity doesn't seem to be linked to employee prosperity. Former Labor Secretary Robert Reich writes of one CEO he faced on *Nightline* in 1996:

If "Chainsaw Al" Dunlap didn't exist, I'd have to invent him. In less than two years as head of Scott Paper, he fired 11,000 employees (one-third of the workforce), slashed the research budget, moved the world headquarters from Philadelphia (where it was founded in 1879) to Boca Raton, Florida (where he has a $1.8 million house), eliminated all corporate gifts to charities, and barred managers from being involved in community affairs. Then he sold what was left of the company to Kimberly-Clark, which promptly announced it would cut 8,000 of the combined companies' workforce and close Scott's new headquarters in Boca Raton. For his labors, Dunlap has just walked off with a cool $100 million.[294]

One of the patterns of change throughout the three economies has been the isolation of leaders of the dominant institution from the realities of "the little people." The Renaissance popes and the monarchs during the Enlightenment lived lives that were preludes to that of today's CEOs. Able to enjoy incredible wealth and privilege that their employees can scarcely comprehend, CEOs undoubtedly feel less anxious about the efficacy of the corporate model in the post-modern world. As long as their fate remains separate from that of their communities and even their employees, they tend not to think about whether the corporation needs reform.

I do think that corporations will become more like countries in this respect: inevitably there are citizens who make more than presidents in democratic countries and once the corporation is transformed, I think the same will be true of employees and CEOs. But still, real differences in pay and leadership roles will persist for the simple fact that real differences between people's capacity for leadership persist.[295]

---

[294] Robert Reich, *Locked in the Cabinet* (New York: Alfred A. Knopf, 1997), 294.

[295] Elliot Jacques, *Executive Leadership: A Practical Guide to Managing Complexity* (Oxford: Blackwell Publishing, 1994).

Corporate Scandals

Given that senior executives are so driven by success as measured by equity value, the corporations they run are susceptible to corruption and scandal. The collapse of Enron is not the first, nor will it be the last, of the corporate scandals that have been made possible by the power of senior executives to delay and distort honest reporting. It does, however, illustrate the insidious ways in which corporations, as the most dominate institution, have become able to circumvent normal government oversight.

Left unchecked, senior executives of organizations work to distort reality in a way that will most positively impact share prices. An investigation into Enron stated, "Many of the most significant transactions apparently were designed to accomplish favorable financial statement results, not to achieve *bona fide* economic objectives or to transfer risk."[296] As the reality of Enron's situation gradually came to light, its stock price fell. Employees worried about this consulted Kenneth Lay. As CEO, it was thought that he might have insight into the true state of the company behind the precipitous drop in stock price from $90 to $25 a share. "Though he had cashed in some $20 million of Enron stock himself over the previous two months, Lay urged his employees to hold on." Those who did lost everything. In the years before its crash, Lay sold about $200 million worth of Enron stock. During that same time, it is estimated that employees lost about $1 billion. Many of his employees lost both their jobs and their retirement savings when the company collapsed.

Perhaps the real crime is that it is possible that Lay's actions weren't criminal. Many Americans felt that running a company to enrich one's self with millions while one's investors and employees lost billions was, quite simply, theft. CEOs don't have to break laws to break people and, in the process, make ridiculous amounts of money.

In 2003, according to *Business Week*, the average CEO in their survey made $8.1 million and the top twenty-five CEOs made an average of $32.7 million—about "900 times the annual pay of the typical U.S.

---

[296] Flanagan, *Dirty Rotten CEOs*, 98–116 for quotes and facts in this paragraph.

worker."[297] In 2010, average compensation for CEOs at S&P 500 companies was $11.4 million, representing a raise of 23 percent in a single year. The ratio of CEO to average employee pay at the top 299 companies was about 342 to 1.[298]

Nor is such pay necessarily a function of creating equity value. Larry Ellison, as CEO of Oracle, lost 54 percent of shareholders' equity from 2001 to 2003, but made $746.7 million during that time. For the top 25, perks alone averaged nearly $1 million in 2003.

It is perhaps not too strong a statement to say that the modern corporation is more focused on the compensation of top executives than on the potential of typical employees, or the quality of life of customers, suppliers, or the community in which it operates. CEOs commonly make millions while presiding over a loss in jobs, being rewarded for actually decreasing total income in a community. The community's goals often come second to management's goal of maximizing their compensation. This is just one of the reasons that the reform of the corporation is central to progress for the community. The good news is that market forces could help with reform more than theological debate helped with the reforms of the first economy. It is possible the CEOs are as likely to resist reforms as kings and popes before them, but doubtful; there is simply too much competition between companies for CEOs to successfully resist better models for long.

If a reform corrects abuses and a revolution transfers power, what is needed is revolution – just as it was needed in each of the previous three economies. Power could be transferred to the many who own the corporation.

The new owners of a corporation need mechanisms to shape its policy, and to gain control of the corporation. The new owners of publicly owned corporations are the public—specifically, and most notably, the average worker through pension funds. Although many corporations are currently run by elites, they are owned by the masses. The transformation of banking and financial markets during the third economy has created this new reality.

So far, though, the mechanisms for controlling the corporation are

---

297 *Business Week Online*, "Special Report—Executive Pay," <http://businessweek.com/magazine/content/04_16/b3879010.htm>

298 http://www.aflcio.org/corporatewatch/paywatch/

mostly in the hands of the CEO – not so much the owners.

Inheriting Old Goals

After the nation-state emerged as more powerful than the church, it took centuries for it to let go of the idea that its goal was the same as that of the church. The nation-state got its power from control over land, the first economy's limit to progress. Yet for the longest time, monarchs thought it their obligation to also look after the souls of their citizenry. It would have seemed irresponsible not to. "Bloody" Mary used violence to move England towards Catholicism, and her younger sister Elizabeth used violence to move it back towards Anglicanism.

Once the nation-state became a tool for improving one's condition in this life and not the next, once rulers gave up on dictating religion, a great deal of grief was avoided and a great deal of good could be done.

It's probably not surprising that the newly dominant institution would think it should prove itself by meeting the goals of the previously dominant institution. Those goals become so intertwined through all of society that legitimacy depends on at least acknowledging those old goals. It is hard to imagine a Renaissance king dismissing religion as unimportant for policy, saying that he would focus on GDP growth instead, for instance. (For one thing, GDP is a measure we didn't even have until about a century ago.)

So as the corporation emerged to compete with the bank as the most powerful institution in the West, it adopted the goals of the bank. That is, it saw its purpose as profit.

On the surface, this hardly seems problematic. It is, you might say, a fact of life. But as John Abramson points out, the purpose of pharmaceutical companies is not to maximize the health of Americans; it is, instead, to maximize profits. This is problematic. He cites a World Health Organization study that ranks the US health 15th overall in the world, a ranking that drops to 37th if that ranking adjusts for per person spending on healthcare.[299] This in spite of the fact that US

[299] John Abramson, MD., *Overdosed America: The Broken Promise of American Medicine* (HarperCollins, New York, NY, 2004) 46.

healthcare costs per person are double that of any other developed nation. Maximizing profits does not automatically maximize health.

The former management gurus Peter Drucker and Russell Ackoff both have claimed that profit is to a corporation what oxygen is to a person: vital but by no means its purpose. Companies have to make profit but they don't have to subordinate everything to it.

Robert Beyster, a man who helped to create billions in wealth, wrote that profit was a clear goal for the divisions within his company SAIC, but the goal was not profit maximization. He acknowledges that being privately held by employees exempted them from many of the pressures that publicly held companies feel to subordinate everything else to profits. (And curiously, SAIC's performance with such an approach was such that any investor would have been lucky to hold its stock. More on this later.)

To make explicit that something other than profits should direct corporate behavior is to suggest that corporations have to define the kind of life they are trying to create for customers, investors, employees, and their community. This is – it seems – a fairly interesting starting point for any corporation. It suggests that the corporation will more explicitly become a tool for helping the individual to create the life of his own choosing – even if that individual is not a CEO.

Overcoming the Limit of the Fourth Economy

The most powerful social inventions help communities to overcome the current limit to progress. This suggests that the corporation will be adapted to help communities to overcome the limit of entrepreneurship.

One reason is that business is the area in which entrepreneurship is most obviously allowed and rewarded. Although we typically think of entrepreneurship as something that happens within markets rather than within companies, it is not a big shift. But as it now stands, entrepreneurship is not something most companies attempt to cultivate. A typical model in business is for a start-up to define a new market or product and then a big company to buy that start-up and scale it up. They take a local product to a national market, or provide a combination of advertising and manufacturing that creates a surge in demand and supply. Although big companies do *create* new products and services, it is not as common as one thinks. More often they acquire and then scale up.

One compelling example of a company that does blur the boundary between running the business and creating a new business is Google. Google has a curious rule that allows them to promote entrepreneurship from within the company: they ask programmers and engineers to devote about one day per week—on average—to pursuing a project of their own. This is not classic R&D that is approved and funded centrally. These are projects conceived and pursued by individuals without going through central boards for approval. This is Google management showing the same kind of confidence in individual initiative that capitalist governments show in individual initiative. Gmail and Google Earth are just a couple of the initiatives that began as individual projects.

One of the fascinating things about this is that Google is treating the resource of knowledge workers like venture capitalists do money. That is, Google is using a scarce resource—its programmers and engineers—and investing a portion of their time into new ventures that have a very high probability of failure. This seems like a silly short-term policy. Odds are good that they are just diverting precious attention into projects that won't pay back. Long term, however, this seems brilliant. They need only one spectacular success every five to ten years in order to maintain a growth trajectory that even corporate giants like GM and Microsoft have been unable to sustain. And in truth, Google may not pull this off. What I do know is that if this meme catches on and lots of companies try this, we will have more entrepreneurial ventures and as a result will have more products, services, jobs, and wealth created than we otherwise would. It seems a fact that any one venture like this is destined to fail and any larger community that regularly invests in such ventures is destined to thrive.

The important question in the eighteenth and nineteenth century was "how do we create and attract more capital and make it more productive?" At that stage of development, all other advances followed. The important question in the twentieth century was "how do we create and attract more knowledge workers and make them more productive?" At that stage of development, all other advances followed. Now? Now the question ought to be, "how do we create and attract more entrepreneurs and help them to be more successful?" At this new stage of development, all other advances will follow.

The Internet and the End of the Information Age

It is sort of fitting that Google can be used as one kind of example of corporate transformation. It seems likely that the Internet will do for the corporation what the Guttenberg press did for the church. That is, it'll break up structures we had always assumed were simply the way that things are: it'll render temporal what we thought was timeless.

Ronald Coase won a Nobel Prize in Economics for his work on the firm. The question he asked is, "Why, if markets are so effective, do companies have employees?" The simple answer is that information costs are too high to turn every task into a transaction, making it cheaper to rely on contracts than markets. That is, it is simply too hard to coordinate the work that goes on inside of a company any way other than through job descriptions and assignments. Yet Coase's work was largely done long before the Internet as we know it. Information costs have plummeted in the last couple of decades. One consequence of these falling information costs may be a growth in the portion of the economy that is managed by the invisible hand of markets rather than the visible hand of management. Savvy corporations will tap this potential to create e a growth in market forces *within* corporations.

What does this mean in practical terms? If a programmer in the Ukraine should get an idea and can find a designer in Italy and an assistant in India, the work can be done through informal arrangements that may or may not include a corporation. I actually think that one of the social inventions of savvy communities will be the simplification of what is required to form a multinational corporation, if only to make issues of ownership more clear and simple. (It is one thing to say that people from different countries collaborated to create something and quite another to say that everyone is clear and happy about the way its success is shared.) Regardless of how many and what type of social inventions will be necessary for this to work, however, the fact is simply this: technology around the planet has never before so lent itself to self-organizing activities.

Robert Beyster and SAIC

"Much of our business culture is infatuated with power—amassing it, holding on to it, using it to vanquish competitors and dominate markets. In contrast, much of Dr. Beyster's leadership philosophy is about spreading freedom. And freedom, it turns out, packs a bigger wallop than power. Power is about what you can control; freedom is about what you can unleash."

—William C. Taylor

Curiously, SAIC founder Robert Beyster is little known. Beyster attained stunning results by blurring the boundaries between the role of employee and that of entrepreneur.

Robert Beyster articulated a key challenge to his company as being the recruitment, retention, and reward of entrepreneurial employees who are also team players. For Beyster, this was not mere rhetoric. He built a company that had reached the level of hundreds of operating divisions, forty-four thousand employees, and $6.7 billion in sales by the time he retired.[300] Through stock ownership, he made millionaires out of hundreds of employees, and retained only 1.3 percent of the company—an amount still worth about $100 million. SAIC's top management operate more like venture capitalists than a strategic management team anxious to impose strategic and process discipline onto lower-level managers. Market and project success are their own consequences, and shared equity helps to align the interests of shareholders, management, and employees towards the natural consequences of business success. What's more, SAIC shareholders are the employees (and vice versa). Using an internal market for share trading, only SAIC employees, directors, and consultants could own shares. (This changed when Beyster retired.) Few leaders have done as much as Beyster to make explicit the fact that at the close of the third economy, it is the knowledge workers employed by corporations who also own these corporations. A man who buys a machine or builds a factory line and then hires workers to come work on those machines has a very different relationship towards his employees than the man who looks inside the mind of his employees for the capital. Bill Gates was once quoted as saying something to the effect of, "My capital walks in and out of the office every day." Beyster's strategy seems to have worked. From the time that Beyster founded the company to when

[300]"Founder of SAIC steps down from his position as chairman" *The San Diego Union-Tribune*, Saturday July 17, 2004, p. C-1. Numbers reported for the fiscal year ended in January 2004.

he retired, revenues and profits had grown an average of 35 percent per year for thirty-five years, an amazing feat of business growth. It wasn't until his thirty-second year at SAIC that he failed to increase both revenues and profits over the previous year.

In his book, the *SAIC Solution*, Beyster in a sense compares himself to Edison. Or, more accurately, compares his employees to Edison. Instead of experimenting with light bulbs and batteries, SAIC's employees experimented with their organization—adding a new location here, reorganizing a division there—and with its programs, projects, and methods. While other companies worried about maintaining stability across their existing lines of business, SAIC's technical managers were figuring out how they could try new ideas.[301]

This, it seems to me, is one of the simplest examples of social invention becoming as important as technological invention. (And this is not to say that SAIC employees don't generate lots of patents and do their share of technological invention. It is merely to point out that reliance on technological innovation alone is not enough. Sustainable progress always seems to come from a confluence of technological and social invention.)

Fortunately, Beyster is not the only example of treating employees like entrepreneurs. There are others and one of the more interesting ones is Jack Stack.

Jack Stack & SHC

Jack Stack has had impressive business success focusing on teaching his employees *The Great Game of Business*[302]. Put in terms of this book, he's essentially popularizing the duties of management, giving everyone some degree of management responsibility by creating transparency in the financials and tying bonuses to critical numbers.

---

301 J. Robert Beyster with Peter Economy, *The SAIC Solution: How We Built an $8 billion Employee-Owned Technology Company* (Hoboken, N.J.: John Wiley & Sons, 2007), 138.

302 Jack Stack, with Bo Burlingham, *The Great Game of Business: Unlocking the Power and Profitability of Open-Book Management* (Currency Doubleday, New York, NY, 1992).

Every employee sees the numbers and understands how his or her job impacts the organization.

Stack was managing one of International Harvester's factories in 1983, when the recession prompted International Harvester to shut down the plant. He was able to find a loan to keep the plant running and quickly adopted an open-book approach to management. The goal was to unleash the entrepreneur within every employee.

Since then, SHC has created 60-some companies, gone 27 years without layoffs, paid out $50 million on bonuses to date, and seen an incredible rise in equity. Successfully turning employees into entrepreneurs has created wealth.

Start in 1983 when Jack Stack was terrified of going broke with the plant he'd bought from International Harvester. Had you invested $1,000 in the S&P 500, by early 2011 you'd have about $13,000. Had you let the investment genius Warren Buffet invest it instead, buying his Berkshire Hathaway stock, your $1,000 would have become about $87,000. But had you invested in SHC, your investment would now be worth nearly $2 million. Countries that encourage entrepreneurship become wealthier than those that do not; apparently, so do companies.

These examples from Robert Beyster and Jack Stack seem to me worth exploring. It might just be that the biggest waste inside of companies is the waste of the potential of their employees, waste created in no small part by limiting their role and compensation to something defined by others.

The Popularization of Entrepreneurship

As mentioned earlier, knowledge work was not invented in the twentieth century. It was merely popularized. What was once the domain of a few experts became something in which a much larger percentage of the population became involved. And that was enough. We didn't need the entire population to become knowledge workers in order to make huge productivity gains. Neither will we need huge swaths of the employee population to become entrepreneurs in order to see huge gains in productivity. If, say, about one-tenth of 1 percent of the population today are entrepreneurs, think what would happen if even 1 percent, much less 10 percent, became entrepreneurs. In such a scenario, job creation would not be the problem; finding and affording good employees would be the problem. And for most of the West, that would be different from the reality today. Just it was not enough to design good products, but instead was necessary to design products for manufacturability, so might it become with business ventures. That is, it might not be enough to create jobs, but instead it might become necessary to create jobs for which available employees are suited. We might even see organizations designing businesses for employability.

Social Invention as the New Norm

If we manage to pull off this next transformation, it will mean much in the way of progress. It should change every domain, from education to business, finance to politics, and even religion. Most of all, it will mean a real paradigm shift in terms of the individual.

For generations, we've judged individuals by how well they've adapted to institutions. Are they good Christians? Are they good citizens or employees? Now we'll be looking at something different: asking the question, are these institutions as they are now constructed good for the individual? The basis for judgment will shift from the individual's performance within the institution to the institution's support of the individual.

This will mean the ultimate rise of the individual over the institution, which has been the dominant theme of progress throughout the history of Western Civilization since about 1300.

The Modern Corporation: Modeled on the Medieval Church

One of the reasons that it matters that the medieval church became evil is because it is still a model for modern institutions. It is difficult to overcome a blueprint at the foundation of Western Civilization, a blueprint that influences even the design of the modern corporation. The medieval church had popes and priests who discerned the will of

God and directed the congregants; the modern corporation has CEOs and managers who discern the will of the market and direct the employees. The hierarchy of power in either the church or the corporation depends upon a belief in the supremacy of the insight of those at the top, a belief that true understanding does not come from the individual's own experience but from a higher authority. The belief is that a standard process best represents the true path and measurement of conformity to this process is more important than what the individual would report or believe.

The corporation has many flaws. Its primary flaw is that it so poorly fits with its environment and the needs of the people who work within it. No institution has done more to contribute to climate change than the corporation. And in the United States, which for many represents the apex of progress, 84 percent of people are unhappy in their jobs.

Job dissatisfaction hardly compares with burning at the stake. In the grand scheme of history, it is a fairly petty and pathetic complaint to be unhappy at work. It is not the Spanish Inquisition. Yet if one can't enjoy what one does all day—what defines one's life—it makes one question the progress up to this point. Is this really the culmination of thousands of generations of genetic and social evolution? To sit in cubicles, feeling disengaged and frustrated? The church did not have to defend misery, because happiness was to be reserved for the next life. Yet the corporation whose ads promise happiness through consumption can hardly be so dismissive of its own employees' happiness. It might just be that the transformation of work and what it means to create value and to be valued is the next personal frontier, the domain for the next great institutional revolution.

About a decade ago, I went into one of the Big Three automakers to do some training and consulting work. I left dismayed. The managers were conscientious and the employees seemingly sincere, all good people and yet they seemed more like parents and children than consenting adults. It left me thinking that the traditional distribution of power constrains employees from acting like adults and puts managers into the role of parent. Everyone is made less effective.

The corporation could learn something about needed change by looking at the huge transformation of the church over the last half millennia.

Two big changes to come out of the Protestant Revolution were the entrepreneurial approach to religion and the shift in authority to the individual. These two are inextricably linked.

Religion in the wake of the Protestant Revolution has been wildly entrepreneurial. Luther claimed that we are all priests, and the germ of this idea—the notion that individual revelation and conviction ought to be the root of religious belief—continues to spark new denominations. The World Christian Database now tracks nine thousand denominations.

For all the dismissal of churches as archaic, in terms of freedoms granted, the church may be the most evolved and modern of our institutions. Churches either meet the need of their congregants or the congregants go elsewhere—or nowhere. We have freedom not just across religions, but also within. For instance, two people who both call themselves Catholic can profess and practice very different things.

In America, after each presidential election it seems that about half the population feels dismayed and alienated. This less often happens in the church, where people can easily change affiliations or even practices within a church.

In consumer markets, the corporation does an incredible job of facilitating choice and freedom. Just think of the variety of choices one has for food, for instance. Do you want prepared food or raw food? Organic or processed? Do you want a particular ethnic style? The consumer has an incredible array of choices for something even as simple as dinner.

By contrast, think of the paucity of freedom that each employee has. In some companies, employees have more freedom, but still the corporation generally defines for the employee everything from processes to dress code. If the consumer has a choice among a cornucopia of foods, the employee essentially can say that he does or does not want fries with that. The lack of choices and freedom of the employee is in stark contrast to the plethora of choices and freedoms of the modern worshipper or consumer.

If the medieval church is the model for the current corporation, we can hope that the post-Protestant Revolution church will be the model for the future corporation—a place of huge variety and freedom.

A great deal will be different in the next version of the corporation, but most of the changes will begin with a shift in the notion of where authority ought to lie: in central authorities or in the individual. This means trusting the individual with true freedom. All the design changes that may occur in the corporation will be meaningless without this profound and important shift.

Turn the page. The next chapter, about the eclipse of the corporation by the individual, is quite personal.

27 The Rise of the Individual

It would seem to rather miss the point if I were to write this chapter, wouldn't it? I believe that if you've come this far, this is yours to write.

Acknowledgements

The idea for *The Fourth Economy* came out of a serendipitous exposure to three ideas in a short amount of time. I was studying Deming's philosophy for a training role at work, and heard him say, "I don't worry about the future. I know what will happen. Executives will either learn how to manage a system or will go out of business." At this same time, I was teaching macroeconomics at a local community college. James Galbraith, in the textbook, made a simple but really profound statement. He said that before there was a market economy, there were no factors of production, no land, labor, or capital as we know it. And finally, I was reading Paul Kennedy's *Rise and Fall of the Great Powers* and wondering if something more than military overreach might explain rise and fall of the Spanish and British empires. Putting these all together in a quick snap led me to the much slower process of confirmation, refinement and elaboration of the initial idea about different economies being defined by different factors of production.

Since then, various folks have helped to encourage me and the idea. The San Diego Deming User Group was a wonderful place to learn more about the new management and to test *The Fourth Economy.* In particular, conversations with Michael Kaufman, Charlie Mount, Murray Slater, and Phil Monroe helped. At work, I was encouraged by the following people who took the idea seriously: Dave George, Dr. Rick Barker, Rudy Rodolfo, Pete Sterling, Orlin Wetzker, Norman Patnode, Geordie Keitt, and Bill Fulton. Daryl Morey, Eric Winder, Matt Elley, Jim Plant and Rick Jacobsen are buddies whose success in business has not dissuaded them from expressing support for me and my ideas. Jeff Sherling was not just supportive of the idea, but did a great deal to help me with an earlier version of the manuscript. Sandra Judd edited this version.

Thanks to Jerry Johnson and Stephen Covey at the Covey Leadership Center for the unique privilege of facilitating conversations about what sort of life a person would want to invent under the guise of teaching a seminar on 7 Habits. And thanks to Bill Lynch and Rob Newbold at ProChain Solutions, Inc. for making me a part of their adventure to change how quickly and effectively companies can create new products, allowing me to work inside some of the world's best companies.

More recently, I've been excited to see the degree to which the conversation in so many places is shifting towards corporate transformation. Traci Fenton, at WorldBlu, is creating a community of wonderful folks who are exploring what it means to democratize the corporation; companies engaged in various ways in helping to define and create a new kind of business include WD-40 in San Diego, Namaste Solar in Colorado, Podio in Copenhagen, and Zappos in Las Vegas. Organizations like the Kauffman Foundation and Ashoka are encouraging entrepreneurship in the private and public sectors. Gifford Pinchot has been advocating intrapreneuring since the late 1980s. Thousands of organizations are emerging and millions of people are stepping up to take on the task of defining sustainable production and redefining community and what it means to be human.

It is a great time to be alive. And no generation will be a part of more fascinating changes than the generation that is just now beginning its career and must feel as though their timing could not be worse. Short term, that's a reasonable conclusion to reach. Longer term, their timing could not be better.

Finally, my wife Sandi has been wonderfully patient. This project has continuously required me to do tasks for which I'm ill-equipped and would have been too long a project even if I had had a clue about what I was doing. She didn't just tolerate this effort but actually encouraged me.

Ron Davison, July 2011.

Bibliography

Abramson, John, *Overdosed America: The Broken Promise of American Medicine*

Ackoff, Russell L., *Ackoff's Best: His Classic Writings on Management*

Ackoff, Russell L., *The Democratic Corporation: A Radical Prescription for Recreating Corporate America and Rediscovering Success*

Alinsky, Saul D., *Rules for Radicals: A Pragmatic Primer for Realistic Radicals*

Anderson, Walter Truett, *Reality Isn't What It Used to Be: Theatrical Politics, Ready-to-Wear Religion, Global Myths, Primitive Chic, and Other Wonders of the Postmodern World*

Armstrong, Karen, *The Battle for God*

Bakan, Joel, *The Corporation: The Pathological Pursuit of Profit and Power*

Barker, Richard A., *On Organizational Citizenship*

Barzun, Jacques, *From Dawn to Decadence: 500 Years of Western Cultural Life 1500 to the Present*

Beniger, James, *The Control Revolution: Technological and Economic Origins of the Information Society*

Bernstein, Peter L., *Against the Gods: The Remarkable Story of Risk*

Bernstein, William J., *The Birth of Plenty : How the Prosperity of the Modern World was Created*

Beyster, J. Robert, *SAIC Solution: How We Built an $8 Billion Employee Owned Technology Company*

Block, Peter, *Community: The Structure of Belonging*

Bohm, David, *Wholeness and the Implicate Order*

Bookstaber, Richard, *A Demon of Our Own Design: Markets, Hedge Funds, and the Perils of Financial Innovation*

Boorstin, Daniel J., *The Creators: A History of Heroes of the Imagination*

Boyett, Joseph H., *The Guru Guide to Entrepreneurship: A Concise Guide to the Best Ideas from the World's Top Entrepreneurs*

Bruck, Connie, *The Predators' Ball: The Inside Story of Drexel Burnham and the Rise of the Junk Bond Traders*

Buckingham, Marcus, *First, Break All the Rules: What the World's Greatest Managers Do Differently*

Buckingham, Marcus, *Now, Discover Your Strengths*

Calder, Lendol, *Financing the American Dream: A Cultural History of Consumer Credit*

Campbell, Joseph, *The Power of Myth*

Chandler, Jr., Alfred D., *The Visible Hand: The Managerial Revolution in American Business*

Chernow, Ron, *The House of Morgan: An American Banking Dynasty and the Rise of Modern Finance*

Chernow, Ron, *The Death of the Banker: The Decline and Fall of the Great Financial Dynasties and the Triumph of the Small Investor*

Collins, Jim, *Good to Great: Why Some Companies Make the Leap... and Others Don't*

Covey, Stephen R., *First Things First: To Live, to Love, to Learn, to Leave a Legacy*

Covey, Stephen R., *The 7 Habits of Highly Effective People*

Covey, Stephen R., *The 8th Habit : From Effectiveness to Greatness*

Csikszentmihalyi, Mihaly, *Finding Flow: The Psychology of Engagement with Everyday Life*

Csikszentmihalyi, Mihaly, *Creativity: Flow and the Psychology of Discovery and Invention*

Csikszentmihalyi, Mihaly, *The Evolving Self: A Psychology for the Third Millennium*

Csikszentmihalyi, Mihaly, *Flow: The Psychology of Optimal Experience*

Davidson, Mark, *Uncommon Sense: The Life and Thought of Ludwig Von Bertalanffy* (1901-1972, Father of General Systems Theory)

Davis, W. Sumner, *Heretics: The Bloody History of the Christian Church*

Dörner, Dietrich, *The Logic of Failure: Recognizing and Avoiding Error in Complex Situations*

Deci, Edward L., *Why We Do What We Do: Understanding Self-Motivation*

Deming, W. Edwards, *Out of the Crisis*

Deming, W. Edwards, *The New Economics for Industry, Government, Education - 2nd Edition*

Diamond, Jared, *Guns, Germs, and Steel*

Diamond, Jared, *Collapse: How Societies Choose to Fail or Succeed*

Drucker, Peter F., *The Effective Executive: The Definitive Guide to Getting the Right Things Done*

Drucker, Peter F., *Innovation and Entrepreneurship*

Drucker, Peter F., *Managing in the Next Society*

Drucker, Peter F., *Post-Capitalist Society*

Dunn, Richard S., *The Age of Religious Wars, 1559-1689*

Durant, Will, *The Age of Louis XIV* *(Story of Civilization 8)*

Durant, Will, The Age of Napoleon *(Story of Civilization 11)*

Durant, Will, *The Age of Voltaire* *(Story of Civilization 9)*

Durant, Will, *Rousseau and Revolution*(*Story of Civilization 10)*

Durant, Will, *The Age of Faith* *(Story of Civilization 4)*

Durant, Will, *The Reformation* *(Story of Civilization 6)*

Durant, Will, *The Renaissance* *(Story of Civilization 5)*

Dweck, Carol S., *Self-theories: Their Role in Motivation, Personality, and Development*

Ehrman, Bart D., *Lost Christianities: The Battles for Scripture & the Faiths We Never Knew*

Ehrman, Bart D., *Jesus, Interrupted: Revealing the Hidden Contradictions in the Bible & Why We Don't Know About Them*

Epstein, Steven A., *The Economic and Social History of Later Medieval Europe, 1000 – 1500*

Ferguson, Niall, *The House of Rothschild, Volume 1: Money's Prophets: 1798-1848*

Ferguson, Niall, *The Ascent of Money: A Financial History of the World*

Ferriss, Timothy, *The 4-Hour Work Week: Escape 9-5, Live Anywhere, and Join the New Rich*

Freeman, Charles, *The Closing of the Western Mind: The Rise of Faith and the Fall of Reason*

Freud, Sigmund, *Civilization and Its Discontents*

Friedman, Thomas L., *The World Is Flat: A Brief History of the Twenty-First Century*

Fritz, Robert, *Creating*

Fritz, Robert, *Path of Least Resistance: Learning to Become the Creative Force in Your Own Life*

Fritz, Robert, *Corporate Tides: The Inescapable Laws of Organizational Structure*

Gaarder, Jostein, *Sophie's World*

Galbraith, James K., *Macroeconomics*

Gardner, Howard, *Good Work: When Excellence and Ethics Meet*

Gardner, Howard, *Multiple Intelligences: New Horizons*

Gardner, Howard, *Changing Minds: The Art And Science of Changing Our Own And Other People's Minds*

Gardner, Howard, *The Unschooled Mind: How Children Think and How Schools Should Teach*

Gardner, Howard, *Frames of Mind: The Theory of Multiple Intelligences*

Gardner, Howard, *Creating Minds: An Anatomy of Creativity Seen Through the Lives of Freud, Einstein, Picasso, Stravinsky, Eliot, Graham, and Gandhi*

Gay, Peter, *Modernism: The Lure of Heresy*

Gerber, Michael E., *The E-Myth Revisited: Why Most Small Businesses Don't Work and What to Do About It*

Gladwell, Malcolm, *The Tipping Point*

Gladwell, Malcolm, *Outliers*

Gleick, James, *Chaos: Making a New Science*

Gleick, James, *The Information: A History, A Theory, A Flood*

Goldratt, Eliyahu M., *The Goal*

Goldratt, Eliyahu M., *It's Not Luck*

Goldratt, Eliyahu M., *Theory of Constraints*

Goldratt, Eliyahu M., *Critical Chain : A Business Novel*

Goleman, Daniel, *Emotional Intelligence: Why It Can Matter More Than I.Q.*

Goleman, Daniel, *Vital Lies, Simple Truths: The Psychology of Self Deception*

Goss, Tracy, *The Last Word on Power*

Gould, Stephen Jay, *The Mismeasure of Man*

Gray, John, *Black Mass: Apocalyptic Religion and the Death of Utopia*

Heilbroner, Robert L., *The Worldly Philosophers*

Hock, Dee W., *Birth of the Chaordic Age*

Hofstadter, Richard, *Anti-Intellectualism in American Life*

Jacques, Elliot, *Executive Leadership: A Practical Guide to Managing Complexity*

Johnson, Steven, *The Invention of Air: A Story Of Science, Faith, Revolution, And The Birth Of America*

Josephson, Matthew, *The Robber Barons: The Great American Capitalists 1861 - 1901*

Kegan, Robert, *The Evolving Self: Problem and Process in Human Development*

Kennedy, Paul, *The Rise and Fall of the Great Powers*

Kohn, Alfie, *No Contest: The Case Against Competition*

Kohn, Alfie, *Punished by Rewards: The Trouble With Gold Stars, Incentive Plans, A'S, Praise, and Other Bribes*

Korten, David C., *When Corporations Rule the World*

Kramnick, Isaac, *The Portable Enlightenment Reader*

Kuhn, Thomas Samuel, *The Structure of Scientific Revolutions*

Landes, David S., *The Wealth and Poverty of Nations: Why Some Are So Rich and Some So Poor*

Layard, Richard, *Happiness: Lessons from a New Science*

Leach, William R., *Land of Desire: Merchants, Power, and the Rise of a New American Culture*

Lefkoe, Morty, *Re-create Your Life: Transforming Yourself and Your World*

Lewis, Michael, *The New New Thing: A Silicon Valley Story*

Machiavelli, Niccolò, *The Prince*

Mallaby, Sebastian, *More Money Than God: Hedge Funds and the Making of a New Elite*

Manchester, William Raymond, *A World Lit Only by Fire*

Maslow, Abraham H., *Toward a Psychology of Being, 3rd Edition*

Maslow, Abraham H., *Motivation and Personality*

McGrath, Alister E., *Christianity's Dangerous Idea: The Protestant Revolution: A History from the Sixteenth Century to the Twenty-First*

Menand, Louis, *The Metaphysical Club*

Menand, Louis, *Pragmatism: A Reader*

Micklethwait, John & Wooldridge, Adrian, *The Company: A Short History of a Revolutionary Idea*

Morris, Charles R., *The Trillion Dollar Meltdown: Easy Money, High Rollers, and the Great Credit Crash*

Nace, Ted, *Gangs of America: The Rise of Corporate Power and the Disabling of Democracy*

Newbold, Robert, *The Billion Dollar Solution: Secrets of ProChain Project Management*

Nørretranders, Tor, *The User Illusion: Cutting Consciousness Down to Size*

Nocera, Joseph, *A Piece of the Action: How the Middle Class Joined the Money Class*

North, Douglass C., *Institutions, Institutional Change and Economic Performance*

Perrow, Charles, *Organizing America: Wealth, Power, and the Origins of Corporate Capitalism*

Pipher, Mary Bray, *Writing to Change the World*

Pollard, Justin, *The Rise and Fall of Alexandria: Birthplace of the Modern Mind*

Porter, Michael E., *Competitive Strategy: Techniques for Analyzing Industries and Competitors*

Rauchyway, Eric, *Murdering McKinley: The Making of Theodore Roosevelt's America*

Reich, Robert, *The Work of Nations: Preparing Ourselves for 21st Century Capitalism*

Richardson, Jr., Robert D., *William James: In the Maelstrom of American Modernism*

Roberts, J.M., *The Penguin History of the World*

Rosen, William, *The Most Powerful Idea in the World: A Story of Steam, Industry, and Invention*

Schivelbusch, Wolfgang (translated from the Germany by David Jacobson), *Tastes of Paradise: A Social History of Spices, Stimulants, and Intoxicants*

Schulze, Hagen, *States, Nations and Nationalism*

Searle, John R., *The Construction of Social Reality*

Seligman, Martin E.P., *Authentic Happiness: Using the New Positive Psychology to Realize Your Potential for Lasting Fulfillment*

Sen, Amartya, *Development as Freedom*

Senge, Peter M., *The Fifth Discipline: The Art & Practice of The Learning Organization*

Senge, Peter M., *The Fifth Discipline Fieldbook*

Shekerjian, Denise, *Uncommon Genius*

Shermer, Michael, *Why People Believe Weird Things: Pseudoscience, Superstition, and Other Confusions of Our Time*

Smith, Adam, *The Wealth of Nations*

Smith, B. Mark, *A History of the Global Stock Market: From Ancient Rome to Silicon Valley*

Soros, George, *Open Society: Reforming Global Capitalism*

Spong, John Shelby, *Liberating the Gospels: Reading the Bible with Jewish Eyes*

Stack, Jack, *The Great Game of Business*

Strayer, Joseph Reese, *On the Medieval Origins of the Modern State*

Taleb, Nassim Nicholas, *The Black Swan The Impact of the Highly Improbable*

Tart, Charles T., *Waking Up: Overcoming the Obstacles to Human Potential*

Tuchman, Barbara W., *The March of Folly: From Troy to Vietnam*

Tuchman, Barbara W., *A Distant Mirror The Calamitous 14th Century*

Watson, Peter, *Ideas: A History of Thought and Invention, from Fire to Freud*

Weiner, Jonathan, *Long For This World: The Strange Science of Immortality*

Wells, H.G., *The Outline of History: Being a Plain History of Life and Mankind – revised and brought up to the end of the Second World War by Raymond Postgate*

Wessels, Tom, *The Myth of Progress: Toward a Sustainable Future*

Wheatley, Margaret J., *Leadership and the New Science: Discovering Order in a Chaotic World*

Wolfe, Tom, *Hooking Up*

Wright, Robert, *Nonzero: The Logic of Human Destiny*

Wright, Robert, *The Evolution of God*

Wright, Ronald, *A Short History of Progress*

Zander, Rosamund Stone, *The Art of Possibility: Transforming Professional and Personal Life*

Zinn, Howard, *A People's History of the United States: 1492 to Present*

Other resources

Mindwalk, the video

7 Habits of Highly Effective People, seminar

The Landmark Forum, seminar

For more information on accelerating product development, visit ProChain.com

The Author

Working as a business consultant for Franklin-Covey and ProChain Solutions, Inc., Ron Davison has worked with some of the world's largest and best-performing corporations. For Covey, Ron had the good fortune to lead the *7 Habits of Highly Effective People* and *Principle Centered Leadership* seminars. With ProChain, Ron works with project teams inside of Fortune 500 firms to accelerate their development of new products as varied as diapers, computer chips, pharmaceuticals, and stents. Ron's first full time job was to take over the operation of a 22-employee restaurant- bakery when he was 17.

Ron has hosted a radio show, taught macroeconomics, was part of the organization to first host a trade show featuring American companies in Hanoi, and spoken in a variety of venues that include systems thinking conferences and Deming User Groups. Ron has previously created *A Change in Thinking*, a video on systems thinking.

The Fourth Economy: Inventing Western Civilization is his most audacious attempt yet to make this a better world.

http://thefourtheconomy.com

http://twitter.com/#!/iamrondavison

http://www.facebook.com/pages/The-Fourth-Economy-Inventing-Civilization/208588905829036

http://rwrld.blogspot.com/

ron@thefourtheconomy.com

Made in the USA
Lexington, KY
21 September 2011